THE HISTORICAL SERIES OF THE REFORMED CHURCH IN AMERICA
NO. 97

BEFORE THE FACE OF GOD:

Essays in Honor of Tom Boogaart

Dustyn Elizabeth Keepers, editor

REFORMED CHURCH PRESS
Grand Rapids, Michigan

The Historical Series of the Reformed Church in America

The series was inaugurated in 1968 by the General Synod of the Reformed Church in America acting through the Commission on History to communicate the church's heritage and collective memory and to reflect on our identity and mission, encouraging historical scholarship which informs both church and academy.

www.rca.org/series

General Editor
> James Hart Brumm, MDiv, MPhil
> New Brunswick Theological Seminary

Associate Editor
> Andrew Klumpp, MDiv
> Southern Methodist University

Copy Editor
> Jordan Humm
> Grand Rapids, MI

Production Editor
> Russell L. Gasero
> Archives, Reformed Church in America

Cover Design
> Matthew Gasero
> Archives, Reformed Church in America

General Editor Emeritus
> Donald J. Bruggink, PhD, DD
> Van Raalte Institute, Hope College

Commission on History
> Alexander Arthurs, Western Theological Seminary
> Lynn Japinga, PhD, Hope College
> Andrew Klumpp, MDiv, Southern Methodist University
> Steven Pierce, DMin, Grand Rapids, MI
> David M. Tripold, PhD, Monmouth University
> Douglas Van Aartsen, MDiv, Ireton, Iowa

Contents

Contributors   vii

Preface

    Before the Face of God
        Dustyn Elizabeth Keepers   xiii

Part One: Reflections on Dr. Boogaart's Work

1. Dying to Read the Bible
     Carol M. Bechtel   1

2. The Mountains are Full of Horses and Chariots
     Jeff Barker   13

3. Hospitality of the Heart: How Changing Our Metaphor
     Can Change Our Relationship with the Bible
     Travis West   31

4. Love as Pedagogy
     Pam Bush   49

5. Stewarding a Living Tradition: A Case Study
     Benjamin Conner   63

6. Cosmology, Coram Deo and the Camino
     Kyle Small   77

Part Two: Dr. Boogaart Influences Our Work In the Study of Scripture

7. Virtues of a Faithful Reader
     Tim Brown   91

8. Interpreting Scripture
     James Brownson   105

9. The Pastoral Implications of Our Amnesia about
     Believers Resurrection: Learning from
     the Apostle Paul
     Lyle VanderBroek   113

10. The Book of Joel—The Millennial Narrative?
    Jaco J. Hamman   135

11. There is Blood in the Vineyard(s): A Liberationist
    Reading of 1 Kings 21 and Joshua 10-12
    Zac Poppen   157

12. Woman as Disciple: Scripture and the Church as a
    Discipleship of Equals
    Dustyn Elizabeth Keepers   173

13. The God who Elects Leaving
    Alberto La Rosa Rojas   191

Part Three: Dr. Boogaart Influences Our Work in History, Science,
Philosophy and Theology

14. Francis of Assisi's Ministry of Example in
    The Assisi Compilation
    John W. Coakley   207

15. Ben Zoma Shakes the World: Two Sources or Two Powers?
    Christopher B. Kaiser   223

16. Divine Immanence, Newton's Metaphysics, and Just-So
    Stories: The Boogaartian Challenge at the
    Science/Theology Boundary
    Stephen J. Wykstra   239

17. 'History' and 'State' in Karl Barth: Elements of
    an Ontology of Human Being
    Christopher Dorn   265

18. The Saving Work of Christ: Three Offices or
    Three Pilgrim Feasts?
    David L. Stubbs   275

    Index   293

    Historical Series Books in Print   301

Contributors

Jeff Barker is professor of theatre at Northwestern College in addition to a director, playwright, and screenwriter. He has written more than 50 plays, including *Unspoken for Time, September Bears,* and *Kin: The Trial of Carrie Buck,* a finalist for the Arlin Meyer Prize in 2005. In collaboration with Broadway composer Ron Melrose, he created the musical *And God Said,* which, along with *Terror Texts: The Musical, Joseph and His Brothers,* and many others, is part of the Ancient Hebrew Drama Project. Jeff's feature-length films include *Of Minor Prophets,* a modern retelling of the Hosea story. He is also the author of several books, including *The Storytelling Church* (Webber Institute Books, 2011) and *Sioux Center Sudan* (Hendrickson Publishers, 2018).

Carol M. Bechtel is professor of Old Testament at Western Theological Seminary in Holland, Michigan, where she has taught since 1994. Dr. Bechtel studied at Hope College in Holland, Michigan, and Western Theological Seminary before earning her PhD in Old Testament from Yale University. Dr. Bechtel is a General Synod professor of theology in the Reformed Church in America (RCA) and has served as president of the RCA's General Synod. She currently serves as the executive director of the American Waldensian Society. Her publications include a commentary on Esther for the *Interpretation* series and several Bible study books and curricula.

Timothy Brown is the president and Henry Bast Professor of Preaching at Western Theological Seminary in Holland, Michigan. He has served as pastor to several congregations in the Reformed Church in America and as the Dean of the Chapel at Hope College in Holland, Michigan. A General Synod professor, Tim has been a member of the seminary faculty for over 20 years, serving as president since 2008. He is a frequent speaker at pastor's conferences, college and seminary campuses, and church renewal events, and he often contributes to a range of periodicals in preaching and pastoral theology.

James V. Brownson is James and Jean Cook Professor of New Testament at Western Theological Seminary and a General Synod professor in the Reformed Church in America. Jim's scholarly interests include the Gospel of John, the Synoptic Gospels, biblical hermeneutics, contextual theology, and theology in service to the church. A longstanding member of the Gospel in our Culture Network, Jim regularly contributes to its research and publications, and he is the author of several books along with numerous journal and magazine articles.

Pam Bush is a member of the formation for ministry and Hebrew teams at Western Theological Seminary. She is an ordained minister of Word and sacrament in the Reformed Church in America and previously served in campus ministry at Grand Valley State University in Grand Rapids, Michigan. Pam earned her MDiv from Western Theological Seminary as well as her D.Min., which focused on contemplative leadership formation.

John W. Coakley, L. Russell Feakes Professor of Church History, emeritus, at New Brunswick Theological Seminary in New Jersey, is a minister of Word and sacrament in the Reformed Church in America and a General Synod professor emeritus. Among his publications are *Women, Men, and Spiritual Power: Female Saints and Their Collaborators* (Columbia University Press, 2006); *New Brunswick Theological Seminary: An Illustrated History* (Eerdmans, 2014); and (as co-editor), *Readings in World Christian History: Earliest Christianity to 1453* (Orbis Books, 2004).

Benjamin T. Conner is professor of practical theology as well as creator and director of the graduate certificate in disability and ministry at Western Theological Seminary. He has been involved in youth ministry for many years, serving in congregations and through Youth Life. Ben earned his MDiv from Union Presbyterian Seminary in Richmond, Virginia, and his PhD in missions, ecumenics, and history of religions from Princeton Theological Seminary. His most recent book is *Disabling Mission, Enabling Witness: Exploring Missiology through the Lens of Disability Studies* (IVP Academic, 2018).

Christopher Dorn earned an MDiv from Western Theological Seminary and a PhD in religious studies from Marquette University in Milwaukee, Wisconsin. He currently serves as chair of Christians Uniting in Song and Prayer, an ecumenical group in Holland, Michigan, dedicated to organizing community-wide worship events in the interest of promoting unity among Christians. He preaches regularly at First

Presbyterian Church in Ionia, Michigan, and Redeemer Presbyterian Church in Holland, Michigan.

Jaco J. Hamman is associate professor of religion, psychology and culture and is the director of the program in theology and practice at Vanderbilt Divinity School. A South African, he earned his B.Th. and M.Th. from Stellenbosch University in South Africa and a PhD from Princeton Theological Seminary. He also holds certificates in psychodynamic psychotherapy, marriage and family therapy, and group therapy from the Blanton-Peale Graduate Institute in New York City. Jaco is the author of numerous articles and four books: *When Steeples Cry: Leading Congregations Through Loss and Change* (Pilgrim Press, 2005), *Becoming a Pastor: Forming Self and Soul for Ministry* (The Pilgrim Press, 2007/2014), *A Play-Full Life: Slowing Down and Seeking Peace* (The Pilgrim Press, 2011), and *Growing Down: Theology and Human Nature in the Virtual Age* (Baylor University Press, 2017). His current book projects include *The Millennial Narrative: Sharing a Good Life with the Next Generation* (Abingdon Press, 2019) and *The Virtues of Artificial Intelligence: Pastoral Recommendations* (Lexington Books, Forthcoming).

Christopher Barina Kaiser is professor emeritus of historical and systematic theology at Western Theological Seminary. He began his education and professional life as an astrophysicist, earning a B.A. in physics from Harvard University and a PhD in astrogeophysics from the University of Colorado, but he later devoted his life to theology, earning a PhD from the University of Edinburgh in Scotland. His teaching and research aim to build bridges (or dig tunnels) between the two academic disciplines. He is the author of five books: *The Doctrine of God* (Crossway, 1982/2001), *Creation and the History of Science* (Eerdmans, 1991), *Creational Theology and the History of Physical Science* (Brill, 1997), *Toward a Theology of Scientific Endeavour* (Routledge, 2007), and *Seeing the Lord's Glory* (Fortress, 2014). Chris has served on the Theological Commission of the Reformed Church in America and is active in the World Communion of Reformed Churches and the Gospel and Our Culture Network.

Dustyn Elizabeth Keepers is pursuing her PhD in systematic theology at Wheaton College Graduate School while adjunct teaching at Trinity Christian College in Palos Heights, Illinois. Her current research centers on John Calvin, ecclesiology, and feminist theology. Dustyn is also an ordained minister of Word and sacrament in the Reformed Church of America and served as a pastor for several years in Holland, Michigan. She earned her MDiv from Western Theological Seminary where she also taught as part of the Hebrew teaching team.

Alberto La Rosa Rojas is pursuing a Th.D. in Christian Ethics at Duke Divinity School. A member of the Reformed Church in America, Alberto earned his MDiv from Western Theological Seminary. Alberto migrated with his family from Peru to the United States in 2001. His experience as an immigrant informs his work on developing a theological and ethical account of immigration. Alberto is interested in giving a rich account of the way immigrants think about home and belonging in conversation with Christological and creational motifs found in Scripture.

Zac Poppen is a PhD candidate in Hebrew Bible at Brite Divinity School at Texas Christian University in Fort Worth, Texas. He earned his MDiv from Western Theological Seminary. While at Western, Zac worked with Tom Boogaart on a project considering the implications of metaphorical theology and the potential impact of root metaphors on contemporary Christian scholarship that often seeks to demystify aspects of nature. Zac went on to receive an MA in theological studies from Portland Seminary at George Fox University in Oregon before pursuing his PhD His research interests include reception history, decoloniality, and political theory.

Kyle J. A. Small is professor of church leadership and dean of formation for ministry at Western Theological Seminary. He is ordained in the Reformed Church in America and served as a pastor in the Evangelical Covenant Church prior to coming to Western. He earned his MDiv from North Park Theological Seminary in Chicago, Illinois, and a PhD from Luther Seminary in St. Paul, Minnesota. Kyle's teaching and research focus on the church in America, spiritual formation, leading Christian communities, and theological education.

David L. Stubbs is professor of ethics and theology at Western Theological Seminary. After earning BS and MS degrees from Stanford University, David worked as a seismic engineer in San Francisco. While pursuing his engineering career, he also worked in churches and ministries and eventually decided to change paths. He earned an MDiv from Princeton Theological Seminary and a PhD in theological ethics from Duke University. He is an ordained minister of Word and sacrament in the Presbyterian Church (USA) and co-director of the Hope-Western Prison Initiative. He is also finishing a book project, *Table and Temple,* that traces the central meanings of the Lord's Supper from the worship of the Jerusalem temple into Christian worship.

Travis West is assistant professor of Hebrew and Old Testament at Western Theological Seminary. He is an ordained minister of Word and sacrament in the Reformed Church in America and is author of the innovative introductory Hebrew grammar, *Biblical Hebrew: An Interactive Approach* (GlossaHouse, 2016). Travis earned his MDiv from Western Theological Seminary and his PhD from Vrije Universiteit in Amsterdam, the Netherlands, where his dissertation was titled *The Art of Biblical Performance: Performance Criticism and the Genre of the Biblical Narratives.*

Stephen J. Wykstra is professor of philosophy at Calvin College. As a student at Hope College, he double-majored in philosophy and physics, going on to earn a PhD in history and philosophy of science from the University of Pittsburgh in Pennsylvania. He has published numerous papers in philosophy of science and philosophy of religion with a focus on probability, evidence, and evidential arguments from evil and is continuing his research and writing in retirement. His academic interests include epistemology, logic, history of science, philosophy of science, and philosophy of religion.

Lyle Vander Broek is professor emeritus in New Testament Studies at the University of Dubuque Theological Seminary in Iowa. He earned his MDiv from Western Theological Seminary and his PhD from Drew University in Madison, New Jersey. Lyle is ordained in the Presbyterian Church (USA). His publications include *Literary Forms in the New Testament, Breaking Barriers: The Possibilities of Christian Community in a Lonely World,* and *The Life of Paul for Today.* His ongoing interests include the pastoral issues in 1 Corinthians, the nature of Christian community, and the historical setting of the Gospel of Mark.

Preface

Before the Face of God

Dustyn Elizabeth Keepers

According to Tom Boogaart, theology is not merely a way of thinking. It is a way of living. His 33 years of teaching at Western Theological Seminary (WTS) are a vivid example of this fundamental conviction. Through the study of the Scriptures, Dr. Boogaart has worked to lead ministers-in-training on a journey from speaking in the "third person" about God toward a transformative "second person" conversation with God. His deep commitment to engaging the Scriptures as a living Word rather than as a (dead) object of study generated a theological ethos that has affected not only Tom's classroom but the whole WTS community: a call to remember that our life is lived before the face of God.

Recently, Dr. Boogaart told me about a key moment in his self-understanding: some years ago, Western Theological Seminary began the practice of sharing the Lord's Supper in chapel every Friday. As they began to regularly invoke the Spirit's presence among this learning community while sharing these ordinary elements, Tom started to articulate something that was already forming the center of his work—a sacramental view of reality. He thought, "That's my understanding of teaching, of the church. I'd been doing it but hadn't yet worked out all the theology." Tom's approach to his work was characterized by the belief that God is immanently present in creation, even in the ordinary realities of a particular people who open themselves to the Spirit. The presence of God that he saw so clearly through the community's participation in the Lord's Supper pointed to God's nearness in all aspects of life.

According to Tom, this worldview is fully on display throughout the Scriptures, which describe creation as filled with the glory of the Lord. And he dedicated himself to helping students encounter this world and the living God who so intimately animates it. But of course, this sacramental view of reality was not only a curiosity to be visited when we read the Bible; it demands that we adopt it ourselves and thus engage the rest of our material lives and our relationships in a new way, expecting God's presence to be evident all around us. It is this view of the world that drives Tom's interests in justice for the oppressed and conservation of the earth, that drives his commitment to his local community as well as his interests in the findings of science. Tom has invested in relationships, led his community in initiatives for social justice, and cultivated conversations across disciplines from drama to the philosophy of science. All of these areas of interest are explored in the essays that follow, written by Tom's colleagues and friends who span an equally wide range of disciplines.

Tom Boogaart's devotion to formational teaching and his deep roots in the WTS community in many ways stand in stark contrast to an academic guild all too often characterized by disconnected scholars striving for notoriety. Thus, as Ben Conner points out later in this volume, it seems a bit ironic to recognize Tom's retirement with a festschrift—what an academic way to honor someone who has been so suspicious of the temptation to make a name for oneself! And yet I think those of us participating in this volume have felt a deep sense of satisfaction as we set ourselves to the work of describing and reflecting upon the impact Dr. Boogaart has made through his academic work, teaching, and embodied theology. As the essays on the following pages filled my inbox, my anticipation for this volume grew. I began to hope that it would not only demonstrate our thankfulness for Tom and his work but that it could also be an invitation to the reader to consider their own life and work and worship before the face of our loving and ever-present God.

Additionally, there is a sense in which this volume might also serve to record and preserve a snapshot of the character of Western Theological Seminary during Tom's tenure. While we expect the reader will gain a fulsome picture of Dr. Boogaart's passion and work, Tom himself would be the first to point out that he has done all of this within a community who has loved, trusted, and joined him in the pursuit. When other academic institutions might have dismissed his desire to radically alter the Hebrew program as "not scholarly" enough, Western's leadership trusted Tom to lead a pedagogical experiment. (The essays by Carol Bechtel, Travis West, and Pam Bush describe aspects of the program in more detail). This new approach to teaching Hebrew through oral and interactive methods was unorthodox and labor intensive, yet the seminary supported him in the extraordinary efforts it required. Today, this approach to learning biblical Hebrew as a living language has become a centerpiece of the student experience at WTS, indicative of the theological heart of this institution, which, like Tom, has continued to grapple with the question: Who are we, and what are we called to do before the face of God? I know Tom is deeply grateful for the love and trust invested in him and his work by the WTS community, and so are so many of us—his students, colleagues, and friends—who have been shaped by Tom's love for the Scriptures and the living God who speaks in them.

In Part One of this volume, the reader is introduced to some of the key themes of Tom Boogaart's work. Here his friends and colleagues describe and reflect on his approach to Scripture and to teaching along with the theology that guides his life and work. The first entry is from Tom's longtime colleague and fellow professor of Old Testament, Carol Bechtel. She writes about the problem of biblical illiteracy in our society and its impact on the work of training seminarians in her essay. She suggests that Dr. Boogaart's critique of the traditional methodology for biblical language instruction and his use of drama to introduce students to the text as the living Word of God point to a way forward in response to this concern. Next, Northwestern College theatre professor Jeff Barker sheds more light on Dr. Boogaart's understanding of the Old Testament narratives as Hebrew dramas. In his essay, he tells the story of his first encounter with Dr. Boogaart's idea and how it inspired his own efforts at putting the narratives of Scripture on stage.

Travis West further unpacks Dr. Boogaart's approach to the Scriptures. As several of the essays indicate, Tom has frequently drawn attention to the fact that many of the metaphors that describe the study of the Scriptures imply that it is a dead object. Yet as this essay explains, approaching Scripture with a posture of receptivity or hospitality rather than seeking mastery over it can alter our relationship with the text as a living Word and, more importantly, with the living, loving God who meets us in it. Pam Bush's essay shows how Dr. Boogaart's teaching reflects not only a transformed relationship with his subject of study but also with students and colleagues. She describes the team-teaching approach used in Western Theological Seminary's Hebrew courses, where the posture of welcome extends to invite people of all levels and abilities into a community space where transformational learning is made possible by love.

The last two essays in this first section turn toward the theological legacy—a sacramental view of reality—that Dr. Boogaart has received and is passing on to his colleagues and students. Benjamin Conner describes the living tradition Tom has championed: a Reformed, Pietist, experiential theology, summarized in the concept of *coram Deo*—that is, living before the face of God. Dr. Conner connects this tradition to earlier generations of Reformed scholars like Eugene Osterhaven and traces how this approach to theology has been made manifest in various aspects of Tom's work. Kyle Small's contribution gives us a glimpse into Tom's influence through personal relationship and explores coram Deo theology as a lived experience. Dr. Small reflects on his recent pilgrimage experience during a sabbatical and considers the possibilities of that practice to expand our awareness of the presence of God in the ordinary places we find ourselves.

Part Two of the volume turns from direct consideration of Dr. Boogaart's work to a collection of essays that seek to honor him through their own reflections on Scripture. The first two essays by Tom's longtime colleagues at Western Theological Seminary, Timothy Brown and James Brownson, examine broader questions related to our approach to reading and interpreting Scripture, while the ones that follow interact more directly with individual passages. Dr. Brown asks what is demanded of us if we are to become the kind of people who read Scripture rightly. He begins with five virtues found in Colossians 3, which culminates in the call to allow the Word of Christ to "dwell among you richly," and explores how compassion, kindness, humility, gentleness, and patience help us fulfill this command. James Brownson, on the other hand, names the deep divisions in our culture and church that challenge us when it comes to interpreting Scripture and suggests two approaches that may help us to read Scripture together more fruitfully.

Drawing on numerous examples of past debates on the interpretation of Scripture, Dr. Brownson suggests that by reexamining the role of experience and considering the purpose of a given text, we might begin to move past our current impasses in interpreting the Bible.

The next two essays engage Scripture in order to address specific pastoral questions in the church today. Lyle Vander Broek nods to Dr. Boogaart's concern for the practical pastoral implications of biblical studies as he closely reads the apostle Paul's teaching on the resurrection of believers. The frequent failure of contemporary churches to teach a full biblical vision of the resurrection has consequences not only for our understanding of death but also for how we live the Christian life in relation to the world around us, as Dr. Vander Broek carefully parses out. Next, Jaco Hamman credits Dr. Boogaart with inspiring him to look more closely at the book of Joel in response to concerns being raised about how the church will respond to the millennial generation. In Dr. Hamman's reading, the six narrative movements of the book of Joel correspond to various elements that characterize life in the millennial generation, offering an invitation to this generation to find meaning and access to the Good Life through the Hebrew Scriptures.

Three more essays by Dr. Boogaart's former students Zac Poppen, me (Dustyn Elizabeth Keepers), and Alberto La Rosa Rojas directly engage the Scriptures, each with a particular focus on justice for the oppressed. These essays fittingly demonstrate Dr. Boogaart's reverberating reminder that because our lives are lived before the face of God, we are called to an abiding and active concern for all of God's creation. Zac Poppen explores the connection between justice and land, offering a liberation-inspired lens for reading, which he terms the "preferential option for the dispossessed." Examining the narrative of Naboth's vineyard (1 Kings 21) alongside several troubling texts about the destruction of land during the conquests in Joshua, he invites us to read these texts with the poor and dispossessed in order to better grasp the critical tension between these narratives and other texts that extend healing and command justice for the oppressed.

In my own essay, I raise a challenge to the church to reengage the stories of women in Scripture as models for discipleship in the face of modern interpretations that often seem weighted down by sexism. I read the story of the Samaritan woman in John 4 in light of the perhaps unlikely combination of feminist scholarship and pre-critical interpretations in order to reclaim the woman's story as one of dedicated discipleship and inspiring evangelism. Next, Alberto La Rosa

Rojas invites us to take up the questions of the migrant as he rereads the story of Joseph leaving his family in Canaan. Placing this narrative in the larger context of God's journey with Jacob/Israel disrupts our usual way of reading it. In this way, he reminds us that the God of Israel is a God who goes with his people who are marked by the trauma of leaving—a God who is with the migrant on their difficult journey.

In Part Three, our volume branches out to explore how Dr. Boogaart's questions and concerns touch other areas of his colleagues' scholarship. John Coakley notes how he and Dr. Boogaart have often reflected on the surprising grace they encounter in reading the premodern figures of their respective disciplines. Dr. Coakley and Christopher Kaiser each offer here an examination of such a figure. Dr. Coakley begins with the oft-quoted phrase attributed to St. Francis of Assisi, "Preach the gospel, sometimes with words," and turns to examine how the concept of "example" is demonstrated in the records of St. Francis's life as recorded by his fellow brothers. Dr. Kaiser explores the rabbinic tradition of ben Zoma, whose unique interpretation of Genesis 1 was said to have "shaken the world." Following an analysis of ben Zoma's hermeneutical approach, Dr. Kaiser suggests that perhaps we're not meant to take that description of its impact metaphorically. He suggests that Christians, who believe in the living Word of God, should not dismiss too quickly the idea that a performative interpretation of Scripture could actually call forth an experience of what it describes.

Dr. Kaiser's essay helps us draw out a connection between Dr. Boogaart's emphasis on the performative and living reality of the Scriptures as God's Word and his sacramental view of the created world. For many years, both Dr. Kaiser and Dr. Boogaart have been a part of an informal science and theology discussion group. This group attempts not only to keep theologians informed about the secure findings of science but also strives to find language that can bring the scientific findings about the created world into theological articulation of creation. In the next two essays, Stephen Wykstra and Christopher Dorn, both members of this science and theology group, engage aspects of the group's ongoing discussion from the vantage point of their own fields of study.

Dr. Wykstra, a professor of philosophy from Calvin College, honors Dr. Boogaart by specifically addressing his concern over the connection between the spiritual and material worlds that modern people seem to have lost. In an effort to rebuild the bridge between a scientific understanding of the world and a sense of God's immanence in creation, Dr. Wykstra examines Isaac Newton's metaphysics, which may surprise many with its willingness to understand God at work in the properties of matter. Christopher Dorn, on the other hand, suggests Karl Barth as a potential conversation partner in response to Dr. Boogaart's hope that theologians might help us articulate an understanding of the world informed by the findings of science. He describes two concepts, "history" and "state," as used in Barth's discussion of theological anthropology, where Barth describes true human existence as existence in relationship to God, who became like us in Jesus Christ.

The final essay, from David Stubbs, brings our volume back to where it began by placing a theological topic on the saving work of Christ into conversation with the Old Testament. Inspired by Dr. Boogaart's efforts to help students rediscover not only the words but also the rich sacramental worldview found within the Old Testament, he suggests that the pilgrim feasts of Israel might serve as a more fitting lens for our understanding of Christ's atoning work. The three feasts—Passover, Pentecost, and the Feast of Booths—structured the lives of the Israelites, narrating and celebrating God's saving relationship with them. And Dr. Stubbs's argues this same narrative, which the New Testament writers already had partly in mind, can help us avoid the reductions at risk with other atonement theories as we describe Christ's saving work.

I am confident I can speak for each of these contributors when I say that we are all deeply grateful for Tom Boogaart—our friend, teacher and colleague. These essays, whether reflecting on our own work or on Tom's more directly, are offered in his honor and in thanks for all he has taught us. We pray these essays reflect, at least in part, the conversation and community that Tom has cultivated through his work. We also offer them in order to welcome you, the reader, into that community. We hope that as you read you hear the same invitation to live fully coram Deo—before the face of God—that our friend

CHAPTER 1

Dying to Read the Bible[1]

Carol M. Bechtel

Imagine a world before Netflix. Imagine evenings spent together in conversation on the front porch or around the fire. Imagine your days winding to a close doing quiet, companionable tasks while listening to another family member reading aloud, most likely from the Bible. In short, imagine a world very different from that of most citizens of the twenty-first century.

This trip down memory lane is not intended as nostalgia. It is important to acknowledge that the "good old days" were not always that good. (In some parts of the world, they are not even old.) Still, one of the real losses of the last century has been the easy and intimate familiarity with the Bible that was a by-product of such evenings.

As someone who has spent the last quarter-century teaching the Bible to ministers in training, I have had ample time to opine the decline in Bible knowledge and to formulate theories about the causes of that decline. The first two sections of this essay will set

---

[1] This chapter is dedicated to my friend and colleague, Tom Boogaart, who has done so much over the course of his career to nurture in his students a vibrant and formative relationship with Scripture.

forth some observations about the decline and suggestions about contributing causes. While these sections will not break much new ground, they are important for "getting our bearings," as it were. The last section, however, will offer an example of a fresh interaction with an underappreciated biblical story: the book of Jonah. In this section, I hope to help us glimpse a promising path for the road ahead.

When We Can't Distinguish Esther from St. Paul

Gone are the days when one can allude to biblical characters and expect instant recognition from one's audience. More often than not, such name-dropping will garner only puzzled expressions. Even former favorites such as "David and Goliath" are no longer part of our common cultural heritage. This decline is well documented, and though some of the yardsticks pollsters have used to measure it are flawed,[2] references to an "epidemic of biblical illiteracy" are common in both sacred and secular circles. No, Horatio—Joshua was *not* the son of a nun.[3] So far, so grim. But surely this epidemic has not infected seminarians; one would assume that individuals who have discerned a call to Christian ministry would have a fairly good grasp of both biblical testaments. In my experience, however, this is not the case. For many budding seminarians, the New Testament is a fairly new friend, and the Old Testament is a suspicious looking stranger.

I must be quick to add caveats to this claim. It does not apply to *all* of my students—only to enough of a growing number of them to create what is, in my mind, an alarming trend. It is also not intended to call into question the validity of any student's calling; it simply means that many of them have more work to do before they can accept that call. In my experience, most of these biblically-disadvantaged students quickly realize that they have to play catch-up and apply themselves to that task with energy, intelligence, imagination, and love.

At the risk of belaboring the obvious, it is important to ask: Why is biblical illiteracy—especially among Christians—so alarming? Consider the following circuitous illustration, which will eventually address this question.

---

[2]   Leonard Greenspoon, "Bible Literacy Polls," SBL Forum, last modified November 2005, http://sbl-site.org/Article.aspx?ArticleID=470.

[3]   This is an example from a student paper used by Kenneth Berding in his article, "The Crisis of Biblical Illiteracy" (*Biola Magazine*, Spring 2014). Berding goes on to observe, "This student clearly didn't know that Nun was the name of Joshua's father, nor apparently did he realize that Catholic nuns weren't around during the time of the Old Testament. But I'm sure it created quite a stir at the convent!"

Some time ago, I wrote a Bible study on Paul's encouragement to the Christians at Colossae to "let the word of Christ dwell in you richly" (Colossians 3:16). Part of Paul's point in the larger passage (3:1-17) is that it is not enough to simply call ourselves "Christians." We must apply ourselves to the hard work of compassion, kindness, humility, patience, forgiveness, and love.

To illustrate this, I wrote a parody of the ever-popular *VeggieTales* song, "We Are the Pirates Who Don't Do Anything."[4] The original video features a bunch of our favorite vegetable characters dressed up like pirates, sitting around in their recliners, singing a song about how they don't do anything remotely pirate-like any more. The parody invited us to imagine what Christians might sing from our recliners. Sing along if the song fits:

> Refrain: We are the Christians who don't do anything
> We just stay home and lie around
> And if you ask us to do anything
> We'll just tell you, "We don't do anything!"
> Verse: Oh, we never show compassion
> And we never read the Bible
> And we never pray the Lord's Prayer
> Or recite the hundredth psalm
> And we never feed the hungry
> And we never love our neighbor
> And we can't distinguish Esther from St. Paul

Granted, the point of the parody is broader than "Christians don't know the Bible very well anymore." However, since the Bible is where we learn about the elements of Christlike character, it could be argued that being wholly immersed in and formed by Scripture is foundational for everything that falls under the theological heading of "sanctification." Just as pirates risk their identity as pirates when they stop doing pirate-like things, so one has to wonder whether Christians who have stopped reading the Bible may be risking a crucial part of their Christian character.

To summarize: in my experience, even seminarians do not know the Bible very well anymore. This is, at least in part, a reflection of the broader culture, where the Bible is neither read nor studied even by those who profess to be Christians.

---

4   "What Pirates and Christians Have in Common" in *Life After Grace: Daily Reflections on the Bible* (Louisville: Westminster John Knox, 2003), 102–4.

Now I'd like for us to enter more deeply into thinking about why this is the case. What factors—internal and external to the church—have contributed to what is arguably a crisis for both ministry and Christianity?

Why We Can't Distinguish Esther from St. Paul

In the opening paragraph of this essay, I invited readers to imagine a day when Bible reading was a daily part of people's experience. The Netflix analogy was intentional, since one of the reasons people read the Bible with such regularity in pre-television times was for entertainment. This was by no means the *only* reason people read it, but the fact that there are some really good stories in the Bible must have played a role in its popularity. Who wouldn't want to hear the story of Daniel in the lion's den or read about the perils of Paul to break the monotony of a long winter's evening? The story of David's rise to power and the scramble to succeed him in 2 Samuel rivals *House of Cards* for steamy political intrigue. And if that isn't enough to get our attention, this so-called "Succession Narrative" (2 Samuel 9-20; 1 Kings 1-2) is worth a read solely on literary grounds. In fact, its author is sometimes referred to as the Old Testament's Shakespeare.

Nevertheless, the church can no longer rely on the Bible's entertainment value to raise the tide of biblical literacy. There is simply too much competition. If the Bible *is* entertaining, then that quality is secondary to what ought to motivate Christians to read it. At the heart of the matter is this: generations of the faithful have testified to their belief that the Old and New Testaments are somehow, mysteriously, the holy, inspired Word of God. Debates about precisely what that means have kept us busy for centuries, but the centrality of Scripture is not up for debate in most Christian quarters.

Here is an example of how the Reformed Church in America expressed its understanding of "the authority and infallibility of Scripture" in a paper affirmed by that denomination's General Synod in 1963:

> Through the Word the living Christ exercises his lordship over the church and the world, and therefore we test all doctrine and life by this authority. Scripture as the Word of the faithful God is infallible and inerrant in all that it intends to teach and accomplish concerning faith and life. The confession declares, "We believe that these Holy Scriptures fully contain the will of

God, and that whatsoever man ought to believe unto salvation, is sufficiently taught therein...the doctrine thereof is most perfect and complete in all respects" [Belgic Confession, 7]. We recognize that the Bible is written by human authors in human language and thus subject to certain human limitations, but these limitations in no way detract from the infallibility of the message. We hold that neither Scripture nor the Reformed confessions require the extension of these divine attributes of infallibility and inerrancy to the whole human process involved in revelation of the total phenomena of Scripture.[5]

It is a puzzling irony that even those churches that hold so tenaciously to the inspiration of Scripture should still find themselves falling victim to the epidemic of biblical illiteracy.[6] That irony becomes positively painful when we remember the lengths to which Christians, both ancient and modern, have been willing to go in order to read the Bible at all.

One little-known example comes from twelfth-century France. A group of lay Christians, upset by the opulence and hypocrisy of the church in their day, began a movement that emphasized living according to the Sermon on the Mount. (Their enemies referred to them as "Waldensians" after their leader, Valdes of Lyon.) In addition to simplicity, service, and poverty, the Waldensians insisted on reading the Bible for themselves. Tragically, this earned them the attention of the Inquisition, and in the fourteenth and fifteenth centuries, hundreds were denounced as heretics and burned at the stake. In 1532, the survivors met with emissaries from Calvin's Geneva and agreed to join that branch of the Protestant Reformation. Undaunted by persecution, one of their first priorities was to commission a new translation of the Bible from its original languages into French. Today their descendants continue to live out their faith "according to the Word of God" in Italy, Uruguay, Argentina, North America, and other places around the globe.

Such stories "put to shame the casual way we wear your name," as the familiar hymn text puts it.[7] In fact, a whole verse from that hymn bears quoting:

---

[5]   *The Church Speaks: Papers of the Commission on Theology*, Reformed Church in America, 1959–1984, ed. James I. Cook (Grand Rapids: Eerdmans, 1985), 7–8.

[6]   I would note that the mere emphasis of biblical authority does not guarantee a profound familiarity with the Bible's content. In my experience, in fact, the two often occur in inverse proportion.

[7]   Fred Pratt Green, "How Clear Is Our Vocation Lord" (Carol Stream: Hope Publishing Company, 1982).

We marvel how your saints become in hindrances more sure;
whose joyful virtues put to shame the casual way we wear your
      name,
and by our faults obscure your power to cleanse and cure.

If the Inquisition couldn't keep the Waldensians from reading the Bible, what's our excuse? If they were dying *for* reading the Bible, why aren't we dying *to* read the Bible?

The reasons are "legion," as they say, and I will not attempt to be either exhaustive or exhausting in listing them. In an article titled "The Crisis of Biblical Illiteracy," Kenneth Berding suggests the following candidates: distractions (especially technology), misplaced priorities, over-confidence, and the pretext of being too busy.[8] These, in addition to the larger cultural shifts already described in this essay, comprise as good a beginning as any. In what follows, however, I would like to focus on a few explanations (not excuses) that are particularly nettlesome at the seminary level.

Playing Catch-Up

More and more students come to seminary as recent converts. Many find their way to us by way of parachurch organizations. Don't misunderstand—we are happy to get them and grateful that the Holy Spirit is working "in many and various ways" (Hebrews 1:1). And some organizations put more emphasis than others on Christian formation, which includes, of course, getting acquainted with God through the regular study of Scripture. But the fact remains that there is a lot of ground to cover in a relatively short time, and students who come via this route often have a long way to go.

The irony is that seminary students who have been raised in the church often find themselves playing catch-up as well. In their rush to be relevant, congregations have often substituted material judged to be more interesting to young people. I hesitate to be too critical of these efforts since I know from first-hand experience how difficult it is to get the attention of a seventh-grade Sunday school class. On the other hand, I remember feeling deeply insulted as a fifth-grader when I was forced to put on a beanie and sing a song about being a "Jet Cadet for Jesus." Surely, a nice, gruesome story about David and Goliath would have better than that!

---

[8]   Berding, "The Crisis of Biblical Illiteracy."

Curricular Competition

Once students arrive at seminary, there is vicious curricular competition for their time. Faculty members who teach and preach in congregations are constantly greeted with the refrain, "I hope you're teaching them _____ at the seminary." Fill in the blank with all manner of essential subjects: financial planning, non-violent communication, avoiding clergy misconduct, cultural competence, leadership skills, et cetera. I even had an aunt who would bend my ear with amazing regularity about the importance of teaching future ministers good table manners. To be honest, I couldn't disagree with her. But I also knew that if we made room in the curriculum to teach students everything they needed to know in ministry, they wouldn't graduate from seminary until it was time for them to retire.

When "curriculum crowding" meets growing biblical illiteracy, it forms an even more challenging conundrum. Yet too often, seminaries have been slow to recognize the need for more biblical training. How we can create more space for Scripture without eliminating other "essentials" from the curriculum is something we will need to work out with fear and trembling. It may even mean lengthening the number of years it takes to get a degree. But ignoring the problem does a disservice to the church and is nothing short of irresponsible.

Misplaced Methodological Loyalties

One last reason we are not always "dying to read the Bible" even at the seminary level has to do with misplaced methodological loyalties.

In his last public lecture at Western Theological Seminary in Holland, Michigan, retiring Old Testament professor Tom Boogaart spoke for the entire Hebrew teaching team when he said:

> We began to entertain the possibility that the lack of interest that people showed in the Bible, what decades ago was labeled "the strange silence of the Bible in the churches," and the corresponding biblical illiteracy might be due in part to the way we were teaching languages and exegesis at the seminary. Using teaching methods that dated from the 19th century, the same methods by which we the instructors had been taught, we spent the majority of our classroom time focusing on memorizing vocabulary and grammatical tables as the necessary tools that students could use to dissect a text. And what does the image of

tools and dissection suggest? The image suggests that the biblical text is cut up into pieces and laid out on a table before us, that the Bible is a dead object and that we are the living subjects whose task it is to discover its true meaning.[9]

I will say more about Boogaart's innovative approach to improving the teaching of Hebrew at the seminary level in the final section of this essay. For now, I would simply like to highlight his insights and link them to a broader critique, not just of the way we teach the biblical languages but also of historical criticism. This critique was made by Jewish professor and scholar, Jon Levenson. In a 1993 book titled *The Hebrew Bible, the Old Testament, and Historical Criticism*, Levenson points out that in their relentless pursuit of "what it meant," historical critics have often subtly fostered an image of the Bible as a book which "once meant a great deal" but now means "little or nothing."[10]

This critique stings, especially since I owe my faith to a rich encounter with historical criticism during my college years. And it would be foolish to gainsay all the important contributions made by historical criticism and its descendants. I teach and will continue to teach using many of the tools given to me by these methods.

Nevertheless, the guild's tendency to treat the Bible as if it is an object awaiting dissection urges caution at the very least. To make matters worse, those of us who have spent our careers using these methods may have inadvertently given the impression that biblical interpretation was a matter best left to the "experts." If that is the case, then these misplaced methodological commitments may have contributed to "the strange silence of the Bible in the churches."

It is tempting to end this essay with a confession of sin. Everything we have surveyed so far could form the foundation for that confession. In short, biblical illiteracy is real, and even those of us who love the Bible deeply have often contributed to the problem.

But I think I would rather end with a confession of faith. The foundation for that confession is based on the work of my students and colleagues at Western Theological Seminary and their engagement with the book of Jonah. Their work suggests that God may be leading us to discover (or rediscover) ways of engaging with the biblical text that are profound, accessible, and—one hopes—contagious.

---

[9]   From Tom Boogaart's "Last Lecture," Western Theological Seminary, Holland, Michigan, December 13, 2018.

[10] John D. Levenson, *The Hebrew Bible, the Old Testament, and Historical Criticism* (Louisville: Westminster John Knox Press, 1993), 97.

Engaging Jonah

Most people never get past the fish in the Bible's story of Jonah. Perhaps that's what the late Howard Hageman realized when he delivered a speech on Jonah, which is said to have begun: "Today we are not going to talk about either the credibility of the book or the edibility of the prophet."

Commentaries wring their hands over whether it was a "big fish" or a "whale" that swallowed up Jonah in chapter 1. One creative commentator from the early twentieth century even suggested that perhaps the prophet had been rescued from the waves by a ship named "Big Fish." Given how obsessed readers often are by this detail, I sometimes suggest that the fish is really a red herring. If we are not careful, it can distract us from all the wonderful theology in the rest of the book.

Perhaps people's fixation with the fish is part of what prompted my colleague, Tom Boogaart, to search for a new way to engage this Old Testament story in his Hebrew class at Western Theological Seminary. His primary motivation, however, had to do with his frustration with the "dissection" approach to teaching Hebrew alluded to earlier in this essay. In Boogaart's words,

> We needed to find ways to overcome the distance between the student and the biblical text. The words of Scripture needed to make their way to the heart. In order to do this, students needed to involve all their bodily senses in learning the language. They needed to hear words, speak words, and move with words. The bodily senses are doors to the heart, and words can walk through these doors and reside there. Words kept in the heart—knowing by heart as we often say to each other—was the deeper knowing that we desired for our students.[11]

With the help of a teaching team composed of both students and colleagues, Boogaart began to teach in a way that responded to the biblical story as drama.[12] The narrative itself signals the appropriateness of this approach especially through its inclusion of dialogue. As Boogaart points out, "The captain and the crew's words are not being documented; they are speaking for themselves. The presence of dialogue

---

[11] Boogaart, "Last Lecture."
[12] Although the teaching team has varied over the years, the faculty/staff component has included Tom Boogaart, Travis West, Dawn Boelkins, and Pam Bush.

shows that biblical narratives take up past events and present them as happening again."[13]

In the process of memorizing, casting, blocking, and composing songs for the drama that is the book of Jonah, Boogaart and his students discovered much about the book that would have been inaccessible to them through less intimate and interactive methods. Especially stunning from an audience member's point of view were the ways their interpretation allowed them to "get past the fish." Forget whether a prophet could literally be swallowed by a fish; the story of Jonah is a story about the prophet's inability to stomach God's grace to people Jonah doesn't like. He is happy to accept God's grace but furious when God extends that grace to others. The drama of Jonah reveals the violence of the prophet's own theology in contrast to the gracious nature of God. It is a cautionary tale against narrow exclusivism in any age and a pointed reminder that God is indeed "slow to anger, abounding in steadfast love, and ready to relent from punishing."[14] In an age when we are so quick to judge and so slow to show compassion—especially to people we see as "foreign"—there is surely a word from the Lord somewhere in there for us.

While the students in Boogaart's class were working in the original Hebrew language, I think the way they engaged Jonah's story as drama suggests one important way all of us might begin to engage a biblical story as the living Word of God. Consider the following quote from a commentary that seems to be on a similar wavelength:

> If God's revelation came through history alone it would be history that matters; if God's revelation was directly taught to us by every biblical text, it would be the teaching in the text that matters. But God's revelation is not directly from history or text alone. The presence of contrasting and differing texts in our Bible is an invitation to us to think. If communication reveals the communicator, the Bible's communication reveals a communicating God who does not coerce or impose but rather invites. *The invitation is to think, to use imagination, to search the Scriptures, to find where God is offering fullness of life*—life and the joy

---

[13]   Boogaart, "Last Lecture."

[14]   This confession of faith occurs frequently in the Old Testament (see Exodus 34:6; Numbers 14:18; Psalm 86:5, 15; Joel 2:13). Only Jonah (4:2) has the temerity to complain about these habits of God's heart!

of life that implies accepting being loved by God and does not exclude pain and suffering and heartache.[15] [emphasis added]

As the church seeks to turn the tide of biblical illiteracy, this call to a more imaginative engagement with Scripture is one we cannot afford to ignore. We will not succeed without a lot of help from the Holy Spirit, of course. But pledging ourselves "to use imagination, to search the Scriptures, and to find where God is offering fullness of life" may be just what we need to leave people "dying to read the Bible" again.

---

[15] *The International Bible Commentary: A Catholic and Ecumenical Commentary for the Twenty-First Century*, ed. William Farmer (Collegeville: Liturgical Press, 1998), 576.

CHAPTER 2

The Mountains are Full of Horses and Chariots[1]

Jeff Barker

Do you recall the Bible story of the chariots of fire? Here is Tom Boogaart's translation (2 Kings 6:8-23).

Conflict

And the king of Aram, he was warring in Israel. And he held council with his officers, saying:

"At place—such and such[2]—my camp."

And the man of God sent to the king of Israel, saying:

"Be on guard from passing by this place for Aram is waiting there."

---

[1] I previously told much of this story in my book *The Storytelling Church: Adventures in Reclaiming the Role of Story in Worship* (Webber Institute Books, 2011). Portions of this essay will also be included in the book that Tom Boogaart and I will soon release about performing the plays of the Bible.

[2] Since the name of this place is not known, Tom and I decided to insert the Hebrew term for "such and such" into our performance of this play.

And the king of Israel sent to the place which the man of God said to him. And he warned it, and it was on guard there. Not once and not twice.

Development

Scene 1

And the heart of the king of Aram was thunderous because of this thing. And he called his officers, and he said to them:

"Will you not tell me who among us is for the king of Israel?"

And one out of his officers said:

"No. My lord, the king. Indeed, Elisha, the prophet who is in Israel—he tells the king of Israel the words that you speak in your bedroom."

And he said:

"Get going and see where he is. And I will send, and I will take him."

And it was told to him, saying:

"Behold. In Dothan."

And he sent there horses and chariots and a great army. And they came by night, and they surrounded the city.

Scene 2

And early, the attendant of the man of God awoke and got up. And he went out. And, behold, an army surrounding the city and horses and chariots. And his servant said to him:

"Aahh. My lord. What do we do?"

And he said:

"Do not be afraid! For many more are here with us than are there with them."

And Elisha prayed, and he said,

"Lord. Open his eyes, and let him see!"

And the Lord opened the eyes of the boy. And he saw, and, behold, the mountain was full of horses and chariots of fire surrounding Elisha.

Scene 3

And they all descended upon him, and Elisha prayed to the Lord. And he said:

"Strike these foreigners with a blinding light!"

And he struck them with a blinding light according to the word of Elisha. And Elisha said to them:

"This is not the way; this is not the city. Walk behind me, and I will take you to the man whom you are seeking."

And he walked them toward Samaria. And time passed. As they had entered Samaria, Elisha said:

"Lord! Open the eyes of these men, and let them see."

And the Lord opened their eyes, and they saw. And, behold, in the middle of Samaria.

Resolution

And the king of Israel said to Elisha, when he saw them:

"Ha-akay? Akay?![3] My father?"

And he said:

"You shall not strike them down! Will you be killing men whom you have captured with your sword and your bow? Set bread and water before them. And let them eat! Let them drink! Let them go to their lord."

And he prepared for them a great feast. And they ate, and they drank. And he released them. And they went to their lord. And the bands of Aram no longer raided the land of Israel.

---

[3] Hebrew words, rather than their English translation, are used here for their powerful sound. They mean, "Do it? Do it?!" Or, "Shall I strike them down? Shall I strike them down?"

Here is the story of my journey into performing Bible plays. This was long before Tom Boogaart translated the chariots of fire story and long before Bible performance became such a huge part of my life's work.

The story begins at Western Theological Seminary. Karen and I were on sabbatical from our professorships at Northwestern College. We were guest professors at Western, team-teaching a course in worship with Dr. Tim Brown. We had known Tim for several years but only knew Tom as an acquaintance. One day, Tim handed me a printout of an essay that Tom had written. The essay would eventually be published in *Touching the Altar*,[4] but when Tim handed it to me, it was 19 pages on white printer paper. Tim simply said, "I think you'll want to read this."

I read the essay that same night. I could hardly believe what I was reading. Here was a serious scholar of the Scriptures arguing that there are dozens—maybe hundreds—of plays in the Bible. I had long thought there were a few plays in the Bible. The biblical book of Job is written in dialogue form and has plot development. In addition, some of the enactments of the prophets seem to be performance art. Think of Ezekiel publically lying upon his side for over a year to foretell the upcoming siege against Jerusalem. Think of Hosea marrying a sex worker as a metaphor for the LORD's covenant with an unfaithful Israel. But dozens and dozens of playscripts in the Bible? Seriously? Tom concluded his essay with these words: "Apprenticeship to theater includes apprenticeship to Scripture."[5]

If Tom's essay was correct, theatre history must be rewritten—theatre artists the world over have a new book of ancient plays to add to their repertoire. I went to bed and tossed and turned.

I arose early and read through Tom's essay again. I went over to the seminary. I saw Dr. Boogaart in the seminary hallway and called out, "Tom!" I came down the hall toward him and said, "Tim gave me your essay, 'Drama and the Sacred.' I read it last night, and I read it again this morning. I want you to know what I think about it." I knelt on the seminary floor and kissed Tom's shoe.

I was being dramatic. I was trying to say, "This is a big deal. I want to remember the start of this journey." Tom sort of giggled and said, "Well, this is not how my Bible scholar friends have reacted to my essay." I asked Tom if we could meet and have a conversation. Even though I wanted Tom's thesis to be true, I had lots of questions.

---

[4]   Thomas A. Boogaart, "Drama and the Sacred: Recovering the Dramatic Tradition in Scripture and Worship," in *Touching the Altar: The Old Testament for Christian Worship*, ed. Carol M. Bechtel (Grand Rapids: Eerdmans, 2008).

[5]   Boogaart, 58.

Tom invited Karen and me over for dinner. Later that week, we joined Tom and Judy at their charming, older, two-story home set back from State Street, which cuts diagonally through Holland, Michigan. The Boogaarts pointed us toward carefully prepared hors d'oeuvres and iced tea, but Tom and I plunged immediately into the subject of his essay. Judy and Karen had to put up with our singularity of focus throughout dinner and late into the evening as we mused over the ancient plays of the Hebrew people.

I asked Tom how many plays he thought there were in the Old Testament. Tom said, "Most of Bible up to the Psalms is playscripts."

I said, "We have Greek theatres. Where are the Hebrew theatres? Where did the ancient people perform their plays?"

Tom answered, "We don't know. We have so little archeological evidence from the time of these dramas. These stories come down to us from a people that experienced dislocation and threatened annihilation. The Bible is what's left. We have to draw conclusions from these texts themselves. And these texts are written in the form of dramas."

I said, "Just as Bible scholars don't readily agree with you, theatre scholars are not likely to agree with you either. First, they're going to say that Bible stories are for religious gatherings rather than artistic events."

Tom replied, "Yes, but the Israelite culture didn't distinguish between the sacred and secular. To them, all of life was religious."

I went on, "And next, theatre scholars are going to say there is a difference between a story and a play. They're going to say these are stories rather than plays."

"What's the difference?" Tom asked.

"A play brings the audience into the presence of an action. The event is taking place in front of us. A story, on the other hand, recounts something that happened in the past."

"Well, I don't know why that distinction should matter. There have always been storytelling performances."

I responded, "It's not only about performing; it's about acting. That's at the core of what makes theatre art distinct—enactment. Doing as opposed to describing. Showing as opposed to telling."

Tom sort of threw up his hands. He seemed to be struggling with whether such a distinction between storytelling and enactment really mattered. To Tom's thinking, storytellers and actors were both performers. But with his usual graciousness, Tom acquiesced, saying, "You know more about that than me." Then he added, "What I know is that these ancient Bible stories have dialogue and plot structure. They suggest movement that underscores the meaning of the story. They needed to have been performed in order to be kept alive through pre-literate times. Otherwise, they would have been lost. Many in my field also call them stories, but they seem like plays to me."

As the evening ended, I felt as if I had taken a step back from Tom's central idea. I readily agreed that the Bible was part of an ancient storytelling tradition, but I was no longer sure that the Bible was full of plays.

My sticking point was the verbs.

I am a playwright, and I teach playwriting. I write a lot of plays with narrators, and I teach my students that narrators in plays need to speak mostly in the present tense. The reason they do this is because, as I said to Tom in his living room, drama brings us into the presence of an action. The event is not over and done; it is here and now.

I am not alone in this view of dramaturgical technique. In his essay, "Some Thoughts on Playwriting," the great American novelist and playwright Thornton Wilder, explains, "Novels are written in the past tense. [The] constant running commentary of the novelist ('Tess slowly descended into the valley'; 'Anna Karenina laughed') inevitably conveys to the reader the fact that these events are long since past and over. The novel is a past reported in the present. On the stage it is always now."[6] A novel or story, Wilder explains, is what *took* place. A play is what *takes* place.

Throughout the remainder of Karen's and my time at the seminary that semester, I learned more about Tom. He is a Hebrew scholar who has studied in the United States, the Netherlands, and Israel. He is in love with the Bible. He says its craft and beauty take his breath away. He is committed to far more than the Bible; he is committed to the God of the Bible. He is a person of prayer and worship. He is a preacher. He does his work with care and methodology. He moves slowly. He smiles gently. He speaks softly.

I was glad to meet Tom and work alongside both him and Tim. I continued to ponder Tom's essay. Was the Bible full of plays or merely stories? I found my answer in Japan.

Late that fall, Karen and I joined a group of emissaries from our church back home. We traveled to a church that we have a sister

---

6   Thornton Wilder, "Some Thoughts on Playwriting," in *The Intent of the Artist*, ed. Augusto Centeno (Princeton: Princeton University Press, 1941).

relationship with in Kamakura. While visiting there, a 70-ish-year-old Japanese man named Hiroshi took my family and me to the Kabuki-Za in Tokyo. We watched a Kabuki play, an ancient theatrical form. Kabuki has fascinating conventions, including the fact that all the women characters are played by men, just like in Shakespeare's day. I noticed that during the play the actors would sometimes speak their lines and sometimes sort of sing them. Kabuki would never be called realism. There was also a performer who sat off to the side, singing a great deal. After the performance, I asked my Japanese hosts about the singer off to the side.

"Oh," they said, "That's the narrator."

"What's the narrator singing?" I asked.

"Well, they connect the parts of the story together and sometimes tell us what the character is feeling."

I immediately began thinking about the narrator in the Bible stories. So I asked my hosts to tell me if the narrator in Kabuki was singing in present tense or past tense.

One of them, Kuniko, looked at me curiously and said, "Your question doesn't make a lot of sense with the Japanese language. It's pretty much the same."

When I got back to the States, I excitedly contacted Tom to ask a similar question to the one I had asked our Japanese hosts: "The narrative lines in ancient Israelite dramas, in the Hebrew—are those present tense or past tense?" Tom gave me a similar answer to the one that my Japanese hosts had given me. Past and present are not handled the same in biblical Hebrew as they are in English. The Hebrew storytellers draw us into the presence of their ancestors, and their stories are told in a continuing present.

Tom explained that the term for this "continuing present" Hebrew verb is *vav*-consecutive. Over the years, Tom and I have continued to converse about the ways English and Hebrew writers use verbs differently. I come at this question from a dramaturgical perspective, and Tom comes at this question from a linguistic and cultural perspective. Here is how he explained it to me in a recent email.

> There is considerable debate about the meaning of the Hebrew verb form that we call *vav-consecutive*. Most scholars realize that the Hebrew view of time was different than the western one and that the *vav-consecutive* is conveying something significant about this Hebrew view of time. Lacking a better understanding of the

use of this form, scholars suggest that the best way to proceed is to invert the meaning of the verb from imperfect (present and future tense) to the perfect (past tense). This inversion conveys, in their opinion, adequately the basic meaning of the narrative.

I want to explore another way to proceed that takes into account the fact that the culture of the Hebrew people was oral and that the narratives were not documenting the lives of the Hebrew ancestors but performing them so that their memory did not die and their influence on their descendants lived on. In such a culture, the use of the imperfect with the *vav-consecutive* would make sense. In the time and space of the performance, the Hebrew people were communing with the ancestors, and they were hearing and seeing them again.[7]

In my first year of thinking about Tom's thesis, I found further clues in Young's Literal Translation, a version of the Bible whose point was to provide English readers with a word for word match to the Hebrew language. Robert Young did his work in the nineteenth century, so his language choices are similar to the King James Version. I cannot pretend to vouch for Young's overall biblical scholarship, but I can observe him suggesting that the English translations of his time had not adequately represented the verb tenses as the Hebrews used them. For example, the King James says in 2 Kings 6:

"Then the King of Syria warred against Israel and said unto his servants ...."

Young translates the same verse as follows:

"And the king of Aram hath been fighting against Israel, and taketh counsel with his servants, saying ...."

Why did the present tense verbs in Kabuki theatre and biblical Hebrew matter so much to me? They helped me see that the narratives of the Old Testament use the techniques of playwrights the world over. The verbs themselves affirm that the Old Testament historical narratives are plays.

But why do translators use past tense verbs in so many of our Bibles? Typical stories in English are told with past tense verbs: "Once upon a time, there was a ...." English translators of the Bible have looked at the narrative voices in Hebrew and said, "Oh, it's a story, so in our culture that should be translated in past tense." If, conversely, a

---

[7]   Tom Boogaart, email message to author, July 24, 2018.

translator were to say, "This Bible passage is a play," then that translator might allow the verbs to lean into present tense, because that is what plays do. Maybe this difference does not matter to you, but it matters a great deal to the theatre artists of the world.

Some theatre artists who are Christians function within contexts that do not affirm their life's calling. In their churches, theatre is unmentioned at best and outlawed at worst. I grew up in such a context that was guided by a *regulative principle* view of the Bible. Such contexts argue that if certain artistic forms are not explicitly modeled in Scripture, those forms are questionable. The most sincere of such churches do not permit certain musical instruments in their public gatherings. Those same churches would never permit the performance of a biblical drama, even one that uses only the biblical text. I know this to be an ongoing issue because I have been explicitly told by some pastors in my own current town that my touring theatre company would not be welcome at their churches specifically because of the regulative principle. Their assumption is that the Bible is a book: intended to be read, or perhaps sung, but never enacted. As Tom wrote in his essay, "The relationship between the church and the theater has often been compared to a troubled marriage."[8]

In my own life and at the college where I currently teach, theatre is a treasured artistic endeavor. My college (a Christian college) has built a new theatre complex containing two theatres to support an energetic and vital theatre program. But not all of my students come from families and churches that embrace their artistic gifts. And many of my Christian theatre colleagues from around the country operate in schools, churches, and communities where their life's work is constantly challenged.

Think about it this way. What if you opened the Bible to read Psalm 150. What if, instead of telling you to praise God with trumpet and guitars and drums and organs, Psalm 150 said this:

> *Praise the LORD!*
> *Praise him with monologue and dialogue.*
> *Praise him onstage, backstage, and down in the pit.*
> *Praise him in the green room and dressing room,*
> *Coatroom and seats!*
> *Praise him with scenery, lights, costumes, and props.*

---

[8]   Boogaart, "Drama and the Sacred," 36.

Praise him in laughter and tears, from Act one, scene one until "Ring down the curtain!" Let everything that breathes praise the LORD! You praise him!

What freedom there would be if the Bible were that explicit about our art form. Tom Boogaart, a serious Bible scholar, was telling me that the Bible was begging, page after page, for theatre artists to take it seriously.

Do you see why I fell to my knees in the seminary hall?

Karen and I returned home from our sojourn at the seminary and our journey to Japan. Sabbatical was over. My attention was drawn away from the ancient plays of Israel, attending to all those things left unattended when one is away for a long time. The Iowa winter eventually receded, and late that spring, I took my touring company to the library. I told them to go find nine different versions of 2 Kings 6. This was before you could easily find nine versions on your phone. We reconvened at the theatre and read our versions of the story of the chariots of fire.

My students surprised me by saying their favorite was the King James rendition of the story. I am not certain we could have articulated the reason at the time. It may have been because the KJV was written with orality in mind. The seventeenth-century translation team knew that their work was not so much for private reading but for hearing in the churches. Our team also affirmed that the antiqueness of this translation would remind our audiences that even though the form of our presentation would seem to be an adaptation of the Bible, we were speaking directly from the Bible. We wanted to affirm that we were attempting to perform precisely what we found. We were reclaiming something lost: the lost plays of Israel.

The King James places the story not in Aram but in Syria. Our first version of the play was called *The Bands of Syria*. We had a text and a title. Then one of our team members spoke up. He said, "I'm confused. What happens in this story?" We had just read the story aloud nine times! I asked, "Does anyone want to explain the story?" I looked around the circle. Silence.

I acknowledged that this was a confusing drama. I told my students that most dramas are confusing when you just read them. Plays spring to life and clarity when they get on their feet. We would need to pick a playing space, assign the parts, and try to act out the story.

One of my students said, "Where did the ancient Israelites perform their plays?"

I shook my head and said, "I don't know. No one does." I had asked Tom if he knew, and he had reminded me that the ancient people spent much of their lives threatened and on the run. Most of the physical record of the Old Testament people has been lost. What we have left is the Bible.

Then I said, "The ancient Hebrews probably performed their plays outside. Let's go outside." We went out in front of our theatre and sat in a circle on the grass. I said, "What are the places in the story, and who's there?" My students quickly listed the locations: Syria and Samaria were the locations of the kings. Dothan was where Elisha and his servant lived. Dothan was surrounded by mountains where chariots of fire would appear.

"Is that all the places?" I asked. No. There was "such and such a place." That was the secret encampment where the king of Syria would be trying to attack the king of Israel. It was the place that Elisha warned Israel about. There was also the king of Syria's bedroom. There were planning places where the king of Syria met with his spies and where the king of Israel met with Elisha's servant. There was a gathering place where the king of Israel would surround the Syrian soldiers to kill them, and there was another gathering place where the king the Israel would see to it that the Syrians would be fed before they were sent home. There was inside Elisha's house, and someplace for his servant to come out in the morning. About ten different places! No wonder my students had found the story confusing.

I said, "Collect some objects from the grass." We found some leaves, sticks, and a cigarette butt. We used the leaves to create the locations of Syria, Samaria, and Dothan. Then we broke off different shapes of sticks to represent the kings and the prophet and all their servants and soldiers. We used the cigarette butt to represent the chariots of fire. Then someone read the story, pausing while someone moved the various sticks to the locations of the story.

There in the grass, with leaves, sticks, and a cigarette butt, the story came to life! We saw it clearly.

We were excited and eager to begin assigning parts. We raced to a copy machine to make multiple copies of that page of the Bible so we could mark up the script. I decided that for our first Bible play, we would use a single narrator separate from the other characters. Every character who spoke was assigned to a different actor. We only had eight actors, so we couldn't worry about gender. As for casting, I said, "Who wants to play the king of Syria? The king of Israel?" going down the line through all the speaking parts: the two kings, a Syrian soldier, Elisha, and his servant. Along with the narrator, that accounted for six parts. Since we had eight actors, we had two actors left over. Who could they play? We decided pretty quickly that we could use another Syrian soldier since the text says that the king of Syria speaks to servants plural. And we could use a messenger for the king of Israel since the king "sent to the place which the man of God told him and warned him of."

We had identified the roles. We had chosen the actors. We marked up the scripts accordingly.

Then I decided to make a change. My students who are reading this will now be laughing. They know that I am always making changes. I hope everyone reading this is open to making changes. That is the nature of artistic process. You must try something and then try something else. The first way is almost never the final way. This is a difficult lesson that can be an obstacle to our work with Bible plays. We are used to treating the Bible with such respect that we rush to certainty. To speak of "experimenting" with the Bible seems sacrilegious. However, we must come to understand that rehearsal of Bible dramas in a respectful but playful manner is proper Bible study.

I said to my students in that first rehearsal process, "The ancient people were tribal people. Tribal people insert music into all the rhythms of their lives. The ancient Hebrews must have had music with their plays."

"Do you mean add songs?" asked one of the students.

I said, "Maybe. But since we're trying to stick to the text, let's not do anything extra-biblical in terms of words. Let's try to speak and do precisely what's on the page. But let's support it with sound." Then I asked who could play the drums. One of the students raised his hand. I sent him off to find something to drum on. I pointed to another student and said, "You're our singer for this play."

"What should I sing," she asked.

I said, "I have no idea. Just don't use words, and support what's happening on stage." She grinned because, like ancient tribal people, she loved to sing.

Then I asked an analytical question: "Who are the protagonist and antagonist of this play?" We thought initially that the protagonist must be Elisha. Then we applied a few classical tests for determining the opposing forces of a drama. We knew that contemporary analytical tests might not suit 3,000-year-old dramas, but we reasoned that we were telling these stories to audiences of today. We should at least acknowledge what our contemporary audiences expected of a story. So we plowed ahead.

We applied these simple analytical guidelines to deciding the protagonist and antagonist of *The Bands of Syria*.

1. The protagonist and antagonist should each show up early in the drama.
2. While the protagonist is usually singular, there can be many antagonists. The principle is that a greater antagonistic force creates a greater threat and therefore evokes greater sympathy for our protagonist.
3. The protagonist and antagonist should both be physically present at the climax of the drama.
4. The climax of the drama should be a physical action.
5. The protagonist is changed as a result of the climax of the drama.

When we applied the above analytical guidelines, we decided that the main character who actively changes in this drama is the king of Israel. The other characters intrude into the king of Israel's life, causing him to test his options in a variety of ways. Eventually he makes a decision to feed his enemies, which ends his war with Syria.

We were startled to discover that we identified the climactic moment as the king of Israel's faceoff with Elisha. The king of Israel wants to kill the Syrians, but Elisha demands that they be fed and set free. It is Elisha who facilitates the blinding of the Syrians and who leads them into the presence of the king, intruding into the king's life with a life-changing confrontation. This means that, like most dramas, there is a physical action hidden at the climax of the play. In this case, it is the moment of confrontation between the prophet and the king. That was the moment we would need to discover in our rehearsal process.

The king of Israel would be our protagonist. Since Elisha is the antagonist present at the moment of climax, that means that Elisha is among the intrusion forces, along with nearly everyone else in the play: Elisha's servant, the king of Syria, the Syrian soldiers, and even the chariots of fire all come crashing into the king of Israel's life, inviting a change of perspective.

The choice of the king of Israel as protagonist led us to introduce him in the first image of the play. We chose to introduce him in an image of being served. He sat upon his throne reaching for something that a kneeling servant was holding out on a tray. This would be a setup for the upending of the world after the climax of the drama, at which time the king of Israel would be the one kneeling to the Syrian soldiers, offering them a meal before sending them home. These two images would clearly depict the arc of our story.

Next, we asked ourselves how we should physically show what happens at the king's moment of decision in his face-off with Elisha. The setup is that Elisha and his servant have led the miraculously blinded Syrian soldiers into the king of Israel's presence. The king of Israel asks Elisha for a cue to kill. Two or three times, he urges Elisha to give the signal.

The physicality of the climactic moment is in the details. What is the king planning to kill the Syrians with? Elisha tells us: "with your sword and your bow."[9] We realized that the bow might be most dynamic for this moment. Here's the sequence: The Syrian soldiers are standing there, blind. The narrator tells us that the LORD opens their eyes. This is at least the third time in this story that a miracle has occurred concerning seeing: the servant sees the chariots, the Syrians are blinded, and the Syrians' sight is restored. The narrator can pass a hand over the eyes to suggest these miracles. Syrian soldiers suddenly regain their sight, see that they are trapped, and fall to their knees. The actor playing the king of Israel mimes putting an arrow to the string of his bow. He puts tension on the string and points the arrow at the Syrian soldiers. If the king of Israel lets his arrow fly, all the Israelite arrows will fly, and all the helpless Syrians will die. The prophet has only to give the word. The king says, "Shall I smite them?" No answer. The bow is still drawn. The question is asked a second time. "Shall I smite them?" Still no answer. The Hebrew interlinear, Young's Literal Translation, and Tom Boogaart's translation all place the salutation at the end of the king's speech, asking for attention and approval one last time: "My father?!"

The scene we have been in may rightly be called the catastrophe. In dramatic analysis, the catastrophe is an event that is paired with and immediately precedes the climax. The catastrophe is a structural signal that tells the audience, "Watch! The climactic scene is about to start." The catastrophe scene began when the Syrian soldiers' sight was restored and concluded when the king made his final appeal. Now our protagonist and antagonist(s) will fully engage. The climax is the protagonist's final struggle and change.

The way that our production helped the audience to notice this climactic struggle was to orchestrate a series of careful dramatic beats.

9   2 Kings 6:22.

The script provides dialogue to be sure, but more important was for our production to provide a physical representation of the change. A produced play always helps the audience see the change. That visual/physical change requires our protagonist to make a decision that includes great effort and, ideally, emotion. In our production, we chose to support the protagonist's emotional journey musically.

Here is what we did. After the king asks for approval a third time, Elisha steps in front of the king's arrow. This is dangerous, so the king quickly lowers his bow. Elisha tells the king not to kill his prisoners of war. He must feed them and send them home. Now comes the king's moment of decision. The decision is not in the text! The ancient playwright leaves this moment to the performers to physically enact the moment of change. If the decision is too easily and quickly made, the stakes of the decision are lessened. If there is struggle and even danger, the value of the decision and its connected character change is more meaningful to the audience.

In our production, the king of Israel decided to test Elisha. The king raised his bow, pointed the arrow directly at Elisha's heart, and pulled the string to full extension. Elisha's servant covered his own eyes. The Syrian soldiers were aghast. The drums built and built. Elisha looked the king in the eyes and did not move. Everyone on stage (except the frightened servant) stared at the prophet and king, and the prophet and king stared at one another. The king's muscles began to shake. The drums suddenly quit. Silence. The sharp click of a clave tried to break the tension. The moment held. One more sharp click of the clave, and finally the king made a decision. He slowly relaxed the string and lowered his bow. He set the bow down. He walked over and mimed picking up a large tray of food. Elisha and his servant led the Syrian soldiers to sit on the king's very own throne. The terrified Syrians were still not certain if they were not about to be killed, but they sat down. Then the king knelt, bowed his head, and held out the plate of food to serve his enemies. One of the Syrians took a chance and reached for something to eat. Freeze. Finally the narrator broke the long silence with, "And he prepared great provision for them."

The change in our protagonist is finally clear, and we breathe a sigh of relief. The climax is passed. All that remains is the play's resolution, a scene that always hints at the future. On this occasion, the Syrians are well fed and released. They arrive home, followed by a time of peace between the two countries.

The following summer, the performers, Tom, and I convened in Virginia at the Christians in Theatre Arts national conference to share our discoveries and investigate some other Bible plays. Our work was affirmed in this surprising way. We were leading a workshop with a group of directors from around the country. We were watching a director attempt to stage a version of the burning bush text. God tells Moses to take off his shoes. The director said, "Stop, Moses. You should obey God and take off your shoes." The actor obeyed the director, but we all realized in that moment that the Bible never says whether Moses took off his shoes. An artistic choice must be made to obey God or not. The performance immediately makes clear that which the text leaves vague. The rehearsal continued and the actor playing God told Moses what was going to happen to him, and then he told him to get going. So Moses left, and Tom leaned over and said to me, "Look! He left his shoes." On the last day of the conference, the play was performed for a final time, and that bit of business remained: the shoes were left behind—a powerful reminder of a protagonist's changed life. The image of Moses's shoes was also a powerful reminder that there is so much to be discovered in any play when you stop reading and put it on its feet.

At the end of that summer conference, there was a performance of Ron Melrose's one-woman musical *Early One Morning*, the story of Mary Magdalene told in a cycle of nine beautiful songs. Ron is a Broadway musician and an incredibly gifted composer and lyricist. I contacted him and asked if he would compose a score for a musical cycle of Old Testament stories verbatim from the Bible. He said yes, and the result was our first full-length Old Testament drama: *And God Said*.

Shortly after the Christians in Theatre Arts national conference, I received this email from Tom:

> What a moving experience it was to see *The Bands of Syria*. I have worked [privately] with texts like this for a long time, and in doing so I had to imagine how it might have looked to the people of Israel. The text suggested a performance, and imagining the performance helped me to "see" the text. But ... seeing it, really seeing it ... I was not prepared for the impact it made on me. It is not enough to read the texts and imagine. We need to perform them. And this is not just for me, it is true for everyone in the church.[10]

---

[10]   Tom Boogaart, email message to author, July 22, 2003.

Leap forward a dozen years or so. On a Sunday evening in a church sanctuary in western Michigan, a group of my students performed seven Bible stories. That particular Sunday evening, I was sitting behind a ten-year-old girl and her grandmother. After an hour of dramas performed verbatim from the Scripture, the ten-year-old girl turned to her grandmother and whispered, "Oh Nana, I hope there are a lot more stories!"

One week later, our team visited a stately, two-story house on the west side of Chicago. The family of one of my students had invited us all over for supper. After supper, we picked up the living room sofa and moved it to the other side of the room. We scooted end tables, lamps, and the rocking chair. We pushed open the sliding door between the living room and dining room and turned all the chairs toward an open playing space by the piano. The neighborhood gathered in, several generations, 25 strong. The kids sat on the floor. The grownups sat on the sofa and the dining room chairs at the back of the room.

My students performed the Bible, verbatim, story after story.

Over an hour passed with the children calling out, "Do another one!" Finally, one of the parents said, "This is the last one." After all, the next day was a school day.

The next morning, we drove to Judson University in Elgin, Illinois. Just before chapel, I watched as an emeritus professor fell on the stairs coming in. I raced over to him. He had hurt three of his fingers, sprained his neck, and cut his lip. Nevertheless, he stayed for chapel. When my students announced at the end of chapel that they could stay and perform a few more stories, a small group lingered, including the elderly professor, who joined the post-chapel stories and conversation with enthusiasm and joy.

Since when do we sit still for an hour, sometimes on a hard floor, sometimes in pain, to listen to the Bible word for word? Perhaps the better question is, when did we stop?

CHAPTER 3

Hospitality of the Heart: How Changing Our Metaphor Can Change Our Relationship with the Bible

Travis West

Introduction

When I was a kid, I loved going to my grandparents' house. They lived on a small lake about a 90-minute drive from my house, and we would spend hours swimming in the water during the summers or skating on top of it during the winters. My grandpa is the consummate jokester and always had us kids in stitches. My grandma is the consummate host and always made us feel loved, appreciated, and cared for.

My grandparents' home was also a sanctuary for me, a place of quiet and calm in the midst of the chaotic and stressful world I inhabited at home. This sacred quiet I experienced there was due, at least in part, to my grandparents' abiding faith. They had been lifelong members of a Reformed church in Kalamazoo, and their piety was palpable in the peaceful serenity of their home.

At the center of their piety was my grandmother's relationship with the Bible. She read it from cover to cover every year, often in different translations. She seemed to love the Bible as much as she loved my grandpa, which I could hardly fathom as a child. In the center

31

of their living room in a prominent place atop their coffee table sat an embodiment of my grandmother's devotion to the Word: a gargantuan Bible bound by an ornately carved, three-dimensional cover made of wood with silver-plated letters spelling out "Holy Bible" and gold-lined pages. The thing must have weighed 20 pounds at least. I wouldn't know, because I was forbidden to touch it! It was too holy to be placed in the hands of an unruly and unpredictable child. In addition to all the ornamentation, the Bible had two great metal clasps that connected the edge of the back cover to the edge of the front cover, which effectively served as locks, preventing the Bible from being opened. It may have sat open during the week, but the only way I recall seeing that Bible is lying heavy and holy on the table, locked tight!

This image of my grandmother's Bible has become a metaphor for me of the relationship many people of faith have today with the Bible, particularly with the Old Testament. It is clearly an important book, holy and sacred, weighty and to be treated with respect, but it is locked tight, and we do not have the key to unlock its meaning or comprehend its significance in our daily lives. This is the relationship with the Bible that I brought with me to seminary. Twenty-five years of Sunday school lessons, Christian school education, a degree in religion from a Christian college, and a full year of seminary education had taught me an enormous amount of information *about* the Bible, but rarely had I *experienced* it as a resonant source of spiritual vitality; rarely had it ushered me into the presence of the living God. And then I entered my second year of seminary and took a class from Tom Boogaart.

In this essay, I will attempt to articulate some of the ways Tom's teaching and life have (trans)formed me over the past 13 years since I first walked into his classroom. More than any of my former teachers, Tom has shaped the way I approach Scripture, the relationship I have with it, and now the way that I teach it as a colleague of his on the faculty at Western Theological Seminary (WTS).

Tom's approach to the Bible can best be described through the metaphor of "hospitality of the heart," which he developed in the early days of our collaboration on an interactive and embodied approach to teaching biblical Hebrew at WTS over 12 years ago.[1] After explaining the metaphor and some of the pedagogical embodiments of it in

---

[1]   This began in the summer of 2006 and has continued to today. Many others participated in varying degrees in this collaboration. Dr. Carol M. Bechtel taught the class during its first year while Tom was on sabbatical and helped shape the vision of the class and our collaborative teaching model. Since that first year, the

Tom's teaching, I will identify three implications that this metaphor offers the church and the academy. These three implications are as follows. First, hospitality involves the whole person; it implies an embodied relationship with Scripture. Second, hospitality assumes an epistemology that offers a corrective to the overly analytical, cerebral, and objective view of knowledge that prevails in the academy and in many churches. And finally, hospitality prioritizes the role of the Holy Spirit in our understanding of biblical authority. I believe these implications, if taken seriously, could help shift the view of the Bible—and especially the Old Testament—away from being a holy-yet-inaccessible book and restore it to its rightful place as a vital spiritual resource for the church. But before I discuss the metaphor itself, we need to revisit the prevailing metaphor we presently have for the Bible—namely, that it is a book.

The Bible Is (Not) a Book

For most people who have grown up in the modern West, the Bible is a book. The image of my grandmother's Bible may be a fancier (and heavier) version of the one(s) you have, but the basic components are the same: pages filled with ink and bound together beneath a cover. It is so obvious that the Bible is a book that it almost feels embarrassing to write it. The textual nature of the Bible has dictated the way it has been read in homes, interpreted in churches, and taught in seminaries for a long time.

The Bible is assumed to be a book for a very good reason: it *is* a book. It is an object we can hold in our hands and purchase from our local bookstore. By some estimates, the Bible has sold more copies than any other book in history.[2] But it is also *not* a book. It was not a book to the people of Israel. They belonged to a primarily oral culture in which

---

core teaching team at WTS has been Tom, myself, Dr. Dawn Boelkins, and Dr. Pam Bush. In addition to this core team, many students have contributed in significant ways over the years, some as instructional assistants in the classroom and others as tutors and lab leaders, and still others in developing curriculum through writing the songs we now use to teach Bible passages in the class. There are far too many to name them all here since literally dozens of students have contributed to this program over the years. A few who taught with us for several years and made important contributions are: Rev. Dustyn Keepers, Rev. Megan Hodgin, Rev. Josh Cooper, Matt Veenstra, Abby DeZeeuw, and Kyle Lake. Rev. Noah McLaren wrote the tunes for the passages we require our students to internalize.

2   "Best-Selling Book of Non-Fiction," Guinness World Records, accessed December 24, 2018, http://www.guinnessworldrecords.com/world-records/best-selling-book-of-non-fiction/. According to the site, the Bible has sold more than 5 billion copies since 1815.

very few could read or write. As Jon Levenson has said, "The basis of religion in biblical times was not a Bible: the religion *in* the Book is not the religion *of* the Book."[3]

Is it possible that, in becoming "the religion of the Book," we have fundamentally altered our relationship with the Bible in ways that are not altogether positive? Was Hans-Ruedi Weber onto something when he decried the "Gutenberg captivity of the Bible"?[4] Why is it that everybody "has" a Bible but so few read it? Tom has asked these questions repeatedly throughout his career. He feels deeply the crisis the American church is in with regard to Scripture, particularly the Old Testament. For Tom, the crisis plays itself out in the objectification of the Bible, the reduction of its contents to propositions and moralisms, and profound biblical illiteracy. But behind and beneath each of these symptoms is a larger theological and cultural reality: the desacralization of the world. That is to say, "the inability of Western Christians to imagine how the Spirit of God is present in the material world."[5] The biblical personages lived in the "middle world" where heaven and earth overlapped, but that world is becoming less and less imaginable in our increasingly secularized society. Thus, it becomes more challenging to imagine the Bible coming alive in one's heart or life, or the Holy Spirit authenticating the Bible in the heart of a believer or congregation. And so, the Bible gets reduced to an object or a list of dos and don'ts rather than being a gateway to God's presence—or, as I will argue here, a friend to invite into one's heart.

Tom used the occasion of his recent "Last Performance"[6] to reflect on what has animated his long career in teaching and service to the church. In his description of why he chose to transform the Hebrew

---

[3]   Jon Levenson, "The Bible: Unexamined Commitments of Criticism," *First Things* 30 (February 1993): 24. Edgar Conrad made a similar assertion by playing off a different common phrase: "'books' in the Old Testament are for the *ear*, not for the eye of the silent reader; unlike the proverbial child, they are to be heard and not seen." Edgar Conrad, "Heard But Not Seen: The Representation of 'Books' in the Old Testament," *Journal for the Study of the Old Testament* 54 (1992): 59.

[4]   Hans-Ruedi Weber, *Experiments with Bible Study* (World Council of Churches, Geneva: Switzerland, 1981), 10.

[5]   Tom Boogaart, email message to author, February 7, 2019.

[6]   Instead of conducting a "Last Lecture" before his retirement, as is the typical practice of retiring professors at WTS, Tom conducted a "Last Performance," which involved a dramatic presentation of the entire book of Jonah along with a number of his students and colleagues in order to draw attention to the transformative potential of Scripture enactment—one embodiment of his metaphor of "hospitality of the heart"—and to highlight the formational potency of WTS's Hebrew program, which is one of his pedagogical legacies.

curriculum at WTS from the traditional "grammar and translation" method to the embodied, interactive, performative pedagogy that characterizes it today, he spoke of the objectification of the Bible as a central component in the present crisis, which, he argued, "might be due in part to the way that we were teaching languages and exegesis at the seminary."[7] Not an easy criticism to make for someone who dedicated their life to teaching the languages and exegesis at a seminary!

He went on to describe how the previous approach focused on memorizing vocabulary and grammatical tables, which were seen as the

> necessary tools that students could use to dissect a text. *And what does the image of "tools" and "dissection" suggest?* The image suggests that the biblical text is cut up into little pieces, laid out on a table before us; it suggests that the Bible is a dead object and we are the living subjects whose grand task it is to discover its true meaning. We began to realize that this approach to teaching the languages was subtly undermining what we were hoping to accomplish.[8]

In the face of such a realization, Tom felt a deep conviction that the church was not confined to the pedagogies and metaphors it had been given. He believed that in the face of the present crisis new metaphors and pedagogies were needed. His hope (and mine) is that hospitality— as a metaphor for discipleship and a classroom pedagogy—would equip pastors not to feed their souls and their flocks with the dissected parts of a cadaver-Bible but would invite them to commune with the "living and active"[9] Word of God, and, in so doing, would usher them into the presence of the living God.

Hospitality of the Heart

Hospitality is a compelling metaphor to describe the practices that characterize people of faith's relationship with the Bible. It has implications for the church and the academy. Tom has developed some of these implications explicitly, and others are latent in the metaphor itself that I will attempt to draw out. After a brief description of the metaphor, I will describe the practical implications of the metaphor in Tom's teaching.

---

[7]   Tom Boogaart, "Jonah: Standing Before the Face of God," (lecture, Western Theological Seminary, Holland, Michigan, December 13, 2018).

[8]   Boogaart, "Jonah."

[9]   Hebrews 4:12.

Consider the process of meeting and making a new friend. At first, the two of you are strangers to each other, connected by nothing more than mutual humanity. After awhile, the face of the other becomes familiar. Fifteen minutes earlier, this person was a statistic, a stranger, perhaps someone to be feared. Now they are a human being. Over time, you come to know them better. Eventually, you invite them to your home.

Hospitality is a sacred activity. To prepare for the arrival of your guest, you follow a set of rituals. The rituals may differ depending on cultural context, but they may include some or all of the following elements. You clean your house, plan the meal, purchase and prepare the food, set the table, light the candles. You prepare a place for your guest. When they arrive they are overcome by your preparations. Over the meal, you talk, laugh, cry, share silence. Eventually, your friend looks at the clock, and it is far too late—they must be going. Two hours later, you usher them out the door and bid them goodnight. When you close the door behind them, you turn around and see your kitchen—now empty save for the artifacts of the evening's meal. Surveying the scene, you realize what just took place. You have made a new friend. And though their gratitude was unending, you know in your soul that you were the one who received the greatest blessing.

Practicing hospitality of the heart follows a similar arc with the Bible. The ultimate goal is to befriend a passage, to welcome it into your heart and life in a way that creates space for it to speak, and that gives up some control over when it is allowed to speak and what it is allowed to say.

Hosting the Word involves a process of internalization. Internalization goes beyond the traditional sense of memorization, which so often maintains a *visual* relationship with the passage by writing the words on the backs of the eyelids. In this context, a recitation is still an act of reading; one just reads the words from an imagined page rather than a physical one. The Bible remains an object, abstracted into letters and words. By contrast, internalization involves the whole body and all of the senses. It "entails deep immersion in the text, the internalization not just of sounds but of feelings, images, complexes of visualizations of setting, character, and narrative structure, all of it 'clothed' with the words of the text."[10] Internalization is engagement with the words to

---

[10]   Dennis Dewey, "Performing the Living Word: Learnings from a Storytelling Vocation," in *The Bible in Ancient and Modern Media: Story and Performance*, eds. Holly E. Hearon and Philip Ruge-Jones (Eugene: Cascade Books, 2009), 154.

the degree that they become a part of the interpreter. Internalization fundamentally changes the interpreter's relationship with the Bible, lifting the words off of the page and planting them in the heart. The Bible is no longer an object; it is a living and active subject. This bridges part of the gap between the modern literate interpreter and the non-literate people of Israel. The biblical passage is no longer something external, something the scholar can choose when to think about and when to analyze. She and the passage have become one, and each has agency to exert on the other.

Internalization plays a substantial pedagogical role in the Hebrew class at WTS. First year Hebrew students learn the *Shema* (Deuteronomy 6:4-9), Aaron's Blessing (Numbers 6:24-26), the Ten Commandments (Exodus 20), and many other passages by heart—*in Hebrew*—throughout the two-semester course. All of the passages have been put to music—much of it written by former students—to deepen the emotional impact of the passage and indefinitely extend the period of time in which the student can recall the passage. Hand motions help connect words to meaning and involve the whole body in the process.

Another pedagogical embodiment of the practice of hospitality of the heart is Scripture enactment. If internalization is getting the script inside the disciple, enactment is getting the disciple inside the script. In a sense, this flips the hospitality image on its head. We begin by making room in our hearts for the Word only to find that it makes room in its heart for us as well; we host the Word and discover we are being hosted by it.

In the context of enactment, the text, the script, is internalized for a purpose—namely, to be presented (typically in a worship setting) through the body, voice, facial expressions, postures, gestures, and movements of the performer(s). The process of blocking[11] out the performance raises a whole set of questions that would never occur to the silent reader, revealing gaps in the biblical stories that literary approaches often miss.[12] The performance brings the passage to life by

---

[11] "Blocking" refers to the various staging decisions required to facilitate a performance.

[12] For example, how does Isaac get off the altar between verses 12 and 13 in Genesis 22? The moment is not narrated, but the entire drama breaks down if Isaac never gets off of the altar to be replaced by the ram. Performance requires the interpreter to ask this theologically consequential question because the person playing Isaac, who is laying "bound" upon the altar, likely asks, "How do I get off of this thing?" when the Narrator glides past it following the biblical script.

moving it from the page to the stage. This process, as Tom has developed it along with theatre professor Jeff Barker, is best done in community as an ensemble performance, which engages the spatial elements of the story latent in the script and democratizes the interpretive process by creating a community of interpretation. This approach is one aspect of an interpretive approach called biblical performance criticism.

Three Implications of Tom's Approach to the Bible

Inherent in everything I have said thus far are three implications of Tom's approach to interpreting the Bible and the craft of teaching, which I believe offer the church and the academy resources to revitalize the Old Testament as a vital spiritual resource. In the remainder of this essay, I will identify each implication and then offer my own reflections on them to show how they have impacted me and how I believe they can impact the church and the academy.

Embodied Exegesis

In the fall of 2007, Tom embarked on (another) pedagogical experiment. The previous school year, we had begun to implement the brand-new Hebrew curriculum, which would go through many iterations before becoming what it is today.[13] But during this semester, Tom tried out something he had been considering for many years, which had finally become possible through the new interactive, oral-style Hebrew class. He took the Hebrew Reading class—traditionally focused on translating a passage each week and discussing its significance—and made it the Hebrew Reading *and Performance* class, which was less about reading and more about performance. We took the first chapter of Jonah, internalized it in Hebrew, and developed a performance of the story to present in chapel at WTS, in local churches, and in other gatherings.

---

[13]   In the first few years, we recreated the curriculum every year, making resources from scratch and analyzing its effectiveness from week-to-week. Our first metaphor for the class was that we were "building the plane while flying it." After a year of "white-knuckle" teaching this way, we transcended the plane metaphor and graduated to a culinary one: "baking fresh bread" every week. After a year or so of this, one of our long-term student assistants playfully lamented: "I appreciate the fresh bread, but can we at least use the same recipe?!" The curriculum we developed is now supported by an introductory grammar, which facilitates a dynamic, interactive engagement with the language through various exercises and a host of companion audio/visual resources. See Travis West, *Biblical Hebrew: An Interactive Approach* (Wilmore: GlossaHouse, 2016).

The class was a revelation. By embodying the characters in the story, they came to life in a way none of us had ever experienced before. By putting them on a stage, we attended to the physical and spatial elements latent in the story that had previously gone unnoticed or seemed irrelevant. Everything from character development (Jonah consistently does not respond when spoken to by God or other characters[14]) to locations on stage (God locates Godself in Nineveh, setting up a vertical and horizontal axis through which the drama's theology is revealed[15]) to physical postures (the number of times Jonah lies down on the floor, the sailors' growing desperation) to tone of voice (the captain actually shouts his command to Jonah in 1:6 so the audience *feels* his desperation, while Jonah dispassionately recites his confession in 1:9 so the audience feels the irony between his words and his actions) contained and communicated the theological affirmations the story was making. The words in the script are but the trailhead that ushers you into the strange new world of the Bible, and you cannot enter this world with your eyes alone; your whole body is necessary for the journey.

Around the same time that Tom was experimenting with this class, others in the academy were exploring similar terrain. In 2006, David Rhoads, a now-retired New Testament professor from the Lutheran School of Theology, published a two-part article in the *Biblical Theology Bulletin* titled "Performance Criticism: An Emerging Methodology in Second Testament Studies" in which he articulated some of the historical, biblical, cultural, and hermeneutical foundations of

---

[14] The first and most substantial discovery happens in between verses 6 and 7. In verse 6, the pagan captain echoes God's initial call and tells Jonah to "get up" and "cry out" to his god for help. In verse 7, the sailors are reverting to "Plan B" and cast lots to discover who is at fault for the storm. In between these two verses is an implied gap: Jonah does not reply to the captain's plea. What does the gap imply? Is he so deeply asleep that the captain's cries can't wake him? Is he so apathetic that he cannot muster the energy to respond, and so lies there as if struck dumb? Is he so uncaring that the pagan sailors' fears cannot move his heart to respond and so he just rolls over in his "sleep"? Et cetera.

[15] For example, God's profound and scandalous compassion for the people of Nineveh, that God would identify with them as their God (cf. Jonah 3:3); the tension between God's particularity and ubiquity: God is located in Nineveh, but Jonah's flight away from Nineveh is futile because you can never flee from the face of the Lord; Jonah's flight away from God's face is mirrored by successive "descents": Jonah "goes down" three times in chapter 1 before finally "laying down" and "falling" asleep (cf. Jonah 1:3, 5); the sailors' prayer to the Lord is tantamount to a conversion and involves them *turning* from the sea where their gods reside back toward Nineveh whence God hears their prayer and accepts their worship (cf. Jonah 1:14, 16).

performing the New Testament.[16] Since then, he has become the series editor for the Biblical Performance Criticism series from Wipf and Stock/Cascade, which so far contains 16 volumes, mostly dedicated to the New Testament world.[17]

The Old Testament, somewhat strangely, has been largely unexplored through this medium, but Tom has published two articles[18] and has a forthcoming book with theatre professor Jeff Barker that makes this approach accessible to the church. My dissertation, titled *The Art of Biblical Performance: Biblical Performance Criticism and the Genre of the Biblical Narratives*, develops a generative methodology for performing Old Testament narratives, rooted in the cultural and historical realities of the oral character of Israelite society. Performance Criticism, which involves the whole person in the act of interpreting the Bible —one concrete expression of the practice of hospitality of the heart—when taken seriously calls for a shift in the way biblical studies is conducted, from a singularly mental/visual/intellectual focus to include more embodied/multi-sensory/experiential elements. This shift includes a critique of the prevailing epistemology that guides so much of the way modern, Western Christians—in the academy and in the church—engage their Bible.

An Epistemological Corrective

Hospitality as a metaphor shifts our understanding of the Bible from an object to a subject, from a book we hold in our hands to a friend we welcome into our hearts. But more is at stake in the metaphor than a different way of imagining or *thinking about* the Bible. Implicit in the metaphor is a critique of the traditional epistemology that prevails in the academy and the church—particularly in Western churches

---

[16] See David Rhoads, "Performance Criticism: An Emerging Methodology in Second Testament Studies—Part I," *Biblical Theology Bulletin* 36, no. 3 (2006): 118–33; and David Rhoads, "Performance Criticism: An Emerging Methodology in Second Testament Studies—Part II," *Biblical Theology Bulletin* 36, no. 4 (2006): 164–84.

[17] One recent publication in this series is an interesting study of Ruth and is the only volume so far that is committed to the Old Testament. See Terry Giles and William Doan, *The Story of Naomi—The Book of Ruth: From Gender to Politics* (Eugene: Cascade Books, 2016).

[18] Thomas A. Boogaart, "Drama and the Sacred: Recovering the Dramatic Tradition in Scripture and Worship," in *Touching the Altar: The Old Testament for Christian Worship*, ed. Carol M. Bechtel (Grand Rapids: Eerdmans, 2008); and Thomas A. Boogaart, "The Arduous Journey of Abraham: Genesis 22:1-19," in *Yes! Well ... : Exploring the Past, Present, and Future of the Church: Essays in Honor of John W. Coakley*, ed. James Hart Brumm (Grand Rapids: Eerdmans, 2016).

influenced by the Enlightenment. The term epistemology refers to theories of knowledge; it has to do with how we know what we know, what it means to know, and what kind of knowledge is valid (or not).

The philosophical and cultural movement known as the Enlightenment left a lasting impression on the way knowledge is understood in the West by creating a hierarchy that prioritized reason, logic, and empirically verifiable data over all other forms of knowing. It elevated the intellect over experience, the mind over the body. *True* knowledge became external to the knower and was abstracted into facts, data points, and propositions. This brand of disembodied, abstracted, objective epistemology has ruled supreme not only in the sciences but also in theology and biblical studies from around the late eighteenth century until today, though its reign is beginning to erode. Hospitality of the heart challenges this objectivist hegemony directly by advocating a more democratic approach to knowledge and emphasizing the essential roles played by the body, experience, personal relations, and community in the process of knowing.

Michael Polanyi, the twentieth-century scientist-turned-philosopher, made an early contribution to the coup against objectivity through a compelling critique of the objectivist position. He argued that all knowledge is personal and is framed by commitments, whether stated or not, whether the scientist or scholar claims to engage in purely objective research or not. It is impossible, in any field of research, to engage in one's work without being guided by commitments that are personal—and this is a good thing. He also argued that there are many valid ways of knowing; he emphasized two in particular: focal and tacit knowledge.

Focal knowledge is gained and expressed through explicit focus, such as in developing a skill or the act of observation. For example, a musician applies focal knowledge to learn the scales on the bass guitar, repeating them over and over with fastidious attention. But eventually the scales become instinctive, and instead of playing scales, the musician makes *music*. The scales—and the necessary muscle movements—now form part of the musician's tacit knowledge. Similarly, as a blind person learns to use a seeing stick, they are acutely aware only of "the impact of the stick against the palm," but eventually the "awareness of its impact ... is transformed into a sense of its point touching the objects [they] are exploring."[19] Tacit knowledge is inherently embodied

---

[19]   Michael Polanyi, *The Tacit Dimension* (New York: Anchor Books, 1967), 12.

and is achieved through a process of indwelling.[20] The example of the "seeing" stick is an apt analogy for what indwelling the Scriptures makes possible. As Lesslie Newbigin, who was influenced by Polanyi, put it, "The important thing in the use of the Bible is not to understand the text but to understand the world *through* the text."[21] The Scriptures become the "lenses" through which we can truly see and make sense of the world around us.[22]

Another scientist advocated a similar approach to Polanyi. In *The Courage to Teach*, Parker Palmer relates the story of Barbara McClintock, the Nobel prize-winning biologist whose unorthodox research into the genetic makeup of corn "changed the map" of modern genetics and posed a direct challenge to the prevailing objectivist approach of her peers.[23] McClintock did not objectify the ears of corn she studied; she "did not approach it with the textbook notion that her task was to analyze it into data bits. Instead, she approached genetic material on the assumption that it could best be understood as a communal phenomenon."[24] McClintock eschewed the strict dichotomy between object and observer that governed scientific inquiry and proved that subjective engagement could lead to new discoveries. She, of course, remained committed to scientific integrity, practiced careful analysis, and kept accurate data. "But data and logic and the distance they provide are only one pole of the paradox of great science. When McClintock, arguably the greatest biologist of our century, is asked to name the heart of her knowing, she invariably uses the language of

---

[20]   On this point, Polanyi is quick to say this applies equally to the sciences as to the humanities. "But my analysis of tacit knowing shows that they were mistaken in asserting that this sharply distinguished the humanities from the natural sciences. Indwelling, as derived from the structure of tacit knowing, is a far more precisely defined act than is empathy, and it underlies all observations." Polanyi, *Tacit Dimension*, 17.

[21]   Lesslie Newbigin, *The Gospel in a Pluralist Society* (Grand Rapids: Eerdmans, 1989), 98.

[22]   John Calvin applied the metaphor of "spectacles" to the Scriptures, which sharpen our view or understanding of God that comes through the natural world. "Just as old or bleary-eyed men and those with weak vision, if you thrust before them a most beautiful volume, even if they recognize it to be some sort of writing, yet can scarcely construe two words, but with the aid of spectacles will begin to read distinctly; so Scripture, gathering up the otherwise confused knowledge of God in our minds, having dispersed our dullness, clearly shows us the true God." John Calvin, *Institutes of the Christian Religion*, trans. Ford Lewis Battles (Louisville: Westminster John Knox Press, 1960), 1.vi.1.

[23]   Parker Palmer, *The Courage to Teach: Exploring the Inner Landscape of a Teacher's Life* (San Francisco: Jossey-Bass, 1998), 55.

[24]   Palmer, 55.

relationship."[25] According to her biographer, in relation to her ears of corn, McClintock achieved "the highest form of love, love that allows for intimacy without the annihilation of difference."[26]

An epistemology like the one Polanyi advocated and McClintock embodied, which takes the body and experience seriously, is far closer to what could be called the Hebraic epistemology assumed in the pages of the Old Testament and expressed in the Hebrew language. The verb "to know" in Hebrew (ידע *yada'*) and its noun form, "knowledge" (עדת *da'at*), are related to another, unexpected word: "hand" (יד *yad*). This suggests that, for the people of Israel, knowledge was related to touch. This connection suggests that knowledge is relational as opposed to abstract, mutual as opposed to isolated. When I touch you, you touch me back. Knowledge is reciprocal. The fullest expression of the mutual, reciprocal character of knowledge is seen in the use of ידע (*yada'*) for sexual intimacy, the physical act in which two become one as each gives of themselves fully and receives the other fully.

To "know" the Bible, then, through the practice of hospitality, is to incorporate it into our hearts and lives—to indwell it—in such a way that "our spirit becomes synonymous with a passage," as Abraham Joshua Heschel once wrote.[27] The closest biblical example of this transformational encounter with the Word of God comes in Ezekiel 3 when God commands Ezekiel to "eat this scroll" and then to "speak my very words" to the house of Israel.[28] The words on the scroll were

---

[25] Palmer, *The Courage to Teach*, 55.

[26] Palmer, 55.

[27] Abraham Joshua Heschel, *God in Search of Man: A Philosophy of Judaism* (New York: Meridian Books, 1955), 242.

[28] Ezekiel 3:1, 4. Ezekiel was not the only prophet to have this culinary encounter with God's word. Jeremiah also ate God's words (Jeremiah 15:16), as did the apostle John as recorded in the book of Revelation (10:9). In his reflections on these encounters, the late Eugene Peterson wrote: "The act of eating the book means that reading is not a merely objective act, looking at the words and ascertaining their meaning. Eating the book is in contrast with how most of us are trained to read books—develop a cool objectivity that attempts to preserve scientific or theological truth by eliminating as far as possible any personal participation that might contaminate the meaning. But none of us starts out reading that way. I have a granddaughter right now who eats books. When I am reading a story to her brother, she picks another off of a stack and chews on it. She is trying to get the book inside her the quickest way she knows, not through her ears, but through her mouth. ... But soon she'll go to school and be taught that that's not the way to go about it. She'll be taught to get answers out of her book. She'll learn to read books in order to pass examinations, and having passed the exams, put the book on the shelf and buy another. But the reading that John is experiencing is not of the kind that equips

incarnated in Ezekiel's body to the extent that when he spoke, he spoke God's words, for they were now a part of him; the two had become one. Hospitality of the heart has a deep sacramental impulse. Each passage we internalize is like a piece of bread held in the hand—"this is my body, broken for you"—and dipped in a cup—"this is my blood, shed for you"—that mediates to us in some mysterious way the very presence and power of God. Internalizing the text, like taking the Eucharist, opens us to the Word so it can speak to the deepest parts of us, calling us to become who we were created to be, calling us out of the insecurities and pretentions we hide behind and beckoning us to live beyond our wants, beyond our fears, from death into life, and so to encounter the power of the Spirit to "rebuild in us the defaced image of Himself."[29]

Ultimately, hospitality of the heart is about formation, which takes place by the power of the Spirit through our encounter with the text. It is about changing our relationship with the Bible in order to deepen our relationship with God and empower us to love both God and neighbor more and more each day. A consistent emphasis on the Spirit's power to form us through the Scriptures is an important part of Tom's legacy at WTS.

A Reformed View of Biblical Authority

The transformational power of hospitality shines a light on an under-emphasized aspect of a Reformed view of the authority of the Bible: the role of the Holy Spirit. For John Calvin, the authority of the Scriptures was rooted in a robust Pneumatology. However, Reformed theology—particularly those parts influenced by Calvin—is not often associated with giving a substantial role to the Spirit. That association is generally reserved for Pentecostal and charismatic theologies and the communions that grow out of them. Better-known Reformed emphases are the doctrines of election and predestination, the practice of infant baptism, and God's radical sovereignty. These "headier" doctrines have helped create monikers like "the frozen chosen" and the sense that Reformed types are little more than brains on sticks. Discipleship practices and preaching styles in many Reformed and Presbyterian churches reinforce this stereotype, which, in turn, is reinforced by the teaching practices in many seminaries.

---

us to pass an examination. Eating a book takes it all in, assimilating it into the tissues of our lives. Readers become what they read." Eugene Peterson, *Eat This Book: A Conversation in the Art of Spiritual Reading* (Grand Rapids: Eerdmans, 2006), 20.

[29] C. S. Lewis, *Reflections on the Psalms* (Orlando: Harcourt Brace & Company, 1986), 114.

Tom Boogaart sees it differently. He stands in a long line of WTS professors who have celebrated the prominent role played by the Spirit in Reformed theology, particularly in John Calvin's work. As the late I. John Hesselink, former president and professor of systematic theology at WTS once wrote, "the Reformed tradition—at least certain strains of it—has placed great emphasis on the person and work of the Holy Spirit. Not only that; I am convinced that in Reformed theology there is a greater appreciation, deeper understanding, and more comprehensive and balanced presentation of the full-orbed power and work of the Holy Spirit than in any other tradition, including the Pentecostal tradition!"[30]

One area that Hesselink identified as a unique and lasting contribution of Calvin's Pneumatology relates to the authority of the Bible. Calvin taught that the "testimony of the Spirit is more excellent than all reason. For as God alone is a fit witness of himself in his Word, so also the Word will not find acceptance in [people's] hearts before it is sealed by the *inward testimony of the Spirit* [emphasis added]."[31] Calvin maintained that the same Spirit that hovered over the waters of creation in Genesis and animated the voices and ministries of the Hebrew prophets must also "penetrate into our hearts" to convince us of the truth and power of the Word.[32]

Tom sees Calvin's emphasis on the Spirit as a refreshing and generative counter to the rational foundation of fundamentalist or inerrantist positions on biblical authority. According to Tom,

> The inerrantist theory of *Scripture is based ultimately on a syllogism: God is perfect, the Scriptures are the word of God, therefore, the Scriptures are perfect.* Based on this syllogism, people assume that the Scriptures contain perfect knowledge in all areas of human inquiry and that its factual accuracy "authenticates" the Scriptures. Accepting what it says about God is a rational act that human beings can make on the basis of their own powers of reasoning, a deduction made in the head not a movement of the heart [emphasis original].[33]

---

[30]   I. John Hesselink, "The Charismatic Movement and the Reformed Tradition," *Reformed Review* 28 (Spring 1975): 148.

[31]   Calvin, *Institutes*, 1.vii.4.

[32]   Calvin, 1.vii.4.

[33]   Tom Boogaart, "Steeping Ourselves in the Scriptures: A Reformed Approach" (unpublished papers, 2013), 9.

In contrast to this rational deduction that must be defended and proven to secure the Bible's authority, which places the ultimate authority of the Scriptures in human hands (or, rather, minds), Calvin's position places it in a higher authority—namely, the Spirit. Further, through the Spirit, the Scriptures themselves bear witness to their authority in our lives. For Calvin, Scripture is self-authenticating and therefore need not be subjected to "proof and reasoning."[34] It "owes the full conviction with which we ought to receive it to the testimony of the Spirit."[35]

This begs a more fundamental question: What is meant by "authority"? How are we to understand the authority that the Bible, by the power of the Spirit, exerts on us as we read, internalize, and ultimately indwell it? Bill Brown helps answer the question by drawing from the etymology of the word "authority." It comes from the Latin *auctoritas* ("origination"), from which the word "author" also comes. According to Brown,

> "Authority" in the biblical sense takes on a different nuance from its normal usage in contemporary legal discourse. ... The Bible's "authority" ... connotes a generative, provocative power that elicits a response and, in so doing, shapes the conduct, indeed identity of the reader or reading community. Simply put, biblical authority is reader responsive: through our genuine engagement of Scripture, God "authors" us.[36]

God alone has the power, by the Spirit, to "author" us into existence, to engrave us in—and engrave in us—the image of Christ. We cannot *think* ourselves into being the image of Christ in the world. Insofar as the Spirit witnesses to the Bible's authority in our lives, so too our lives, transformed by the Spirit, bear witness to the Bible's authority as we work to bring shalom to the earth through acts of love and justice.

Conclusion

I believe that hospitality of the heart is a robust and timely metaphor that offers practices to both the church and the classroom that

---

34 Calvin, 1.vii.5.
35 I like the way the older translation by Henry Beveridge words this. John Calvin, *Institutes of the Christian Religion*, trans. Henry Beveridge (Grand Rapids: Christian Classics Ethereal Library, n.d.), 1.vii.5., http://www.ccel.org/ccel/calvin/institutes/.
36 William P. Brown, *Engaging Biblical Authority: Perspectives on the Bible as Scripture* (Louisville: Westminster John Knox Press, 2007), xiii.

can liberate the Bible from its "Gutenberg captivity" and reestablish it as a vital spiritual resource. But in order to truly appreciate hospitality of the heart, we need to think carefully and critically about the epistemological assumptions we bring to the Bible, which dictate to a great extent how we relate to the Bible, what we expect from it, and the role it plays in our lives. Hospitality of the heart reminds us that the Bible is not a book; not ink on wood pulp; not a collection of historical facts, outdated law codes, or theological propositions; not stories written down to keep children in line and help adults avoid vices. The Bible is more like a friend who has the potential to transform our lives by speaking hard truths in the face of our self-righteousness, and words of comfort in the face of our pain—if we but open our hearts and let it in. When we do so, we participate in an ancient tradition, joining the likes of biblical sages, desert mothers and fathers, reformers like John Calvin, and beloved teachers like Tom Boogaart. And when we host the Word in our hearts, we may come to a new understanding of that hidden and mysterious reciprocal blessing the writer of Hebrews connected with hospitality: when you practice it, you may be entertaining "angels unawares."[37]

---

[37]   Hebrews 13:2, ASV.

CHAPTER 4

Love as Pedagogy

Pam Bush

Dr. Tom Boogaart was my Hebrew and Old Testament teacher at Western Theological Seminary (WTS). He led me into a world that changed the way I encounter life and Scripture—a world that is intriguing and integral, magnificent and mysterious, a world enlivened by the presence and breath of God. The God of the Bible became bigger and livelier and infinitely more connected with humankind. Something came alive in me, which animates me to this day.

I have been blessed for the past decade to be part of the Hebrew teaching team. The team has been carrying out Boogaart's grand experiment for unleashing the incredible formative capacity of biblical Hebrew with an interactive and altogether creative pedagogy. I marvel as Boogaart—a seasoned and respected professor—steps into utter vulnerability in the classroom with activities that look more like preschool than grad school. My own creativity and passion have blossomed on a team where every person, whatever their title, has an equal and welcomed voice at the pedagogical table. Everyone flourishes in this environment because Boogaart is not in it for purposes of notoriety, image, or control but rather because of awe of God, concern for the church, and love for students.

One of the pedagogical tools the Hebrew team employs is assigning unusual Hebrew names to students from the texts we encounter in class. Soon students began to love their names and live into them. Boogaart too, has a Hebrew name, which he loves and constantly lives into, Tehom. In Genesis 1:2, darkness covers the face of the deep (*tehom*). One of the beauties of team teaching with Tehom is that I get to hear, over and over, exquisite and unique expressions about the God of the Hebrew Scriptures—the very sort of "deep" insights that opened my heart in the first place.

Love as Pedagogy

Tehom sometimes says, "All creativity is born of love." The implications of such a statement are far reaching. They cast back into Genesis 1 and draw forth the suggestion that all that came into being in the germinal story of the Bible must be the result of an immense and expressive love. God, who *is* Love, speaks, and the words become material, creating a reality dripping with divine love and shalom. The ancient psalmist bears this out in asserting that the whole earth is full of the steadfast love of God.[1] Tehom has repeatedly suggested that Reformed theology is fundamentally about love, expressed through *coram Deo*—God the monarch lowering the scepter and lovingly bringing humankind into God's presence.

Henry Nouwen connects the loving creativity of God specifically to humankind: "God has created and redeemed us in love and has chosen us to proclaim that love as the true source of all human life."[2] Not only did God create humanity *with* love; God created humanity *to* love. Marianne Williamson says it this way: "When we were born, we were programmed perfectly. We had a natural tendency to focus on love. Our imaginations were creative and flourishing and we knew how to use them."[3] Love and creativity are linked.

Love, however, is a reality too mysterious and too mighty to be demarcated. We are shaped for it, ache for it, and chase it, but we are clumsy in defining it. Williamson, who spent a lifetime teaching about

---

[1]   Psalm 33:5.
[2]   Henry Nouwen, *In the Name of Jesus: Reflections on Christian Leadership,* (New York: The Crossroad Publishing Company, 1989), 30.
[3]   Marianne Williamson, *A Return to Love: Reflections on the Principles of a Course in Miracles* (New York: HarperCollins, 1992), xxi.

love, says her instruction "does not aim at teaching the meaning of love, for that is beyond what can be taught."[4] In *attempting* to wrap the meaning of love with words, Williamson says, "Love is the intuitive knowledge of our hearts."[5] Love is a way of being in the world. Love is a posture toward others. Love is a way of perceiving the world. "It's the same world we see now, but informed by love, interpreted gently, with hope and faith and a sense of wonder," says Williamson.[6]

Love is energy, and it invigorates our lives and our world. Love generates reality in everyday life on planet Earth, yielding authenticity, hospitality, healing, commitment, forgiveness, and trust. Therese of Lisieux posits that the effects of love are both concrete and ordinary: "Love is shown in how we go about living our lives in a practical level here and now."[7] Sister Therese recognized that "in the end, love—responding to God's love and loving others—is the only thing that matters."[8]

How then is love linked to learning? bell hooks explains it this way:

> Love [is] a combination of care, commitment, knowledge, responsibility, respect, and trust. All these factors work interdependently. When these basic principles of love form the basis of teacher-student interaction, the mutual pursuit of knowledge creates the conditions for optimal learning.[9]

Tehom's refrain, "all creativity is born of love," draws aptly into the very particular arena of teaching. The power of creating spaces of transformational learning flows from love. The springs of love that shape pedagogy are multiple. They include love of teachers for each other, love of teachers for students, love of students for each other, and love for the subject.

Love of Teachers for Each Other

Tehom also often says, "The effectiveness of the teaching is directly related to the love of the teaching team for each other." Parker Palmer phrases it this way: "Relational knowing ... turns our human capacity

---

[4] Williamson, xvi.

[5] Williamson, xxiii.

[6] Williamson, xxiv.

[7] Elizabeth Ruth Obbard, *Therese of Lisieux's Little Way for Everyone* (Hyde Park: New City Press, 2007), 52.

[8] Obbard, 15.

[9] bell hooks, *Teaching Critical Thinking: Practical Wisdom* (New York: Routledge, 2010), 159.

for connectedness into a strength."[10] Teachers who are connected to each other can more readily enter into the creativity expressed by God. Love fosters trust, which encourages each person's ideas to bubble up. Love then becomes a crucible in which ideas are vetted, contested, and sharpened, often evolving into something far more effective and enlivening than any teacher could have produced in isolation. Finally, the generativity afforded by love enters the classroom, awakening the hearts and minds of the students.

When professors teach together, students have the opportunity to see how leadership built on trust and love leads to agility, account-ability, and joy. Teachers who love and trust each other also bring students a valuable model for ministry via team teaching—namely, col-laboration. Henry Nouwen shares how he was raised up in seminary to think of ministry as a solo affair in which pastors and teachers were autonomous.[11] It took living at L'Arche for him to see that "ministry is a communal and mutual experience."[12] Just as Jesus sent out his disciples two-by-two, Nouwen discovered that:

> We cannot bring good news on our own. We are called to proclaim the Gospel together, in community. ... I have found over and over again how hard it is to be truly faithful to Jesus when I am alone. I need my brothers or sisters to pray with me, to speak with me about the spiritual task at hand, and to challenge me to stay pure in mind, heart, and body.[13]

In the multi-faceted interactive classrooms of Boogaart's Hebrew team, a pair of teachers prepares and leads each class session together. Because of the high level of trust, if one teacher has a spontaneous idea in the middle of a class period, the other teacher will most likely follow the lead of their partner even if it means relinquishing a planned activity that was carefully crafted. These team teachers come to love each other well enough to bring their full, authentic selves to the teaching. Consequently, they desire and facilitate each other's success and bring a light-hearted demeanor that facilitates learning. They can also rec-ognize when one is floundering and would benefit from the other

---

[10]   Parker Palmer, *The Courage to Teach: Exploring the Inner Landscape of a Teacher's Life* (San Francisco: Jossey-Bass, 1998), 98.
[11]   Nouwen, *In the Name of Jesus*, 51–52.
[12]   Nouwen, 57.
[13]   Nouwen, 58.

stepping in. Boogaart's hope is that students will bring the power of collaborative leadership to bear in the ministry context, inviting others to join them in many of the tasks that are often considered solitary. In so doing, ministry leaders can build community, empower others, and unleash generative missional potential.

Team teachers who love and trust each other can disagree and even work through conflict in view of the class, a model that can be hard to come by in regard to ministry leadership. They can show students how to cooperate, compromise, and come to consensus in ways that respect everyone's presence and contribution, even in the midst of disparate opinions. Stephen Brookfield explains:

> This is where students see the faculty attempt to model what respectful disagreement and a critical analysis of each other's positions look like. ... Often the greatest moment of delight that students note on their Critical Incident Questionnaires are when two instructors publicly disagree on something. This immediately gets their attention and wakes them up.[14]

Team teaching is not the only avenue for the pedagogical power of love. It comes through even between teachers who are not in the classroom together. Boogaart's belief about the potency of love for effective teaching applies to the entire faculty of the institution to which he has dedicated 32 years. In staying connected and knowing each other well, competition and shame can be abated and communication can be honest and life giving. In an environment where teachers feel appreciated and undergirded by each other, their energy can flow toward the flourishing of students and the quality of learning. Plus, it could be argued that students learn more about leadership from who their professors are and how they are present in the world than from what their professors say. 2012 leadership research at WTS found:

> Modeling Matters - Seminary is that temporary place where students have access to real life practices via the people in the community. ... [Seminary] becomes their location of experiencing reality—both in personal relationships and institutional modeling.[15]

---

[14]   Stephen Brookfield, *Powerful Techniques for Teaching Adults* (San Francisco: Jossey-Bass, 2013), 42.
[15]   Megan Mullins and Kyle J.A. Small, "Learning to Follow, Learning to Lead," (report, June 2012), 17.

The researchers "discovered that leadership formation occurs in an ecosystem or web. ... Modeling in and through the seminary experience becomes a deeply formative aspect of the ecosystem."[16] Students intuit the condition of the ecosystem even if specific issues are kept secret. When teachers live into the epistle plea to "love one another, because love is from God," the atmosphere becomes alive with grace and authenticity.[17] In such an environment, teachers love not only each other but also students.

Love of Teachers for Students

A rather pragmatic educational outcome results from students experiencing love and compassion in the classroom as explained by Daniel Barbezat and Mirabai Bush. Referring to a study from the University of Southern California, they assert that "positive feelings and compassion have ... been found to stimulate and increase learning" and that "we should redesign learning environments and pedagogy to reap the benefits of greater self-awareness and social connection."[18] While increasing the learning potential of students may be a worthy outcome of love as pedagogy, a more bedrock motivation comes from the greatest commandments.[19] Loving each other is simply the horizontal result of the vertical and reciprocal love between God and humankind.

We need only look as far as Jesus to see a prototype of a teacher loving his or her student. Jesus repeatedly calls his disciples to love each other *"as I have loved you."*[20] Jesus compares his love for his students to the Father's love for Jesus—an intense and intentional love, to be sure.[21] Even onlookers were able to perceive Jesus's love for his students, as witnessed by the Jews at the death of Lazarus: "See how he loved him."[22] The apostle Paul, too, was motivated by love for his students. Paul ached for his people, pleaded for their faith, and prayed for their well-being. "I do not write these things to shame you, but to admonish you as my beloved children."[23]

---

[16]   Mullins and Small, 2.
[17]   1 John 4:7.
[18]   Daniel Barbezat and Mirabai Bush, *Contemplative Practices in Higher Education: Powerful Methods to Transform Teaching and Learning* (San Francisco: Jossey-Bass, 2014), 32.
[19]   Matthew 22:37-39.
[20]   John 13:34; 15:12.
[21]   John 15:9.
[22]   John 11:36.
[23]   1 Corinthians 4:14-15.

In our spiritual tradition, loving and knowing are tightly connected. Parker Palmer says it directly: "The origin of knowledge is love."[24] He goes on to say:

> The goal of a knowledge arising from love is the reunification and reconstruction of broken selves and worlds. A knowledge born of compassion aims not at exploiting and manipulating creation but at reconciling the world to itself. The mind motivated by compassion reaches out to know as the heart reaches out to love. Here, the act of knowing *is* an act of love, the act of entering and embracing the reality of the other ... .[25]

Knowing as an act of love moves the lover and the loved—the knower and the known—toward healing and wholeness.

Teachers who love students know them. Because they do, they discover areas of pain and vulnerability in students as well as areas of passion and strength. A teacher can adjust content, pedagogy, and personal interactions according to what will create the most effective learning environment. The analogy of a fire in a fireplace can help us envision this. The early sparks of a fire are hesitant and timid. A hearth-warming flame may develop, and it may not. If the fire builder determines that air is needed, she must breathe ever so gently on the tiny glimmer in order not to extinguish it but to infuse just enough oxygen to ignite and sustain a flicker. In the same way, some students overcoming hurts or being exposed to new ideas, however true or life giving, may need to be gently tended and supported. Jesus is said by Matthew to be one who will not extinguish a smoking wick.[26] At other times, a fire that has been untended and allowed to burn down to glowing embers needs a bellows in order to incite a blaze. Sometimes students need a burst of challenge or confrontation to ignite what already smolders in their souls. The teacher who knows and loves students can discern how much fanning will best support the fire of learning and growth. As bell hooks put it:

> When we teach with love we are better able to respond to the unique concerns of individual students, while simultaneously integrating those concerns into the classroom community. When teachers work to affirm the emotional well-being of students, we are doing

24 Parker Palmer, *To Know as We Are Known: Education as a Spiritual Journey* (San Francisco: HarperCollins, 1983), 8.
25 Palmer, 8.
26 Matthew 12:20.

the work of love. ... Teachers are not therapists. However, there are times when conscious teaching—teaching with love—brings us the insight that we will not be able to have a meaningful experience in the classroom without reading the emotional climate of our students and attending to it. ... Actually, when we teach with love we are far more likely to have an enhanced understanding of our student' capabilities and their limitations.[27]

Love for students also influences teachers to engage vulnerably in and out of the classroom even though vulnerability is countercultural in the academy. Teachers who love their students take the risks they ask their students to take: making mistakes, being honest, and confessing their shadows and their struggles. bell hooks says, "I do not expect students to take any risks that I would not take, to share in any way that I would not share."[28] Risking vulnerability requires courage and per-haps a bit of rebellion, because the overwhelming pressure of academic culture is to maintain objective distance and an image of expertise. "Entering the classroom determined to ... give ourselves over more fully to the mind, we show by our beings how deeply we have accepted the assumption that passion has no place in the classroom."[29]

In some classes at WTS, students and teachers participate anon-ymously in answering five reflective questions at the end of each class period.[30] When the results are shared at the beginning of the next class period, difficult issues sometimes come to light, including criticism of teachers or teaching methods. In such situations, teachers are likely to reveal how they were thinking and feeling when a certain incident happened. They are apt to apologize or to admit that they don't know something and feel insecure. They sometimes take advice from students and change the teaching plan to make learning more effective. They may also challenge the students' interpretation of an incident. Sometimes they choose to continue a practice even amidst loud student

---

27   hooks, *Critical Thinking*, 160.
28   bell hooks, *Teaching to Transgress; Education as the Practice of Freedom* (New York: Routledge, 1994), 21.
29   hooks, 192.
30   The Critical Incident Questionnaire is adopted from Stephen D. Brookfield, *Becoming a Critically Reflective Teacher* (San Francisco: Jossey-Bass, 1995). The questions are 1) When did you feel most engaged with what was happening? 2) When did you feel most distanced from what was happening? 3) What action that anyone took did you find most affirming or helpful? 4) What action that anyone took did you find most puzzling or confusing? 5) What surprised you the most?

protest, acknowledging the discomfort, explaining their motivation, and inviting students to trust the process.

This kind of trusting exchange arises predominantly from the love of teachers for their students. "Do not hesitate to love and to love deeply," pleads Nouwen.[31] Just as love of teachers for each other spills into love for students, students who know they are valued and respected are freed up to love each other.

Love of Students for Each Other

The tone in the classroom shifts when students love each other. Competition morphs into collaboration. Students desire and work toward the success of their classmates. Animosity turns to affection. Suspicion changes into support. Students sharpen each other. When students live into the second greatest commandment, trust blossoms and learning flowers. Mistakes become opportunities for learning instead of onramps to shame. Humor emerges, opening hearts and minds with receptivity. Valuing authenticity replaces protecting image. Trust creates an atmosphere where conflict becomes generative and honesty is commonplace. Perhaps Jesus was recognizing some of these dynamics when he said, "I give you a new commandment, that you love one another. Just as I have loved you, you also should love one another."[32]

bell hooks calls this kind of classroom a *learning community*. "I enter the classroom with the assumption that we must build 'community' in order to create a climate of openness and intellectual rigor."[33] A learning community both requires the intention of the teacher and includes the teacher, as hooks explains:

> When I enter the classroom at the beginning of the semester the weight is on me to establish that our purpose is to be, for however brief a time, a community of learners together. It positions me as a learner.[34]

Often, a classroom is conceived of as a collection of individuals receiving information from an expert. But in a learning community,

---

[31]   Henri Nouwen, *The Inner Voice of Love: A Journey Through Anguish to Freedom* (New York: Random House, 1996), 59.

[32]   John 13:34.

[33]   hooks, *Teaching to Transgress*, 40.

[34]   hooks, 153.

interdependence among participants is recognized and nurtured. Each person's presence and contribution affects the experience of every other. It matters if people don't show up, physically *or* emotionally. Pedagogy becomes about much more than teaching content. It also teaches process, reflection, and relationship. Participants in a learning community come to *know* each other. "Love in the classroom creates a foundation for learning that embraces and empowers everyone."[35]

Early on in Tehom's interactive Hebrew classes, word pictures were introduced because pictures broaden meaning and spark memory of Hebrew words in ways that a single English word often cannot. When students had difficulty understanding the meanings of various word pictures, the Hebrew team created the opportunity for students to find their own word pictures. These assignments, called "Show and Tell," have evolved unexpectedly and delightfully. Students not only choose to find an online picture to represent the Hebrew word of the day but may also bring photos, artwork, objects, and stories from their personal lives. They share their representations in class with honesty and vulnerability. As a result, at least three things happen: First, the meaning of the Hebrew word becomes a matter of the heart. The stories arise from the heart of the "shower-and-teller" and lodge in the hearts of the "seers-and-hearers." Second, intimacy and trust grow in the learning space of the classroom. Increased trust and compassion allow students to engage the interactive pedagogy with a greater willingness to risk mistakes, work collaboratively, and support each other. Third, everyone learns, students and teachers alike. They learn about what is important to each other and why. *And* they learn the depths of the Hebrew word at hand. Love as pedagogy extends beyond human relationships to passion for the subject that is being taught.

Love for the Subject

Passionate teachers have heard the piper's call of the subjects they teach. They show up with bright eyes. They interact with conviction. They effuse joy. And they cannot help but be excited about sharing it with students because the subject is transforming their own lives. Palmer says of one of his own mentors, "The passion with which he lectured was not only for his subject by also for us to know his subject."[36] Many are the times in Tehom's classrooms when students have drawn a sharp breath because they are surprised by a story passionately and

---

[35]   hooks, *Critical Thinking*, 159.
[36]   Palmer, *Courage to Teach*, 137.

vulnerably told. They have been cast headlong into an abyss of meaning and depth of the topic at hand, which they did not have access to five minutes earlier.

Boogaart often speaks of the goal of the interactive Hebrew classes as "changing the students' relationship with Scripture." He wants students to receive the Word with what he calls *hospitality of the heart*: an openness that allows the Word, via the Spirit, to come home to the very being of the student. Tehom wants the Word to take up residence in the student and the student to take up residence in the Word. No longer is the Word an object to be dissected but rather a friend to live with and love. Internalizing Scripture is one powerful way to welcome the words into the heart and begin to love them. Memorization also demonstrates a value in something. We memorize things we care about or are essential to our existence, like names of new students or, in the old days, phone numbers. When teachers internalize and then speak the text, they display the fervor and affection with which they regard the Word.

Students quickly detect a teacher's passion for a topic, whether expressed breathlessly or calmly. The energy is inescapable and invitational. Students are drawn into the glory of discovery, curiosity, and creativity. Passion is contagious. Boogaart's Hebrew team discovered early on that music was a way to help students learn Hebrew grammar and texts. The team introduced several simple songs with lyrics directly from Scripture. Students responded well. In fact, as the years went by and music became more and more integral to the courses, students began to write and teach each other stunning music for other Hebrew texts and blessings they were internalizing. They love the songs they learn, often speaking of them as worship or prayer. Each cohort tends to become particularly fond of songs created by their class, and it is not unusual to hear Hebrew songs being sung in the halls of the seminary by enthusiastic students. Again affections are intertwined as the professors' passion for the Hebrew texts, for music, and for the students contagiously bubbles over into the hearts of the students. In turn, the students love the texts and the community formed by the liturgy the songs create.

Loving the subject enough to let it be at the center of the learning community and the students enough to trust their ability to be active contributors creates a space in which what Palmer calls "a community of truth" flourishes around "a great thing."[37]

---

[37]   Palmer, *Courage to Teach*, 116.

I now listen anew to students' stories about their great teachers in which "a passion for the subject" is a trait so often named. ... I always thought that passion makes a teacher great because it brought contagious energy into the classroom, but now I realize its deeper function. Passion for the subject propels that subject, not the teacher, into the center of the learning circle—and when a great thing is in their midst, students have direct access to the energy of learning and of life.[38]

A literal example of *subject in the center* in the Hebrew classroom involves the creation story from Genesis 1. Students and teachers sit in a circle. The teachers recite the text in Hebrew while students place items in the circle to represent what is happening on each day of creation: a blue cloth with stuffed fish multiplying when God blesses them, craft-foam suns setting and rising as evening and morning make another day, and so on. At the end when God declares everything *very good* and rests on Shabbat, silence often falls over the circle as insights appear like the foam stars that now adorn the silk firmament. *Love* does that.

Conclusion

Love in the classroom is self-perpetuating, like the water cycle of the earth. Evaporation leads to condensation, which leads to precipitation, and the cycle repeats. Similarly, teachers loving students leads to students loving each other. Teachers loving the Scriptures leads to students loving the God of the Scriptures. Students loving Scripture and each other leads to teachers loving students, and so on. And the whole thing originates with God loving humankind in the first place.

Boogaart's Hebrew team invests heavily in student leaders who are affectionately known as *talmorim,* a combination of the Hebrew words *talmidim* (students) and *morim* (teachers). These students attend a ten-day Hebrew retreat in preparation for leading Hebrew labs and tutoring beginning Hebrew students. The retreat is an outpouring of love. Teachers and students study together, eat together, live together, and play and pray together. A hospitality team thoughtfully prepares meals that respect the earth and feed the soul. "Food is God's love made edible," they say. An authentic learning community forms. Students and teachers speak honestly about what they are experiencing and hash things out when necessary. Daily worship, meditation, and silence spark

---

[38]   Palmer, 120.

joy and gratitude toward the triune God. As a result, students grow in their love of the Hebrew language, Scripture, and the God revealed in Scripture. They develop an affection and appreciation for each other and their teachers. Then they take their enthusiasm and love back to the halls of the seminary and lend it to anxious incoming Hebrew students and to the overall spirit of the community.

However, not everyone is comfortable with the notion of love as a substantial element in the academy, as hooks points out:

> Well learned distinctions between public and private make us believe that love has no place in the classroom. ... Professors are expected to publish, but no one really expects or demands that we really care about teaching uniquely passionate and different ways. Teachers who love students and are loved by them are still "suspect" in the academy.[39]

Some argue that love in the classroom removes the possibility of objectivity. But objectivity is a myth anyway. No one comes to any topic without the freight of past experiences and beliefs, childhood upbringing, and temperament. Our vocabulary bears this out in that the courses in the academic setting are called *subjects*. It could be argued that the atmosphere brought about by the engaged pedagogy of love enables students and teachers to more easily recognize and acknowledge their biases and preconceptions.

Others fear that love will prevent the teacher from being able to balance student freedom and good discipline. E.F. Schumacher wonders aloud about such tensions:

> How can one reconcile the demands of freedom and discipline in education? Countless mothers and teachers, in fact, do it ... by bringing into the situation a force that belongs to a higher level where opposites are transcended—the power of love.[40]

Some also wonder if love in the classroom disables teachers from teaching painful things. It could be suggested that love enables learning communities to encounter difficult and controversial topics more honestly and with adequate levels of care and support necessary to sustain anxious or wounded souls.

---

[39] hooks, *Teaching to Transgress*, 198.
[40] E. F. Schumacher, *Small Is Beautiful: Economics as if People Mattered* (New York: HarperCollins, 1973), 97–98.

Boogaart characterizes not only the power of pedagogy but also the heart of Reformed theology as arising from love, the love of God portrayed in the parable of the Prodigal Son. The "open arms of the Father" embrace broken humanity, and we are "drawn into the presence of a loving God."[41] The Reformed theologian I. John Hesselink in his last days shared with Boogaart his conviction that knowledge of God, as expressed in the opening chapter of Calvin's *Institutes*, is not an intellectual knowing but rather a loving personal encounter with God. We love because God first loved us.[42] Loving pedagogy powerfully coaxes students and teachers to be "held in the arms of God," thus knowing who they are and what God has created them to do and to be.[43]

---

[41]   Tom Boogaart, "The Heart of Western Theological Seminary," *The Commons* 22, no.1 (Fall 2018): 4.

[42]   1 John 4:19.

[43]   1 John 4:19.

CHAPTER 5

Stewarding a Living Tradition: A Case Study

Benjamin Conner

According to moral and political philosopher Alasdair MacIntyre, a living tradition is a "historically extended, socially embodied argument" about the goods that constitute a tradition.[1] Educational theorist Craig Dykstra adds that the argument is also about the "truth and reality on which [the goods] are grounded and to which they point."[2] Tom Boogaart has been the steward of Western Theological Seminary's (WTS) living tradition for the past quarter century and has maintained that the "truth and reality" in which that tradition is rooted and out of which it grows is Reformed Pietist experiential theology, summarized for him in the concept *coram Deo*, the sanctification of ordinary life before the face of a welcoming and loving God. In what way can it be said the Boogaart was the steward of a living tradition? How did he do it? Boogaart preserved and transmitted the living tradition of WTS

---

[1]   Alasdair C. MacIntyre, *After Virtue: A Study in Moral Theory,* 3rd edition (Notre Dame: University of Notre Dame Press, 2007), 222.

[2]   Craig R. Dykstra, "Reconceiving Practice," in *Shifting Boundaries: Contextual Approaches to the Structure of Theological Education*, eds. Barbara G. Wheeler and Edward Farley (Louisville: Westminster John Knox Press, 1991), 58.

through his scholarly work, his commitment to experiential theology as representative of a vital and life-giving expression of the Reformed theology, and through his pedagogy.

Form Forms: Scholarly Work

It is a bit ironic that Boogaart would be honored in a festschrift given his ambivalence toward the academy, not that Boogaart has had a completely adversarial posture toward the academy or that he isn't worthy of being honored by his colleagues in a collection of essays that touch upon his scholarly impact. The fact, however, is that a festschrift is a particularly academic and institutional way to honor a colleague, and Boogaart has taken an untraditional path as an academic. As of his retirement, he was the only faculty member at WTS without a CV link on his faculty webpage. His webpage included a link to one published work, a book written for Reformed Church Press. All of his other writings were similarly oriented toward the church and could be found in church or denomination-based magazines and periodicals like *Reformed Review, Church Herald,* or *Perspectives,* for which he served as an editor for years. He didn't publish in the journals of his guild and attended the American Academy of Religion and the Society of Biblical Literature only once in the last 20 years of his professorship.

As a scholar and theologian, Boogaart is reflexive, meaning he understands that he can't stand outside a research field and bracket himself off from it. Therefore, he embraces that fact that he both interprets and creates at the same time. As a Bible scholar, he insists that we must allow "communion" with what we are learning, bringing all of what we are to the text if we are to experience true knowledge. Knowledge is like touch; it is an act of comprehending while being comprehended. From where did such commitments issue? It is important to remember that "all research is, to an extent, autobiography."[3] Boogaart's experience of the academy—and reaction to that experience—shaped his contributions.

While a doctoral student in the Netherlands, Boogaart quickly realized that many European Old Testament scholars weren't in contact with the church. They were so disconnected from worshiping communities, so universally oriented, that they weren't asking

---

[3]   John Swinton, "'Where is Your Church?' Moving toward a Hospitable and Sanctified Ethnography," in *Perspectives on Ecclesiology and Ethnography,* ed. Pete Ward (Grand Rapids: Eerdmans, 2012), 84.

contextually relevant questions anymore. Furthermore, years of bracketing, objectifying, and intellectualizing had emptied their research practices and, consequently, their educational content of personal encounter.

The goal of scholarship seemed to be, in part, to be objective in one's theological exploration, yet there is no true objectivism. Scholars are always navigating the space between objective rationalism and subjective relativism. Parker Palmer confesses, "My formal education ended fifteen years ago, but I continue to reckon with the form it gave my life."[4] Form forms, so states the Boogaart axiom, and objective and distanced approaches to the world have implications for the kind of knowing that students imagine is possible—knowledge of self and of God. In Boogaart's experience of the academy, objectivism had become the reigning worldview governing all plausibility structures. Palmer, similarly, finds objectivism to be deeply rooted in our educational institutions and practices: "Objectivism is institutionalized in our educational practices, in the ways we teach and learn" such that objectivism is the "hidden curriculum" that impacts our students the most no matter the subject matter of study, and these ways of teaching "form students in the objectivist world view."[5] Formation in such a curriculum is especially detrimental for a theological institution. Though not speaking of theological education directly, Palmer clarifies, "From our platform we observe and analyze and assess, but we do *not go into the arena*—for that is how we have been taught to know. This means that virtues like compassion, the capacity to 'feel with' another, are 'educated away' [emphasis added]."[6]

Where in the kind of scholarship that Palmer described above does one find an encounter with the sovereign who "lowers the scepter" and invites people into the welcoming embrace of God? Boogaart became dissatisfied with his received mode of scholarship and became convinced that the reality behind the biblical text has a power that can transform people—one can't live in an "objectivist" bracketed state. Openness and vulnerability are required to open one's heart to experiencing the transforming power of the living God. Boogaart found a conversation partner and spiritual mentor in Abraham Heschel. Heschel gave voice

---

[4] Parker J. Palmer, *To Know as We Are Known: A Spirituality of Education* (New York: Harper & Row, 1983), 20.

[5] Palmer, *To Know as We Are Known*, 29.

[6] Palmer, 34.

to Boogaart's frustrations with the academic environment in which he was (mal)nourished:

> Philosophy had become an isolated, self-subsisting, self-indulgent entity, *a Ding an sich*, encouraging suspicion instead of love of wisdom. The answers offered were unrelated to the problems, indifferent to the travail of a person who became aware of man's suspended sensitivity in the face of stupendous challenge, indifferent to a situation in which good and evil became irrelevant, in which man became increasingly callous to catastrophe and ready to suspend the principle of truth.[7]

The shape of students' theological education shapes them as scholars and pastors, and Boogaart was concerned that his theological training had abandoned what practical theologian Edward Farley termed "theology's primary genre." Theology's primary genre is our encounter with the living God, or, in Boogaart's Reformed theology, coram Deo. In Farley's "*Mea Culpa*," he laments the fact the many of his students have not and will not benefit from the content of his courses because of his "failure to identify *theology's primary genre*" and his "refusal to let the *primary genre* (once I did become aware of it) determine my theological pedagogy [emphasis added]."[8] Consequently, Farley believes that much of theology from the academy will be irrelevant to the congregational ministry of spiritual formation and will be "quickly shed like a heavy coat in hot weather."[9] Seminaries that are teaching theology as, primarily, knowledge about God often miss the practical knowledge that characterized early Christian theology. Rather than the hidden curriculum being objectivism so that students are being taught an objectivist worldview no matter the course of study, Boogaart put theology's primary genre (a spirit, a heart, a genuine encounter with the presence of God) back into theological education. His commitment to theology's primary genre led Boogaart to practice formational teaching.

What is formation? All theological education forms us in some way; the question Boogaart kept before himself and his colleagues is whether or not the ways in which theological education forms us are ways that create the kinds of spaces or arenas in which a community

---

[7]   Abraham Joshua Heschel, *The Prophets*, 1st Perennial classics edition (New York: HarperPerennial, 2001), xxviii.

[8]   Edward Farley, "Four Pedagogical Mistakes: A *Mea Culpa*," *Teaching Theology and Religion* 8 no. 4, (2005): 200.

[9]   Farley, 201.

becomes aware of God's presence and prepared to participate in God's ongoing redemptive mission in the world. Are we objectively dissecting Scripture and theology (controlling, categorizing, and evaluating it in a way that suggests revelation is no longer living),[10] or are we experiencing God through Scripture and theology (reflecting God's love and being transformed by it, growing in self-knowledge and knowledge of others)?

Historically Extended: Coram Deo

It wasn't simply dissatisfaction with the academy that led Boogaart to say no to the received form of theological education; there was something more compelling to which he was saying yes. Boogaart considers himself to be extending the tradition of the experiential theology of early Dutch Calvinism or Reformed Pietism, which promoted the idea that doctrine is not meant "merely for the mind."[11] In the words of Eugene Osterhaven who was the steward of the heart of WTS before Boogaart, knowledge of God "must not only be an intellectual awareness of certain facts about [God], but a knowledge of the heart, which is inclusive of the whole person."[12] Boogaart's career at WTS involved drawing upon and extending two important streams of Reformed Pietism: mysticism, or spiritual elation, and activism. It is not surprising that Boogaart would feel at home in experiential theology as the movement was reacting to "an almost exclusive emphasis upon the intellect in the late reformation,"[13] that is, the bloodless speculative scholasticism that Boogaart encountered in the academy and that pervaded many congregations. Indeed, a theological seminary is an intellectual community, but if it is to stay true to its primary genre, a student's heart must be engaged. Coram Deo is the Reformed concept

---

[10] As Boogaart explained in his final lecture/performance: "Using teaching methods that dated from the nineteenth century, the same methods by which we the instructors had been taught, we spent the majority of our classroom time focusing on memorizing vocabulary and grammatical tables as the necessary tools that students could use to dissect a text. And what does the image of tools and dissection suggest? The image suggests that the biblical text is cut up into pieces and laid out on a table before us, that the Bible is a dead object and that we are the living subjects whose task it is to discover its true meaning." Tom Boogaart, "Jonah: Standing Before the Face of God," (lecture, Western Theological Seminary, Holland, Michigan, December 13, 2018).

[11] M. Eugene Osterhaven, "The Experiential Theology of Early Dutch Calvinism," *Reformed Review* 27 no. 3 (1974): 180.

[12] M. Eugene Osterhaven, *The Spirit of the Reformed Tradition* (Grand Rapids: Eerdmans, 1971), 88.

[13] Osterhaven, "Experiential Theology," 183.

that can call a community to the core value of acknowledging the presence of God and experiencing God's embrace.

How might putting coram Deo at the center of a seminary's corporate life impact that community? While the doctrine of the church, of the persons of God, or about the inspiration of Scripture may be of value, such doctrine is derivative from that which is ultimate—a living encounter with the living God, or existing in the presence of God. The core doctrine and practice of the Reformed tradition for WTS, standing as it does in the Pietistic strand of the Reformed tradition, is coram Deo, life lived before the face of God. As a community of faith, the faith that we proclaim is a living faith. Again, in the word of Osterhaven, "Faith is not arid speculative discussion about this or that theory of theology, philosophy, or life, but it is devout living before the face of the Lord in the consciousness of responsibility to [God]."[14] All of life—work, play, relationships, responsibilities—are performed before the face of God. When a community lives out coram Deo, they experience *gelukzaligheid* and *godzaligheid*, or

> That blessed state of joy in the Lord in which one finds a high degree of perfect contentment and peace. Involving the whole person, his intellect, feeling, and will, it is the ultimate blessing that God can give one in this life and the greatest proof that God is a gracious father to his children.[15]

The spiritual core of a seminary is the experience of being embraced by God, a vision most clearly portrayed in the Lukan parable of the prodigal son.

In an unpublished paper titled "The Heart of Western Seminary," Boogaart recalls his first encounter with the concept of coram Deo, and, I would argue, he also discerned the trajectory of his vocation:

> I remember sitting in Dr. Eugene Osterhaven's theology class and learning from him about WTS's place in the broader Reformed tradition. He told us that soon after the Reformation took hold in the Netherlands, some reformers felt that a Further Reformation (*Nadere Reformatie*) was needed. Beset by theological controversies, they feared that the church was too focused on head-knowledge and right thinking and was losing sight of Calvin's emphasis

---

[14]   Osterhaven, *The Spirit of the Reformed Tradition*, 108.
[15]   Osterhaven, "Experiential Theology," 182.

on the heart and faithful living. The proponents of this Further Reformation were enraptured by the fact that God, the all-powerful Sovereign, had lowered his scepter and drawn his beloved people into his presence, and they celebrated the joy (gelukzaligheid) and peace of heart that came when believers were held in the arms of God.[16]

It was not surprising, therefore, to hear similar words at his final lecture, which, appropriate to his ambivalence toward traditional scholarship, was a not a lecture at all but was instead a final performance or enactment:

> Throughout its long history, WTS has celebrated a Sovereign God who lowers the scepter and draws us his children into his presence. We are not fascinated with the power and control that God exerts over us, but with the love and intimacy God shows us. We understand ourselves as standing before the face of God and being embraced in the arms of God.[17]

Coram Deo is about living a liturgical life; it is the sanctification of ordinary life before the face of God. How does reorienting a seminary's life around such an experiential doctrine impact pedagogy? In short, it means that the classroom is a place of encounter and worship. The goal of pedagogy is that through deeper penetration into Scripture and theology a community will comprehend God while being comprehended. Such pedagogy is the socially embodied expression of the goods internal to the living tradition and issues in a kind of knowledge that can only be gained through active, intimate encounter.

Socially Embodied: Pedagogy

Boogaart contributed to the embodiment of the living tradition of WTS by prioritizing the two streams of Reformed Pietism in his pedagogy: mysticism, or encounter, and activism. Through formative Christian practices, particularly the practice of hospitality, he was able to recover what had been "educated away" by making the classroom and the world an arena of encounter. Though he wouldn't have phrased it this way, Boogaart was following Parker Palmer's well-known definition of teaching: "To teach is to create a space in which obedience to truth

[16]   Tom Boogaart, "The Heart of Western Seminary" (unpublished paper, 2018), 1.
[17]   Tom Boogaart, "Jonah: Standing Before the Face of God."

is practiced."[18] Encounter and obedience are the keys to faithful theological pedagogy.

If theology's primary genre is related to our encounter of God, then the knowledge gained or received in theological education will be transformative and will change the student's orientation to reality. As Farley explains, "Because that knowledge had to do with salvation, it was a practical knowledge, a "habit" (*habitus*) of wisdom: that is, a fundamental way of being disposed toward things."[19] Dykstra, drawing on Farley describes habitus as "profound, life-orienting, identity-shaping participation in the constitutive practices of Christian life."[20] The object of theology is a living and active subject, so true theological and biblical studies can never be comprehended by abstract, impersonal knowledge. According to Palmer,

> Jesus calls us to truth, but not in the form of creeds or theologies or world-views. His call to truth is a call to community—with him, with each other, with creation and its Creator. If what we know is an abstract, impersonal, apart from us, it cannot be truth, for truth involves a vulnerable, faithful, and risk-filled interpenetration of the knower and the known.[21]

When the setting of theological education is the academy, which tends to carry an objectivist worldview, then the instructor must be diligent to ensure that theological formation related to encounter doesn't morph into either clergy education—training in the proficiencies or best practices of the job—or into the abstract reflections on the being of God.

Boogaart avoided the blanched objectivism of the academy by making Christian practices the center of his pedagogy. "Christian practices are things Christian people do together over time in response to and in the light of God's active presence for the life of the world [in Jesus Christ]."[22] Christian practices include ecclesial practices, like

---

[18]   Palmer, *To Know as We Are Known*, 69.
[19]   Edward Farley, *Practicing Gospel: Unconventional Thoughts on the Church's Ministry* (Louisville; London: Westminster John Knox Press, 2003), 4.
[20]   Craig R. Dykstra, "Reconceiving Practice," in *Shifting Boundaries: Contextual Approaches to the Structure of Theological Education*, ed. Barbara G. Wheeler and Edward Farley (Louisville: Westminster/John Knox Press, 1991), 50.
[21]   Palmer, 48–49.
[22]   Dorothy C. Bass, ed., *Practicing Our Faith: A Way of Life for a Searching People*, 1st edition (San Francisco: Jossey-Bass, 1997), 5.

baptism and the Lord's Supper, that are touch points and summaries for all Christian practices. But Christian practices are also ordinary activities that make up a life in the world (forgiving, honoring the body, giving and receiving hospitality, offering testimony, keeping Sabbath as we live as creatures in time, etc.) that address fundamental human needs and "can be shaped in response to God's active presence."[23] More importantly, as I have written elsewhere, "When congregations participate in Christian practices ... they are participating in a social reality in which the Holy Spirit is the agent of change, the shaper of people and communities. Practices are places of encounter that evoke responses."[24]

Practices also bear epistemological weight. According to Dykstra,

> In the context of participation in certain practices we come to see more than just the value of the "good" of certain human activities. Beyond that, we may come to awareness of certain realities that outside of these practices are beyond our *ken*. Engagement in certain practices may give rise to new knowledge.[25]

This knowledge comes from a true encounter with God—it is reflected in the *ethos* of the experiential theology of early Dutch Calvinism.

Following Dykstra, Christian practices are "habitations of the Spirit." He explains it in the following way:

> They are not, finally, activities we do to make something spiritual happen in our lives. Nor are they duties we undertake to be obedient to God. Rather, they are patterns of communal action that create openings in our lives where the grace, mercy, and presence of God may be made known to us. They are places where the power of God is experienced. In the end, these are not ultimately our practices but forms of participation in the practice of God.[26]

In this sense, Christian practices are understood to be "arenas" that "put us where life in Christ may be made known, recognized, experienced,

---

23 Bass, 5.

24 Benjamin T. Conner, "For the Fitness of Their Witness: Missional Christian Practices," in *Converting Witness: The Future of Christian Mission in the New Millennium*, eds. John G. Fleet and David W. Congdon, (Lanham: Lexington Books, forthcoming 2019).

25 Dykstra, "Reconceiving Practice," 45.

26 Craig R. Dykstra, *Growing in the Life of Faith: Education and Christian Practices*, 2nd edition (Louisville: Westminster John Knox), 66. See also xv, 64, and 78.

and participated in."[27] They are the experiential theology by which the presence of God is palpably experienced and by which our doubts, fears, and the "nasty suspicion"[28] that there are no realities behind the language and liturgies of the Christian faith are overwhelmed: "In the midst of engagement in these practices," explains Dykstra, "a community comes to such an immediate experience of the grace and mercy and power of God that the 'nasty suspicion' ... simply loses its power."[29]

The practice that is most evident in Boogaart's formational pedagogy is the practice of hospitality. God's hospitality toward humans offers a framework for answering questions like: How do we receive God in others? How do we bear the welcome of God? How do we teach a foreign language and engage a distant culture in ways that honor our differences as part of God's intended diversity? How do we organize and guide a classroom made up of "strangers"? Whom should we welcome as a student at a theological seminary? How might the practices and patterns of our coursework together need to change in order to receive the blessing of someone who typically experiences marginalization? What can a seminary do about local and global economic inequity? Boogaart's practice of hospitality is not a teaching technique. Instead, Christian practices are arenas of encounter and transformation through which the Holy Spirit can open up a community to new possibilities. David Smith and James K. A. Smith explain in *Teaching and Christian Practices*:

> Christian practices, and their pedagogical analogues, are to be understood neither as theoretical principles to be clinically applied nor as efficient techniques practiced upon students; they depend upon the building of a shared imagination in which students acquire new ways of seeing and understanding their own learning as well as new rhythms commensurate with this renewed imagination.[30]

For Boogaart, the "shared imagination" is a sacramental worldview, and the curriculum is common participation in Christian

---

[27]   Dykstra, *Growing in the Life of Faith*, 43.

[28]   Edward Farley, *Ecclesial Man: A Social Phenomenology of Faith and Reality* (Philadelphia: Fortress Press, 1975), 6.

[29]   Dykstra, 53.

[30]   David I. Smith and James K. A. Smith, "Introduction: Practices, Faith, and Pedagogy," in *Teaching Christian Practices: Reshaping Faith and Learning* (Grand Rapids: Eerdmans, 2011), 23.

practices as arenas for encountering the mystery of God. Participation in hospitality is more than a technique for teaching a worldview. It is, according to Elizabeth Newman, participation in the life of God.[31] The practice of hospitality—following the hospitality of God—is extravagant, crosses human-made barriers, and is inclusive of and accommodates all people.

In the academy, professors rely heavily on sensory perceptions and the capacity to rationally organize and control information. Reason is one tool for knowing, but it's not the only tool and not always the most efficacious. And while the capacities for abstraction and cogitation are important, they are overemphasized in the academy while other aptitudes for knowing are undervalued or never invoked: intuition, empathy, emotion, and faith. It is likely that it is these ways of knowing that shape students in ways that are most important for future ministers.

Theologian Frances Young was challenged by the birth of her son, Arthur, who was born with severe learning disabilities, to imagine vocation in a world that seemed not to value disability. His presence in her life caused her to consider her culture's uncritical acceptance of the values of individualism, dominance, and competitiveness that seemed to undergird a concept of competence that was deemed essential to a fulfilling and successful life. Arthur would never have competence by the world's standards. But he did have something to offer a community. While he lacked the characteristics that society uplifts as being human—"language, intelligence, the ability to read others' minds, a moral sense"—what he had was the capacity to

> call forth those characteristically human qualities of response to one another—indeed the true human values that Paul calls the gifts of the Spirit: love, joy, peace, patience, kindness, goodness, faithfulness, gentleness, and self-control (Gal. 5.22). Indeed, that some persons lack moral autonomy surely highlights that point that true human goodness is never individualistic—it's corporate, something found in community.[32]

Many of our most significant contributions to a community are mysterious gifts that we steward or bear.

[31] Elizabeth Newman, *Untamed Hospitality: Welcoming God and Other Strangers* (Grand Rapids: Brazos, 2007), 13.
[32] Frances Young, *Arthur's Call: A Journey of Faith in the Face of Severe Learning Disability* (London: SPCK, 2014), 76.

Boogart's pedagogy includes not only the mysticism, or encounter, evident in his sacramental worldview; his pedagogy also incorporates the other stream of Reformed Pietism: activism. Responding to global concerns with a missionary response, The Western Bridge, now simply known as The Bridge, is a store in the tradition of the Alternative Trade Organization (ATO) movement. The ATO is a fair-trade organization that attempts to mitigate the impact of poverty in impoverished regions of the world by allowing marginalized and economically vulnerable producers to financially benefit more directly from the sale of their goods. Through affording them fair access to "developed" markets, the store itself provides a ministry that addresses unjust financial structures related to globalization. Boogaart was instrumental in bringing The Bridge to Holland, Michigan. He viewed it as both a ministry of justice and as a theological training ground. Boogaart recognized that participating in the ministry of the store transformed volunteers and students who were experiencing fatigue and exhaustion in other areas of their lives. He reflected, "What does it mean when a group of people experience energy in an activity beyond that which they themselves have put into it? What does it mean when bushes burn, but are not consumed? Are the volunteers of The Bridge somehow standing in the presence of God?"[33] Activism leads to encounter and reinforces a sacramental worldview that expects to find God at work in the world.

The Community Kitchen at WTS, an activist response to local injustices, provides another context for theological formation. When the State of Michigan eliminated general assistance benefits (welfare) for nearly 80,000 adults (twice-monthly payments of around $90 described by one recipient as a "life raft" in *The New York Times*, October 7, 1991) Boogaart and others sought to use seminary resources, both physical and human, to reduce the strain on the community by offering one nutritious meal on a daily basis. They stated, "We believe that we are called to respond to the 'bad news' from the State of Michigan with an announcement of the good news to people who need it most."[34] In the proposal for the Community Kitchen, the ministry of the kitchen is tied to the purpose of the seminary with the following statement of rationale: "We believe our primary calling is to equip students to

---

[33]   Tom Boogaart, "Vital Missions in the Exhausted West," *Urban Mission* 9 no. 5 (1992): 53.

[34]   Tom Boogaart, Pam DeBoom, and Paul Smith, "Memo To: WTS Community Re: Community Kitchen," October 21, 1991.

be ministers in the world. We believe that equipping people requires engagement in mission. Thus, we believe that this new opportunity will enhance our mission."[35] For Boogaart—in following Reformed Pietism—activism and encounter are inextricably united.

Conclusion: The Goods Internal to the Tradition

What better way to honor Boogaart's impact and legacy than by writing a festschrift? Perhaps another way to honor Boogaart's contribution to WTS would be to purchase Rembrandt's painting *Return of the Prodigal Son* and display it prominently, allowing the image to stand beside and orient our doctrinal statements about what it means to be "Reformed." Reformed identity seems to have a script that can't be circumscribed by doctrinal statements and must be enacted: lived, tasted, and experienced. Boogaart, as the custodian of WTS's living tradition, ensured that WTS would never forget this experiential aspect of Reformed identity.

[35] Boogaart, et al., "Memo."

CHAPTER 6

Cosmology, Coram Deo, and the Camino

Kyle J.A. Small

"Taking the first step is recognizing that we will never reach the image of perfection we have been trying to achieve." David Whyte

Tom Boogaart approached me as I returned to the office after a four-day absence attending and speaking at a conference for pre-tenure faculty. He kindly asked where I was and what I accomplished. He listened as I nervously and loquaciously recounted my journey. I commented on the delight of being upgraded to first class on my flight home. In that moment, Tom moved from listening colleague to advising sage. I remember him saying, "Kyle, there is a proclivity of academics (and pastors) to find their value and worth in flying about the country to the acclaim of their unknown listeners. The strangers will applaud your brilliance and grant you special privileges. You can build your resume and become impressive to everyone far from home. This is a temptation, but the journey of discipleship and vocation for a teacher is not leaving home and gaining wings but is remaining home and growing roots. The people here won't applaud you nearly as often, and they will know your proclivities, both the good and ill. It is here, at home, where you need to speak and teach and learn, for the journey isn't out and up but moving close and in." This was one of my first conversations with Dr. Boogaart, and it remains defining (and convicting).

I wasn't exactly sure what Tom meant with his advice. I wanted to dismiss him since he was already secure with tenure, a full professorship, and a fancy title. At the same time, the story would not leave my mind as I began planning my next grant project, speaking gig, or conference. Ever since, I have been trying to understand what he meant by "the journey isn't out and up but moving close and in" and "the journey of discipleship and vocation of a teacher are not leaving home and gaining wings, but remaining home and growing roots."

This is my seventh year at Western Theological Seminary (WTS), and I am still trying to both understand and live Tom's advice. The temptation to achieve ubiquity (to be known by everyone, everywhere) and become significant lingers, but the ambition is waning. This may be due to the fifth decade of life, but it also may be due to the world created in me from the words spoken by Tom. This essay is an attempt to flesh out the intersection of these two worlds through the spiritual discipline of pilgrimage. Pilgrimage is a primary practice for discovering Tom's sacramental view of reality— namely, that the world in front of you is the only world necessary for understanding God's relationship to us and to God's justice in the world. My audience is those who desire to lead the church in mission. I never imagined writing an essay on slow leadership; yet Tom's words, God's character, and the practice of pilgrimage coalesce in a sense that leading in mission is primarily a slow task.

I see the irony that finding roots means taking a pilgrimage, but as I hope to show, pilgrimage is an interim practice for deepening roots and not a way of escaping reality. Tom's advice became clearer to me during my first sabbatical. I went away from WTS and spent my first six weeks of walking the Camino de Santiago de Compostela. The French Way of the Camino is 499 miles across the north of Spain. This 1,100-year-old pilgrimage hosted Teresa of Avila, Francis of Assisi, and Pope John Paul II. I invested 33 days to walk the 499 miles. Yet the Camino is not over, and each day, I invest time deepening my call as a pilgrim. In light of Tom's words several years ago, the pilgrimage is not a repudiation of his advice; indeed, it is a pursuit to understand it. The practice of pilgrimage is as much a spiritual practice for finding home and roots as it is for leaving them.

From Escape Artist to Pilgrim

Much of life invites us to escape the moment and remain inattentive to what matters most, now.[1] The current research on technology consumption elevates distraction exponentially; yet iPhones and iPods are not to blame. Humanity has long remained distracted and asleep to the world. The apostle Paul's invitation to wake up and rise from the dead is one commonly not taken.[2] Richard Foster said it well: "In contemporary society, the adversary majors in three things: hurry, noise, and crowds."[3]

Irish poet David Whyte has become a close companion in my attempt to discover the meaning of Tom's words. He tells a story that underscores my own story of distraction and escape and also the pursuit of ubiquity. David Whyte says, "I was under stress vocationally. I began to see velocity as an answer to complexity. The problem with this is that you cannot see anyone who is not traveling at the same speed as you. Those who go slower become your enemies."[4] Many leaders are flurrying about, exchanging velocity for complexity, and most of the world goes by unnoticed. One of the core acts of being human is to make others visible; speed destroys visibility. This speed is not simply a physical reality of bustling about; it is also true of the overactive brain that spins with anxiety, envy, and anger. Slow in every way is the way of God, the way of the pilgrim, and the way of a rooted leader. In order to move from escape artist to pilgrim, we must learn to see what is in front of us once again and to enjoy it. This is the first act of overcoming the lust of ubiquity and connecting to home by forming roots.

The Addiction to Ubiquity

When I left Holland, Michigan, for Spain, I was an exhausted person who had given himself to his work. I was morally fatigued and vocationally confused. I would check LinkedIn daily for other jobs to save me from myself. I would grasp for the next conference, speaking engagement, or consulting gig. I wanted to be ubiquitous, but God was

[1]   See Thomas Merton, *Contemplative Prayer* (New York: Random House, 1969); and Thomas Merton, *New Seeds of Contemplation* (New York: New Directions, 1971).
[2]   Ephesians 5:6-14.
[3]   Richard Foster, *The Celebration of Discipline* (New York: Harper & Row, 1971), 13.
[4]   David Whyte, "Vulnerability as a Faculty for Understanding," in *What to Remember When Waking: The Disciplines of Everyday Life* (Louisville: Sounds True Productions, 2010), audio CD, Track 2, 1:09–2:33.

calling me to stay put and face the difficulty. My body was inflamed in misery and burnout, and my heart for compassion weakened. My mind was spinning with paranoia. I was frustrated with myself and with everyone I worked with for not being what my institution ought to be. Judgment was my mood, and mercy was missing.

Those first days of walking on the Camino were not healing but disorienting. I was 2,000 miles from home and work; yet unreconciled relationship, unfinished projects, and concerns about the institution plagued me. Vocational perfection and questions like "Am I enough?" haunted me. I worried about what was happening while I was gone. The speed of my brain outpaced the compassion of my heart. I was going too fast, not simply on the Camino but for six years at WTS and probably elsewhere. I was no longer aware of my friends, and most everyone seemed an enemy. I was overwhelmed by Whyte's words and began to realize why the temptation to be a traveling scholar and speaker was so. Being home requires a deep intimacy and connectedness. We cannot be ubiquitous.

Recovery with the Earth

Seven or eight days into walking, I realized how much of the present moment had gone unnoticed in those first days. Most mornings, I would set my gaze at the horizon, seeing the landscape but rarely the ground beneath me. In those first mornings, anxieties and frustrations would occupy my thinking brain, and I would be fighting or worrying about a world thousands of miles away. The present moment didn't matter, and what was closest to me was worlds away.

One morning, I was walking and looking behind me, for the sun was always rising at my back, and I wanted to see the beauty of the sunrise. This particular day, I almost tripped while walking backward, causing an audible laugh amidst my solitude. Even so, the slip caught my attention, and I wondered what it would be to walk forward with my eyes closer to the ground of the path in front of me. Thoughts like these arise on the pilgrimage. It reminds me of Heschel's view of the prophets, where the ecstatic experience isn't what is interesting; indeed, it is the source of the experience that catches one's attention.[5] I turned around and set my eyes on the ground. To the left and right were beautiful snails hanging from rose vines. The glistening of the morning dew was home for the snail. In that very moment, I discovered the calling of the

---

5   Abraham J Heschel, *The Prophets* (Peabody: Prince Press, 2003), 2:206.

Camino through the snail: slow and present is the practice of a pilgrim. I was being asked to come closer to the images and life in front of me. The source of the snail was calling me to notice; this was the source of my clarity.

The pilgrim needs to unlearn the practice of worrying about what's being left behind or what lies ahead; the only thing that matters is what lives in front of our very eyes. As I woke up to snails and flowers and insects, I felt so very grounded in where I was. As I took a few more steps, I realized the path in front of me was shared; it was a snail highway. Snails and slugs flourished under my feet. This moment was my first grounding as a pilgrim; I was unlearning my escape art and finding the pilgrims pose. The creation, the people, and the conversations before me were to be my only concern on the Camino. This is the unlearning necessary when moving from escape artist to pilgrim.

The Power of Wandering and Returning: Pilgrimage as a Practice for Rootedness

The journey into God is rooted, but it doesn't mean we only remain at home or in the land we were granted. There are reasons to depart from home. Pilgrimage is predicated on such travel. However, the purpose of pilgrim travel is always with a *return* in mind. The ancient pilgrim left home either to seek purification for unreconciled sin or to process an ecstatic experience as a prophet or a saint. The latter is what Theresa of Avila, Francis of Assisi, and John Paul II sought on their walk to Santiago. The former is what penitent sinners did on the way to conversion or in pursuit of a fresh start. Whether due to violence, shame, or other fractured existence, a priest or bishop would send *confessors* to Santiago. I am still discovering whether I left for pilgrimage as a saint seeking God or a criminal seeking reconciliation. Either way, the saint and sinner within found life and calling on the Camino.

The Christian pilgrim joins in a long confession of faith, for "my father was a wandering Aramean."[6] The wandering vocation is not to establish God's people as permanent aliens, nomads, or travelers. The wandering for the pilgrim is an interim vocation on the way to finding a land and a home; sometimes this is simply a return to a home once departed.[7] As the confession reminds, the end of pilgrimage is home

---

[6]   Deuteronomy 26:5.
[7]   Patrick Keifert, *Testing the Spirits: How Theology Informs the Study of Congregations* (Grand Rapids: Eerdmans, 2009), 1–5.

(again), whereby the pilgrim can see God's promise anew: "God brought us into this place and gave us this land, a land flowing with milk and honey."[8] And once God delivered the Hebrew pilgrims to a land called home, any further departure from home was either for communion (devotion and *ecstasis*) or repentance (returning from exile due to sin, disobedience, or idolatry). Indeed, God's calling to his people is to be home and to enjoy it as shalom.

There is more to be said about the power of home and land for flourishing, but that is for another essay. The purpose here is to understand how pilgrimage grows roots rather than perpetuating our wandering. The monotony of a pilgrim's walk grows the longing for home deep within. Each day of pilgrimage is waking, walking, wondering, and resting. There are also abundant times of relying on others' hospitality and meeting new friends, and these final two practices cultivate the virtues needed when the pilgrim returns home.

I was roughly 30 days into the 33-day pilgrimage when I felt such a deep longing for home. I received a note from my youngest daughter. She said, "Every time someone mentions your name, I begin to cry." I felt similarly, and throughout the Camino, when my wife or children would come to mind, streams of tender mercy would flood my face. The longing for home is the calling of the pilgrim's journey. This was a common sensation on the pilgrimage. Close friends, relatives, experiences, and the like would find echoes in other pilgrims or moments along the way. I was overjoyed when I could both appreciate the present moment and the memory of home without wanting to make the moment into the memory or vice versa. It's as the Irish poets say, "The thing about the past is, it's not the past. It's right here, in this room, in this conversation."[9] The suspension of time is beautiful, and it allows the pilgrim to dwell in multiple worlds without fighting one for the other. This is beginning of living a cosmology where all things belong and where bifurcated worlds disappear.

Sacramental View of Reality and *Coram Deo*: The Two Bookends of Dr. Boogaart's Teaching

The distance between the earth and the heavens is thin. The ladder between is filled with ascending and descending angels; this is

---

8   Deuteronomy 26:9.
9   David Whyte, "The Conversational Nature of Reality" from *On Being* with Krista Tippet, December 28, 2018, https://onbeing.org/programs/david-whyte-the-conversational-nature-of-reality-dec2018/.

not merely a tale from old but the manner by which faithful people understand the rising of the sun and its setting.[10] Despite the modern world's attempt to expand the distance, teachers like Tom Boogaart have interrupted a secular imagination from continuing to bifurcate the world. Central to Dr. Boogaart's teaching on rootedness is his cosmology and his theological conviction for coram Deo. These are the bookends for his teaching career, and he has offered them to another generation of faculty. My discovery of rootedness came by finding coram Deo and sacramental view of reality embodied on the Camino.

Sacramental View of Reality

Overcoming the myths of bifurcation and time divisions requires a view of the world from another place than the West. Dr. Boogaart calls this view of the world "the sacramental view of reality" or a "biblical cosmology." He offers this way to view the world to his students and colleagues in every lecture, meeting, and conversation. Dr. Boogaart is committed to a way of following Christ that does not seek fame or accomplishment but is daily dwelling with God, with students, and with himself. This dwelling makes him ever more available to the world. This view of the world is best known by its fruits; WTS has several ministries, especially the Friendship House, the Community Kitchen, and The Bridge because his cosmology made him attentive to things that mattered, here and now. He has made the roots of his vocation deep enough that he can see the whole world from home, or as Flannery O'Connor wrote, "The longer you look at one object, the more of the world you see in it; and it's well to remember that the serious fiction writer always writes about the whole world, no matter how limited his particular scene."[11] The closeness of something unfolds the world within it. This is Dr. Boogaart's cosmology.

Dr. Boogaart long taught a course on Galileo where he unleashed his vision for a biblical cosmology. One can learn Dr. Boogaart's cosmology from his lectures and assignments, but it may also be discovered simply by listening to him speak in meetings and hallway discussions or from the images and doodles he creates while others are pontificating during these same meetings and discussions. He proposes a theistic cosmology of the earth that is an aesthetic more

---

[10]   Genesis 28:10-22.
[11]   Flannery O'Connor, "The Nature and Aim of Fiction," in *Mystery and Manners: Occasional Prose*, eds. Sally and Robert Fitzgerald (New York: Farrar, Straus and Giroux, 1969), 67.

than legislation, poetic and evocative more than didactic. Dr. Boogaart teaches from a Hebraic worldview: "The people of Israel believed the Spirit of God was the infrastructure of reality, the power behind all the powers, the authority behind all authority, the system beyond all systems, the basic element that sustains life from moment to moment. They often imaged this infrastructure as words proceeding from the mouth of God," as witnessed in Isaiah 55:10-11.[12]

This cosmology is not new, but it runs counter to the Greek mind that so much of Western thought is built upon. For far too long, that Greek cosmology was the basis for dualistic thinking. The cosmos operated on two orders, one natural and one social or moral.[13] The language morphs over time: material/spiritual, which evolves into facts/values and finally to public/private. The dichotomy is extended to bifurcate the universal and particular, for which the former is the modern Western goal.

This bifurcated cosmology needed a harmonizing mechanism, so it was justified with either allegory or hierarchy. In the allegory, as go the planets, so goes the state. As Stephen Toulmin writes, "If we recognize the existence of a 'rational' order in the planetary system, it can strengthen our confidence in the possibility of achieving a similarly 'rational' order in the ways in which human states and societies can be run."[14] The hierarchy relegated one sphere to the backdrop so that "the natural order is only a backdrop in front of which the human drama follows its own plot. So conceived, our theories of nature have little to do with general theology, let alone moral theology."[15] Even more, science and the natural order take over the moral order, and all things true must be proven by scientific method. Mystery, in this case, is lost, for what cannot be explained does not exist. Materialism is lifted as supreme, and the spiritual world is demoted to the private sphere. Neither world has room for the other.

Regardless of the false dichotomies and false mechanisms to uphold them, Boogaart demonstrates in all of his teaching that biblical cosmology is an integrated view of the world and runs contrary to a cosmology of two separate spheres of material and spiritual. The natural and theistic worlds are one, and even now, the current affairs of religion

---

[12]   Tom Boogaart, "Biblical Cosmology Notes" (unpublished lecture, 2015).
[13]   Stephen Toulmin, *Cosmopolis: The Hidden Agenda of Modernity* (Chicago: University of Chicago Press, 1992), 67–69.
[14]   Toulmin, 67–69.
[15]   Toulmin, 68.

and science are finding home together. For many years, Dr. Boogaart has been dialoging with scientists at New Holland Brewing once a week at midday to gain insight and to question his own cosmology. From what he has told me, his theistic perspective on the cosmos has not shifted, but rather, science has found its senses moving toward his view. John Polkinghorne, a scientist and theologian, articulates this move in the sciences toward a theistic perspective,

> Science offers no help for us in these questions of value. If you ask a scientist as a scientist to tell you all he or she could about the nature of music, they would say that it is neural response—things go off in our brains, neurons fire—to the impact of sound waves on our ear drum. And of course that is true and this way is worth knowing, but it hardly begins to engage with the deep mystery of music, of how that sequence of sounds in time can speak to us—and I think speak to us truly—an encounter of a timeless realm of beauty. I think we should take our aesthetic experience very seriously.
>
> And where do they come from? Where does that aesthetic value come from? And again theistic belief suggests that aesthetic experience is a sharing in the Creator's joy in creation. So I see belief in God as being a great integrating discipline really, a great integrating insight, perhaps I should say rather than discipline. It links together the order of the world, the fruitfulness of the world, the reality of ethical values, the deep and moving reality of aesthetic values. It makes sense. It's a whole theory of everything in that way, which is to me, essentially, most satisfying.[16]

Ultimately, secular science is finding its way toward a theistic cosmology.

In the end, Boogaart offers his students, colleagues, and the church a biblical cosmology that understands the material world as, in his words, "the congealed energy of the transcendent presence of God."[17] This integrative reality has been so since the beginning of creation, when God breathed the cosmos into being. Ever since, God has been breathing life into us that we would be made manifest to join the ongoing creativity of God in material things. God's capacity for creativity is gift to us through the breath or the inpouring energy of God in the *imago Dei* that lives in and through us.

---

16   John Polkinghorne, "On Natural Theology, Part 1," https://biologos.org/resources/audio-visual/john-polkinghorne-on-natural-theology-part-1/.

17   Conversation with author, December 2018.

Coram Deo: What Kind of God Is This?

The world Dr. Boogaart narrates is primarily the conversational nature of reality, where trees, God, and humanity interact with one another beyond the simplicity of what one can see, "get behind," or control. This is similar to the world of Tolkien's *The Lord of the Rings*, yet it is not the stuff of fabulous fiction. It is the way the world continues to orbit.

Some refer to this as the two books of revelation, where creation is revealing one story—namely, a story of glory scripted of theophanies of God's power, which are hospitable and inclusive; and Scripture is revealing the same story, albeit through oral and textual narratives, parables, poetry, and proverbs. Together these two books unfold a God who is ever present to us. Dr. Boogaart defines this as coram Deo, borrowing from the Reformed Pietistic tradition. He describes coram Deo this way: "The Sovereign of the universe lowers the scepter, invites his children into his presence, and prepares a meal for them. God seeks communion with his people. The defining characteristics of the sovereign God are hospitality and love, not exclusion and control."[18] This is the God we find welcoming the prodigal son. In response to such a God, Dr. Boogaart cites his teacher and beloved professor, Eugene Osterhaven, "Faith is not arid, speculative discussion about this or that theory of theology, philosophy of life, but it is devout living before the face of the Lord in the consciousness of responsibility to him."[19]

Presence for a Pilgrim

Two things happen to pilgrims on the Camino. God comes near, and the veil between the heavens and earth disappears. Indeed, coram Deo and a sacramental view of reality are the daily life of a pilgrim on the Camino. There are no natural or social orders but one order, which is witnessed through each step on the earth and through each pilgrim met on the road. There is no distant God but Christ whose presence has been inscribed in the soil of the Way.

This theocentric cosmology is available wherever pilgrims choose to see it. As Augustine said long ago, "Some people, in order to discover God, read books. But there is a great book: the very appearance of

---

18   Tom Boogaart, "Theological Rationale for the Curricular Proposals," (unpublished essay, 2011).
19   Boogaart, "Theological Rationale."

created things. Look above you! Look below you! Read it. God, whom you want to discover, never wrote that book with ink. Instead, He set before your eyes the things that He had made. Can you ask for a louder voice than that?"[20]

The voice and presence of God are made manifest each day on the Camino. I wrote in my journal 14 days into walking, "The other day, I was standing in a park on the edge of a small town. The light was coming up behind over the mountains as I exited a small church door, which led the way around the corner where the vines and branches, wheat fields, and shepherds' territory collided. I laughed at the 'I Ams' ever present around me. Shortly before entering the church, I stood at the fountain filling my water bladder for the miles ahead, and baptism came back. The life of Christ unfolds magnificently on the Camino."

Later that week, I continued sensing the presence of God on the Camino and wrote, "I'll leave El Ganso tomorrow morning for the *Cruz de Ferro*, the Iron Cross. This is the place where ancient pilgrims left their burdens. Even today, pilgrims bring stones from home as symbols of their burdens. They leave them at the cross. The cross is evident throughout the Camino and invites reconciliation with Christ and the world. I plan to arrive quite early in the day and offer Christ my burdens. I don't imagine it to be a light day but a liberating one nonetheless. May I find Christ at home in me over these next hours and days. May the darkness of the world not have any home in me as I leave the mountain. I am amazed, though I shouldn't be, by how Jesus, in the power of the Spirit, seems to say, 'On the Camino, I will draw close to you. Some of you will call me love, truth, beauty, challenge, awareness, or enlightenment. But it is me. I've had many names, but no matter how you know me, I am coming close to you. Whether you see me or not, I see you; I love you. *Buen Camino.*'"

I think that's it—a sacramental worldview, the conversational nature of reality. This is what occurs from Genesis 1 onward; words create worlds, and God's word is one of grace. This is the Bible living in the moment of our life. It's not terribly intellectual, but it is emblematic of Jesus, who comes to us in the moment as fully human and divine, and it is the power of the Spirit, who comes as helper and friend.

---

[20] Augustine of Hippo, "Sermon 126.6," in *The Essential Augustine*, ed. Vernon J. Bourke (Indianapolis: Hackett, 1974), 123.

Spiritual Formation Happens Best at Heart's Home

Dr. Boogaart often says that seminary is asking 20-year-old students to do the work most 40-year-olds are barely ready to consider. I think he is right. He says,

> Of all the work involved in Christian formation, this heart work is the most demanding and the most significant. It is relatively easy to accumulate factual knowledge about all things theological—history, biblical languages, theological propositions; it is harder to know our own hearts and open them to the Spirit's influence. The untoward words, the bad habits of our hearts, are powers that have taken up residence there, and do not want to be evicted. In order to remain hidden, they offer clever and convincing [strategies] and arguments for their continued presence and for approaches to theological education that will leave them alone."[21]

The Camino invites pilgrims to take stock of their hearts. Those first days revealed to me that I was living in the crucible of untoward words, bad habits of the heart, and powers that had taken residence. I wrote the question, "If words create worlds, then how many of my words have created toxic life for others?"

The physicality of the first seven days wears on the pilgrim, and what begins as an adventure and challenge quickly fades as the blisters grow larger and the heart grows tender. I had many questions in those early days and was expecting God to answer them—all of them—in a mere 33 days. I'll spare you the details and simply say that the questions were left not simply unanswered but uninteresting. Once I began to release my hands of everything, including my questions, I could feel my body and mind begin to settle down. The need for perfection and control began to wane, and I was left with a heart yearning for connection. Sadness rose within and began to pour out. The pilgrim is no longer living for himself or herself when sadness emerges. He or she is living toward others, and each pilgrim met is a person from home. The task of the pilgrim is to learn grace and mercy for the other pilgrims on the way. Returning home is a continuation of this encounter, for we are all pilgrims on the way somewhere.

Pilgrims return home, and the eyes that could see Christ calling from the mountains, snails, and sunflower fields are the same eyes to see

---

[21]   Tom Boogaart, "The Context of Formational Grading" (unpublished essay, August 26, 2013).

the same Christ whose presence is at home too. When a pilgrim returns from the walk, her formation is embodied and cannot be escaped without willful denial. I was happy to come home, and now each day, the Camino remains as I encounter strangers, colleagues, and students. The Camino is alive when I walk into a classroom as a teacher and a student, for even that bifurcation gets messy in this Boogaartian world. I think Wallace Stevens says it best: "Sometimes the truth depends upon a walk around the lake."[22] I walked 500 miles to discover God near and the thin veil between heaven and earth; now home is granting me the eyes to see in this same way, here and now. I am grateful to Tom for interrupting my incessant speech and desire for ubiquity. I'm here now and trying each day to stay put, that I might see the God who has lowered his scepter and said, "Welcome home."

[22] Wallace Stevens, "Notes Toward a Supreme Fiction, 1942," in *Wallace Stevens, Selected Poems*, ed. John Serio (New York: A.A. Knopf, 2009) 195–220.

CHAPTER 7

Virtues of a Faithful Reader
or
On Becoming the Kind of Person Who Can
Read the Bible the Way it was Meant to be Read

Timothy Brown

*The Bible is the perpetual motion of the Spirit, an ocean for meaning,
its waves beating against man's abrupt and steep shortcomings, its echo
reaching into the blind alleys of his wrestling with despair.*

*No sadder proof can be given by a [person of their] own spiritual
opacity than insensitiveness to the Bible. ...*

*Irrefutably, indestructibly, never wearied by time, the Bible wanders
through the ages, giving itself freely to [all], as if it belonged to every soul on
earth. It speaks every language and in every age. It benefits all the arts and
does not compete with them. We all draw upon it, and yet it remains pure,
inexhaustible and complete. In three thousand years it has not aged a day.
It is a book that cannot die. Oblivion shuns its pages!*

Rabbi Abraham Heschel

If Western Theological Seminary had a Mount Rushmore, Tom
Boogaart's face would be prominently displayed. But where in the
order of the four would it properly belong? It probably would not be
displayed in the place that belongs to George Washington (front and

91

center), because Tom's genuine humility would never allow for that to happen, and besides, he would really want to see one of his beloved teachers in that place (Eugene Osterhaven, Lester Kuyper, and Jim Cook). His face could possibly go in the second place where Thomas Jefferson resides, but I think Tom would object to that, too, thinking that it should belong to his dear colleague Chris Kaiser. And it certainly wouldn't be in place of Teddy Roosevelt, because he was a Republican—no, I think it would belong in the fourth place, the place of Abraham Lincoln. Why? Because Abraham Lincoln was our most noble, soulful, justice-seeking president, and Tom Boogaart is all of those things to us and so much more.

Tom Boogaart is noble, always holding to the highest ideals and never for a second trying to work the system or cut a deal for himself. Just think of the tireless hours he has put into the revision of learning the Hebrew language. He turned it on its head, making it an oral phenomenon rather than a literary one.

Tom Boogaart is soulful; he is the one who tirelessly calls into our darkness, "*Coram Deo*"—before the face of God. Tom insists and insists loudly that the Sovereign One has lowered the scepter and stunningly welcomes all into his luminous and holy presence, or, perhaps better, like the father of the squandering prodigal, he stands at the boundary lines urging the rebel to come home!

Tom Boogaart is justice seeking; who in our life together has been a more vital advocate of social justice change than Tom Boogaart? None! To shift metaphors for a moment, Tom declares from every pore of his being what the Statue of Liberty has declared from Ellis Island since 1886:

> "Give me your tired, your poor,
> Your huddled masses yearning to breathe free,
> The wretched refuse of your teeming shore.
> Send these, the homeless, tempest-tost to me ...!"[1]

And if I may end on a more personal note, I owe my life at Western Theological Seminary to Tom Boogaart. Twenty-five years ago when the seminary was in need of a professor of preaching after the untimely death of Prof. Jay Weener, Tom went to then-new president, Dennis Voskuil, and urged him to consider me. He did, and my life has been dramatically different ever since.

---

[1]   Emma Lazarus, "The New Colossus," National Park Service, last modified January 31, 2018, https://www.nps.gov/stli/learn/historyculture/colossus.htm.

Introduction

Abraham Joshua Heschel once said, "A Jew is asked to take a leap of action rather than a leap of thought. He is asked to ... do more than he understands in order to understand more than he does."[2] Tom Boogaart has held these words in our midst at Western Theological Seminary for over 30 years, and for that reason and many more, I am eager to contribute this chapter to his well-deserved festschrift.

So what kind of person do I have to become to read the Bible in the way that it was intended to be read? Are there certain virtues that I must possess to navigate the adventures that the Bible will constantly bid me to pursue? These questions are almost as old as the act of Bible-reading itself and have been deeply considered by Christian writers for centuries. One of the earliest and most influential considerations was written by a thoughtful North African poet and theologian named Prudentius (348–405 A.D.). Living essentially at the same time as other leading Christian thinkers like Augustine of Hippo and the fearless of preacher of Constantinople, John Chyrsostom, Prudentius was appropriately anxious about the well-being of Christian believers in a world of chaotic social change and wildly competing truth claims. In response, he wrote a riveting allegory about the struggle to survive in a world spun out of control. He gave his little work the mysterious title, *Psychomachia*, which means "the battle for the soul." Tucked away in the beautiful lines of his poetic theology is an exposition of the kinds of virtues we need to possess in order both to read the Bible well and, in fact, to survive as whole and consistent Christian thinkers in just such a world. Actually, the whole thing sounds eerily as though it were written for our ears today.

The virtues that Prudentius saw as non-negotiable for this battle were humility, kindness, abstinence, chastity, patience, liberality, and diligence. These virtues correspond to still more ancient lists that Prudentius had at his disposal: the classical virtues of the Greek philosophers, particularly those chiefly attributed to the works of Aristotle—prudence, temperance, courage, and justice; and the theological virtues of the New Testament— faith, hope, and love. All of this tells us, centuries later, that only a peculiar kind of person is capable of reading the Bible in the way that it was intended to be read. If we come to the act of reading the living Word of God impatient, proud,

---

[2]   Abraham Joshua Heschel, *God in Search of Man: A Philosophy of Judaism* (New York: Farrar, Straus and Giroux, 1955), 283.

and unwilling to change, the door of understanding will be slammed in our faces. If, however, we come eager to learn, humble in spirit, and ready to change in whatever way necessary to more fully conform to the image of God, then the doors of Scripture will swing open on their hinges. There is an unavoidable relationship between the character formation of the reader of the Bible and the capacity to receive the things that are written there in the first place.[3]

While Prudentius's list of virtues is an important one—as are other even more ancient ones from which he was drawing—I would like us consider still another list, this one written by the apostle Paul. Writing to the brothers and sisters in Christ in the ancient city of Colossae, the apostle Paul challenged them, "As God's chosen ones, holy and beloved, clothe yourselves with compassion, kindness, humility, meekness, and patience."[4] These virtues were the ones necessary, in Paul's vision of things, to fulfill five succeeding commands: to forbear with one another, to forgive one another, to allow the peace of Christ to rule in our hearts, to be thankful, and, lastly, to let the word of Christ dwell in us richly. The apostolic logic is undeniable; only people who are compassionate, kind, humble, meek, and patient can reasonably hope to fulfill these commands.

The last command in this list—the one enjoining us to "let the word of Christ dwell in you richly"—seems to me curious on several different levels. On one level, it is curious to me because it is so homey—literally, homey. The word for "dwell" in the heart language of the New Testament, Greek, is a compound word: *en-oikos*. The prefix *en* simply means "in," and the root word, *oikos*, interestingly enough means "house." The apostle is asking our Colossian brothers and sisters—and us in turn—to allow "the word of Christ dwell in our houses!" And when you take in to account the force of the adverb "richly," you get the sense that the apostle wants the Bible in every room of the house!

This, of course, is all figurative language for allowing the word of Christ to dominate everything about us: the way we think, the things

---

[3]   I found an essay in Gordon Fee's *Listening to the Spirit in the Text*, titled "Exegesis and Spirituality: Completing the Circle," to be extremely helpful at this point (Grand Rapids: Eerdmans, 2000; 3–15). For instance, listen to this: "The aim of [reading the Bible is] to produce in our lives and in the lives of others true Spirituality, in which God's people live in fellowship with the eternal and living God, and thus in keeping with God's own purposes in the world. But in order to do that effectively, true 'Spirituality' must precede exegesis as well as flow from it."

[4]   Colossians 3:12.

we do or choose not to do, and the kinds of people we are becoming. To do this, we must consciously and courageously live in a "Word-shaped world."[5] And doesn't this sound strangely familiar to something that ancient Israel cut their spiritual teeth on every day? "Keep these words that I am commanding you today in your heart," resounds the ancient *Shema Israel*, "Recite them to your children and talk about them when you are at home and when you are away, when you lie down and when you rise. Bind them as a sign on your hand, fix them as an emblem on your forehead, and write them on the doorposts of your house and on your gates."[6]

The second thing that strikes me as curious is the way that all of the other commands speak to the way we relate to people: bearing, forgiving, being grateful, and being peaceful. This command seems to speak to the way we relate to a thing—the word of Christ—but to move ahead with that assumption would be a serious mistake. The Bible is much less like a "thing" and much more like a person, and correspondingly, we must behave ourselves in relationship to the Word much like we would behave ourselves in the presence of another person. Writing to young Timothy in Ephesus, the apostle said, "All Scripture is God-breathed and profitable ...."[7] The Bible, as the Word of God, is the very breath of God. It is far more like a person than a thing. This is such a dramatically Jewish way of thinking about the Bible.

Abraham Heschel, one of the most important Jewish thinkers of the twentieth century, sees it this way and speaks in such deeply personal, relational terms when he speaks of the Bible:

> Irrefutably, indestructibly, never wearied by time, the Bible wanders through the ages, giving itself with ease to all men, as if it belonged to every soul on earth. It speaks in every language and in every age. It benefits all the arts and does not compete with them. We all draw upon it, and it remains pure, inexhaustible and complete. In three thousand years it has not aged a day. It is a book that cannot die![8]

---

5   This draws on the title of a helpful—and provocative—book by Old Testament scholar Walter Brueggeman (*The Word That Redescribes the World: The Bible and Discipleship* [Minneapolis: Fortress Press, 2011]) who makes a point similar to one made powerfully by Abraham Heschel that point of reading the Bible is not to merely know thinks "about" it but rather to know things "through" it!
6   The Shema Israel, Deuteronomy 6:4-9.
7   2 Timothy 3:16, DLNT.
8   Heschel, *God in Search of Man*, 242.

Heschel writes as though he were speaking of another living person, because, in a very real sense, he is. Only a living person can "wander" or "give itself to all"! The point in all of this is to echo as loudly as I can what the apostle Paul seems to being saying by including the command to "let the word of Christ dwell in you richly" alongside the commands to "forbear and forgive." The virtues required to live in relationship to others are the virtues required to read the Bible. Isn't that curious?

Compassion: The Virtue That Helps Us to Feel Our Way into the Story

The first virtue of a faithful reader of the Bible is compassion. Paul's word for compassion is actually two very interesting sounding words in the language in which he wrote this letter: *splanchna oiktirmou*. The earliest translators of the Bible had a particularly difficult time rendering this two-word phrase into English. They chose "bowels of mercy," which, if it helped people to understand the term then, it certainly does not now. They chose this awkward, but colorful, phrase for good reason though. *Splanchna* refers to the liver, kidney, and bowels of a human being, or as we would crudely say today, our *guts*. The word *oiktirmou* refers to deep feeling, or the action of crying out with a loud lamentation—the sort of crying out that you might expect to hear at a funeral home through the broken heart of someone who has loved and lost. Taken together, the phrase means something like *gut feeling*. Compassion then, in this odd way of speaking, is the peculiar capacity to feel as deeply as you possibly can with and for another person. It actually functions like empathy.[9]

Readers who read well will have a large capacity for feeling. Some years ago, I came home after my wife Nancy had gone to bed. I went to the bedroom to see if she was still awake. I found her curled up next with a book she was reading. It was obvious that she had been crying. She quickly began to tell me how moving the book was that she was reading. It was actually a book written by friends of ours, Bill and Helen Brownson. Bill and Helen have four sons, two of whom suffered lifelong debilitations. Billy suffered from the effects of childhood encephalitis, and David lived with mental illness. Each of them died at the end of their long journeys. Bill and Helen wrote to tell their story of the long, painful struggle of their sons in a book titled *Billy and Dave: From*

---

[9]   Paul T.P. Wong, "Introduction to the Virtues Series," 2004, http://www. psychjourney.com/The%20Virtues%20Series.htm.

Brokenness to Blessedness.[10] They were excruciatingly honest about their anxieties and discouragements, and they were honest, too, about God's steadfast love and mercy that met them in strange and unexpected ways every day. It was not possible for Nancy to read their story without weeping, and her tears were ample evidence of her faithful reading. She read it compassionately.

Reading the Bible at a distance—with an air of aloofness or objectivity as if the Bible were a thing to simply look at or talk about—is a colossal mistake. It can be read this way and regularly is in some settings—like it so often is in the academy where I have spent much of my vocational life—but this is neither satisfying nor transforming. Reading compassionately "is in contrast with how most of us are trained to read books—develop a cool objectivity that attempts to preserve scientific or theological truth by eliminating as far as possible any personal participation that might contaminate the meaning."[11] Imagine yourself telling a friend about a particular struggle that you have been having, and all the while, they keep looking at their watch or out the window, and from time to time they yawn. Their body language alone will stick your conversation in a deep freeze. However—and this is a sizable however—if they lean forward in their chair and look into your eyes with eagerness, seeming as though they have all the time in the world just for you, your deepest feelings rise up like a morning sun. The sympathetic listening of a keenly caring friend—eyes focused, body leaning forward, nodding at just the right moments—is an example of compassion and good reading too!

Kindness: The Virtue That Makes Us Good Listeners

The second virtue of a faithful reader of the Bible is kindness. This particular virtue might seem, on first glance at least, an unnecessary one for readers to assume when they sit down to read, but if we stay with it for a moment, it might bear some unanticipated fruit. The word *kindness* is almost exclusively used in the New Testament to describe the work of the Spirit in a believer's life allowing them to enter into loving relationships with others in the community of faith. It is a prized relational quality, and it is the very quality that allows us to put up with the shortcomings of others.

[10]   Bill Brownson and Helen Brownson, *Billy and Dave: From Brokenness to Blessedness* (Grand Rapids: Credo House, 2006).
[11]   Eugene Peterson, *Eat This Book* (Grand Rapids: Eerdmans, 2009), 21.

Most often the Bible reserves this word to describe God's loving disposition toward us even when we are indifferent. God's compassion becomes the catalyst or rationale for kindness. This was the logic that St. Paul used with the Ephesians, "Put away from you all bitterness and wrath and anger and wrangling and slander, together with all malice, and be kind to one another, tenderhearted, forgiving one another, as God in Christ has forgiven you."[12] When we are being kind toward others, we are thinking the best of them, giving them the benefit of the doubt, and staying connected with them even when we want to bolt and run. Kindness, the virtue that keeps us on the line when we want to hang up, is necessary for reading the Bible, because when we do, we are likely to hear things that we do not want to hear, like our sins being confronted, or hear things that we cannot figure out why we have to hear at all, like the genealogies in Genesis 5 or Matthew 1. The Bible, like our mothers, will make us eat things we don't want to eat all because it is good for us! Kindness is the virtue required to help us swallow.

There is a moving scene in Augustine's *Confessions* where this virtue of kindness is put in a picture window for everyone to see. Before Augustine of Hippo became a Christian, he was an obnoxious, annoying, and self-absorbed playboy. He was unquestionably brilliant and filled with potential, but he was not the kind of person you would want your child to date. His mother, however, was a devout follower of Jesus and longed for his salvation. She knew that he aspired to becoming the world's greatest orator, so she baited him into meeting Bishop Ambrose of Milan, who was not only a great preacher but a great man of God too! She told her son that as long as the saintly Ambrose was living, he could never fulfill his dream. For young Augustine, that was like saying "fetch it" to a golden retriever!

Augustine, along with some of his friends, set sail for Milan, Italy, simply to size up Ambrose for himself. The young Augustine wanted to see whether or not Ambrose was as good as his reputation and what he would have to do to be better than Ambrose. The trip would prove to be the most important one of his life but for reasons he could never have anticipated. He swaggered into Ambrose's presence only to find something he hadn't expected. as he later wrote:

> This man of God welcomed me with fatherly kindness .... I began
> to feel affection for him, not at first as a teacher of truth, for that

---

[12]   Ephesians 4:31-32.

I had given up hope for finding in your Church, but simply as a man who was kind to me. ...

... He would go on to spell out the consequences of this kindness; I hung keenly upon his words, but cared little for their content .... Yet little by little, without knowing it, I was drawing near. ...

... As his words which I enjoyed penetrated my mind, the substance, which I over-looked seeped in with them, for I could not separate the two. As I opened my heart to appreciate how skillfully he spoke, the recognition that he was speaking the truth crept in at the same time.[13]

There was a relationship between the kindness of Ambrose and the spiritual retooling that happened in Augustine's life after his encounter with Ambrose. It led to Augustine's new life in Christ, which in turn gave the church one of its most important teachers.

In order to read the Bible, we are going to have to listen to things we would rather not have to listen to. The Bible can be bloody, chauvinistic, and can seem hopelessly out of touch with what I have to deal with day in and day out. But kindness keeps me listening—keeps me listening to what I may not be interested in or may even be offended by—until I hear what the Spirit is saying to the church!

Humility: The Virtue That Gets Us Out of Our Comfort Zone

Another virtue of a faithful reader of the Bible is humility. Humility is the stunning capacity to think more highly of others than you think of yourself, while at the same time not disparaging yourself either. Humility is much less like thinking poorly of yourself and more like not thinking of yourself at all. A humble person is almost always thinking about other people. This, of course, is why humility is so clearly associated with Jesus Christ. The earliest Christians sang songs about Jesus as a way not only to honor him but also to set in motion the possibility of emulating him. One of those songs in particular highlights his breathtaking humility: "Who, though he was in the form of God, did not regard equality with God as something to be exploited, but emptied himself, taking the form of a slave, being born in human likeness. And being found in human form, he humbled himself and became obedient to the point of death— even death on a cross."[14]

---

[13] Augustine of Hippo, *Confessions* (New York: Vintage Books, 1997), 93.
[14] Philippians 2:5-11.

But there is something really curious about the logic of this early Christian hymn that reveals an enormously important aspect of humility: humility was the flywheel that set in motion Jesus's obedient actions. "He humbled himself and became obedient ...." Humility is to obedience what a starter's pistol is to an Olympic race, what an ignition is to an automobile engine, or what a rocket booster is to a spacecraft; it is what sets things in motion. And setting things in motion is what the Bible is all about. This is what Rabbi Abraham Heschel is driving at in his famous conviction:

> A Jew is asked to take a *leap of action* rather than a *leap of thought*. He is asked to surpass his needs, to do more than he understands in order to understand more than he does. In carrying out the word of Torah he is ushered into the presence of spiritual meaning.[15]

Only the humble will "take a leap of action rather than a leap of thought"—only the humble can!

There is a wonderful scene in C.S. Lewis's *Screwtape Letters*, his fanciful account of efforts of demons to wreak havoc in the lives of believers. An underling demon named Wormwood writes his superior, named Screwtape, for advice on what to do now that his patient—that is, the believer he is assigned to mess with—has undergone a personal spiritual renewal. Screwtape's advice is hugely instructive on how important humility that jump-starts acts of obedience is to reading the Bible. Listen to this:

> My dear Wormwood ... the situation is very grave ... a repentance and renewal of what the other side call "grace" on the scale which you describe is a defeat of the first order. It amounts to a second conversion—and probably on a deeper level than the first. ...
>
> It remains to consider how we can retrieve this disaster. The great thing is to prevent his doing anything. As long as he does not convert it into action, it does not matter how much he thinks about this new repentance. Let the little brute wallow in it. ... No amount of piety in his imagination and affections will harm us if we can keep it out of his will. ... The more often he feels without acting, the less he will be able ever to act, and, in the long run, the less he will be able to feel.[16]

---

15   Heschel, *God in Search of Man*, 283.
16   C.S. Lewis, *The Screwtape Letters* (New York: Harper Collins, 1996), 63, 66–67.

"The more often he feels without acting ...." C.S. Lewis is trying to tell us precisely the same thing as Abraham Heschel, which is precisely what Jesus was trying to tell his disciples after he had washed their feet as a call to a towel-and-basin way of living: "If you know these things, blessed are you if you do them!"[17] Reading the Bible requires a readiness to act, and humility is the virtue that empowers us to put our overalls on and head out the door to do the will of God in the world!

Meekness: The Virtue That Opens the Door

The word "meek" is easily left on the shelf in our pushy and self-assertive culture. Someone once said that there are only three kinds of people in the world: people who make things happen, people who watch things happen, and people who wonder what happened! Living in a land fixated on money, sex, and power—emblemized best by the images of the Nike swoosh, the Kardashians, and the Blackhawk helicopter—there can be little question what kind of people we ought to want to be. All of us are trained from childhood to sit tall in the saddle of opportunity and make the high horse of self-determination run like the wind. Meekness, however, is the cure for this cultural disease and a virtue necessary for reading.

We are all quite familiar with the importance that Jesus places on meekness as evidenced by his inclusion of it in the Sermon on the Mount, "Blessed are the meek, for they shall inherit the earth."[18] But it is easy when you look at this Beatitude in isolation to misconstrue the image of meekness as helpless or docile. However, nothing like this quite fits the image Jesus is commending. Actually, Jesus himself—especially standing at his trial in silent defiance as he refused to speak to Pilate—is the best example of meekness. [19] He was chained but clearly in charge. Meekness is not so much a quality as it is a capacity. Meekness refers

---

[17] John 13:17.

[18] Matthew 5:5.

[19] F. Dale Bruner, *The Christbook: Matthew 1–12* (Grand Rapids: Eerdmans, 2004), 166. Prof. Bruner's two-volume commentary is extremely helpful, and he is a remarkably wonderful example of a "meek" person in just the way I am construing the term. Here are his comments on Jesus and meekness more fully: "Jesus himself is the best definition of meekness particular at his trial (Matt. 26–27). We do not exactly see weakness there, but we do not see many claims there either, and not a great deal of aggression. The overall impression of Jesus on trial is an impression of poise. It is the poise of not having to assert oneself. ... There is a meekness that is almighty and a gentleness that is strong. In a world threatened by terrorist holocaust macrocosmically and by the destruction of the family microcosmically, the great need of the age may be this Beatitudes gentle-men and gentle-women."

to the capacity to receive a gift; hence, the blessing of meekness is the inheritance of the earth. We might have a better sense for its meaning if we altered the translation a little to say, "Blessed are the meek, for they alone have the capacity to inherit the earth." The opposite of meekness in not boldness as you might expect but self-sufficiency. If Jesus is the best example of meekness as he stands on trial waiting to fulfill his call, then the Laodicean brothers and sisters, in their utter self-sufficiency, are its opposite: "We are rich, we are prosperous. We need nothing!"[20]

The idea of meekness as a capacity to receive shows up again in the epistle of James: "Welcome with meekness the implanted word that has the power to save your souls."[21] Can you see how easily James couples meekness with welcoming? Meekness is the practice of welcoming. And this is why it is such an important virtue for readers to possess. Readers of the Word are asked to open the door and welcome into their lives a new family, a new faith, a new set of convictions about God, and a new set of practices that makes all of this sustainable and observable.

Patience: The Virtue That Slows Us Down

The Bible was not written to be read in a hurry. It wants to be read slowly, audibly, word-for-word, and with our imaginations ready to take us wherever it wants to lead us. When Jesus bids us, "Consider the lilies of the field ..."[22] he wants us to actually think about flowers, how they push their way through stubborn soil in the spring, open their hidden beauty to the warming sun, and quietly bow their heads at the cool of the evening breeze. When he says, "Behold, I stand at the door and knock ..."[23] he is not expecting to hear us say, "Sure, come on in, but I only have a few minutes, so make it quick!" If the reader does not take time to luxuriate in these images, they will miss the point. A hurried reader of the Bible is a poor one. Speed-readers, feverishly looking for the main idea with eyes darting from one thing to the next like frenzied Christmas shoppers trying to get one last gift, have no idea what they are missing. Speed-reading, the kind of reading prized and taught in

---

[20]   The city of Laodicea was completely destroyed by an enormous earthquake in 78 A.D. The Emperor Nero offered to pay for the entire cost of reconstruction. Staggeringly wealthy through their large pharmaceutical industry, rich textile industry, and stunning natural resources, the Laodiceans responded to his offer by writing back to Rome, "We are rich, we are prosperous. We need nothing." They lacked the capacity to receive a gift. This is the opposite of meek!

[21]   James 1:21.

[22]   Matthew 6:28.

[23]   Revelation 3:20, ESV.

most of our schools, is the polar opposite of the kind of patient reading that this virtue provides. As Carl Jung once said, "Hurry is not *of* the devil, it *is* the devil."[24]

Twentieth-century archaeology has uncovered several curious things about the ancient Temple Mount in Jerusalem. Among them is the random design of the southern stairs that carried weary pilgrims from the Tyropoeon Valley several hundred feet up to the temple itself. It was discovered that the steps were an engineering nightmare. The rise of each step varied in some instances by several inches, while the stretch of each step varied in some instances by several feet. The conclusion was as painful as it was obvious; the design engineers were either incompetent or intoxicated! The ancient rabbis, our primal teachers in spiritual formation, however, had a different take. They thought theologically about this matter just as well as every other. In their view of things, the engineers of the ancient Temple Mount knew that to ascend the hill of the LORD hurriedly and without thought would be a spiritual nightmare. You must approach the temple as you would approach God: cautiously and with measured steps. These uneven steps to the presence of God are a metaphor for reading with patience. Read it slowly and cautiously, or else you will fall!

Conclusion

If you are like me, you are already feeling hopelessly inadequate for the task of reading, and you are certain that all of these virtues elude you entirely. I have some good news for all of you, who, like me, are by nature too tired to be compassionate, too disinterested to be kind, too lazy to be humble, too self-sufficient to be meek, and too much in a hurry to be patient. All of these virtues, stunningly embodied in the person of Jesus of Nazareth, are—wonder of wonders!—made available to us through him. If you have a copy of C.S. Lewis's wonderfully helpful book *Mere Christianity*, go get it and turn to the chapter titled "Let's Pretend." Actually, it will be easier if I just quote it for you to hear:

> Very often the only way to get a quality in reality is to start behaving as if you had it already. That is why children's games are so important. They are always pretending to be grown-ups—playing soldiers, playing shop. But all the time, they are hardening

---

[24] Quoted in Richard Foster, *The Celebration of Discipline* (New York: Harper Collins, 1998), 15.

their muscles and sharpening their wits, so that the pretence of being grown-up helps them to grow up in earnest.

Now, the moment you realize "Here I am, dressing up as Christ," it is extremely likely that you will see at once some way in which at that very moment the pretence could be made less of a pretence and more of a reality. ...

You see what is happening. The Christ Himself, the Son of God who is man (just like you) and God (just like His Father) is actually at your side and is already at that moment beginning to turn your pretence into a reality.[25]

In Jesus Christ, we can become so much more than we ever imagined possible. We can, in fact, become compassionate, kind, humble, meek, and patient, and as we become all of these things, we will finally begin to realize that we are reading the Bible more and reading it better!

---

[25]   C.S. Lewis, *Mere Christianity* (New York: Macmillan, 1952), 161–62.

CHAPTER 8

Interpreting Scripture

James V. Brownson

I am increasingly proud of and grateful for the many years I have spent working with Dr. Tom Boogaart at Western Theological Seminary. Tom has not only brought a distinctive presence to the classroom, but he also has contributed in many additional ways to the seminary. In particular, Tom started a number of projects that continue to give the seminary vocation and to shape its identity. These additional projects include The Bridge, a store owned by the seminary selling crafts from third-world producers; the Community Kitchen, which has served over a million meals on the campus of the seminary to people in need; and a distinctive way of teaching Hebrew focusing on oral mastery of the language. We are deeply grateful for these important contributions to the life of the school in addition to Tom's excellent teaching career.

But I want to focus in this essay on some distinctive issues on interpreting Scripture. We have seen in recent times deepening divisions in our culture and in our churches over how to interpret Scripture. In some ways, these deepening divisions are very closely related to the proliferation of sources of information in the age of the Internet. When people get their information from sources that are distinct and separate from each other, they don't all hear the same information, and their responses to the information that they receive are quite diverse. When you add to that the rise of social media and the emergence of deep conflict in settings like Facebook and Twitter, the situation looks even worse. The world (at least in these platforms) seems to be filled with trolls who make it their job to oppose each other in the most vehement ways possible, and the result is an increasingly divided population.

We saw these divisions play out dramatically, for example, in the midterm elections in the United States in November of 2018. A huge number of people participated in that election, but the electorate was deeply divided. "Red" states and "blue" states looked very different, and those differences were reflected in divisions between urban and rural electorates and between electorates with different levels of education.

But these conflicts have appeared similarly—and sometimes in even more pronounced ways—in the churches, particularly in disagreements over how to interpret and apply the Bible to contemporary issues. We see deep dissension over sexual ethics, and, more particularly, how LGBTQ people should function in the church. These disagreements were compounded by the Supreme Court's Obergefell decision in the middle of 2015 legalizing same-sex marriage throughout the country. Suddenly, churches had to decide not only if LGBTQ people could be members in good standing of congregations but also whether those congregations would allow LGBTQ people to be part of same-sex marriages conducted in their sanctuaries. This requirement of a more public position has compounded older disagreements and moved them to center-stage, forcing either/or sorts of decisions that don't allow congregations to develop more nuanced positions over longer periods of time. The end result is deeper polarization.

These disagreements have, in turn, ignited older disagreements, which have also become more pronounced in recent years. For example, older disagreements over women in leadership have more recently become more divisive again. In my own denomination (the Reformed Church in America), the issue of the ordination of women to all the offices of the church was settled by a judicial case in the summer of 1979. For quite some time after that, women moved progressively into wider and wider circles of leadership within my denomination. But in more recent years, the tide seems to have turned, and women are encountering more resistance than even ten years ago. For example, ever since the start of my time on the faculty of Western Theological Seminary in 1989, I have taught an exegetical and theological course on women in leadership. But the last time I taught it, in the fall of 2016, I saw unmistakable signs of deeper divisions than I had seen before. For example, two-thirds of the women in that 2016 class had an immediate or extended family member who did not believe that they should have been in seminary, preparing for ordination. In all my years of teaching, I have never seen opposition to women in leadership occurring this way, with this strength and pervasiveness.

Similar disagreements have also appeared in other areas of the church's life, such as the practice of infant baptism, even though these disagreements do not always fall out along the same liberal/ conservative lines. This issue has, at least at an objective and doctrinal level, been resolved in our denomination for centuries. However, at the level of the actual practice of churches, we have seen more conflict over this issue in recent years (though divisions on this issue are not nearly so pronounced as divisions over questions of sexual ethics.)

I have no expectation of being able to resolve all these conflicts, but I want to speak to them and to suggest some possible constructive ways forward. Rather than debating the exegetical issues directly, I hope to shed light on broader issues that may illumine the ongoing conversations from different angles. For if I have learned one thing over the years with respect to conflicts like these, it is that they do not arise primarily from rational disagreements. If we are going to deal with them constructively, we need to have a broader vision than merely an exegetical or rational concern.

The first of these broader issues that I want to explore focuses on the role of experience in formulating various theological positions. This question, we must acknowledge, is not very welcome in many Reformed circles. These Reformed circles have historically differentiated themselves from positions like that of the Wesleyan quadrilateral, which sees experience as an integral part of theological formulation (even though most Wesleyans don't place experience on the same level as Scripture.) Reformed types, by contrast, have been suspicious of any sorts of appeals to experience and have focused instead almost exclusively on what Scripture has to say on a topic. This expresses itself, in the Reformed tradition, in the claim that Scripture is the only rule of faith and life, quite apart from any other considerations.

I embrace this tradition of refusing to place experience on the same level of authority as Scripture. I am convinced that if we fail to see Scripture calling us to a deeper place than merely our experience, we will miss something important and essential about Christian faith.

The gospel is the norm for Christianity, not human experience. At the same time, however, this does not mean that experience is irrelevant to various theological formulations. In this sense, Wesleyans are correct. But many Reformed theologians need more clarity about specifically what sort of role experience plays in our theological formulations. One of the ways this happens focuses on the risk, time, and energy it takes to develop new readings of the biblical text. It takes a lot of work to develop a new way of reading the Bible, even if that new way of reading is based on the texts themselves.

We see this most clearly when we look back at some of the issues that divided the church in earlier times. Let's consider, for example, the shift away from a geocentric view of the universe that occurred after the work of Galileo in the sixteenth century. For centuries, the geocentric view of the universe was regarded as self-evident, and that view was articulated by such greats as Aristotle. Moreover, there are multiple biblical texts that also seem to assume such a view. Psalm 93:1 speaks of how God has "established the world; it shall never be moved." Joshua 10:13 speaks of how the sun and moon "stood still" by divine command. So when Galileo articulated a heliocentric—rather than a geocentric—view of the universe in his study, he stirred up a real controversy. When he published his "Dialogue Concerning the Two Chief World Systems" in 1632, he was tried for heresy, convicted, and spent the rest of his life under house arrest.

Of course, in our context today, even though a tiny minority may continue to advocate for a geocentric view of the universe, Galileo's alternative view is nearly universally embraced, even by the Roman Catholic Church that had earlier placed him under house arrest. In particular, scientific investigation has now made this view both normal and normative, and space exploration has confirmed it even through visual images. The spherical—rather than flat—character of the earth is now the basis of navigation, whether by planes, trains, ships, or other means of transportation. What was once seen as heretical is now regarded as self-evident. Thus, while it took a long time, people eventually came to see a geocentric view of the universe, even though that geocentric view seems to be assumed in many biblical texts, as *not* part of what Scripture teaches with authority. It is still there in the texts, but those texts are now read differently, with a different understanding of how they authoritatively speak to our lives.

We see the same pattern with respect to the institution of slavery. Again here, many biblical texts seem to simply assume the existence of the institution of slavery. Paul offers advice and counsel to slaves at numerous points in his letters. 1 Corinthians 7:21ff. suggests that one's status as a slave is irrelevant to one's identity in Christ (even though a preference emerges for freedom over slavery in this passage). We see the same perspective in 1 Corinthians 12:13 and in Ephesians 6:8. An enormous amount of energy was devoted to exploring these and other passages during the Civil War, when Americans were killing each other over the question of whether slavery was a valid institution. But now, at this later point in human history, we accept as self-evident that slavery is not a valid institution according to Scripture. What was once a point of controversy in the interpretation of Scripture is now regarded as self-evident.

In both of these cases, experience played an enormously significant role. In the case of Galileo and the question of the order and shape of the universe, biblical interpretation focused on the experience of scientific inquiry in observation and its relationship to our interpretations of Scripture. In the case of slavery, it was the experience of an increasingly commercialized form of slavery prior to the Civil War that forced people to ask much more basic and fundamental questions about the institution of slavery itself. In both of these examples, the church changed its mind about what Scripture teaches, and it did so in response to compelling cases brought (at least in part) from human experience, which forced Christians to reread the biblical texts and to inquire more deeply into what those texts actually said and didn't say. In neither of these cases did experience *replace* Scripture, but in both cases, it forced Christians to read Scripture more carefully in order to arrive at a fresh reading of the text that was compatible with specific dimensions of human experience.

I believe that this is the dynamic that appears in the Reformed slogan "ever reforming according to the Word of God" (*semper reformanda*). It is human experience that drives us back to the Bible to make sense of things that seem not to fit even though they may be long established in terms of tradition. Reformed theology has always taken this somewhat ambivalent approach to "tradition," on the one hand using it as a framework for reading Scripture but also subjecting tradition to a fresh critique from Scripture itself. It is issues such as a geocentric view of the universe or slavery that illustrate this dynamic.

That leads to a second issue I want to explore, focusing not on experience but on how we interpret Scripture itself. In particular, I want to talk about the "why" question. It is not enough for us simply to read a text and to assert that Scripture teaches this or that practice of belief. We have to ask *why* Scripture says what it does on any particular topic and how the answer to that question can and should inform our interpretation.

For example, let's return to the problem of a geocentric theory of the universe over against a heliocentric view. In light of the work of Galileo and many others, readers of the Bible were forced to return again to the question of *why* Scripture says what it does about the earth, the moon, and the sun. Over against a normative view that states that Scripture simply teaches these things, the church came more and more to the view that Scripture simply *assumed* a geocentric view rather than teaching it authoritatively. This was based in large part on the awareness that Scripture never drew further conclusions or ethical obligations from its assumptions about a geocentric view of the universe. The geocentric view was not the basis of further reflection or application in the text. This made it easier, of course, to set aside its normative character when experience suggested that this view was mistaken.

The "why" question comes into play in almost all the contemporary conflicts over biblical interpretation. For example, on the question of women in leadership, one might note that there are a variety of passages that deal with women in leadership and that they can be roughly divided into two groups. On the one hand, there are a variety of texts that simply point to the *practice* of the early church and indicate that women played a variety of significant roles in that church. One might point to the many women who are greeted in Romans 16, including Phoebe in verse 1, who is identified as a deacon, and Junia in verse 7, who is declared to be "prominent among the apostles." Moreover, there are a number of women who are acknowledged as hosting churches in their homes as well as occupying other prominent roles. On the other hand, we see texts that seem more *prescriptive* in scope, such as 1 Corinthians 14:34-35, which declares that "it is shameful for a woman to speak in church." One might also consider 1 Timothy 2:12, which declares that a woman must never teach or hold authority over a man, or a variety of other texts as well.

Now here is a way to formulate the "why" question: Should we read the so-called "practice" texts as marginal and focus instead on the "prescriptive" texts, acknowledging that the early church didn't always live up to its own prescriptive guidelines? Or shall we instead put the "practice" texts in the center and assume that the so-called "prescriptive" texts are dealing with unusual situations that are not universally normative for all women? I don't have the time or space to lay out the entire argument here, but I believe that the latter option is the better one that provides a more integral view of all the texts in the canon. These larger issues then feed back into the interpretation and application of specific passages.

So for example, let's consider 1 Timothy 2:12. The text reads (in the NRSV): "I do not permit a woman to teach or to have authority of a man, she is to keep silent." However, the word used for "have authority over" in this text (the Greek verb αὐθεντέω) is not the usual word for exercising authority in the New Testament (that Greek verb is ἐξουσιάζω). The word used in this passage (αὐθεντέω) is much rarer, and most of the parallel instances that occur are negative. Thus, if one takes the negative parallels seriously, one might paraphrase this passage, "I do not permit a woman to tell a man what to do or to boss him around; she is to be calm." So this is not talking about universal roles for men and women in the church but rather addressing a particular church in which specific forms of excessive behavior are manifesting themselves. The issue is not universal practice but excess. Asking this sort of "why" question reframes the discussion.

We see a similar phenomenon occurring in the realm of sexual ethics. What is at issue here are two competing views of what Scripture teaches authoritatively about gender roles. Conservatives tend to read the "one flesh" union of Genesis 2:24 as a sexual union that is normatively constituted in a marriage between one male and one female. In my book *Bible, Gender, Sexuality*,[1] however, I argue that simple lexical study suggests instead that "one flesh" is a way of speaking not about a heterosexual union in its essence but rather about a kinship bond (and kinship doesn't focus at all on gender). A heterosexual union is assumed, but that is not what the authority of the text is focusing on.

Hence, at least as I frame the argument, the critical witness of Genesis 2 is not that it points to a unique heterosexual marriage bond but rather that it points to the vital connection between sex and kinship and sees the first marriage as the beginning of this kinship relation. At the heart of a biblical sexual ethic, then, is the principle that one ought not to say with one's body (by uniting sexually with someone) what one is unable or unwilling to say with the rest of one's life (by living

---

[1]   James V. Brownson, *Bible, Gender, Sexuality: Reframing the Church's Debate on Same-Sex Relationships*, (Grand Rapids: Eerdmans, 2013).

out a lifelong kinship bond). Hence both sides take Genesis 2 seriously but come to very different assumptions about what is authoritatively taught here and its applicability to contemporary life. Asking *why* a text says what it does begins to explore these more complex questions.

This points us to a possible way forward from many of our current dilemmas. We simply will not make much progress at all dealing with our disagreements over how to interpret Scripture unless we engage in serious and ongoing conversations that not only integrate a reading of the details of the texts in dispute but also incorporate our understandings of our experiences, our rationales for reading the text as we do, and how we view alternative readings of the biblical text. In all of this, it is enormously important to be as explicit as we can be in articulating our own position and in exploring the positions of others. Purely rational discussion of evidence and argument is important, but it is not the only thing that is important. We need to be honest about the way in which experience drives our explorations and also honest about the sorts of "why" questions that also inform our reading of the text. Further conversation about these wider issues can be helpful in facilitating more productive dialogue.

This can take extremely practical and concrete forms. In a Sunday school class, people can be invited—before even attempting to interpret a biblical text—to share what their own experience is related to this text and how that experience shapes the way they come to the passage in question. They then can be invited to share how those prior experiences shape their particular ways of reading specific biblical passages. The ensuing conversation will take into consideration not only differing readings of the text but can also consider how those alternative readings are shaped by different experiences and different assumptions. The result is that people still may not always agree with each other, but they will understand more deeply *why* they disagree and what some of the crucial differences are.

The resulting conversations will have a clearer sense of purpose and direction. It's not simply that we disagree about how to read the text; we can also talk about *why* we disagree and how various experiences help to explain that disagreement. In so doing, we may find a more profitable line of engagement than the church has yet known.

CHAPTER 9

The Pastoral Implications of Our Amnesia About Believers Resurrection: Learning from the Apostle Paul

Lyle Vander Broek

What a joy it is to be able to participate in this celebration of Prof. Boogaart's gifts for ministry! In part because our personal and professional lives had so many parallels, maintaining a long-term friendship has always been incredibly easy and fulfilling. My family and I—as well as my colleagues here at the University of Dubuque Theological Seminary—wish you God's blessings as you enter this new phase of life. The body still needs your biblical and pastoral input. We look forward to hearing more of the thoughtful critique of the church we have found so helpful in the past.

Our Topic: Paul and Pastoral Issues Concerning Resurrection of the Body

I have always been impressed with Dr. Boogaart's pastoral approach to biblical studies. My topic here honors that ministry-focused methodology. So I want to discuss an important biblical and theological issue in the church with special focus upon its pastoral implications. The issue is this: contemporary mainline Christianity has almost universally ignored what the Bible teaches about believers' resurrection. When the New Testament discusses the new life believers experience after this life, it almost never speaks about what happens immediately after death. Its focus is not on "heaven," at least as most Christians I know use that term, but on what happens when Christ returns at the end of the age. At that time, believers will be raised from the dead and creation will be transformed. The Christian promise of life after death should be understood primarily in terms of resurrection of the body.

Obviously, I could devote this entire article to substantiating the above assertions. But I hesitate to use this precious space for even such foundational topics because so much has already been written about them.[1] I will speak briefly about how and why the church fails to embrace the resurrection of the body, and I will do a short analysis of two passages from Paul that go to the heart of his teaching about believers' resurrection. But these discussions will really be introductions to my main concern, which is the pastoral and theological issues that surround our failure to anticipate resurrection and how Paul's words inform these pastoral concerns. Put simply and in question form: How, according to Paul, is believers' resurrection important for church and ministry?

What Resurrection?

I became acutely aware of mainline Christianity's limited under-standing of life after death while teaching an adult church class several years ago. Our topic was the Apostles' Creed, and the class went well until we came to the confession, "I believe in the resurrection of the body." The ten women in the group were mostly longtime Christians, baptized, educated, and nurtured in the church they now attended. So when I asked them what resurrection of the body meant, the blank look on their faces was truly amazing. Yes, they knew that Jesus had been raised, but they had no idea how Jesus's resurrection impacts our lives as Christians or that "resurrection of the body" refers to what will happen to believers! Imagine celebrating a lifetime of Easters without a

---

[1]   Let me mention here three books every pastor should read: N.T. Wright's *The Resurrection of the Son of God*; his lighter volume, *Surprised by Hope: Rethinking Heaven, the Resurrection, and the Mission of the Church*; and a quite different kind of book (less theological and more analytical) by Lidija Novakovic, *Resurrection: A Guide for the Perplexed*. As is often the case, the church's amnesia about a theological topic is not because there are no resources to guide and correct it!

clear understanding of the incredible good news: Jesus's resurrection is the "first fruits" of our resurrection![2]

This reaction is not limited to lay people. I vividly recall one instance when I was addressing a group of pastors on the meaning of 1 Corinthians 15. They seemed to be less than engaged until I asked the question, "What do you say about Jesus's resurrection on Easter morning? Why is it important to the people in your congregation?" They admitted that it was difficult and sometimes boring to preach about Jesus's resurrection. This was so because they usually explained it in terms of Jesus's divinity and his atoning power. In other words, they spoke of the resurrection of Jesus as "proof" that what we believe happened on the cross is real. Almost to a person, they confessed that their Easter sermons usually did not draw a link between Jesus's resurrection and ours. This anecdotal evidence is supported by historical studies of Christian views of the afterlife.[3]

Perhaps the best indication of what believers think about life after death can be seen at funeral services among those who have lost loved ones. Invariably, they speak about the new life of their loved ones as they are now experiencing it, that is, as they exist in heaven with God. What is often missing, whether in liturgy or song or sermon—and especially in the deepest longing of their sorrowing hearts—is any sense that what happens to a believer immediately after death is only an intermediate state that will be far surpassed by the coming resurrection and restoration.

The amnesia about believers' resurrection, a teaching that is so foundational and biblical, is perhaps the most surprising and dangerous theological aberration I have encountered during my years of teaching in mainline denominations. Why is it that we ignore this essential doctrine? My research points to three reasons. First, Christians have grown hardened to a promised coming that has not arrived.[4] If Christ's return appears unlikely—and with it the promised resurrection and

---

[2]   1 Corinthians 15:20.

[3]   For a more substantial overview of the contemporary Church's amnesia about believers' resurrection, I suggest you read the first few chapters of N.T. Wright's *Surprised by Hope*, Colleen McDannel and Bernhard Lang's *Heaven: A History*, or Jeffrey Burton Russell's *A History of Heaven: A Singing Silence*. They show how Christianity has often affirmed views of the afterlife that are almost indistinguishable from its pagan neighbors and ignored the Bible's teaching about eschatology and resurrection.

[4]   The excitement about Christ's return, found everywhere in the New Testament, seems naive. "Heaven"—our experience of eternal life after we take our last breath—becomes our comprehensive and only way of speaking about life after this life.

restoration—then it is very tempting to condense a future disclosure of salvation into what happens immediately after death. Second, many contemporary Christians are quite comfortable with the Greek concept of immortality of the soul.[5] The third reason for our failure to recognize believers' resurrection is obvious but not unimportant. I would call it "the weirdness factor." We know what happens to bodies when they die, and we have a hard time imagining how resurrection would work.[6] Rejection of believers' resurrection based upon the physics of death indicates, in my opinion, a failure to understand what the New Testament says about the nature of our new bodies.[7]

I want to make it very clear that I am not rejecting the teaching of "heaven" as it is typically used to describe believers' experience of continued life in God's presence immediately after this life. The New Testament is full of allusions to a heavenly existence after death but before the return of Christ.[8] Paul is our best teacher about the nature of believers' resurrection, as we shall see in the following passages, but he also has many references to the intermediate state, almost always

[5]   Contrary to the holistic understanding of body and soul typically found in Jewish thought, Greek thought tended to see humans dualistically. Humans are composed of two parts, body and soul. Life after death is concerned with the soul: it is immortal, a divine spark that during a person's lifetime is trapped within the body. When a person dies, the soul is freed from the body and is able to reunite with the divine. From this point of view, the body is relatively unimportant and death is liberation. I am always amazed at how fully Christians adopt this pagan doctrine.

[6]   In the entertainment industry, life after death is often pictured with reanimated bodies that are ghoulish and seek to destroy human beings. People may come back to life, we are being told, but there is always something very wrong with them. Go back and watch Stephen King's *Pet Sematary* if you need to be reminded of how this view of resurrection plays out in our culture. Resurrection appears improbable and very messy in the modern imagination.

[7]   See 1 Corinthians 15:35-57.

[8]   Jesus's teachings and his stories often refer to the ongoing existence of the Patriarchs (Mark 9:2-13 and parallels; John 8:48-59), and the allegory of the rich man and Lazarus reflects the common assumption among Jews that life after death for the faithful would be "with Abraham" (Luke 16:19-31). Jesus appears to make two specific references to the intermediate state as resting places on the way to resurrection and restoration. N.T. Wright argues that the word for "mansions" in John 14:2 is intended to designate a "temporary resting place," here used by Jesus to refer to what he has prepared for believers immediately after death but not to be confused with the more glorious salvation that comes at the end (Wright, *The Resurrection of the Son of God*, 445–46). So also, according to Wright, Jesus's promise to the man on the cross that "today you will be with me in paradise" must not be interpreted to mean that what he experiences upon death is final or complete (Luke 23:43). The word for "paradise" is more accurately translated as "a garden that is a temporary resting place for the dead as they await the dawn of the new age" (Wright, *Surprised by Hope: Rethinking Heaven, the Resurrection, and the Mission of the Church*, 150).

defined simply as an ongoing relationship with Jesus or God. In 1 Thessalonians 4:16, he labels the deceased as those who are "sleeping in Christ." In 1 Corinthians 15, Paul refers to them as those who have "died in Christ" (15:18) or "those who belong to Christ" (15:23). Philippians 1:19-26 is interesting because, there, Paul speaks about the possibility of his own death before the return of Christ. Again, the essence of this intermediate state is that he will be "with Christ" (1:23). Paul does show a strong willingness to enter this existence: "living is Christ and dying is gain" (1:21) and "my desire is to depart and to be with Christ" (1:23). Contrast this desire for life immediately after death with what he says in 2 Corinthians 5:1-5, where Paul prefers not to be "naked" or "unclothed" but to be "further clothed" with the resurrection body. Perhaps the passages in Paul about life after death most often used to comfort the bereaved at funerals are Romans 8:31-39 (no alien powers, not even "death or life" "will be able to separate us form the love of God in Christ Jesus our Lord") and Romans 14:8-9 ("If we live, we live to the Lord, and if we die, we die to the Lord. So then, whether we live or die, we are with the Lord"). For Paul, the intermediate state is one that anticipates the resurrection, but he does not feel compelled to detail this existence other than to say that it is life under God's care.

Christians rightly use these passages to comfort themselves when they have lost a loved one. It is true that we are given few specifics about this post-death/pre-resurrection life, and there is often the temptation to embellish what has been left vague. But surely the promises we have are enough: God does not abandon us in death. We continue to be "with God" or "with Christ." We are safe in God's love. But here is the issue: what happens to us immediately after death should not be the primary or only concern. The problem in the church is not that we cherish God's care for us in both life and in death. Biblical writers do the same. Our problem is that we speak about life immediately after death as if it were the fullness of the promise, somehow forgetting about our future lives in resurrected bodies. And that amnesia has significant theological and pastoral ramifications.

Paul as Pastor in Two Passages that Deal with the Resurrection of Believers

1 Thessalonians 4:13–5:11

Paul consoles this group of former pagans by carefully explaining what happens to those who die before Christ returns. Jesus's resurrection is the basis for believers' hope for life after death (4:14). Through Jesus,

God will bring to life those who are now dead (4:14). When Christ returns, the dead in Christ will rise first (4:16); like those who are alive when the end occurs, they "will be with the Lord forever" (4:17). Paul's pastoral word is that the Thessalonians' grief is more than offset by a hope (4:13) for the resurrection brought about by the return of Christ. The dead in Christ are not somehow gone or lost; they will experience bodily transformation and fully participate in the restoration that Christ brings.[9] We might wish that Paul had said more about the nature of existence after death but before the resurrection (although he does make it clear that this post-death existence is "in Christ"), but the consolation Paul, the pastor, offers is future-oriented and focused on believer's resurrection.

Paul involves the congregation in the eschatological drama that is unfolding in Christ. Using typical Jewish apocalyptic language, he tells his hearers what Christ's return will be like. There will be unmistakable cataclysmic announcements of the Messiah's return to earth: the Lord's voice will be heard as well as that of the angels (4:16) and the end-times trumpet will sound (4:16[10]). These images continue in the next paragraph: Christ will come "like a thief in the night" (5:2), the sudden and radical upheaval will be "as labor pains come upon a pregnant woman" (5:3), and believers must stay awake and choose "light" over "darkness" (5:4-8[11]).[12]

Paul's description of Christ's earthly arrival and the welcome offered by believers (4:15-17) relates directly to the nature of life Christ brings. We are told that both those who have died and those who are still alive will be "caught up in the air" and will "meet the Lord in the air" (4:17). Some have assumed that this refers to Christ's coming again to earth and gathering believers "up" to heaven and away from earth, something like the so-called "rapture" spoken of in Revelation 20:1-6. Rather, Paul is using apocalyptic imagery to describe the arrival of the divine King or Messiah and his establishment of God's kingdom. Believers look forward to the Christ's "coming" or "presence" (Greek:

---

9   See 1 Corinthians 15:51-52.

10   Compare Mark 13:14-15 and parallels; Isaiah 27:13; 30:10; Zephaniah 1:16; Ezekiel 32:7-8; etc.

11   Compare Mark 13:17; 32-37; and parallels.

12   Commentators occasionally wonder why Paul would employ such foreign, Jewish apocalyptic language with a Gentile audience. I think the answer is simple: Paul, as pastor, knows that if the Thessalonians are ever going to grasp the meaning of Jesus's resurrection in relationship to God's larger salvific plan, they must be schooled in the biblical imagery that gives structure to the beginning, middle, and end of this narrative.

parousia, 4:15),[13] a word that is often used in ancient literature to indicate the arrival of a kingly figure. After the figure's appearance is announced (via angels and trumpets) and he is seen approaching, the people go out to greet their guest and escort him to his new kingdom. In this passage, believers who are caught up in the clouds to meet their heavenly king do so to honor his arrival to our transformed earth and its resurrected inhabitants. Paul is not describing a divine arrival to take people up to heaven. His point is consistent with what it is elsewhere. Our hope lies in what God will make happen here on earth.

Paul's words in 5:1-11 are consistent with his pastoral approach above. He relieves the community of the worrisome task of anticipating when Christ will return. Christ will come "as a thief in the night" (5:2)[14]. The time of Christ's return cannot be known, but the Thessalonians can take comfort in the fact that it will come in its time, like "labor pains come upon a pregnant woman" (5:3). Most importantly, Paul informs them that their work here and now is not "wasted," a biding of time until a future event. Paul is encouraging these new Christians to anticipate Christ's return, but their work in the meantime is good and meaningful, a way of building now what will be fully experienced in the future. I see in Paul's encouragement a wonderful balance between the present and future. The future does not make the present meaningless, and the present does not blind us to the glory of the future.

1 Corinthians 15

It would be hard for me to imagine a more sensitive pastoral approach to the pivotal theological issue in 1 Corinthians 15.[15] Paul begins by reminding the Corinthians of how they had accepted the testimony of the church that Christ was "raised on the third day" (15:4).

---

[13]   Note how the word for "coming" (parousia) is used by Paul in 2 Thessalonians 2:1; 1 Thessalonians 2:19; 3:13; 5:23; 1 Corinthians 15:23.

[14]   Compare Mark 13:28-35 and parallels.

[15]   1 Corinthians is an incredibly complicated and powerful response to a group of believers in that church who deny believers' resurrection (v. 12). Their denial amounts to a rejection of the importance of body, both in terms of individual morality (5:1-8; 6:12-20) and corporate integrity (1:10-31; 11:17-34; chapters 12-14). It's a classic example of how a failure to accept resurrection affects almost every aspect faith and life, not least of which is a skewed grasp of eschatology and an over-inflated sense of their own wisdom (1:18-31; 4:8-21; 8:1-13). Paul is extremely pastoral throughout the letter, even toward issues that are often assumed to indicate a rejection of the gospel (i.e., their blatant immorality, their haughtiness, and their failure to understand communal love). Paul treads lightly as a loving pastor, as a father feels compelled to reprimand but who is wary of pushing too hard (4:14-21).

The Corinthians have a direct link with this testimony through the proclamation of their church father, Paul (15:3, 8). Paul is effective as a teaching pastor here not only because he draws the congregation into the power of this corporate witness but also because he sets that witness in the context of God's larger plan: a narrative of salvation is unfolding![16]

But Paul's real genius as a pastoral theologian comes when he insists that Jesus's resurrection cannot be separated from believers' resurrection. The argument in verses 12-18 is that if one denies that people can be raised from the dead, then one is also denying that Jesus could be raised from the dead.[17] And if Jesus has not been raised, then there has been no atonement for sin—the whole Christian endeavor falls like a house of cards. The argument here is a *tour de force* of how our rejection of essential beliefs plays out theologically. It would have been incredibly powerful for the Corinthians, because the apostle starts with his own stance and makes its heretical consequences unavoidable.

Paul is very patient with those who reject believers' resurrection. His own argument shows that their stance nullifies the faith, and yet he persists with a positive argument (15:20-58), being very careful to show how human resurrection is *necessary* (15:20-28), *possible* (15:35-41) and *desirable* (15:42-49). Christ is "the first fruits of those who have died" (15:20). The key sign of Jewish end-times— resurrection—has occurred, and Jesus's resurrection is the guarantor of ours, an indication that the wheels have been put in motion. Paul makes it clear that believers' resurrection is necessary because it comes after and is linked with the final destruction of death and evil power.[18] For the Corinthians (and for us as well), this eschatological statement is powerful because it shows the seriousness with which God takes the resurrection of believers and, of course, death, the reason it is necessary. Resurrection is not an

---

[16]   Note how what happened to Christ was in accordance with Scriptures (15:3-4). Paul himself is witness to the unpredictability and unstoppability of the story. As one who was "untimely born" (15:8) and whose past record toward the church made him an unlikely candidate for his call (15:9-10), he exemplifies God's radical, grace-filled actions.

[17]   Presumably because Jesus too was human, although Paul does not explicitly say that here.

[18]   Notice the very concise story of salvation in verses 21-28, first told through the typology of Adam/Christ (15:21-22) and then given in specific details about the end (15:23-28). After the cosmic forces of evil have been destroyed (rulers, authorities, and powers; 15:24) and after the last great enemy, death, has been subdued (15:26), Christ hands over the kingdom to the Father (15:24), and all things are subjected to him (15:27-28).

addendum, a minor theological oddity that one can accept or reject. Christ came into this world in response to death, an intolerable enemy that mars God's creation. The bodily resurrection of believers is the necessary corporate result of the cross and empty tomb and is proof of the final victory over death.[19] The work of salvation is not yet "finished" on the cross!

Paul needs to employ a high level of cultural sensitivity, because everything in the Greco-Roman background of the Corinthians would have declared the resurrection of people anathema (15:5-41). The Corinthians' rigid definition of resurrected body is not consistent with the plurality of substances and bodies observable in their own world.[20] Paul makes the meaning of his body-analogies explicit in the next paragraphs: "So it is with the resurrection of the dead" (15:42). There he uses a series of word pairs to compare the body before and after it has been raised, careful to use the word "sown" in each case to remind the Corinthians of the continuity and discontinuity between plant and seed, earthly and spiritual body (15:43-44). Paul, the contextual pastor, goes out of his way to explain the new body in terms that would have been appealing to these gentile Christians. The new body is raised in glory (15:42), a term Paul had previously used to describe the eschatological wisdom of believers (2:7) and the reign of Christ (2:8; compare Philippians 3:21). It will be raised in power (15:43), a word Paul has employed to describe God and his wisdom (1:18, 24; 2:4-5). Perhaps most attractive of all, based especially upon what we see in chapters 12–14, is Paul's description of the resurrected body as a *spiritual* one (15:44-45). Think of the appeal of this list to those at Corinth who may have thought that a body could rise after death but could only imagine it in terms of ghoulish Greco-Roman myths (very much like ours). Life in the new age will be in a body, with all the good things that that implies,

---

[19]   See 1 Corinthians 15:54-55.

[20]   The apostle begins by trying to get the Corinthians to understand "body" in terms other than the purely physical. The "fool" (15:36; diatribe language, but not very pastoral!) who asks questions about the nature of the resurrected body can be answered by pointing to something as simple as a seed and the plant it produces (15:36b-38). We cannot anticipate what kind of plant a seed might generate: God designs them according to his creative will (15:36-38). That God gives "to each kind of seed its own body" (15:38b) implies an endless variety of bodies, and Paul proceeds to illustrate this diversity for the Corinthians. Paul argues that there is no single kind of flesh in the animal world (15:39) and that there are both heavenly and earthly bodies (15:40). He even asserts that there is a hierarchy of bodies in the celestial realm, with each having its unique glory (15:40-41).

but it will be transformed as well, imperishable, filled with God's power and glory, a truly spiritual existence.

Paul's logic and conclusions are powerful, but he knows that if "spiritual body" is to be anything other than an oxymoron for the Corinthians it must have a Christological foundation. In fact, his contrast between mortal body (*psychikos,* 15:44) and spiritual body (*pneumatikos,* 15:44) grows out of a Christological interpretation of Genesis 2:7. Adam, the first man, was a mortal or living being.[21] He was dust, bound to this earth in all its corruptibility and transience (15:47). Christ, the last Adam, is from heaven, God's realm (15:47); he has become a life-giving spirit (15:45). There are two types of body, and they determine the nature of our bodies in this life and the next. Now we are bodies determined by this age, bearing Adam's image (15:48-49); in the new age, we will be bodies determined by God's Spirit (15:44), bearing the image of the man from heaven (15:49). Christ's resurrected body not only models what our new bodies will be like, but his resurrection makes such transformation possible.

Paul's affirmation that neither flesh and blood nor what is perishable can inherit the kingdom of God (15:50)—his conclusion to the above argument—sounds like a statement by those who advocate immortality of the soul. But there is an essential difference: Paul is talking about new bodies, made in the image of the resurrected Christ. If flesh and blood cannot inherit the kingdom (15:50), then what happens to those who are still in their earthly bodies when Christ returns? As in 1 Thessalonians 4, Paul affirms that no believers are left out. The dead will be raised, and those still alive will be "changed" (15:52).[22] Once again, Paul reminds his congregation about the eschatological drama[23] of which resurrection and victory over death are central (cf. 15:23-26). Here the vision of death's demise is perhaps even more powerful because Paul's use of two Old Testament passages (15:54-55). Christ's resurrection and therefore our bodily resurrection fulfill Isaiah's longing that death itself will be destroyed (15:54; Isaiah 25:8). In a free allusion to Hosea 13:14, Paul taunts death as a once powerful but now doomed enemy (15:55). As in 15:23-28, Paul is affirming that only at the end, when believers are raised and we experience victory over death (15:57), can Christ's saving work be considered complete.

---

[21]   See the LXX of Genesis 2:7.

[22]   Paul here calls this a "mystery," indicating perhaps that he is telling the Corinthians about this transformation of the living for the first time.

[23]   Note the phrases "twinkling of an eye," and "sounding of the trumpet"; 15:52.

Very much like his conclusion to the story of salvation found in 1 Thessalonians 5:4-1, Paul must remind the congregation what such a grand narrative with its promised victory over death means for the present Christian life. Paul is never escapist. There is work to be done in our communities and world. If Christ returns to this world to effect resurrection and transformation, then what we do now is not insignificant. Sure of our future, we excel "in the work of the Lord" (15:58). Our "labor is not in vain" because we are working on the same project that will find its completion in the return of Christ.

Pastoral Issues Related to Paul's Proclamation of Believers' Resurrection

It needs to be stressed that not only Paul but also the entire New Testament witnesses to the future resurrection of believers. Even books like the Gospel of John, known to emphasize the present reality of eternal life, point indisputably to this future resurrection as the consummation of God's kingdom. The two passages analyzed are not, by any means, the only places where resurrection is a topic. But they are key passages, and they certainly do form a helpful specific foundation from which to make a few comments about pastoral issues that relate to believers' resurrection.

The Desire to Offer Comfort and the Failure to Educate about Resurrection

In our desire to speak words of comfort and begin the process of healing, there is a strong temptation to go beyond the biblical teachings about life after this life, especially concerning the intermediate state.[24] Too often, we as pastors mouth what the world says about those who have passed: that they are enjoying their favorite hobby, that they are "smiling down" on their loved ones, or even that they have become the guardian angels of family members still alive. I can't tell you how many times I have heard the recently-bereaved speak about "signs" that the deceased is watching over them. None of this is biblical, and we as pastors bear a good part of the blame for perpetuating this popular

---

[24] Funerals or memorial services based upon the message of Christ have three basic purposes. First, they witness to resurrection, both Jesus's and ours, as the essence of the Christian message. Second, they console the bereaved with the good news of Jesus Christ. Third, they thank God for the life and ministry of the deceased. This appears to be a rather straightforward task, but these ends are often compromised by the influence of traditional views of the afterlife and by the pastoral urge to console.

notion of heaven. It might surprise some that John Calvin warns that we must be content with the very good but minimal description of life immediately after death conveyed to us in God's Word.[25]

Denominational funeral liturgies usually do properly stress resurrection as the essential way to think about life after this life, but we as pastors need to take care how this resurrection language is heard. For those who have grown up with the typical, culturally defined notion of heaven, resurrection often means generically "what happens to people when they die." For these people, the only conception of life after death imagines the soul leaving the body behind and making its solitary journey to God's realm. Christians may not understand what resurrection means even when they hear it proclaimed!

Pastors need to see this narrow view of the afterlife as a call to regularly teach about the nature of believers' resurrection. When a family loses a loved one, the accompanying counseling and funeral are important opportunities for teaching about death and new life in Christ. A new pastor who hopes to reclaim resurrection theology for his or her church quickly realizes that the funeral service is ground zero for conflict around this issue. The bereaved come to the service hoping to have what they have heard about heaven confirmed. Often the deceased has chosen hymns or passages for the service, ones that might lead in quite a different direction than resurrection. The challenge will be to minister to these people in terms of what they understand while beginning to translate language about life immediately after death into statements about resurrection.

But if this is the only time these issues are addressed in the life of the church, the instruction will fall short. Crisis instruction is always limited by the bereaved's ability to hear. Pastors should feel compelled to address this distortion of a key teaching as a regular part of church life, not just during funerals. Death and resurrection lie at the heart of the Christian message and should not only be discussed in hushed tones at the end of life.

We have no record of Paul conducting a Christian funeral service, although he probably did. With his clear focus on the hope for resurrection, imagine how different his service might be than the ones

---

[25]   Calvin says that "it is neither lawful nor expedient to inquire too curiously concerning our immediate state. It is foolish and rash to inquire concerning unknown matters more deeply than God permits us to know. Scripture goes no further than to say that Christ is present with them. ... What teacher or master will reveal to us that which God has concealed? (Calvin, *Institutes of the Christian Religion*, II. iii. 2:997).

we often attend. Paul clearly believed that followers of Christ are with him immediately after they die. Nothing can separate them from God's love. But, as important as this is, Paul does not consider it the key to our comfort: it is not the "best part" that we are to celebrate most when confronted with death. What distinguishes our sorrow from that of the pagans is "hope" (1 Thessalonians 4:13) for a future resurrection that comes when Christ returns.

Triumphalism Concerning Death

What attitudes toward death do you see in the Christian funeral services you attend? If the service is attuned to biblical teachings, your answer should reflect the paradox of what we learn there. Put simply, we are taught both that death is an ongoing reality and that we have begun to experience its conquest in Jesus Christ. This tension has its theological foundation in the simple fact that Christ has already risen; he is the "first fruits" (1 Corinthians 15:20) of an eschatological event that has not yet happened. As we have seen in Paul, death is the greatest of all enemies (1 Corinthians 15:26, 54b-55), and its final defeat comes only at the end of the age, when Christ returns. But it also true that we have, in the present, the promises that come to us in Christ.[26] It is impossible to overstate how important this tension concerning death is. If the balance is tipped toward an emphasis on future victory over death, then the present can be drained of its joy and power. It would be easy to become obsessed with calculating the time of Christ's return[27] or simply to become an "idler" (1 Thessalonians 5:14; compare 2 Thessalonians 3:6-13). If the balance is tipped toward a present victory over death, then the result is a kind of triumphalism that overestimates our current empowerment (like the "wise" and victorious Corinthians, 1 Corinthians 1:18-31; 4:8-13) and deemphasizes the ways in which we are still bodies.[28]

---

[26] This includes, as the Gospel of John puts it, an abiding relationship with Christ (John 15:1-11) *now* that can be called eternal life (John 5:24). We experience, in the present, the empowerment and comfort of the Holy Spirit (John 15:26; 16:5-12; Romans 8:1-17). Paul loves to speak about the transformation that occurs in believers through the power of Christ: we are new creations (2 Corinthians 5:17); our old nature has been buried with Christ in our baptism (Romans 6:1-4); we have been adopted as children of God (Romans 8:14-17; Galatians 4:5-7).

[27] See Mark 13:32 and parallels; 1 Thessalonians 5:1-2.

[28] See 1 Corinthians 5:1-13; 6:13-20; 7:1-5; etc. I am always impressed with how carefully Paul balances present and future victory in his letters. In Romans 8, he quickly moves from our present reality as adopted children and recipients of the

I have been to many funeral services where the emphasis upon present victory has been so great that it is hard to imagine that death is a problem. Our loved one is in heaven and already experiencing the fullness of the new life! Death is a feature, a welcome transition to a place prepared by God to meet all our need and wants! When believers' resurrection is forgotten, death is trivialized. Paul shows clearly that death is the greatest of enemies, akin to the evil powers in the universe (1 Corinthians 15:24-26[29]). And it is not overcome until Christ's return. Our parishioners know that when we declare victory over death in the case of someone who has passed, we are ignoring the battle with death they continue to fight. Becoming a Christian does not mean that we are freed from the consequences of living in a body. Proclaiming "heaven" at the expense of resurrection becomes a way of stifling the intense sorrow that is present at every funeral service. Triumphalism concerning death is a common belief among contemporary Christians, but it can also become a pastoral ploy for those of us who want to avoid the topic of death and its consequences.

It is so important for us as pastors to be aware of our culture's understanding of death and how that conception is influencing the people in our church. Contemporary American society responds to death in two related but quite different ways. On the one hand, our culture expresses a deep fear of death, which usually manifests itself in a denial of its reality and power. The isolation of the dying, the medicalization of death, extreme efforts to prolong life, cremation, our obsession with youth, and so on, all point to our unwillingness to deal with death. On the other hand, this fear of death can ironically lead to a fascination with its power and morbid qualities.[30]

Spirit to talk about "the glory about to be revealed to us" (8:18ff). In Romans 6, Paul speaks about our baptism into Christ's death, a graphic way of speaking about how we have been changed, but he is clear that resurrection is a kind of newness that comes only in the future (Romans 6:5: "so we might walk in newness of life"). And note the wonderful paradox of what Paul is saying in Philippians chapter 3. Paul considers his own achievements under the law "rubbish" (Philippians 3:4b-8) relative to the new righteous that he now has in Christ (3:9). But even this present experience of salvation does not diminish his desire for what the future brings ("if somehow I might attain the resurrection from the dead," 3:11)!

29   See also Colossians 1:13, 16; 2:10; Ephesians 6:12.
30   Think of the movies that have come out in the last 30 years that tempt us by portraying our worst nightmare: the evil dead, corpses, dead but somehow also alive, desiring to feed on our flesh. And what of the video games that allow a young person to "kill" a thousand combatants in one afternoon, or the way the "skull and bones" has become a stylish element of design? The church's proclamation of death and resurrection can become a foundation of hope in the midst of this fear

In his Pulitzer prize-winning book *The Denial of Death*, author Ernest Becker gives a classic description of modern humanity's response to death. Becker states that humanity reacts to death in three ways. The first—that of the person who lacks any filters to obscure the reality of death—is insanity. Death strips life of ultimate meaning, and it is ironically the deeply depressed person who sees this truth most clearly. The second—the path most humans choose—is to live fully in the present, ignoring their mortality. Survival depends upon the ability to make death a remote concern. The third way is that of the heroic individual, one who attempts to do something, anything, to combat the forces of death. Unwilling to let the reality of death incapacitate them and unwilling to simply hide the reality of death, those who fall into this category usually "project one's problems onto a god-figure, to be healed by an all-embracing and all-justifying beyond."[31] Since Becker rejects the existence of God, let alone his ability to save us from death, this, too, is seen as an act of futility.

However, reading Becker reminds us what should be recognized by Christians and non-Christians alike: there is something very wrong with us and with our world. We are dying. Our world is being tainted and may not be inhabitable forever. We cannot ignore this reality. Only when we wrestle honestly with the fragility and temporality of our bodies and the evil power that would destroy us can we begin to grasp what God has done for us in his Son. It is impossible to experience the wonder of the resurrection unless one first understands the power of the enemy it overcomes. The biblical story of salvation is a drama of conflict between life and death. Death is not God's will for humankind: it is the product of our rebellion and of evil forces. Death is so significant an enemy that God chooses to address it through the death and resurrection of his own son.

An Escapist Theology That Belies What We Say about the Christian Life

One of the fundamental ironies of the message proclaimed in many of our churches is the tension between what we say about life

---

and trivialization. As we proclaim it, the resurrection of the body is not an object of fear but God's ultimate victory over death and the beginning of a new age marked by his love.

31 Becker, *The Denial of Death*, 287. It is not a Christian book, but it is one that can be immensely valuable to the pastor as he or she tries to understand the bleak reality of death apart from Jesus Christ.

after death (an individual experience and a movement away from this earth) and what we say about our current mission as followers of Christ (a corporate expression of love for humanity and God's creation). If it is true that the Christian life has its "end" in an individual transformation at death that leads away from this world, how do we as pastors justify all the energy our churches expend to build God's kingdom here on earth? Is our task as Christians simply about getting individuals into heaven when they die, or do we have a wider arena of concern? What we say about the nature of life after this life is far from being theologically innocent; it very much affects how we live as Christians in the present.

Have you ever wondered how to account for your attraction to this world, both its natural aspects and the products of human industry such as art, architecture, technology, and scholarship? I think the best answer for Christians is that this world is God's good or beautiful (*tov*) creation (Genesis 1:31). It and we have been affected by sin, but God's image and glory have not been obliterated. A clear affirmation of the value of the world comes in the Bible's emphasis upon God's desire to restore his creation. In Jewish thought, the end-times is also a time of cosmic recreation. Several New Testament texts point to this common assumption among early Christians.[32] But the most emphatic way of describing God's desire to save his beloved creation comes in the specifics of the work of his Son, Jesus Christ. The incarnation and resurrection of Christ are the ultimate affirmations of the value and redeemability of human life and the stuff of this earth. Salvation is

---

[32] In Romans 8:18-25, Paul says that creation longs for liberation from its "bondage to decay" so that it too might experience the "freedom of the glory of the children of God" (8:19-21). It groans for its future transformation, just as humans long for a future bodily redemption (8:23). Both creation and humans anticipate what is to come (8:24-25). Ephesians and Colossians also speak of cosmic renewal. In Ephesians, we read that God's mysterious plan for redemption includes gathering up "all things in him, things in heaven and in earth" (1:10). Colossians says that it is God's plan to "reconcile all things to himself, whether on earth or on heaven, making peace through the blood of [Christ's] cross" (1:20). Revelation 21 describes the new age as a time when the earth will be renewed and God will be with his people in a new and intimate way:

> And I heard a loud voice from the throne saying,
> "See, the home of God is among mortals.
> He will dwell with them;
> they will be his peoples,
> and God himself will be with them;
> Death will be no more;
> mourning and crying and pain will be no more,
> for the first things have passed away." (21:1-4)

not a rejection of the world and a flight to a far-off place. Salvation is about God entering our world in all its messiness and restoring it to its original glory. Jesus comes proclaiming the kingdom of God, an anticipation of God's end-time rule on earth. When we pray the prayer he taught us, we echo the hope that our holy God will someday be here among us in a new and powerful way: "Our Father in heaven, hallowed be your name. Your kingdom come, your will be done, on earth as it is in heaven" (Matthew 6:9-10).

Jesus command that we love our neighbor (Luke 10:25-37) is nothing if not a command to love the world as God loves it. All of the Christian message is a movement toward the world, not away from it. What we do in this life, in these bodies, is a participation in God's building of this future kingdom. Unless we understand this, it is easy to be confused by the way Paul follows his words about resurrection with ethical exhortation. In 1 Thessalonians 5:1-11, Paul concludes his encouragement about believers' resurrection with orders to live as "children of light" (5:4). But this combination of eschatological and ethical language makes sense if you see a continuity between this world and the one occupied by these resurrected bodies. This is even more obvious in 1 Corinthians 15:58, where Paul's final comment after a long discussion about resurrection is the exhortation "be steadfast, immovable, always excelling in the work of the Lord, because you know that in the Lord your work is not in vain." The only legitimate way to read this comment in light of the context of resurrection is to see it in terms of the foundational value of our present lives. What are doing now is not "left behind." We are building something that will stand in God's future!

What we believe about the nature of life after death shapes our current lives as disciples. If we anticipate nothing more than a spiritual existence with God apart from this world, then it will surely affect how we express our love for this world. Can we be passionate about God's desire to end racism, poverty, war, hunger, and abuse if our final resting place is an escape from this earth? There is a fundamental tension between the Christian mandate to love and an amnesia about God's plan to resurrect and restore. Grasping the fuller vision of God's plan for us empowers us to live with purpose in the present: in bodies that need to be cared for (1 Corinthians 6:12-20) and in a world that is worth redeeming.

Our Failure to Teach the Larger Story

I am convinced that our amnesia about believers' resurrection and restoration indicates a truncation of the biblical narrative. Even with the guidance of lectionary readings, a kind of theological selection is operative (conscious or unconscious) that indicates what the main points of the "valued" narrative are. In many of the mainline churches I have attended, the narrative is focused on how Jesus Christ saves us from our sins. This is a very good theme indeed, but unfortunately, it often grows out of a relatively limited narrative. The focus is on sin and human disobedience and how God saves us through the cross of Jesus Christ. The bookends of the story are the entrance of sin and death into the world and how we are retrieved from this realm of corruption when we die. The second story is longer and more complicated. Its essential focus is God's love for his creation and how he redeems and restores it through Jesus Christ. In its emphasis upon the story of Israel, the incarnation, and Jesus's proclamation of the kingdom of God, it has a stronger focus on the plight of humanity and issues of corporate justice, both of which are addressed in the second coming of Christ. The bookends of this story stretch from the beginning of the Bible to the final scenes found in the book of Revelation: God creates the world in all its goodness, and, in the end, restores it.

These two stories are not in any way mutually exclusive, nor do they exist in this "pure" form in any given church. And yet is it clear in various churches that I attend that often one or the other of these narrative structures serves as the primary touchstone for the gospel proclaimed in that place. We as pastors need to be very aware of how the biblical story implicit in our sermons will impact our congregations' ability to hear the gospel message. If we preach, week in and week out, that the biblical story is all about an individual's salvation from sin and her or his entrance into heaven, then how can we expect our members to make sense of Jesus's resurrection and ours? The story of salvation ends, in effect, when a person dies and goes to be with Christ. The narrative has no place for later chapters.

Of course, we must preach the contents of the first story. But the story of my salvation in Jesus Christ is only comprehensible in the context of the larger biblical narrative. Jesus not only dies on a cross; he also rises from the dead. Jesus not only pays for our sins; he also enters our world as a human being. Jesus saves not only you and me; he also shows love for and seeks to redeem the entire world. Jesus not only brings a new righteousness with God; he also builds the kingdom of

God and addresses issues of justice. If we ignore the larger story, we lose the sense that God has a larger plan for the world and that he clearly has the power to implement it. Without the biblical beginning and end, we forget the ways God loves our world and is operative in it.

I love the way Paul models a fuller use of the biblical narrative. He constantly schools his gentile readers about God's creation, his relationship with his chosen people, and the way God will lead the story to its conclusion. In 1 Corinthians 1, Paul shows the necessity of Christ's work by comparing him to Adam (1:21, 45-49). Here, Paul gives a sense for the logic of God's plan going all the way back to the beginning. The order and divine necessity of the final events become clear in 1 Corinthians 15:23-28. Christ's resurrection is the "first fruits," an agricultural term that decisively links his resurrection with ours (1:23, 20). The next step in this carefully ordered series of events is Christ's return ("at his coming," 1:23) followed by the resurrection and transformation of believers ("those who belong to Christ," 1:23).[33] Finally, Paul describes a series of events that abolishes evil and death and subjects all things under God (1:24-28). Death, the ultimate enemy, is fittingly the last to be destroyed (1:26). There is a clear sense that these events are a necessary conclusion to the drama of salvation and that the end is final; God will then be "all in all" (1:28).[34]

We need to teach the biblical narrative in a way that makes room for a fuller picture of salvation in Jesus Christ. Christ's resurrection, and all that it implies in terms of our lives and ministry, is not disposable. This does not diminish in any way the centrality of what happens on the cross, but it is an affirmation that both cross and empty tomb are important. The church's amnesia about believers' resurrection can only be addressed if it realizes that there is a final chapter that must take place even after the death of individual Christians.

---

[33] Note the reference to the transformation or "change" that will occur in those still alive in verses 51-52.

[34] As we see above, in both 1 Thessalonians 4:16-18 and 1 Corinthians 15:52, Paul emphasizes the drama and importance of Christ's return by using standard Jewish apocalyptic terminology. Christ will return with "the cry of command, with the archangel's call, and with the sound of the trumpet" (1 Thessalonians) and "in a moment, in the twinkling of an eye, at the last trumpet" (1 Corinthians). Neither of these Gentile congregations knew very much about Jesus's return and may well have never heard this language before. Paul's use of it shows how important it was for him to bring these new Christians into the company of those who understand the details of the larger story. This urge to give the story of Jesus Christ a biblical context, especially in terms of the issues of faith, law, and righteousness, is everywhere present in Paul's letters.

In Conclusion

The resurrection of Jesus, which we think of as the end of the gospel story, is really the beginning, both in terms of how the message goes forward in the Church and of how it goes "backward," so to speak, in terms of understanding who Jesus really was and what his words and acts meant. The very strange and wonderful event of Jesus's resurrection is the impetus for the message of salvation we preach in the Church.

Certainly the contemporary church understands the meaning of Jesus's resurrection on several important levels. It validates Jesus's work and sacrifice; it confirms that he is God's Son, empowered in all that he does. Jesus's resurrection is rightly used to describe the new life we now have as Christians: the eternal life, as Jesus puts in in John, that has transformed us. And Jesus's resurrection is rightly employed to speak of how he conquers that great enemy death, but this victory is almost always applied to our life with Jesus immediately after physical death. What is often lacking in mainline churches is an understanding of Jesus's resurrection that defines the "end-times." Mainline churches too often forget that the New Testament links Jesus's resurrection directly with believers' resurrection. Jesus's resurrection must not be separated from the indispensable conclusion to the story: believers will be raised, creation will be transformed, and evil, including that old enemy death, will finally be destroyed.

I have tried to speak about this amnesia concerning believers' resurrection in terms of pastoral issues, especially as they are raised by Paul. We as pastors are sometimes too anxious to console, often with definitions of heaven that come more from our culture than from the Bible. We have failed to properly instruct about believers' resurrection in a way that integrates it with our larger theological message. We are often triumphalistic about death, emphasizing the victory that occurs when a believer dies and goes to be with Christ but ignoring the ongoing battle against death in our world. Too often, our message about life after death comes across as escapist and individual-centered, and it can belie what we try to say about God's love for this world. We as pastors can be tempted to operate under a truncated version of the biblical story, one that focuses only on the cross. But there is a fuller, more nuanced biblical narrative that helps make sense of both cross and empty tomb. We need all of the chapters of the story of salvation, not least of all the ones that show how God loves his creation and seeks to redeem all of it.

It is very important for us as Christians to know what the Bible does and does not say about life after death. How we speak about new life in Christ affects how we as pastors preach and how we do ministry. From our earth-bound point of view, understanding resurrection and God's transformation of this creation quickly strains logic. But we must not avoid proclaiming resurrection simply because our limited intellects cannot fully explain it. Discussion of life after death must include both a strong biblical foundation and a good dose of humility. And one of the best reasons for this humility is the surprising and unpredictable nature of God. What human could have anticipated that God's own Son, our Messiah, would die on a cross (it's "foolishness," 1 Corinthians 1:18-25)? And no one thought that a single person, even Jesus, would be raised from the dead far in advance of the general resurrection (Mark 9:10). The larger biblical story is one that shows God regularly doing things that, from a human point of view, seem impossible or foolish or reckless. Our biblical understanding of resurrection is a wonderful, improbable vision of life after death! And it lies at the heart of the salvation we proclaim.

CHAPTER 10

The Book of Joel: The Millennial Narrative?

Jaco J. Hamman

This essay, like the others in this festschrift, honors Tom Boogaart, whose friendship, teaching, scholarship, and ministry touched many lives, including mine. Specifically, I want to recognize Tom as a creative and innovative teacher, a transformative mentor, a prophetic change agent and community builder, a wonderful colleague, a great friend, and a person whose spirituality dwells in thin places. Still, I am unable to capture the person, son, brother, husband, father, grandfather, pastor, teacher, and friend who is Tom Boogaart. Tom unlocked the Hebrew Scriptures for many pastors and thousands of faithful. It was Tom who first shared with me that the locusts in the book of Joel were both locusts *and* caterpillars, sparking an interest that led to articles and a book.[1] I am deeply grateful for the life and ministry of Tom Boogaart and for the providence that brought us together as colleagues for 11 years and as friends for life.

"Churches are dying in numbers we hadn't conceived, and most millennials want nothing to do with a dying civic club or community

---

[1] This essay draws on my book: Jaco J. Hamman, *The Millennial Narrative: Sharing a Good Life with the Next Generation* (Nashville: Abingdon Press, 2019).

135

organization."[2] With these provocative—yet honest—words, millennial pastor Rob Lee voices his concern. Mainline Christianity is struggling to reach young persons as denominations age on an unsustainable path. Can the Hebrew Scriptures be meaningful to millennials? This is the question that drives this inquiry. As a "dying civic club," the future of mainline Christianity is bleak. Still, there is hope, for the revitalization of the church may come from unexpected places.

One reason for the church's dire situation is that the church has not reckoned with changing spiritualities. Sociologist Robert Wuthnow describes three distinct spiritualities co-existing in the United States today: spiritualities of *dwelling*, *seeking*, and *practices*. A *spirituality of dwelling* sees God as occupying "a definite place in the universe and creates a sacred space in which humans too can dwell ... [and] feel secure."[3] Here, church, doctrine and tradition are important. A *spirituality of seeking* "emphasizes negotiation: individuals search for sacred moments that reinforce their conviction that the divine exists, but these moments are fleeting ... and they may have to negotiate among complex and confusing meanings of spirituality."[4] Pilgrimage, even to other religions, rather than place, is important. *Practice-oriented spirituality* "put responsibility squarely on individuals to spend time on a regular basis worshiping, communing with, listening to, and attempting to understand the ultimate source of sacredness in their lives."[5] Increasingly, individual practices such as prayer and meditation, yoga, reading texts, and communing with nature, but also eating and serving, are important. Practitioners discover discernment or deep reflection; personal reward; social connections; a moral dimension; and duty, obligation and service in their practices.[6] "Faith," Wuthnow concludes, "is no longer something people inherit but something for which they strive. ... It provides security ... by plugging them into the right networks, and by instilling the confidence to bargain for what they need."[7] Spiritualities of dwelling typically offer *good news*, whereas spiritualities of practice—as practiced by the majority of millennials— seek the *Good Life*.

2   Rob Lee, *Stained-Glass Millennials: Coincidental Reformers* (Macon: Smyth & Helwys, 2016), xvi.GA: Smyth & Helwys Publishing, 2016.
3   Robert Wuthnow, *After Heaven: Spirituality in America since the 1950s* (Berkeley: University of California Press, 1998), 3–4.1998.
4   Wuthnow, 3–4.
5   Wuthnow, 16.
6   Wuthnow, 179ff.
7   Wuthnow, 8.

In this essay, I suggest that the very lives of today's young adults overlap with the narrative we discover in the book of Joel. Millennials are telling us that loss and trauma cannot be lightly brushed away or ignored, that loneliness is too painful to tolerate and they are good at building community, that the freedom to define one's own communal experience where vulnerability can be risked is essential, that nurturing one's spiritual life is important, that we need to hold each other accountable while working toward social justice, and that they seek to make a positive difference in the world. Joel's narrative envisions decimated persons longing for and meeting the compassionate God who restores. It anticipates spirit-filled persons dreaming dreams and seeing visions, even as they face accountability. The narrative concludes with hope and blessing that flows to others. We thus find a 2,500-year-old narrative that resonates deeply with the lived experience of young adults.

The essay first offers a brief snapshot of millennials, risking the generality such depictions bring. Next, our narrative existence—that we live by stories—is highlighted. Contemporary culture is faulted for providing few life-giving narratives. I then briefly introduce the book of Joel as a neglected book in the Hebrew Scriptures. Joel's narrative divided into six acts, each corresponding with a core element in the lives of many millennials. I conclude by arguing that the book of Joel offers a narrative that promises the *Good Life* to all, a message that complements—and possibly supersedes—receiving *good news*.

Who Are the Millennials?

Given a year or two on either side, the young adults envisioned in this essay are those born 1980–2000, called millennials, though strict generational lines are usually not helpful. In the United States, millennials are the largest generation with more than 75 million persons. With 43 percent of young adults as non-white and 6.4 percent identifying as lesbian, gay, transgender or queer, they are also the most diverse generation to date.[8] With only 14 percent living in rural America, young adults are mostly found in suburban (54 percent) and urban (32 percent) areas. Millennial households have a median pre-tax income of $35,300, implying that one in five young adults live in poverty. Gener-

---

8   Pew Research Center, "Millennials Overtake Baby Boomers as America's Largest Generation" (2016), accessed October 12, 2016, http://www.pewresearch.org/fact-tank/2016/04/25/millennials-overtake-baby-boomers/.

ally, millennials are less connected with traditional institutions than earlier generations.[9] Those who came to the United States as children show higher levels of cultural affiliation, with significant connection to family, heritage, community, and language compared to young adults born in the US."[10]

Much has been written on the millennial generation, including their relationship with the Christian tradition and how they approach faith.[11] Whereas the generation received initial affirmation in *Millennials Rising: The Next Great Generation,* recent works show a more critical stance, even overtones of judgment.[12] Research provides an ambivalent picture about this generation best described by professors of education Arthur Levine and Diane Dean, who studied 5,000 freshmen across 270 diverse colleges and universities matriculating between 2005 and 2014 and found young adults being tension filled, "struggling to maintain their balance as they attempt to cross the gulf between their dreams and the world in which they live. They seek security but live in an age

[9]   Pew Research Center, "Millennials in Adulthood: Detatched from Institutions, Networked with Friends" (2014), accessed October 12, 2016, http://www.pewsocialtrends.org/files/2014/03/2014-03-07_generations-report-version-for-web.pdf.

[10] Ad Age Insights and Univision, "The Cultural Connection: How Hispanic Identity Influences Millennials" (2012), accessed October 11, 2016, http://gaia.adage.com/images/bin/pdf/Hispanic%20Millennials.pdf.

[11] Ronald Alsop, *The Trophy Kids Grow Up: How the Millennial Generation Is Shaking up the Workplace,* 1st ed. (San Francisco: Jossey-Bass, 2008); Joshua Best, *Y: Christian Millennial Manifesto* (Holland: Unprecedented Press, 2017); Danita Bye, *Millennials Matter: Proven Strategies for Building Your Next-Gen Leader* (Racine: BroadStreetPublishing 2017); Neil Howe and William Strauss, *Millennials Rising: The Next Great Generation* (New York: Vintage Books, 2000); Rob Lee, *Stained-Glass Millennials: Coincidental Reformers* (Macon: Smyth & Helwys Publishing, 2016); Craig Kennet Miller and MaryJane Pierce Norton, *Making God Real for a New Generation: Ministry with Millennials Born from 1982 to 1999* (Nashville: Discipleship Resources, 2003); Victor Shane, *The Authentic Life: A Guidebook for Millennials* (Bloomington: Westbow Press, 2017); Tim Elmore, *Generation Iy: Our Last Chance to Save Their Future* (Atlanta: Poet Gardener Publishing, 2010); Thom S. Rainer and Jess W. Rainer, *The Millennials: Connecting to America's Largest Generation* (Nashville: B & H Pub. Group, 2011); Monte Sahlin and David Roozen, *How Religious Congregations Are Engaging Young Adults in America* (Hartford: Hartford Institute for Religion Research, 2015); David P. Setran, *Spiritual Formation in Emerging Adulthood: A Practical Theology for College and Young Adult Ministry* (Grand Rapids: Baker Academic, 2013); Howard Gardner and Katie Davis, *The App Generation: How Today's Youth Navigate Identity, Intimacy, and Imagination in a Digital World* (New Haven: Yale University Press, 2013); David Kinnaman, *Unchristian: What the New Generation Really Thinks About Christianity ... and Why It Matters* (Grand Rapids: Baker Books, 2007).

[12] Howe and Strauss.

of profound and unceasing change...."[13] Millennials find economic opportunity, autonomy, intimacy, flux, social regression, and more to be challenging.

Today's young adults received a world unlike the one that welcomed their parents. Global forces come with profound personal, emotional, relational, and professional costs. The millennial experience is amplified by the reality of constant change, changing familial ties, increased racial tension, limited employment opportunities, debt burdens, and a widening class gap. The shift from an analog to a digital world and an information economy has not been easy. Many millennials live and experience an "epidemic of anguish."[14] Can the Judeo-Christian tradition speak into their world?

Living According to an Opera with Many Acts, Not by Hit Singles

Psychologists, sociologists, and linguists remind us that narratives are found in every culture.[15] Popular culture provides many narratives, including: "You can be whatever you want to be," "Technology will save us," and "Guns do not kill; people do." Epic American narratives include "how the West was won (and lost)," "the American Dream," and "the entrepreneurs of Silicon Valley." Gender, race, class, and sexuality come wrapped in these cultural narratives, which orient our lives. With no exception, cultural narratives fail despite the promises they hold or the wisdom they claim.

Linguist Bradford Hall reminds us that narratives "are essentially *actions* taken by *characters* in relation to a *problem* and the perceived *outcome* of those actions."[16] Through characters, problems, actions, outcomes, and by providing information, narratives inform and give meaning. Narratives 1) teach us the ways the world works, giving general principles and also particular contexts; 2) describe our place

---

[13] Arthur Levine and Diane R. Dean, eds., Generation on a Tightrope: A Portrait of Today's College Student, 3rd ed., Jossey-Bass Higher and Adult Education (San Francisco: Jossey-Bass, 2012), x–xi.

[14] Robin Wilson, "An Epidemic of Anguish," *Chronicle of Higher Education*, no. Special Issue: Today's Anguished Students—and How to Help Them (2015): 4.no. Special Issue: Today's Anguished Students—and How to Help Them (2015.

[15] Joseph De Rivera and Theodore R. Sarbin, *Believed-in Imaginings: The Narrative Construction of Reality*, 1st ed. (Washington, DC: American Psychological Association, 1998); Theodore R. Sarbin, *Narrative Psychology: The Storied Nature of Human Conduct* (New York: Praeger, 1986).

[16] Bradford J. Hall, *Among Cultures: The Challenge of Communication*, 2nd ed. (Belmont: Thomson Wadsworth, 2005), 73.2nd ed. (Belmont, CA: Thomson Wadsworth, 2005.

in the world as it shapes personal and communal identities—who we are and what we are like; 3) advise us how to act in the world, both effectively and appropriately; and 4) provide a framework on how to evaluate or judge what goes on in the world—what is good or bad and what might be safe or dangerous.[17] Narratives are always personally appropriated. The Hebrew prophets knew the power of appropriation as they sought to bring "[an] alternative consciousness ... [expressing] new realities against the more visible ones of the old order."[18] As one commentator writes: "The Bible shapes readers by showing them what lies beyond the self."[19]

A significant problem we face in this age of technology, however, is the loss of narratives in our lives. Media theorist Douglas Rushkoff reminds us in his *Present Shock: When Everything Happens Now* that

> experiencing the world as a series of stories helps create a sense of context. It is comforting and orienting. It helps smooth out obstacles and impediments by recasting them as bumps along the way to some better place—or at least the end of the journey. As long as there is enough momentum, enough pull forward and enough dramatic tension, we can suspend our disbelief enough to stay in the story.[20]

As we live notification to notification, driven by a multiverse where one newsflash or text replaces another, we lose the deeper connections to stories. The moment, captured in a selfie or a few lines, becomes all-important. Rushkoff provides a lovely image, saying that *we need to live by operas with many acts, when most persons choose to listen to hit singles.*[21]

Joel: A Person, a Book, and a Narrative

The book of Joel offers a narrative with a powerful plot: there was a people whose lives and landscapes were devoured by different kinds of locusts. They were in crisis and mourning, lamenting their losses and coming together as a sacred assembly. The people cried out to God,

---

[17] Hall, 74–81.
[18] Walter Brueggemann, *The Prophetic Imagination* (Minneapolis: Fortress Press, 2001), 14.2001.
[19] Anthony C. Thiselton, "Reception Theory, H. R. Jauss and the Formative Power of Scripture," *Scottish Journal of Theology* 65, no. 3 (2012): 289.no. 3 (2012.
[20] Douglas Rushkoff, *Present Shock: When Everything Happens Now* (New York: Current, 2013), 39.2013.
[21] Rushkoff, 77.

who met them as a compassionate Being who does not anger easily but rather abounds in love. God responded: "I will repay you for the years that the cutting locust, the swarming locust, the hopping locust and the devouring locust have eaten ...."[22] The restoration includes God pouring out God's spirit on all people, young and old, men and women, slave and free. Empowered by the God now dwelling over and in persons, the people are held accountable, especially where injustices are found. As some expect judgment for their actions, others experience water flowing from God's throne, nurturing the earth wherever it flows, a powerful metaphor of blessing that flows from God through persons to others.

We know that Joel's name means "YHWH is Elohim/God" and that he was the son of Pethuel, though Pethuel is unknown. In ancient Near East culture, Joel was a "mysterious prophet."[23] Many questions surround the book. Joel probably lived in or around Jerusalem, given the frequent references to the temple.[24] Authorship, dating (suggestions span 500 years, but probably written in the fifth century B.C.), genre, and how to understand the content are all disputed categories. [25] Commentator Aaron Schart states that "[since] Joel's superscription has no date, this implies that his message is not related to a specific situation within the history of Israel, but to something more far-reaching and thus to a more important phenomenon."[26] Does the book address a locust plague, warn about the Day of the LORD, or lament a drought brought on by dry Sirocco winds?[27] Is it prophecy, theodicy, lament, or apocalyptic literature? It is easy to identify Joel as a "problem child," wedged between Hosea and Amos.[28]

A short book—merely 73 verses composed of 957 words—Joel has been contained in three chapters since the early thirteenth century,

---

22   Joel 2:25a.
23   Mordecai Schreiber, "I Will Pour out My Spirit on All Flesh (Joel 3:1)," *Jewish Bible Quaterly* 41, no. 2 (2013): 123.no. 2 (2013).
24   Elie Assis, *The Book of Joel: A Prophet between Calamity and Hope*, The Library of Hebrew Bible/Old Testament Studies (New York: Bloomsbury T&T Clark, 2013), 3.<style face="italic">Library of Hebrew Bible/Old Testament Studies</style> (New York: Bloomsbury T&T Clark, 2013).
25   Assis, 216.
26   Aaron Schart, "The First Section of the Book of the Twelve Prophets: Hosea-Joel-Amos," *Interpretation*, no. April (2007): 148.no. April (2007).
27   James L. Crenshaw, Joel, 1st ed., The Anchor Bible (New York: Doubleday, 1995), 35.
28   Ronald L. Troxel, *Joel: Scope, Genre(s), and Meaning, Critical Studies in the Hebrew Bible* (Winona Lake: Eisenbrauns, 2015), 38; John Barton, *Joel and Obadiah: A Commentary*, 1st ed., The Old Testament Library (Louisville: Westminster John Knox Press, 2001), 1.

departing from Hebrew texts that have the same number of verses placed in four chapters.[29] There are two clear sections, with the first two chapters dealing with the destruction of locusts and the second section with the political restoration of a people. Were the two sections written by different authors or by a single author at different times?[30] Structural and linguistic considerations as well as the use of similar terminology support the view that Joel's two sections form a unit and were probably written by a single author. Joel's compelling message calls on his listeners to hear, weep, awake, sound an alarm, return, rejoice, fast, lament, assemble, and more. It is a "demanding" book with 43 commands and "a relatively high overall rate of use of imperatives, approximately three commands in every five verses."[31]

As a story, the book of Joel has "information gaps"—information we need in order to understand the text is not given.[32] We do not know, for example, why God calls on Judah to return to YHWH. No sin is mentioned, and God is not portrayed as an angry God. Whereas Hosea is clear that natural disasters come from God, Joel does not follow Hosea's tradition. We do not know why God would become "jealous of the land" (2:18). Furthermore, we do not know if the people returned to the Lord as called upon. We do know, however, that in Joel, God's compassion turns against God's heart of anger and triumphs. Joel historically has been identified as a significant narrative, with the church father Jerome (347–420 A.D.) seeing the book of Joel as a *"narratio"*—a narrative—teaching *sacramenta*—the mysteries.[33] Like the first listeners of Joel, we, too, cannot remain neutral to Joel's "fantastical story," which is best approached as one story with six distinct acts.[34]

Joel, Act One: Recognize the Locusts, Lament Your Loss

Millennials are intimately aware of loss and trauma: parents who divorce, grandparents who die, moving cities or towns, pets that die—expected losses. They also know interpersonal violence and date rape, painful sexual experiences, friends who die by suicide, bullying, illness,

29   Crenshaw, 11. Seven biblical books are shorter: Obadiah (21 verses); Haggai (38 verses); Nahum (47 verses); Jonah (48 verses); Zephaniah (53 verses); Malachi (55 verses); and Habakkuk (56 verses).
30   See Assis for a discussion of these theories. Assis, 23–39.
31   Ronald T. Hyman, "The Prophecy of Joel: The Prophet's Message, Beliefs, and Prophetic Style," *Jewish Bible Quaterly* 39, no. 4 (2011): 225.no. 4 (2011).
32   Troxel, 11.
33   Troxel, *Joel*, 11.
34   Troxel, 69.

and learning disabilities—unexpected losses. For many teenagers and young adults today, life arrives early, bringing isolation, despair, hopelessness, and the search for meaning.

Joel's opening act, which is for "everyone in the land" (1:2), declares the uniqueness of his narrative:

> Has anything like this ever happened in your days, or in the days of your ancestors? Tell it to your children, and have your children tell their children, and their children tell their children. What the cutting locust left, the swarming locust has eaten. What the swarming locust left, the hopping locust has eaten. And what the hopping locust left, the devouring locust has eaten.[35]

Joel recognizes the locusts of life. He summons all to attend to the very things that are happening in our midst.[36] The locusts, which may have been received from an older hymn dedicated to the Assyrian goddess Nanaya, tells of agricultural failure, which, for an agrarian people, is personal and social failure.[37] Whether real or metaphorical, the destruction by the locusts is all encompassing.[38]

The Hebrew text identifies four different plagues. There is the *gazam*, (the cutter; that which cuts off) and the *gasil* (the chewers; devouring palmerworms), *slow moving* but devastating. And then there's the *yelek* (the eaters; that which consumes) and the *arbeh* (a swarm of locusts), *fast moving* but just as deadly.[39] Whether a crawling worm or the flying locust, Joel describes a fierce enemy. The locusts have teeth (and can pounce) like a lion (1:6), make sounds like chariots coming to launch an attack (2:5), enter a house through a window like a thief (2:9), or constitute a mighty army (2:11).[40] As a metaphor, the locusts describe crises, some slowly unfolding in our lives and others surprising us, possibly with a tweet, a phone call, or a text message. Collectively, the

---

[35] Joel 1:2-4. All Scripture references: *The Common English Bible* (Nashville: Abingdon Books, 2011).

[36] Christopher R. Seitz, Joel, The International Theological Commentary (New York: Bloomsbury, 2016), 116.

[37] Victor Avigdor Hurowitz, "Joel's Locust Plague in Light of Sargon Ii's Hymn to Nanaya," *Journal of Biblical Literature* 112, no. 4 (1993): 597.no. 4 (1993).

[38] Assis, *The Book of Joel*, 41.#5L

[39] Crenshaw, *Joel*, 88; John Wesley, *Joel: Explanatory Notes & Commentary* (Lexington: Hargraves, 2015), 11; Assis, 76. Exodus 10 tells of "*arbeh*," Psalm 78:46 describes the "*gāsil*" and the "*yelek*," and Amos 4:10 links *gāzām*" to God's judgment.

[40] Hyman, "The Prophecy of Joel," 223.

locusts are intricately tied to personal, social, political, and ecological destruction.[41] "Nothing can remain after a four-fold assault."[42]

Joel describes four responses to devouring locusts: lament, build community, return to God, and fast. These practices prevent denial and nostalgia as acts of resistance. The call to a prayer of lament is not a traditional prophetic response to calamity, for tradition is most likely to say that what happened was deserved, retribution for sinful ways. *Joel is a different prophet.* There is no reason given for the presence of the locusts. Rather than being punitive, he is empathetic and calls on Judah to pray, another novel step. In Joel's time, established prayer—as seen in the book of Lamentations—was neither custom nor institutionalized. Rather, "prayer is seen as a spontaneous outburst of a person in need."[43] Lament—to bring your pain into God's presence— is a powerful prayer and act of resistance in the face of tragedy. The teenagers who named their losses practiced lament, sought community, and engaged the work of mourning. The latter implies seeking meaning in the midst of loss.[44]

Joel, Act Two: Gather and Discover Life-Giving Community

Millennials find hope in belonging. All people do. While other generations might find belonging at church, millennials gather outside the church's vision. In their report "How We Gather," Angie Thurston and Casper ter Kuile explore the varied ways millennials build community.[45] Written while they were graduate students at Harvard Divinity School, the authors state that "churches are just one of many institutional casualties of the internet age in which young people are both more globally connected and more locally isolated than ever before. Against this bleak backdrop, a hopeful landscape is emerging. Millennials are flocking to a host of new organizations ...."[46]

Thurston and Ter Kuile identify The Dinner Party, a grass-roots community "of 20- and 30-somethings who all have experienced a significant loss and who get together over homemade food to talk

---

[41]   Assis, *The Book of Joel*, 11.

[42]   Seitz, *Joel*, 122.

[43]   Elie Assis, "The Structure and Meaning of the Locust Plague Oracles in Joel 1,2–2,17," Zeitschrift für die alttestamentliche Wissenschaft 122 (2010): 407.

[44]   J. William Worden, *Grief Counseling and Grief Therapy: A Handbook for the Mental Health Practitioner*, 3rd ed. (New York: Springer, 2009), 18ff.3rd ed. (New York: Springer, 2009).

[45]   Angie Thurston and Casper ter Kuile, "How We Gather," 2015, accessed June 11, 2015, https://www.howwegather.org/reports.

[46]   Thurston and Ter Kuile, 2.

about it and how it impacts their lives." The Dinner Party seeks "to transform life after loss from an isolating experience into one marked by community support, candid conversation, and forward movement."[47] Millennials are gathering elsewhere, too, in gyms and as activist communities.[48] "Overwhelmingly," Thurston and Ter Kuile conclude, "[millennial] organizations use secular language while mirroring many of the functions fulfilled by religious community. Examples include fellowship, personal reflection, pilgrimage, aesthetic discipline, liturgy, confession, and worship. Together, these groups encourage friendship, promote neighborhood welfare, and spread messages for the betterment of individuals and society."[49]

Sociologist of religion Elizabeth Drescher reminds us that millennials are "believing in belonging."[50] Building community is a spiritual practice and a way of living. As one of her respondents told her, "Community *is* religion. Family *is* religion."[51] Drescher anticipates groups like The Dinner Party, as she asserts that "preparing and sharing food" not only cultivates "intimacy, empathy, compassion, and connectedness" but also defines "contemporary spirituality."[52]

Joel, recognizing the devastation left by the locusts, calls on the people to gather: "Demand a fast, request a special assembly. Gather the elders and all the land's people to the temple of the Lord your God, and cry out to the Lord" (1:13). Three times Joel calls on the people to gather (Joel 1:13-14; 2:1-2, 16). Joel merely commands: "Gather!" The Hebrew used, "*korah*," suggesting the calling of a sacred assembly.[53] Gathering, Joel argues, is necessary, even if there is no

---

[47]   The Dinner Party, "About Us," accessed September 1, 2017, http://thedinnerparty.org/about/.

[48]   The other communities "How We Gather" discuss, are: CTZNWELL, a group mobilizing the well-being industry to change the world and increase practices of personal transformation; The U.S. Department of Arts and Culture, an action network of artists and cultural workers whose creativity serves social justice; The Millennial Trains Project (leads crowd-funded train journeys across America for diverse groups of young innovators); Live In The Grey (now: Live Grey) seeks to inspire purpose and meaning in employment; Juniper Path, bringing meditation to modern life; and Camp Grounded, a summer camp for adults.

[49]   Thurston and Ter Kuile, 5.

[50]   Elizabeth Drescher, *Choosing Our Religion: The Spiritual Lives of America's Nones* (Oxford: Oxford University Press, 2016), 122.2016 Drescher draws on the work of sociologist Abby Day in her discussion of "believing in belonging."

[51]   Drescher, 123.

[52]   Drescher, 123.

[53]   Crenshaw, *Joel*, 47. Similarities between Joel and the Cult of Baal includes references to spears, honey flowing in streams, locusts, mourning like virgins, rain-making rituals, mourning rites, oracles of salvation in a vegetative cult, and more.

temple to visit, for it has been destroyed. With the temple destroyed, this was possibly heard with some confusion.[54] One cannot but wonder about the correlation with a millennial people—for whom there is no church and who gather in spinning classes, around tables, on yoga mats and elsewhere—and the narrative of Joel. Still, Joel reminds his people that they can pray to God and engage in religious practices despite God not having a house to live in (for it has been destroyed). Commentator Elie Assis sees Joel motivated in his command to gather "as one of strengthening the people's identity following their deep despair after the destruction of the temple." For a people who had no temple to go to, Joel's message of assembling, fasting, and praying—spiritual practices of his day—awakened hope. It gave purpose and structure to their lives as they stared at devastated lands. The absence of the temple did not sever the people's relationship with God, for it is God's covenant with God's people that keeps their relationship with God alive. This relationship is not mediated by the temple.

In this second act, Joel addresses the priests. "The priesthood in Joel," commentator Christopher Seitz writes, "is without personal name or future specification, which may serve to make the text available for future generations."[55] Joel's priests are to dress, lament, spend the night, and gather. Joel, as stated, does not join the other minor prophets, who are very critical of the priests as the ones who led the people of God astray. The "ministers of the altar," "servants of my God," and "the elders" show a progression but speak of one group of people, the priests. It is the priests, with their funeral clothing, who model mourning.

As leaders among the millennial generation gather their peers to reflect and go on spiritual journeys through ritual and even song, one can rightly ask: Who are the priests for the millennial generation?

Joel, Act Three: (Re)Discover the Compassionate, Restorative God

The prophets, Hebrew Bible scholar Abraham Joshua Heschel reminds us, acted from and communicated God's *pathos*—God's endearing love for humanity. "The central message of the prophets is the insistence that *the human situation can be understood only in conjunction with the divine situation* [emphasis added]," Heschel writes. "The pathos and judgment of God transcend the human dimension."[56] A basic feature

---

[54] Troxel, Joel, 44
[55] Seitz, *Joel*, 135.
[56] Abraham Joshua Heschel, *The Prophets*, 1st Perennial classics ed. (New York: HarperPerennial, 2001), 242.

of God's pathos is "divine attentiveness and concern," with perception and apprehension driving God's involvement with humanity and all of creation.[57] Acting with pathos God is never neutral when engaging us.

Our text, in the pathos-tradition that Heschel identifies for us, continues:

> Yet even now, says the Lord, return to me with all your hearts, with fasting, with weeping, and with sorrow; tear your hearts and not your clothing. Return to the LORD your God, for he is merciful and compassionate, very patient, full of faithful love, and ready to forgive. ... *I will repay you for the years that the cutting locust, the swarming locust, the hopping locust, and the devouring locust have eaten ... my great army, which I sent against you.* You will eat abundantly and be satisfied, and you will praise the name of the LORD your God, who has done wonders for you; and my people will never again be put to shame [emphasis added]. (2:13, 25-26)

By following a demand ("tear") with a metaphor ("hearts and not your clothing"), Joel both draws upon but also diverts from a Genesis 37:18-30 (Reuben tearing his cloak anticipating Joseph's death; parallel text). Such use and deviation of older texts are Joel's signature style.[58] The call to return to God should not be heard as repenting but rather as sadness, mourning and lamenting, and a willingness to hear God's voice.[59] "Not the slightest casuistry and moral criticism can be felt" as Judah's sin is not important to Joel.[60] The people are restored, not forgiven. Here, Joel distinguishes himself from the other prophets. By placing the call to return to God in the context of the pending Day of the Lord, God is thrust into the narrative. The reality of the Day of the Lord, Joel believes, can be averted as Israel experienced at Mount Sinai. Here, "God who is compassionate and merciful, very patient, full of great loyalty and faithfulness, showing great loyalty to a thousand generations ..." appeared to Israel (Exodus 34:6-7).

The "mercy formula" is arguably one of the most evocative and generative texts of the Bible.[61] Biblical scholar Phyllis Trible shows us

---

57 Heschel, 618.

58 Hyman, "The Prophecy of Joel," 228.

59 Barton, *Joel and Obadiah*, 77.

60 Hans Walter Wolff and S. Dean McBride, Joel and Amos: A Commentary on the Books of the Prophets Joel and Amos, Hermeneia: A Critical and Historical Commentary on the Bible (Philadelphia: Fortress Press, 1977), 52.

61 Nathan C. Lane, The Compassionate, but Punishing God: A Canonical Analysis of Exodus 34:6-7 (Eugene: Pickwick Publications, 2010), 1

that feminine traits describe God. The word translated as "compassion" is "womb" in the Hebrew text (adjective *rahum,* compassion; *rehem,* womb; plural *rahmim,* wombs or compassion).[62] God is womb-ish, and, as the Creator God, not only loves with the intensity of a mother for her child but also selflessly participates in life! In Scripture, *rahum*-language is used only pertaining to God, never people.[63] "In many and various ways," Trible writes, "the maternal metaphor of *rahum* witnesses to God as compassionate, merciful, loving."[64] God, beholden to no one, grants mercy, a fact Jonah found especially aggravating. God is not only slow to anger but also offers continual restoration and removal of shame (Hebrew: *yēbōšū*).

This essay argues that millennials touched by the locusts of life long for the compassionate God Joel offers. They have no difficulty imagining the restoration God promises.

Joel, Act Four: Receive the Spirit

Millennials often find spiritual meaning in ways that perplex older generations. Ask a millennial about their sleeve of tattoos and you are likely to hear that the ink has significant personal and spiritual meaning, often tied to transformative relationships or moments. Spirituality anticipates experiencing transcendence, searching for and finding the sacred in the ordinary, and communicating deeply personal values, purposes, and meanings. Experiences, possessions, spaces, places, and relationships witness to something bigger and beyond us.

Sociologist of religion Nancy Ammerman, in exploring the spiritual lives of ordinary Americans, found that for many, everyday activities, rituals, and practices perceived as secular were fused with a sense of spirituality.[65] Her research shows that the typical distinction between "religious" (as the organized, institutional, public, and that which focuses on theological beliefs and traditions) and "spiritual" or "spiritual but not religious" (as the personal, individual, private, and experiential) does not reflect most people's experience.[66] Persons who are religious are also spiritual, and persons who are spiritual are

---

[62] Phyllis Trible, God and the Rhetoric of Sexuality, Overtures to Biblical Theology (Philadelphia: Fortress Press, 1978), 35.

[63] Trible, 38.

[64] Trible, 39.

[65] Nancy T. Ammerman, Sacred Stories, Spiritual Tribes: Finding Religion in Everyday Life (Oxford: Oxford University Press, 2014)

[66] Ammerman, 24.

also religious, even if they never attend church. "The one thing almost everyone agrees on is that real spirituality is about living a virtuous life, one characterized by helping others, transcending one's own selfish interests to seek what is right."[67] Ammerman's subjects fault religion for not practicing what it is preaching.

Spiritual meaning and experiencing transcendence can be found and experienced in many ways. In her research, Elizabeth Drescher found that many of her interviewees had a special corner or table in their apartment or house with objects that had significance for them; others had special places they returned to often for spiritual nurture.[68] Many of the sacred objects were gifts received from persons of importance: a parent, a grandparent, a favorite uncle or aunt, a friend. Other objects were acquired during a vacation or while traveling. For Drescher, the objects and practices are "the raw material for stories of the self that narrate what a person understands as her or his own identity, including spiritual or religious identity."[69]

In Joel's fourth act, a shift is about to occur. Whereas the previous verses were mostly preoccupied with agriculture and the land and its people, the second half of Joel is personal and sociopolitical; it is concerned with individuals, society, social justice, accountability, and the political salvation of Judah. Agricultural renewal opens the possibility for political and societal renewal. God is interested in holistic transformation and renewal, and the promised restoration is seemingly incomplete. Lacking God's essence, the spirit enters the narrative:

> [After I restored you and abundance reigns again,] I will pour out my spirit upon everyone; your sons and your daughters will prophesy, your old men will dream dreams, and your young men will see visions. In those days, I will also pour out my spirit on the male and female slaves. (2:28-29)

The outpouring of God's Spirit was an established tradition in Israel (Hebrew: 'ešpôk 'et-rûḥî', to pour out; rûaḥ, wind, vital life force; see Genesis 2:7; Numbers 11:29; Isaiah 31:15; and Ezekiel 39:29). God's vital life source revitalizes and restores, even a heap of dry bones (Ezekiel 37). Persons come alive!

Our text suggests that what is poured out is precious. Elsewhere in Scripture, shapak is used for the spilling of water, blood, and even

---

67 Ammerman, 45.
68 Drescher, *Choosing Our Religion*, 152.
69 Drescher, 8.

emotion (Psalm 62:9; 79:10). This form of outpouring-as-blessing—or anointing—which includes "everyone" or "all flesh" (Hebrew: kola bāśār) was alien to the world of Joel and is also alien to ours.[70] Cultures of shame such as ours do not do blessing well. God upsets human-made hierarchies by gifting the powerless and hopeless with God's vital life force. Privileges and dichotomies based on gender bias ("sons and daughters"), ageism ("old men ... and your young men"), and class ("the male and female slaves") are obliterated. God's vision for reality was radical then as it is radical now. Joel democratizes prophecy.[71] In case we have any doubts, Hebrew scholar Ronald Troxel writes that "all flesh may mean all mankind, and we should interpret it thus."[72] Having God's life force "actually means the divine inspiration which leads one to an enlightened and uplifted state .... One is reminded of the Latin saying, Vox populi vox Dei ...."[73] That God's redemptive actions flow to all people—and not just some—easily offends.

Reading Joel, one can wonder whether today's church leaders are equipped to catch the visions young adults bring. Vision casters— as some leaders aspire to be—are poor vision catchers!

Joel, Act Five: Be Accountable, Says the Just God

Around the world two groups of people are being formed, often around social, political and environmental concerns. They are the Yimbys —an acronym for YES IN MY BACKYARD—and the Nimbys—NOT IN MY BACKYARD. The latter is "a pejorative characterization of opposition by residents to a proposal for a new development because it is close to them (or, in some cases, because the development involves controversial or potentially dangerous technology) often with the connotation that such residents believe that the developments are needed in society but should be further away."[74] Nimbys band together around a number of issues: affordable housing, homeless shelters, bike lanes, rapid transport, chemical plants, airports, wind turbines, landfill sites, prisons, nuclear waste sites, and even recreational cannabis shops. When a woman com-

---

[70] Steven E. Runge, "Joel 2:28-32a in Acts 2:17-21: The Discourse and Text-Critical Implications of Variation from the LXX," in *The Library of New Testament Studies: Early Christian Literature and Intertextuality*, ed. Chris Keith (London: Bloomsbury, 2009).ed. Chris Keith (Bloomsbury, 2009).

[71] Troxel, *Joel*, 82.

[72] Troxel, 80. Troxel quoting commentator Julius A. Bewer.

[73] Schreiber, "I Will Pour out My Spirit on All Flesh (Joel 3:1)," 128.

[74] Wikipedia, s.v. "Nimby," accessed December 19, 2017, https://en.wikipedia.org/wiki/NIMBY.

plained at a City of Berkeley Council meeting that her zucchini garden will receive no sun should a planned housing development be approved, she heard an indignant Victoria Fierce, a millennial, say, "You're talking about zucchinis? Really? Because I'm struggling to pay rent."[75] Rather than retreating and suffering in silence, millennials are rallying and increasingly hold city and national leaders accountable.

Drescher's research supports Ammerman's indication that millennials fault Christianity—and especially religious leaders—for "hypocrisy, greed, judgmentalism, sexual abuse, sexism, homophobia, [and] anti-scientific ignorance."[76] Millennials are not as concerned with inner sin—an emphasis of tradition—as they are with outward sins, an awareness the church often lacks. Hebrew Bible scholar Aaron Schart names this tendency when he writes, "A Christian understanding of sin often has a tendency to be understood as something restricted to the individual and to one's inner life before God. ... Foreign policy, juridical matters, economic exchange and social behavior are fields where God wants God's people to act according to [their] covenant relationship with God."[77]

Seeking justice reflects the Day of the Lord. Commentator Mordecai Schreiber finds a connection between us and this day, where

> social protests that have begun to effect profound changes in certain countries and which will probably have their impact on the rest of the world. This, indeed, may be the ultimate meaning of "the Day of Adonai," a time when the divine spirit is awakened among people, inducing them to take action and thus "perfect the world through the sovereignty of God" (le-takken olam be-malkhut Shaddai).[78]

Traditionally seen as a day of *judgment* and vengeance by a righteous God, we see the day as a day of *accountability*, opening new possibilities for engaging Joel. God's afterthought, in which God promises the outpouring of the Spirit (Joel 2:28), continues:

> Truly, in those days and in that time, I will bring back to Judah and Jerusalem those who were sent away. I will gather all the

---

75   "Rise of the Yimbys," *The Guardian*, October 2, 2017, https://www.theguardian.com/cities/2017/oct/02/rise-of-the-yimbys-angry-millennials-radical-housing-solution.
76   Drescher, *Choosing Our Religion*, 45.
77   Schart, "The First Section of the Book of the Twelve Prophets," 150.
78   Schreiber, "I Will Pour out My Spirit on All Flesh (Joel 3:1)," 128.

nations, and I will bring them to the Jehoshaphat Valley. There I will enter into judgment with them in support of my people and my possession, Israel, which they have scattered among the nations. (3:1)

In the book of Joel, the Day of the Lord (Hebrew: *yôm YHWH*)—a day of God's political and social restoration of Judah and judgment over nations—features prominently.[79] It appears 19 times in the Old Testament and four times in the New Testament.[80] The day's meaning is contested. Historically, the Day of the Lord was an invitation to live responsibly and with accountability in the present. It was not seen as a future event, as many today interpret the day.[81] After God promised agricultural restoration, which also restored the families and communities in Judah, God continues and promises political restoration in Judah's relationship with its neighbors. The shame the people of Judah (Hebrew: *'ammî*, my people) experienced was not just tied to their lack of food and therefore not being able to give food to their children and to God in worship. Shame burdened them as a people in exile.

As the nations (Hebrew: *gôyîm*) gather, the people of God need not fear this day, for "everyone who calls on the LORD's name will be saved; for on Mount Zion and in Jerusalem there will be security...." (Joel 2:32). Referencing "Jehoshaphat," meaning "YHWH judges," implies that Joel did not have a specific place in mind.[82] Rather, it is a symbolic place. In laying a claim against the people, God confirms, "Hurt my people and you are hurting me."[83]

The Phoenicians and Philistines, Israel's long-standing enemies, are implicated. The charges are fourfold: the scattering of Judah and breaking up of families, taking possession of the land, enslaving the people, and stealing the silver and gold sacred objects that belonged to

---

[79]   References for the Day of the Lord: Isaiah 13:6; Ezekiel 13:5; Amos 5:18; Obadiah 15–17; Zephaniah 1:7, 14–16. See: Crenshaw, *Joel*, 48.

[80]   The New Testament passages are: Acts 2:20; 1 Thessalonians 5:2; 2 Thessalonians 2:2; and 2 Peter 3:10). See also indirect references to the Day of the Lord in 2 Peter 3:10; 1 Thessalonians 1:10; 1 Corinthians 1:8; 5:5; 2 Corinthians 1:14; 2; 2 Timothy 1:12; Matthew 25:13.

[81]   Troxel, *Joel*, 87.

[82]   Leslie C. Allen, *The Books of Joel, Obadiah, Jonah, and Micah, The New International Commentary on the Old Testament* (Grand Rapids: Eerdmans, 1976), 109; Assis, *The Book of Joel: A Prophet between Calamity and Hope*, 216.

[83]   Allen, 109.

God's temple (Hebrew: *hêkēlêkem*).[84] With poetic justice, "the sea-loving Phoenicians and Philistines will be sold by Judahites to desert dwellers (Sabeans)."[85] As God enters into judgment, visions of a holy war (Hebrew: *qaddēšû*) arise. "The nations [are] presented as warmongers who prefer military violence over the agricultural labor with which they were occupied."[86] Beating plows into swords and relying on military power will be futile.[87] The experience Judah had with the devouring locusts, Joel warns, pales in comparison to God's judgment.

Joel's call to accountability resists the anonymity and lack of community so common in our world. God is clear that choices and actions, even of omission, have consequences and will be judged.

Joel, Act Six: Be Blessed and Be a Blessing

We have been looking at the book of Joel as a narrative or opera that has six spiraling acts. We have reached the final, open-ended act. Whereas we began with scenes of despair, we end with hope. Again, we discover a significant correlation between the book of Joel and the lives of millennials.

The *2017 Millennial Impact Report*—a report researching millennial cause engagement—is a hopeful read.[88] The current report, surveying 3,000 millennials, found that "millennials [are] quietly redefining terms long accepted in the cause and philanthropy space: Activist. Cause. Social issue. Ideology."[89] The researchers were interested in the social issues attracting millennials, measuring their level of engagement and looking at the traits of millennial social involvement. We learn that the majority of millennials are seeking to serve the greater good, a fact also

---

84   Douglas Watson, "Divine Attributes in the Book of Joel," Journal for the Study of the Old Testament 37 (2012): 125.

85   Paul R. Raabe, "The Particularizing of Universal Judgment in Prophetic Discourse," *The Catholic Biblical Quaterly* 64 (2002): 665.

86   Assis, The Book of Joel: A Prophet between Calamity and Hope, 228.

87   Will Kynes, "Beat Your Parodies into Swords, and Your Parodied Books into Spears: A New Paradigm for Parody in the Hebrew Bible," Biblical Interpretation 19 (2011): 307.

88   The report is sponsored by The Case Foundation, a non-profit supporting and researching change-makers (https://casefoundation.org/), and conducted by Achieve, a research firm (http://www.achieveagency.com/). The report, released in three phases, can be downloaded from its own website: http://www.themillennialimpact.com/; accessed December 24, 2017.

89   The Millennial Impact Project, "The Millennial Impact Report—Phase 1: Millennial Dialogue on the Landscape of Cause Engagement and Social Issues" (2017), accessed December 24, 2017, http://www.themillennialimpact.com, ii.

attributed to the divisive 2016 presidential election in the United States. Millennials have been motivated and galvanized by many social issues, which they address with concrete behavior. The researchers found that millennials care especially about the following social issues: racial discrimination, civil rights, and social justice; employment, poverty, and homelessness; education and literacy; children (mentoring and early education); higher education (access to and payment for); women's health and reproductive issues; healthcare reform; environmental issues; mental health and social services; criminal justice reform; and immigration.[90] The report maintains that the interviewees "wanted to give all people—but especially marginalized or disenfranchised individuals or groups—early interventions and opportunities that would ensure increased prosperity later in life."[91]

Whereas Joel begins with despair, it ends with hope as it draws on a pervasive image in Scripture: of water that flows from the temple as God's throne or house to nurture parch lands and lives.[92] Joel concludes his narrative by revisiting this striking image:

> In that day the mountains will drip sweet wine, the hills will flow with milk, and all the streambeds of Judah will flow with water; a spring will come forth from the LORD's house and water the Shittim Valley. (3:18)

The land will erupt in abundance and fertility as water reaches desert soil.[93] Joel echoes the ending of Amos: "The mountains will drip wine, and all the hills will flow with it" (9:13). He refers to food to metaphorically show the richness of God's continual renewal.[94] Upon hearing God speak through Joel, Judah, no doubt, would recall the promised land and the milk and honey discovered there.[95] Commentator Elie Assis writes that "the closing describes a new, rectified situation, completely different from what it has been."[96] In a reversal of fortunes,

---

[90]   The Millennial Impact Project, "The Millennial Impact Report—Phase 2: The Power of Voice: A New Era of Cause Activation & Social Issue Adoption" (2017), accessed December 24, 2017, http://www.themillennialimpact.com/, 13.

[91]   Project, The Millennial Impact Report—Phase 1: Millennial Dialogue on the Landscape of Cause Engagement and Social Issues., 8.

[92]   See Genesis 2:10; Psalm 36; Zechariah 14:8; Ezekiel 47:9-12; and Revelation 21:1-2.

[93]   Barton, *Joel and Obadiah*, 108–9.

[94]   Seitz, *Joel*, 219.

[95]   For references to "milk and honey," see: Exodus 3:8; Leviticus 20:24; Numbers 13:27; Deuteronomy 6:3; and Joshua 5:6.

[96]   Assis, The Book of Joel, 254.

Judah and its wine drinkers, who knew desolation and shortage after the locusts, now experience abundance. Judah's enemies, Egypt and Edom, once renowned for their might, are now desolate.

As we follow the water from God's house, we enter the Valley of Shittim (or the Valley of Acacias). The Valley has an ambivalent history for Israel. Here they had illicit sex with Moabite women and worshiped Baal of Peor (Numbers 25:1-3). It was also from the Valley of Shittim that Joshua sent his spies to explore the potential of Jericho and the promised land (Joshua 2:1). Joel's Wadi Shittim, however, is not easily identified and may not be the one Israel frequented on their sojourning.[97] Rather, Joel sees a barren valley and envisions it a place of promise.

A pastoral reading of our text is both challenging and hopeful. Simply put, as we seek to live into the narrative of Joel, we are called to "flow" to our neighbors, to our communities and cities, to all of creation, in mercy and compassion, with patience and love, always ready to forgive. Many millennials are already doing this when faith communities dam themselves up or become flash floods. As we participate in the world's personal, social, political, and ecological renewal, we need not fear, for our choices and actions will be kept in mind on the Day of Accountability. It is not easy work, but Joel reminds us that the people of God will not be shamed. Having tasted the abundance of God, we have plenty to share. God's economy is not a closed economy such that if we share God's abundance with others we'd have less to ourselves. The blessing of water will never stop flowing. And thus ends the narrative of Joel—with blessing. The locusts do not have the last word.

Conclusion

The book of Joel brings promise to a world that has come of age, described by theologian Dietrich Bonhoeffer in 1944 as a "religionless" time.[98] This world may not have ears to hear the good news: that you are a sinner in need of salvation; Jesus is the Savior. Joel's narrative invites one into a narrative that is life-giving, a narrative that resonates especially deeply, but not exclusively, with the lived experience of the millennial generation. This then, is Joel's narrative:

> There was a person who knew the locusts of life. The locusts caused devastation, loss, and trauma. They mourned the losses

---

[97] Crenshaw, *Joel*, 200.

[98] Dietrich Bonhoeffer, *Letters and Papers from Prison*, 1st American [enlarged] ed. (New York: Macmillan, 1972), 279.[1st American] enl. ed. (New York: Macmillan, 1972).

and sought healing for the traumas by building life-giving communities and nurturing their spirituality. They discovered the compassionate God who promises restoration and pours the Spirit over all. They embraced accountability, knowing that decisions made and actions taken have consequences. They participated in God's restorative work toward a just society and a sustainable earth. The person lived the Good Life.

By inviting a generation to discover this neglected narrative in Scripture, the Hebrew Scriptures may come alive to a new generation seeking the Good Life. Furthermore, it can assist the church and her leadership to relation to millions of people. The result may very well be that the church is restored, too, for the water that flows from God's temple will flow through a church into a neighborhood.

CHAPTER 11

There is Blood in the Vineyard(s): A Liberationist Reading of 1 Kings 21 and Joshua 10–12

Zac Poppen

Throughout the history of Israel, the concept of land has always been a leading character in its story. But this concept of land has been locked in a seemingly endless state of conflict. Beginning with the exodus from Egypt, through the wandering in the desert following a divine promise, to the narratively violent entry into Canaan and the subsequent battles and struggles with the reigning world powers of Assyria and Babylon, the land of Palestine-Israel is a site of both ethical and political volatility for those in the past and the present. One major source of this volatility stems from the interpretation of Old Testament/ Hebrew Bible texts regarding who is allowed to exist in the land. The socio-politico-economic dimensions of these texts are in desperate need of attention, especially considering the treatment of Palestinians with regard to land and water rights.[1] My own concern for the well-being of life—for the land itself and those in the land—is indebted to Dr. Tom Boogaart. The questions of his life and work[2]—namely, a call to carefully

---

[1]   For this essay, I will be primarily considering the work and writing of Naim Stifan Ateek and Mitri Raheb, both of whom are Palestinian Christians.

[2]   Much of this essay was inspired by Boogaart's piece titled "Eve's Two Sons" in *Performing the Plays of the Bible* (forthcoming). His section on the implications of a

consider what it means to be a steward of the Earth—have pushed me to construct a liberationist reading of both Naboth's vineyard and the destruction of Canaanite cities and people through the eyes and experiences of Palestinian/indigenous[3] folks. Building upon Gustavo Gutierrez's iconic phrase of a "preferential option for the poor," I will cultivate a method of reading that foregrounds a preferential option for the dispossessed to interpret the accounts of forced depopulation of land in the Old Testament/Hebrew Bible. This critique of both the epistemic and material violence against vulnerable neighbors found in the biblical texts will present a reading of liberationist solidarity with those who are presently suffering in Palestine.

To construct a reading centered on what I will call a preferential option for the dispossessed, I will need to take you, the reader, on a walk through several different sections. The first section is that of liberation theology, particularly the main branches produced by Latin American priest-scholars Gustavo Gutierrez and Leonardo Boff. These thinker-activists, while providing an overview of the important tenets of Latin American theologies of liberation, also constitute important interlocutors as I interpret the troubling texts of 1 Kings 21 and Joshua 10–12. The second section we will walk through is a brief theoretical workshop to link how I understand a preferential option for the dispossessed with Gutierrez's preferential option for the poor. More importantly, I hope to show how poverty and dispossession of land and depopulation are connected in this section. In the third section, I will carefully read through both 1 Kings 21 and Joshua 10–12 through the lens of Palestinian/indigenous experiences. The fourth and final section synthesizes the previous sections in attempt to promote justice-for-each.[4]

---

blood economy versus a consumerist economy, in which he argues that a blood economy, while seemingly brutal, values life whereas the consumerist economy values money over human life, has compelled me to study how the interpretation of biblical texts have affected the ways in which people groups have been dehumanized.

[3]   I use the slash here to indicate the lack of boundary between two terms—Palestinian and indigenous—as some folk in the Levant might identify as both. I also use this term throughout this essay since I draw not only from indigenous folks from Palestine but also from First Nations contexts in North America (e.g., Robert Allen Warrior).

[4]   This is a phrase I modified from the oft-used "justice for all" and figures prominently in my conceptualization of liberation. "All," as a category, is too monolithic to be of use in issues of justice, where each individual situation or case must be evaluated. "Justice for all" reproduces what Albert Memmi calls "the mark of the plural"—a tool of colonial oppression that reductively freezes the identity of a group of people,

Some Reflections from Latin American Theologies of Liberation

As Leonardo and Clodovis Boff say in *Introducing Liberation Theology*, it is vitally important to understand that liberation theology is not "a theological movement but a theology in movement."[5] While much could be said about the history of liberation theology, its connection to Marxism, and several other aspects, these are far beyond the scope of this essay.[6] For the purposes of my study here, I will discuss two major ideas from liberation theology: the conceptualization of compassion ("suffering-with") and the marks of a theological-liberative hermeneutic.

The idea of compassion, with its basic Latin components meaning "suffering-with," is the point of entry for the project of liberation theology.[7] This suffering, then, constitutes the basis of a liberationist reading. It is the "minimum of 'suffering with'"—the presence of suffering in the world by the "great majority of the human race"—that makes liberation theology necessary and intelligible.[8] As the Boffs put it, "Underlying liberation theology is a prophetic and comradely commitment to the life, cause, and struggle of these millions of debased and marginalized human beings, a commitment to end this historical iniquity."[9] This ties back into a theology of movement as the lived experience, the suffering that has happened and continues to happen, not only justifies but also *requires* a liberationist reading in suffering-solidarity with the poor.

Perhaps the most critical characteristic of liberation theology is that its hermeneutics are oriented toward application. Liberation theology constructs its hermeneutics to "favor application rather than explanation" in contrast to other modern modes of reading that prefer "a rationalistic exegesis concerned with dragging out the meaning-in-itself."[10] This practicality of application includes reading biblical

---

which signals the depersonalization of the colonized. While well intentioned, "justice for all" misses the important nuance that "justice-for-each" disruptively captures.

5   Leonardo Boff and Clodovis Boff, *Introducing Liberation Theology* (Maryknoll: Orbis Books, 1987), 83.

6   For a concise overview of the history of liberation theology, see L. Boff and C. Boff, *Introducing Liberation Theology*, 66–75; for liberation theology's connection to Marxism, see *Introducing Liberation Theology*, 27.

7   Boff and Boff, *Introducing Liberation Theology*, 2.

8   Boff and Boff, 3.

9   Boff and Boff, 3.

10   Boff and Boff, 33–34.

texts as "book[s] of life" in that, while the textual meaning is certainly important, the textual is subordinated under the practical meaning.[11] The goal of this praxis-oriented hermeneutic is to find what the Boffs describe as "contemporary actualization for the textual meaning."[12] This is precisely the aim of the study at hand: to read the biblical texts to suffer-with those in the text while searching the text to discover a contemporary actualization of the violence regarding the land in the Palestine-Israel context.

The idea of action also plays a central role in Gutierrez's formulation of liberation theology. He writes that "faith is a commitment to God and human beings," meaning that faith is more than a mere affirmation of God but a "loving response" to a God who loves us.[13] This commitment finds its activity in the present ("I commit myself here and now") as it navigates not only an "existential stance" but also the progressive nature of theology.[14] By defining theology as a "continuous and progressive understanding," Gutierrez insists that theology is always specifically located for a specific reason: "If theology is the understanding of an existential stance, it is progressive, it is the understanding of a commitment in history concerning the Christian's location in the development of humanity and the living out of faith."[15]

Perhaps most importantly, theology is secondary—a reflection that occurs after action. This is Gutierrez's riff on the ancient philosophical maxim: *primum vivere, deinde philosophare*.[16] He stresses that it is the commitment—not theology—that must be first; theology is a turning-back-to-reflect the embodied existential understanding of that commitment made to both God and humans.[17] He concludes this line of thinking by stating:

> If faith is a commitment to God and human beings, it is not possible to live in today's world without a commitment to the process of liberation. That is what constitutes a commitment today. If participation in the process of human liberation is

---

[11]   Boff and Boff, 33–34.
[12]   Boff and Boff, 33–34.
[13]   Gustavo Gutierrez, *Gustavo Gutierrez: Essential Writings* (Maryknoll: Orbis Books, 1996), 24. He adds here that this commitment is fully expressed in the command to love the neighbor.
[14]   Gutierrez, 24.
[15]   Gutierrez, 24.
[16]   Gutierrez, *Essential Writings*, 25. "First you must live, and then philosophize."
[17]   Gutierrez, 25.

the way of being present in the world, it will be necessary for Christians to have an understanding of this commitment, of this process of liberation.[18]

In other words, faith calls Christians to be present in the struggle for liberation.

Gutierrez's famous statement—that God shows "a preferential option for the poor" (and therefore so should Christians)—also deserves some attention. While he writes at length about the various pieces of the phrase (preference, option, and poor), my focus here is on his discussion of "poor." Poverty is not limited to the economic but also includes both the social and political spheres.[19] Yet these contexts of poverty reveal a far more terrible meaning for those who are poor— "poverty means death: unjust death, the premature death of the poor, physical death."[20] This death extends beyond the physical since poverty includes cultural death as well (e.g., despising a people or repressing a people, Gutierrez writes, results in the death of those people).[21] To be poor is to be equivalent to a non-person, those who "do not count in society."[22] This marginalization is compounded by the fact that to be poor is to be a number, a statistic without a name.[23] However, even though society has willfully "othered" the poor to be non-persons without names, Gutierrez reminds us that they are not insignificant before God.[24]

A Preferential Option for the Dispossessed

Reading (i.e., interpreting) the Palestine-Israel conflict requires that I make a modification to liberation theology's preferential option for the poor. In order to sharpen the focus on the issue of the land and its connection to the life and death of those who live upon it, I suggest a transmutation of a preferential option for the poor into a preferential option for the dispossessed. I recognize that dispossession certainly fits within the framework of Gutierrez's interpretation of poverty in the

---

[18]   Gutierrez, 25.
[19]   Gutierrez, *Essential Writings*, 144.
[20]   Gutierrez, 144.
[21]   Gutierrez, 144–45.
[22]   Gutierrez, 144.
[23]   Gutierrez, *Essential Writings*, 145. Gutierrez poignantly describes the epistemic plight of the poor: "We do not know the names of the poor; they are anonymous and remain so."
[24]   Gutierrez, 145.

original phrase, but this modification emphasizes some significant distinctions. Because the conflict involves the land, "dispossession" crystalizes the struggle that Palestinians face (even if their struggle is more broadly contextualized as one of poverty). A second emphasis is that the passive construction of "dispossessed" identifies Palestinians as the unwilling recipients of the actions carried out by the State of Israel. A third yet equally important emphasis of "dispossessed" is that it implicitly forces the conversation to deal with the issue of depopulation. If groups of people are being dispossessed of land by military force, then we must talk about the injustice, terror, and danger that depopulation brings to folks who depend on the land to survive. This last emphasis also demonstrates how a liberationist perspective recognizes the linked nature of social injustice and ecological injustice, meaning that anything that disrupts the balance of well-being between animals, plants, the atmosphere, the water, the land, and human beings poses a planetary threat to all.[25]

A Critical Liberationist Reading of 1 Kings 21 and Joshua 10–12

If liberation theology's preferential option for the poor is rooted in the politics of what might be called neighbor-love (i.e., solidarity, commitment, action), the narrative of 1 Kings 21 is a text concerning the necropolitics[26] of neighbor-death. Naboth's vineyard is located next to the palace of King Ahab of Samaria, catching the eye of the ruler. Despite Ahab's offer of silver, Naboth refuses to relinquish his land. His refusal is grounded in ancestral inheritance: "LORD forbid that I give you my family inheritance." Walter Brueggemann highlights the competing views of land in this section between Naboth (traditional covenantal language)[27] and Ahab (tradable commodity), noting that "kings characteristically think everything is to be bought and sold and traded and conquered."[28] Jezebel's plan (that results in Naboth's

---

[25]   Leonardo Boff, *Ecology & Liberation: A New Paradigm* (Maryknoll: Orbis Books, 1995), 14.

[26]   Broadly speaking, necropolitics is a term coined by Achille Mbembe (*On the Postcolony*, 2001) that describes the use of social and/or political power to determine whether someone lives or dies. The term is often used alongside the concept of "biopower," which was developed by French historian and philosopher Michel Foucault (it features prominently in his lecture *Security, Territory, Population*, 1978).

[27]   What is so critical about Naboth's use of covenantal language is that inheritance is understood as a "dimension of family history." (Walter Brueggemann, *The Land* [Philadelphia: Fortress Press, 1977], 93.)

[28]   Walter Brueggemann, *The Land* (Philadelphia: Fortress, Press, 1977), 93.

death by stoning) reflects what Brueggemann describes as "an alien view of Torah which makes the king immune from its demands." These demands are clearly articulated throughout the Old Testament/Hebrew Bible. Theft of land is something that the writers and redactors of Deuteronomy condemned. Deuteronomy 19:14 reads: "Now in the land the LORD your God is giving you, in your allotted property that you will receive there, *you must not tamper with your neighbor's property line*, which has been *previously established*."[29] Deuteronomy 27:17 reads: "'Cursed is anyone who tampers with their neighbor's property lines.'" In the NRSV, the translation of "property lines" is made even more explicit: "boundary marker." These property lines, or boundary markers, were established when the land was allotted to each tribe after the Israelites had arrived in Canaan. The injustice of the action of Jezebel (and Ahab by proxy) is the annexation of land by force, resulting in the loss of life. Naboth's vineyard has been depopulated in order to allow Ahab to take possession. By using necropolitical power to unjustly accuse and murder Naboth, Jezebel and Ahab were guilty of committing both epistemic (Torah prohibitions regarding boundary markers) and material (the murder of Naboth) violence. God enters the narrative, angered by Ahab's greed, and sends Elijah to deliver a message (1 Kings 21:17-19). What is particularly important about the message is the grave indictment of Ahab's actions, potentially reflecting a preferential option for the dispossessed: "So you've *murdered* and are now taking ownership, are you [emphasis added]?"[30] It is abundantly clear that God has chosen Naboth's side against Ahab's attempt at a land grab. But this conclusion raises a canonical question: What about the instances in the text when God is the one commanding that the land be taken from another people?

The book of Joshua is a complicated member of the Old Testament/Hebrew Bible canon. On the one hand, the text paints a picture of a moment when the children of God were faithful and renewed their covenantal vows. On the other hand, Joshua contains some of the most disturbing accounts of genocidal warfare in the entire Bible. Even more troubling is that most of the violence, according to the text, is not only condoned but instigated by God. Through enacting the "ban" (*ḥērem*)—a total "devotion" (destruction) to God—the Canaanite cities, the people inside, and all living things in and around were annihilated.[31]

---

29   All English translations are CEB unless otherwise noted. Emphases are added.
30   1 Kings 21:19.
31   I fully recognize that the archaeological record disputes the accounts of Joshua (e.g., most conservative dating frameworks show that Jericho was destroyed long before

Despite the land being promised to the Israelites, God commands the army of Joshua to weaponize the land against the Canaanites so that there would be no trace of any foreign influence. The land itself was often weaponized against those trapped inside the city: "the attackers might attempt to ruin fields by littering them with stones and by blocking water sources. ... Trees might be cut down for siege works and equipment."[32] This form of warfare reached its zenith, however, when it weaponized the helpless civilians against the land itself by leaving their corpses to rot in the open. Whether from battle, disease, or famine, "the bodies would be torn apart and scattered by scavenging birds and animals ...."[33] This purge would then allow the Israelites to seize the land. Since I am reading for a preferential option for the dispossessed, it is necessary to analyze the effects of the ban and to survey the damage caused by a group of people commanded by God to take the land by overwhelming force.

Picking up in the middle of chapter 8, Joshua raises his weapon,[34] which is the signal for the ambush to commence, continuing to hold his weapon in place until the entire population of Ai has been slaughtered.[35] According to the text, 12,000 people died that day. Unlike the narratives that will follow, the animals ("cattle and other booty," Joshua 8:27) were not slaughtered this time. But the land itself was not so lucky. Joshua 8:28 tells us the fate of the land: "Then Joshua burned Ai. He made it a permanently deserted mound ...." The JPS translation of the same verse is even more chilling: "Then Joshua burned down Ai, and turned it into a mound of ruins for all time, a desolation to this day." The land's agency has been terminated, and its survival has been seared shut. Since the designation of a city often included the area directly around the city proper, the land in and around Ai may have been scorched badly enough to the point where the lack of vegetation would mean that severe erosion would take place over the coming years—earth being separated from earth by wind and water.

---

the Israelites would have ever stepped foot in Canaan). My concern in this essay is to sift through the narrative accounts to assess the ideological consequences—both for those in the text and for people today—of believing that God's command was to kill and to take.

[32] Jeffrey R. Zorn, "War and Its Effects on Civilians in Ancient Israel and Its Neighbors," in *The Other Face of the Battle*, eds. Davide Nadali and Jordi Vidal (Münster: Ugarit-Verlag, 2014), 82; Jeremiah 6:6. Eph'al 2009, 53–54.

[33] Zorn, 88; Deut 28:26; 1 Sam 17:44-46; Psalm 79:2-3; Jer 7:33; 16:4, 6; Ezekiel 29:5; 39:4, 17–20.

[34] Some translations list "dagger"; others use "javelin."

[35] Joshua 8:18-29.

Joshua 10:28-43 lists the so-called victories in the southern regions of Canaan where the text presents a rhythmic formula of the Israelite extermination of kings and cities. In each location, God gives power to Israel so that Joshua and his army can completely destroy the settlement, its people, and everything within the area. The text often reassures the reader that the annihilation is total with the repeated phrase "until there were no survivors left."[36] Though they are not mentioned here, the destruction at Ai leads the reader to assume that those sacrificed under the ban more than likely included the land and the animals. This is somewhat confirmed in a later verse in this section. In Joshua 10:40b, the text reads: "[Joshua] wiped out *everything that breathed* as something reserved for God, exactly as the LORD, the God of Israel, had commanded." The significant word in this phrase is the word for "breath" since it is the exact same term used for the "breath" of life breathed into humanity in Genesis 2:7.[37] The breath is the breath of humanity and the breath of living things. This breath that was extinguished was breath that had emerged into that spatiotemporal field—life that emerged from matter—much like the waters that were delegated the power to bring forth life in Genesis.

The land, too, is under attack in this final section of Joshua 10. Joshua 10:40a reads: "Joshua *struck* at the whole land: the highlands, the arid southern plains, the lowlands, the slopes, and all their kings. He left no survivors." Though the antecedent of "survivors" is likely referencing "kings," there is no reason it cannot also reference the land-masses listed. The ban—this religiously devoted act to God—sacrifices humans, animals, and entire lands to the deity. The agency of the land is canceled, foreshadowing its relegation to a long cycle of occupation and destruction at the hands of other imperial powers for the rest of ancient Israel's time in the Levant.

While most animals were either completely destroyed (e.g., when "everything that breathed" was put under the ban) or were taken as plunder (e.g., in the cases of Ai and the cities surrounding Hazor in Joshua 12), there is one account where Joshua and the Israelites directly attack an animal. In Joshua 11:6, God speaks to Joshua saying, "Don't be afraid of them. By this time tomorrow, I will make them all dead bodies in Israel's presence. *Cripple their horses! Burn their chariots!*" Joshua, then, fulfills this command against the king of Hazor and

---

[36] Joshua 10:33.
[37] Hebrew: *nisˇmat.*

his allies in Joshua 11:8-9: "they struck them down until no survivors were left. Joshua dealt with them exactly as the LORD had told him. He *crippled their horses* and burned their chariots." The verb for "cripple" is *ahqehr*,[38] meaning approximately "uproot" or "hamstring."[39] These translations do not illustrate the brutality of violence done to these living beings. When used in the context of horses or bulls, *ahqehr* is the act of severing the pasterns (the space between the hoof and the fetlock). Modern veterinary procedures identify pastern lacerations as medical emergencies that, if left untreated, could render the horse "chronically lame" or even "require euthanasia."[40] By severing the pasterns of the horses, not only did Joshua ensure that these horses could never stand again—they were consigned to death. It is important to note at this painful juncture that throughout Joshua 8–12, every single act of destruction of the ban was done "without mercy," 11 times in total.[41] The destruction of the people—those fighting and those civilians—was done without mercy. Setting fire to the land of the cities, leaving corpses to rot and spread disease, severing the pasterns on horses, butchering the living beings that provided milk and worked alongside humans—all sacrificed under the ban and without mercy. Though not human, the land and animals are part of those dispossessed by invading violence. The creation accounts of Genesis speak about the particular spaces available for the flourishing of life in all its forms. The violence in Canaan, however, is a stark reminder that death-dealing power removes any form of life from where it has taken root.

Up until this point, I have been reading through the eyes of a Latin American theology of liberation as a basis for a preferential option for the dispossessed, but in order to address the concerns in 1 Kings 21 and the slaughter of the Canaanites in Joshua 10–12, I will transition to an integrated discussion of Naim Stifan Ateek and Mitri Raheb's articulation of a Palestinian theology of liberation. Ateek locates the genesis of such a theology in two moments: in 1948 (the Nakba: "catastrophe") and in 1967 (The War of 1967). Much like the Israelites entering Canaan in Joshua, the Zionist militias of 1948 drove out "approximately 750,000 Palestinians" by means of fear and force.[42] A

---

38   Hebrew: *'qr*.
39   s.v., "*'qr*" in the Hebrew Aramaic Lexicon of the Old Testament.
40   South Dakota State University, "Pastern Lacerations," accessed December 2018, http://igrow.org/livestock/horse/pastern-lacerations/.
41   Josh 8:24; 10:28, 30, 32, 35, 37, 39; 11:11-12, 14, 20.
42   Naim Stifan Ateek, *A Palestinian Theology of Liberation: The Bible, Justice, and the Palestine-Israel Conflict* (Maryknoll: Orbis Book, 2017), 25.

total of 418 Palestinian villages were destroyed so that the areas marked for Jewish settlement were "clean of Arabs."[43] In 1967, the State of Israel occupied the West Bank, the Gaza Strip, and many other locations.[44] By the mid-1970s, as the Israeli government moved from a secular body to a far more religiously-oriented state that put a high emphasis on Torah, the State of Israel carried out a forced dispossession of Palestinian land into the control of the government while the Jewish settler movement rapidly gained traction.[45] This movement has not slowed; if anything, it has only increased in scale and violence. As of 2018, the Israeli occupation controls 85% of the water in Palestine, blocking Palestinians from accessing any water that runs under their land.[46] Yet, Ateek cites the Palestinian Christian people as the enduring source of their own liberation theology, drawing upon their experiences and their study of the biblical texts alongside current political analysis.[47]

Several Old Testament/Hebrew Bible texts continue to be weaponized against the Palestinians, both Muslim and Christian. Ateek highlights several (e.g., Numbers 33:50-53; Deuteronomy 7:1-3; 23:3-4, 6) that are used to justify the expulsion or murder of vulnerable Palestinians.[48] His repudiation of these texts, particularly the command that Moses gave to the Israelites to "utterly destroy [the Canaanites]" and to "show them no mercy" (Deuteronomy 7:1-3), is grounded in the post-exilic shift found in biblical texts that reflects a movement from isolated communities to one of more inclusivity.[49] This inclusivity can be seen in texts like Ezekiel 47:21-23, where Ezekiel is urging the returning communities of Jews and non-Jews to eschew the ancient boundary markers, evidenced by his insistence that even "the strangers" (*ha-gerim*) should be considered "citizens of Israel" and be given an inheritance of the land.[50] While the majority of the Old Testament/Hebrew Bible

---

43   Walid Khalidi, *All That Remains: The Palestinian Villages Occupied and Depopulated by Israel in 1948* (Washington, DC: Institute of Palestine Studies, 2006); Rochelle A. Davis, *Palestinian Village Histories: Geographies of the Displaces* (Palo Alto: Stanford University Press, 2011).

44   Khalidi, 34.

45   Khalidi, 35.

46   Saed Bannoura, "PCBS: 'Israel Controls More than 85% of the Land of Historical Palestine'," International Middle East Media Center, last modified May 15, 2016, https://imemc.org/article/pcbs-israel-controls-more-than-85-of-the-land-of-historical-palestine/.

47   Ateek, *A Palestinian Theology of Liberation*, 38.

48   Ateek, 49–52.

49   Ateek, 51.

50   Ateek, 60.

texts do not accept the colonialist ideology of a settler state that wishes to violently expunge people from the land for profit, the depopulation and trauma in Palestine remain constant.

When reading for a preferential option for the dispossessed in Palestine, the necessary question is "who is my neighbor?" Throughout the history of Palestine, the question of "neighbor" has been a question of the peoples who have lived there. Mitri Raheb identifies a common theme among many theological (Old Testament) writings as the "triangle of God, land, and people."[51] The problem with the third category of "people" is that Palestine has always been home to more than one people group at a time, thus further complicating the question of neighbor and compounding the implications for political and ethical engagement with the conflict that arises between neighbors. Raheb suggests that one path forward to answer this question resides with Jesus's non-political politics. While neither creating a party himself nor leading a Jewish revolt-protest to the streets of Rome, Jesus's travel and work centered the periphery. In other words, Jesus rejected the structure of the empire and focused his attention on the people living in marginalized villages and towns: "those who were possessed by demons, people who were not in control of their lives, people who had to fear for their lives, people who could not walk upright because they were under so much pressure and oppression."[52] Though I disagree here with Raheb that Jesus was non-political (since any act of rejecting the hegemony of Rome is *inherently political* in its subversion of the power of the emperor), I agree that Jesus's understanding of liberation began with supporting, healing, living among, and working in solidarity with the marginalized.[53] Reading with Palestinian eyes today, it is evident that imperial Rome's control of resources, water, and freedom of movement and so many more of its forms of oppression are mirrored in the control that the state of Israel is exacting upon Palestinian communities.

The conflict between Jesus's liberationist work on the periphery and Rome's oppressive power provides a useful lens to discuss the problem of power found in the Joshua texts I have discussed above. For Joshua and his army, the biblical account mirrors a similar program to that of Roman subjugation. For example, the natural resources of the land are used with the intent of eliminating those in the land

---

51   Mitri Raheb, *Faith in the Face of Empire: The Bible Through Palestinian Eyes* (Maryknoll: Orbis Books, 2014), 70.
52   Raheb, 105.
53   Raheb, 105.

(i.e., weaponizing them against the native population). In this brief sketch, God mirrors the position of the Roman emperor at the pinnacle of the hierarchy, the one who determines who lives and who dies, what is destroyed and what can be enslaved (whether people or whole landmasses). Also like the emperor, it is by God's decree that all of violence transpires in the book of Joshua; without God "giving them into [Joshua's] hand," the military campaign to seize Canaan would have never happened nor been successful. And yet this account sits within the same corpus as the account of a person who was born of a virgin, traveled to the communities marginalized by the Roman empire, performed works of miracles, healings, and teaching, and stood firmly in opposition to the imperial forces that dominated the life of Judeans in the second century B.C. This seeming contradiction brings the discussion back to the question of hermeneutics: How do we read about God who colonizes as an emperor and God who liberates and heals in the face of an empire?

To understand the complex reality of complicated texts sitting in the same tradition, it is imperative to determine the relationship that each text has to each other. Are all the texts of the Old Testament/ Hebrew Bible interrelated? Yes, to some degree. They appear together in the canon, meaning that clerical leaders, scholars, and other figures from across time have decided that they bear the mark of a genuine text that ought to be included in the tradition (whether Jewish or Christian). But do these texts necessarily agree with each other epistemologically? Unfortunately, they do not. The best description of the Old Testament/ Hebrew Bible I have ever heard comes from a former professor of mine, Dr. Carol M. Bechtel. She said that the Old Testament/Hebrew Bible is a "collection of faithful witnesses." While remaining faithful to their own experiences with God and with the people of God, these witnesses do not always agree on the character of God. Extending this definition to the New Testament, the witness of God as conquering emperor leading an army to annihilate the Canaanites does sharply contrast the witness of God in Jesus Christ who, at every turn, resisted and subverted the power of the Roman Empire. With this conceptualization of the biblical texts, I suggest that it is possible to critically read and condemn the violence found in the book of Joshua while recognizing the probable *Sitz im Leben* as a post-exilic text that attempts to grapple with the shambles of a nation that is now a vassal state to Persia. The book of Joshua does not need the assent of the reader. What is required, however, is a hermeneutic of tension that can read both a text of terror alongside a text of resistance and healing in order to better conceptualize the extent of the violence and to register the specific contexts that gave rise to that violence.

Before I offer some concluding analysis, I would like to introduce you to one more interlocutor. His name is Robert Allen Warrior, and he wrote an article titled "Canaanites, Cowboys, and Indians." In this short piece, he writes concerning the possibility of a Native American theology of liberation, and yet how that project would be co-opted by so many well-intentioned Christians, resulting in danger for Native communities because most American Christians have decided that *their* models of leadership, *their* idea of what constitutes "rescue," *their* political frameworks, and *their* solutions are what is needed after they survey the conditions of struggle for Native Americans.[54] The other problem, notes Warrior, is that most Native folks find themselves identifying with the "Indians" in the story of the promised land against the Israelite "Cowboys."[55] When we read with Canaanite eyes, the story of the exile beginning in Exodus and ending with the violent entry into Canaan in Joshua condemns the ideological positions of settlers in places like India, present-day United States, Canada, and Latin America. Warrior's continued warning throughout is that, to be involved in the struggle for liberation, one must always know the layers of (reception) history behind the story being told and to learn how to "participate in the struggle without making their story the whole story."[56]

Some Concluding Thoughts about Justice-For-Each

At the end, let us return to the beginning of this conversation: What is a preferential option for the dispossessed? I argue that, utilizing a framework that understands poverty as a multi-tiered death, a preferential option for the dispossessed reads in solidarity with the people who face oppression, depopulation, violence, and uncertainty in the struggle for survival (physical, emotional, spiritual, psychological). If action must precede theology (in that theology reflects praxis), it is of utmost importance to read the biblical texts, especially those that contain narratives of depopulation, with a two-fold strategy: to bracket oneself[57] first so that the reader can then see with borrowed

---

[54] Robert Allen Warrior, "Canaanites, Cowboys, and Indians," *Christianity in Crisis* 49 (September 11, 1989): 261–62.

[55] Warrior, 261–62.

[56] Warrior, 265.

[57] "Bracket yourself" is one of Tom Boogaart's critical phrases that he used in his courses. To bracket oneself, one must understand one's socio-political location

eyes and hear with borrowed ears. To read texts like 1 Kings 21 and Joshua 10–12 with Palestinian/indigenous eyes is to be overwhelmed with the powerlessness and brutality facing oppressed peoples. State-sanctioned terror against a man with a vineyard, using legal power to condemn him to death, is eerily reminiscent of the bloody purges of Palestinian villages in 1948. When the Canaanite cities were sacked and burned, their people massacred, and their land weaponized and left for dead, Palestinian and indigenous experiences cry out in horror as their homes are razed before their eyes, knowing that the land they live on is occupied by a force that does not see them as humans. In the contexts of suffering, both past and present, the question of "who is my neighbor?" immediately begs a second question rooted in the concern of justice-for-each: Whom do I consider to be worthy of life? A preferential option for the dispossessed must actively and resolutely reject the control of withheld land and water necessary for Palestinian well-being. It demands that Palestinians be allowed to live in peace and safety. And this preferential option for the dispossessed does not find its foremost support in a political party or a movement—this preference is found in the Old Testament/Hebrew Bible's understanding of neighbor, of the stranger, of those who are allowed an inheritance of the land so that they might live.

---

and the modes of reading one has been taught, so that one might create a critical distance with which to read a text with an open mind. This process does not suggest that we can ever eliminate our biases when we read. However, it is a useful concept to remind the reader to understand the internal reactions to a narrative as part of our location-training-culture and to be receptive to new meanings and perspectives.

CHAPTER 12

Woman as Disciple: Scripture and the Church as a Discipleship of Equals

Dustyn Elizabeth Keepers

In her 1987 essay "A Discipleship of Equals: Past, Present, Future," Joann Wolski Conn laid out four areas that require action for the church to build a "new Christianity beyond patriarchy." She writes:

> First, every Christian must participate in the ongoing conversion of religious institutions. Second, we need prophetic insistence upon initial conversion of sinful structures. Third, theologians should continue to enlarge the discipline of Christian feminist theology. Fourth, Christians must appropriate a feminist spirituality.[1]

More than 30 years later, in the era of the #MeToo movement and its counterpart #ChurchToo, it is evident that we are far from finished with this task which calls for "every Christian" to participate. Despite the progress in some denominations toward women's ordination, women as leaders are still seen as exceptional cases. The sexual harassment and abuse of girls and women points to the ongoing and pervasive view of

[1] Joann Wolski Conn, "A Discipleship of Equals: Past, Present, Future," *Horizons* 14, no. 2 Fall (1987): 244.

173

the purpose of female existence as servant to the male. Challenging this deep-seated assumption is not only the work of feminist theologians and scholars. Rather, transformation of our churches into a "discipleship of equals" requires that even the average Christian in the pew must "appropriate a feminist spirituality."

Each week in worship, Christians turn to Scripture to look for the vision of God's kingdom and hear the call to the life of service and discipleship they are to embody. If we believe that women as well as men are created to "glorify God and enjoy him forever"[2] and thus equally called to participate in this life of discipleship, then we must continue to look to the Bible as a vital source of transformation for every Christian, highlighting models of discipleship that include both men and women.

For many feminists, engaging Scripture as a tool for the task of converting the sinful structures of oppression in the church seems an impossible task. After we carefully navigate the male language for God and find a way to deal with the texts that seem most violent or oppressive to women, we might wonder what is left to work with. The women whose stories are given to us in Scripture are often read as flat minor characters whom we are told very little about. Many of the women Jesus interacts with in the Gospels are left unnamed and seem to serve as little more than foils for Jesus as he reveals his understanding or miraculous power. Perhaps we don't fault the author's rightful focus on Christ, yet we are left with so many questions about the women he met and how they responded to him in faith.

And when one digs deeper to learn more about the women in Scripture, a surprising (or perhaps not too surprising) pattern emerges. Again and again, we find that some aspect of the woman's sexual history becomes a point of fixation for commentators, and often it deems the woman suspect or even becomes the defining characteristic. Reminders that Rahab was a prostitute shade how we read about her risky, life-saving work for the sake of Israel's spies. Mary Magdalene, whose story was once conflated with that of the "unnamed sinful woman" in Luke 7, carries the burden of this reputation despite her Christianity-defining role as "apostle to the apostles." As so many women today struggle with the fallout of their #MeToo stories being shared, a conscientious reader can't help but wonder how culture's view of women and sex colors the fact that these women of the Bible aren't celebrated alongside the male

---

[2]   This language comes from the Westminster Catechism Q&A 1.

disciples and heroes of the faith. Women and men in our churches need to hear the stories of faithful women learning and serving as disciples of Jesus in the past as well as in modern settings in order to appropriate a fully biblical and feminist spirituality. More constructive engagement with the Scriptures through a feminist lens is needed for the discipleship of equals to become the normative vision for every Christian.

As a student at Western Theological Seminary, I was profoundly shaped by the deep engagement with the Scriptures I was invited into by Tom Boogaart, one of my many beloved professors. Tom's work exploring the narratives of the Old Testament as dramas shaped our work with the texts, especially in the elective Hebrew reading and exegesis course, where we spent an entire semester working with one narrative by preparing to enact it. The process of considering how a text might look "on its feet" urged us all to slow down and consider each character and aspect of action in the story. Often this transformed our understanding of a character or their place in the story. For example, we often encountered a "minor" character, such as a servant who is mentioned but given no lines or specific actions to move the story forward; yet we still had to consider the possible reaction of this observer to the events as someone took on this role in our play. For more major characters, we had to think about tone, inflection, and facial expressions that might surround their spoken words, deciding whether they executed their actions quickly and enthusiastically or reluctantly. Such cues are often not given to us in the text, yet whether we are enacting a narrative or just reading, we imagine them, and they become a part of our interpretation. Slowing down the interpretive process to consider each of these decisions forced us to carefully examine our assumptions about these details in light of the narrative itself, its historical context, and the activity of God within it—often with surprising results. I have carried these lessons with me as I study and teach the narratives of Scripture and the stories of women in particular.

While I will not be describing an enactment of the scene at the well in John 4, I am inviting us to slow down and consider the female character of the Samaritan woman, including all the assumptions that we tend to carry into our reading of her interaction with Jesus. Two alternative approaches to the text will be used to assist this reexamination. First, by engaging the work of feminist biblical scholars, I will challenge the usual modern interpretations of the Samaritan woman and explore what we've perhaps neglected to observe about this narrative and its historical context. Secondly, I will invite the reader to contemplate how pre-critical theological interpretations of the text offer a fresh way to consider how God might be at work in this woman's life.

To some feminists, looking to the church "fathers" or even expecting Scripture to be a resource for enhancing the role of women in the church may seem naively hopeful. But as Dawn DeVries argues, "Christians—including those who are Reformed and feminist—have every reason to trust that precisely these texts will continue to work as means of grace, or as vehicles for conveying the Word of God."[3] Pre-critical authors regularly approached the text with this same expectation, that it would be God's Word to God's people. I, too, share this fundamental trust that God in Scripture is speaking God's life-giving Word to *all* God's people. So in this essay, I suggest that when the Samaritan woman's story is freed from the burden of patriarchal assumptions and read with an eye toward how God is at work in and through this woman as she meets Jesus, we discover a story of a female disciple. This sort of theological reading of Scripture can help Christians appropriate a feminist spirituality as we work toward a discipleship of equals in the church.

A Legacy of Moral and Intellectual Criticism

Though she is without a name, the Samaritan woman who meets Jesus at the well certainly has a reputation among modern scholars and preachers. Jesus's description of her marital status has often been interpreted to imply his condemnation of her lifestyle. Modern exegetes have made much of her presence at the well at noon—apparently she's alone—to make negative judgments about her "sinful and deceptive nature,"[4] painting her as an outcast in the community because of her lifestyle and thus adding reasons for her surprise at Jesus's request for water that extend beyond what the text itself provides as the explanation (the relationship between Samaritans and Jews). Even those who read her history more charitably often understand her as simply a foil for Jesus's revelation about himself in this chapter rather than as a true theological conversation partner who grows in understanding. This

---

[3]   Dawn DeVries, "'Ever to Be Reformed According to the Word of God': Can the Scripture Principle Be Redeemed for Feminist Theology?" in *Feminist and Womanist Essays in Reformed Dogmatics*, eds. Amy Plantinga Pauw and Serene Jones (Louisville: Westminster John Knox Press, 2006), 56.

[4]   Adeline Fehribach, *The Women in the Life of the Bridegroom: A Feminist Historical-Literary Analysis on the Female Characters in the Fourth Gospel* (Collegegrove: The Liturgical Press, 1998), 45.

type of reading "remains deeply androcentric insofar as it declares her fate to be a marginal issue in the text."[5] Here her "unfortunate" situation is not even asked about because the point is to reveal Jesus's knowledge in order to attract the townspeople to him.

The most enduring issue is that many modern interpretations are quick to pass moral judgment on the woman for her many marriages. The dominant reading was popularized by Rudolf Bultmann, who says, "Perhaps one may go as far as to say that the married life of the woman 'who reels from desire to pleasure' portrays not only the unrest, but the aberrations of the desire for life."[6] This interpretation assumes—based on a stereotype[7]—that the woman's many marriages come from her discontented pleasure seeking, and it frequently serves as the starting point for understanding her encounter with Christ. The NIV Application Commentary opens its comments on this passage by noting that the new character on the scene is "a person of questionable moral character," going on to insist that Jesus judges her statement "I have no husband" as untrue, despite Jesus's words in the text, "You are right in saying, 'I have no husband.' ... What you have said is true!"[8]

Other interpretive issues arise around how to understand the woman's role in the dialogue of 4:7-26. "She usually appears as someone who misunderstands Jesus and merely gives him key words for his revelatory discourse, not as an active partner in the dialogue who introduces her own ideas and moves the discussion forward."[9] She is generally seen as too attached to the material or sensual world to pick up on Jesus's spiritual talk about the water of life. This reading fits together with the assumption that she is trapped in sensual desire and sexual sin. Altogether, this serves to discount her response to the revelation of Jesus as an unwitting sign that points to Jesus rather than describing her as a faithful student of the Word who goes out to proclaim the good news she has received. Her evangelistic proclamation, which points her entire town to faith in Christ, is often minimized as

---

5   Luise Schottroff, "The Samaritan Woman and the Notion of Sexuality in the Fourth Gospel," in *What is John? Literary and Social Readings of the Fourth Gospel*, vol. 2, ed. Fernando F. Segovia (Atlanta: Scholars Press, 1998), 160.

6   Rudolf Bultmann, *The Gospel of John: A Commentary* (Philadelphia: Westminster, 1971), 188.

7   Luise Schottroff, "The Samaritan Woman and the Notion of Sexuality in the Fourth Gospel," in *What is John? Literary and Social Readings of the Fourth Gospel*, vol. 2, ed. Fernando F. Segovia (Atlanta: Scholars Press, 1998), 158.

8   Gary M. Burge, *John: The NIV Application Commentary* (Grand Rapids: Zondervan, 2000), 139, 145; John 4:17-18.

lacking full understanding and is discounted in light of the people's response to Jesus himself.

Feminist Critique

Though many modern commentators root their interpretations of this passage in historical-critical analysis, the harsh view of the woman's moral and intellectual status seems more likely to be grounded in negative stereotypes than on evidence in the text. I will begin to address some of the interpretations described above by laying out some modern feminist readings, addressing the woman's marital status first and then her participation in the discussion with Jesus. In the second part of the chapter, I will work toward a theological rereading of the Samaritan woman by examining pre-modern approaches. By bringing together a theological reading of the text with consideration for the concerns raised by feminist scholars, I will describe the woman's role in the narrative (and for the church today) as a disciple.

Marriage

Sandra Schneiders views the discussion of the woman's husbands as occurring in the midst of a theological dialogue and therefore concludes that the woman's husbands should be understood as figural, not literal. She argues that the Samaritan woman is presented as a representative figure; she is a symbolic character representing her nation; therefore, her husbands are the gods of occupying nations that Samaria has worshiped idolatrously. The woman is not bringing up theological questions to distract from Jesus's questions about her personal life, as many modern commentators suggest. Rather, we should understand the conversation as flowing naturally from religious questions about water to the question of the religious fidelity of her nation's worship. The woman perceives Jesus as a prophet because he speaks prophetically about the fidelity of the nation in verse 18. She asks about worship out of her suspicion that Jesus might be the Messiah who, in Samaritan theology, would be a prophet and would restore true worship.[10] Schneiders argues, "The entire dialogue between Jesus and the woman is the 'wooing' of Samaria into full covenant fidelity in the new Israel

---

9   Schottroff, 161.
10   Sandra M. Schneiders, *Written That You May Believe: Encountering Jesus in the Fourth Gospel* (New York: The Crossroad Publishing Company, 1999), 138.

by Jesus, the new Bridegroom. It has nothing to do with the woman's private moral life, but with the covenant life of the community."[11]

Like the allegorical interpretations offered by pre-modern commentators, Schneiders's figural interpretation draws our attention to some interesting ideas, though I would argue it should be held loosely alongside a more literal reading. By not giving this woman a name, the text invites us to identify her with her nationality and to understand her as symbolic in some way as the first evangelist to the Samaritan people. Yet I don't think we can read the discussion of the woman's marriages as entirely symbolic. A significant aspect of the entire conversation between the woman and Jesus is that it flows back and forth between literal objects, like water, and theological symbols. We must also consider her marriages as a literal part of this woman's history, which Jesus addresses in order to invite her into deeper knowledge of himself.

F. Scott Spencer reads this whole narrative much more literally and sees the shift in conversation to the woman's marital status as very abrupt. He does acknowledge that it suits the well setting, which would bring up thoughts of marriage for first-century readers familiar with betrothal scenes like the one in Genesis 24. Playing on this expectation, Jesus sets the woman up to confess, "I have no husband," and takes the opportunity to display his knowledge of her history. Spencer notes both the "astonishing 'exegetical extravaganzas'" about the woman's past inspired by this revelation and the allegorical reading that Schneiders and others take, but prefers a "kinder and simpler reading."[12] He points out that Jesus makes no moral judgments about her and concludes that we shouldn't either. Her multiple marriages could easily be due to widowhood and legal remarriage, like the case considered in Mark 12:18-23. If she out-lived all her brothers-in-law, she could be living with a more distant relative who is unable or unwilling to marry her. He also points out that the woman is not at all put off by Jesus pointing out her past, which neither of them acknowledges as troubling.

I find Spencer's more straightforward reading of the woman's marriages a helpful rereading of the text. As he observes, the narrative itself does not give us any indication that Jesus's comments cast judgment on the woman. He does not tell her to "go and sin no more." Spencer reads her situation within the context of this narrative and the larger set

[11]   Schneiders, 141.
[12]   F. Scott Spencer, "You Just Don't Understand (Or Do You?): Jesus, Women, and Conversation in the Fourth Gospel," in *Feminist Companion to John*, vol. 1, ed. Amy-Jill Levine (London: Sheffield Academic Press, 2003), 35.

of evidence in Scripture and does not find evidence that the woman's marriages are an indication of her sinful character. Luise Schottroff agrees: "The interpretation of the Samaritan woman's successive marriages as the result of her lustfulness—that is, as immoral behavior—is astonishing in light of the fact that the Bible often speaks of women's consecutive marriages without regarding them as immoral."[13] In fact, she argues, successive marriages for men and women were common in that context, as we can tell from the discussions of mourning periods and limitations of the marriages of widows in literature of the time.

Schottroff admits that these laws demonstrating the possibility of multiple marriages were very biased against women. Nonetheless, there were good reasons for women to marry multiple times. Economic security was one major reason to seek marriage or re-marriage, as there was not much opportunity for a woman to survive by working to earn a wage. Because of this economic situation, a woman could even be forced to accept a non-marriage relationship of sex and work, which provided even less security than marriage.[14] Schottroff suggests that the woman in this story is working as a water bearer (which explains her appearance at the well at noon, often interpreted as demonstrative of her moral outcast status in her community) while living with a man who won't marry her.[15] According to Schottroff's reading, "The Samaritan woman is described as a woman in an extreme situation of sexual exploitation .... Her encounter with Jesus gives her the courage to put an end to her degrading situation."[16]

Schottroff frames the woman's experience of her encounter with Jesus in terms of liberation from this burden of dependence on a man for security. The woman's statement "I have no husband" is a statement in which she frees herself, deciding to live independently of the man she lives with by not acknowledging him as a husband. Jesus praises her twice for saying she has no husband. According to Schottroff, Jesus reveals himself to her as a liberator rather than as all knowing. "The Samaritan woman can leave her water jar (v. 28) and her non-husband, because she has found new sisters and brothers and a new household in which she can survive—in the economic sense as well—as an independent woman."[17]

---

13   Schottroff, "The Samaritan Woman," 162.
14   Schottroff, 163-4.
15   Schottroff, 165.
16   Schottroff, 174.
17   Schottroff, 169.

Here, I think Schottroff goes beyond the text and describes the woman's potential freedom in Christ a bit anachronistically. The Samaritan woman is still subject to the expectations of a patriarchal culture, and it is not at all clear that she would have the support of a community of believers to care for her in her economic vulnerability. Yet her examination of the woman's social and economic situation is helpful, standing in marked contrast to the portrait of the wanton woman that has been offered by other modern exegetes.

Lynn Cohick examines evidence from archives of documents that record the arrangements for marriages, dowries, and inheritances in the Greco-Roman period. She suggests that the Samaritan woman's history of marriages, though surprising in number, could plausibly be explained as the result of being widowed or divorced. "Because neither situation necessarily casts a shadow over one's character, we cannot assume that her marriage history made her a social pariah."[18] Further, there are several possible explanations for the woman's current status. She may be in a concubine relationship due to an inability, under Roman law, to marry someone of higher social status, or in order to prevent the man's estate from being diluted if any children were born to their relationship.[19] She could also be a second wife and thus not legally recognized,[20] or simply living with another male relative who is acting as her guardian. Ultimately, there are a number of scenarios that could explain the Samaritan woman's history, and neither Jesus nor her neighbors, who accept her testimony about Jesus without qualification, seem to judge her as promiscuous or immoral.[21]

Conversation with Jesus

The conversation between the Samaritan woman and Jesus stretches from verse 7, when Jesus asks for a drink, to verse 26, when he reveals his identity as Messiah saying, "I am he, the one who is speaking to you." Jerome Neyrey studies the conversation rhetorically, arguing that it follows the typical Johannine pattern of "statement ... misunderstanding ... clarification." This pattern may either invite Jesus's conversation partner to become an "insider" by offering insight or it may distance his dialogue partner, confirming him or her as an

---

[18]   Lynn H. Cohick, *Women in the World of the Earliest Christians* (Grand Rapids: Baker, 2009), 124.
[19]   Cohick, 125.
[20]   Cohick, 126.
[21]   Cohick, 128.

"outsider." While some modern commentators consistently interpret the woman as "misunderstanding" Jesus throughout, Neyrey sees this conversation between Jesus and the Samaritan woman as an invitation in which she is led step by step to deeper insight and becomes an "insider."[22]

Many other feminist writers also present the Samaritan woman as coming to a new understanding through this conversation with Jesus. Fehribach sees the woman's understanding transformed. The woman begins with a "from below" perspective, in which she understands the water Jesus talks about literally, but then she follows Jesus up to the discussion on a higher level where he reveals himself. In Fehribach's view, Jesus's reference to the husbands is an attempt to bring the discussion to a higher level. And at this point the Samaritan woman understands and proclaims Jesus as a prophet.[23]

Other authors, like Sandra Schneiders, highlight the fact that this scene is the longest and most in-depth theological dialogue in the Fourth Gospel. Indeed, often Jesus's clarifications of misunderstandings elsewhere turn into monologues in which Jesus builds on foils. The confused conversation partner drops out of the conversation, like Nicodemus in chapter 3, to whom the Samaritan woman is often compared. However, the Samaritan woman "is not simply a 'foil' feeding Jesus cue lines like some of these other characters. She is a genuine theological dialogue partner gradually experiencing Jesus's self-revelation even as she reveals herself to him."[24]

Stephen Moore goes further, arguing that even this view leaves a hierarchical structure in place, where Jesus "retains his privileged role as dispenser of knowledge ... while the woman retains her traditional role as the complacent recipient of knowledge, a container as empty as her water jar, waiting to be filled."[25] Both Moore and F. Scott Spencer entertain the possibility that the woman is in fact exceeding Jesus in insight along the way rather than trying to keep up with his knowledge being poured out at the well. As Moore puts it, "The female student has

---

[22]   Jerome Neyrey, "What's Wrong with This Picture?" in Feminist Companion to John, vol. 1, ed. Amy-Jill Levine (London: Sheffield Academic Press, 2003), 112.

[23]   Fehribach, *The Women in the Life of the Bridegroom*, 61–64.

[24]   Schneiders, *Written That You May Believe*, 141.

[25]   Stephen D. Moore, "Are There Impurities in the Living Water that the Johannine Jesus Dispenses?" in *Feminist Companion to John*, vol. 1, ed. Amy-Jill Levine (London: Sheffield Academic Press, 2003), 84.

outstripped her male teacher, even though he himself was the subject of the seminar. She has insisted, in effect, that earthly and heavenly, flesh and Spirit, figural and literal, are symbolically related categories."[26]

Presenting the woman as exceeding Jesus in insight along the way, as Spencer describes, seems to go beyond the theological intention of this dialogue within the Gospel, which is to reveal Jesus as a prophet and as Messiah. But certainly this conversation is unlike many others in the gospels where many characters ask a single question initiating a monologue of teaching. The Samaritan woman is a true theological conversation partner to Jesus, growing in understanding as they discuss religious history, worship, and the coming of the Messiah.

From the perspective of these modern feminist interpretations, new possibilities open up for understanding the woman's marriage and her participation in the conversation. Yet in order to truly reclaim this woman's story as one that invites us into a discipleship of equals, we need more than a rebuttal to sexist readings. So in the following section, I begin to develop a constructive theological reading of the Samaritan Woman as a model of discipleship. If we press further back into the history of interpretation, we discover that earlier commentators, who employed figural and theological readings of the text, were often more charitable to this woman's story and more focused on her role as an example of discipleship for the reader to follow.

Exploring Theological Readings from the Past

While pre-modern writers were certainly not immune to sexism and misogyny, their theological reading of the Samaritan woman's role as an apostle or evangelist seems to keep them from applying to her the troubling rhetoric the same writers might have used speaking about women more generally. Though some, like Calvin, do interpret her many marriages as indicative of sinfulness, they do not necessarily discount her as a preacher or downplay the significance of her evangelism, as some modern interpreters seem to do. Despite the fact that each of these pre-modern theologians wrote long before feminist sensibilities were available to critique them, their theologically-focused interpretations offer possibilities for a modern feminist hermeneutic, helping to reclaim the Samaritan woman's narrative as a model of discipleship and ministry for women and men in the church.

---

[26]   Moore, 95.

Origen

According to Origen, this woman is called by Jesus to be an apostle to her city.[27] He points to her zeal, arguing that the leaving of her water jar shows her "tremendous eagerness" to share the benefit of faith with others.[28] Origen declares that the Evangelist recorded her story as an example to challenge us to imitate this woman, to leave behind concern for the material, and to "be eager to impart to others that benefit of which we have been partakers."[29] Origen makes special note of the role of this woman who preaches Christ to the Samaritans and connects her action to that of Mary, the first to see the resurrected Jesus and proclaim what she saw to the other apostles.[30]

Augustine

Augustine of Hippo takes an allegorical approach to this passage and describes the Samaritan woman as "a figure of the Church, not yet justified, but now about to be justified."[31] He points out the relevance of her foreign nationality for a church made up of non-Jews; by this hermeneutical move, he calls his readers to hear and recognize themselves in this woman.[32] Once again, she is a model for followers of Christ today.

Augustine symbolically interprets the "husband" of the woman's soul as "understanding." Christ tells her to call her husband because he wants her to grasp what he is revealing to her. In Augustine's allegorical interpretation, the five husbands she has had are her five senses. And the one who is not her husband is error, an adulterer who corrupts her. Jesus "is also saying to our soul, 'Call your husband,'" Augustine writes. She, and thus every follower of Jesus, needs to grow in understanding. And the woman's understanding does come in the course of the conversation. When she learns that the one to whom she is speaking is the Messiah, she hurries to preach the gospel. Here again Augustine holds her up as a model, "Let them who want to preach the gospel learn;

---

[27] Origen, *Commentary on the Gospel According to John: Books 13–32*, Fathers of the Church, vol. 89 (Washington, DC: The Catholic University of America Press, 1993), 104.

[28] Origen, 105.

[29] Origen, 105.

[30] Origen, 106.

[31] Augustine of Hippo, *Tractates on the Gospel of John: 11–22*, Fathers of the Church, vol. 79 (Washington, DC: The Catholic University of America Press, 1988), 84.

[32] Augustine, 84.

let them cast aside the water jar at the well."[33] Augustine praises the tact of her preaching as she leads the listeners step by step, that they might not become angry and persecute her. Her approach is effective, and the people of the city listen to her and respond with faith themselves.[34]

John Chrysostom

John Chrysostom calls his readers to imitate the Samaritan woman in her persistence and conversation with Christ. He recognizes in her partial knowledge about the spiritual significance of water when she asks Jesus about Jacob who gave the well, which shows her seeking further understanding.[35] The "prudent soul" goes on to place Jesus ahead of the patriarch she admired, though her questions show that she was "not gullible."[36] For Chrysostom, she is a true seeker of understanding and a theological conversation partner with Jesus.

Chrysostom spends a considerable amount of time in his homilies on John comparing the Samaritan woman to other characters. Compared to Nicodemus, Chrysostom calls her wiser and more courageous, for "she engaged in apostolic work, spreading the good news to all and calling them to Jesus, drawing a whole city from outside the faith."[37] He praises her zeal in leaving behind her water jar and compares her to the apostles, who "left their nets after being called, while she of her own accord, with no summons, left her water-jar and did the work of an evangelist."[38] She is a model for faithful response to the good news and is compared to—and even exceeds—the example of some male disciples.

Calvin

Compared to the earlier interpreters above, John Calvin's reading of the Samaritan Woman seems harsh. He sees the woman as acting reproachfully toward Jesus throughout their conversation, even being facetious when she understands what Jesus is saying. Calvin seems inclined to attribute all sorts of immoral motives to this woman. The most troubling aspect of Calvin's interpretation is where he takes the

---

[33] Augustine, 96.
[34] Augustine, 97.
[35] John Chrysostom, *Commentary on Saint John The Apostle and Evangelist: Homilies 1–47,* Fathers of the Church, vol. 33 (New York: Fathers of the Church, Inc. 1957), 309–10.
[36] Chrysostom, 315.
[37] Chrysostom, 314.
[38] Chrysostom, 332.

mention of her husbands as Jesus reproaching the woman for her wickedness toward him.[39]

Calvin assumes the worst for this woman's moral standing. Yet that does not disqualify her from being viewed as a faithful example. According to Calvin, Christ's reproof of her sin was effective, and the conversation that follows shows that the woman is ready and prepared to learn. She is a model for growth in faith, and we should learn from her example in discipleship "that when we meet with any teacher, we ought to avail ourselves of this opportunity, that we may not be ungrateful to God."[40] Once she learns who Christ is, she is sparked with great zeal and hurries to tell others. In Calvin's reading, then, ultimately the woman is to be admired. When confronted by her sin, she responds to Christ, changing from reproachful to a willing disciple. In fact, one might argue that for Calvin her "sinfulness" is what makes her actions representative of the response all (sinful) human beings should have. Every person should respond to Christ by turning from his or her old ways and following him—growing in knowledge and responding in faith. The Samaritan woman, then, is a model for discipleship held up for our imitation.

The pre-modern interpreters briefly surveyed above give us hope for reclaiming this story in John 4 as a model story of a female disciple. They each invite us to identify with her growth in understanding and her faithful response of preaching the good news in a way that parallels the function of male disciple stories. A modern theological interpretation can build on similar themes to more fully develop the story of the Samaritan woman into a call to discipleship for both women and men.

A Woman Disciple

Many modern interpreters and preachers have dismissed this woman's role as a disciple and an evangelist to her city by calling her morality and intellectual ability into question. Yet, as we have seen, there is evidence elsewhere in Scripture that could explain this woman's marital situation as the troubling result of her vulnerable position as a widow. We do not know from the text whether her multiple marriages were the result of divorce or death, nor do we know what circumstances have led her to living with a man outside of marriage. What we do know is

---

[39] John Calvin, *The Gospel According to St. John, 1–10*, eds. David W. Torrance and Thomas F. Torrance. (Grand Rapids: Eerdmans, 1961), 94.
[40] Calvin, 94.

that "Jesus calls attention to her problematic situation, but he does not condemn her. Subsequently, commentators and preachers have filled the void!"[41] Neither Jesus nor the woman acknowledges her situation as troubling; in fact, Jesus praises her for speaking the truth about it. She does not express shame when Jesus names her situation, but instead she drives the conversation forward, asking theological questions and seeking to grow in her faith and understanding. Based on the text, I don't believe we have enough evidence to pass moral judgment on this woman's past, but what is clear is that her story is told by the Gospel writer as an example of faithful response to Christ.

Her participation in theological conversation shows her desire to learn, which is the proper response of a disciple. She, like other women in John's Gospel, is "among those who while not explicitly identified as 'the disciples,' nevertheless satisfy the Gospel's criteria for discipleship."[42] The Samaritan woman seeks understanding, and, once she learns that Jesus is the Messiah, she responds in faith, rushing to do the work of an apostle to her city. This is an unconventional act for a woman of that period, and I believe that act even more firmly seals her in the category of a disciple. Her faith response is so strong that it compels her to action even beyond her culturally assigned role.

Gail O'Day sees the role of the woman in evangelizing the town as a "persuasive counterbalance to any attempts to diminish the woman's identity and role"[43] earlier in the story. One concern might arise, as the woman's witness is superseded when the townspeople see and hear Jesus for themselves, but this pattern is appropriate to the pattern of discipleship and faith as demonstrated in the Gospel of John. O'Day proclaims that the woman is a witness and disciple like John the Baptist, Andrew, and Philip, whose testimonies are also overshadowed by converts encountering Jesus in person.[44] Schneiders agrees that this pattern is characteristically Johannine and is seen repeatedly in the disciples' own stories, such as Andrew's bringing of Simon (1:41-42), Philip's bringing Nathanael (1:44-51), and the disciples' group witness of the resurrection to Thomas (20:18-25).[45] The woman's witness

---

[41] Marianne Meye Thompson, *John: A Commentary* (Louisville: Westminster John Knox Press, 2015), 103.

[42] Margaret M. Beirne, *Women and Men in the Fourth Gospel: A Genuine Discipleship of Equals* (New York: Sheffield Academic Press, 2003), 7.

[43] Gail O'Day, "John," in *Women's Bible Commentary*, eds. Carol A. Newsom and Sharon H. Ringe (Louisville: Westminster John Knox Press, 1998), 384.

[44] O'Day, 385.

[45] Schneiders, *Written That You May Believe*, 143.

is not diminished by the response of her townspeople, but rather, her comparison to the male disciples is confirmed. Furthermore, the positive response of her townspeople shows that her preaching has been effective!

Adeline Fehribach also notes that the parallels between the Samaritan woman and the male disciples are part of the reason some second wave feminists view her as a disciple. Jesus's knowledge of the woman (in some way) brings her to faith, much as it brings Nathanael to faith in John 1. She, like the disciples in the Synoptic tradition, leaves something behind (her water jar) to take up her role as a witness. And she calls others to "come and see," just as Jesus invited John's disciples and as Philip called Nathanael in chapter 1 (though different words are used in the Greek).[46] These comparisons echo the connections made by pre-modern interpreters and help us understand the woman's role in the Gospel as a model of faith. Margaret M. Beirne contributes to this scholarship by pointing to a pattern of gendered pairs in the construction of John's Gospel. Through the pairing of the stories of the Samaritan woman and Nicodemus, the Gospel demonstrates a model of faith growth from first awareness to full discipleship for both men and women.[47]

Early commentators saw this woman as a figure of the church and a model to be imitated. They remind us that the theological purpose of her story in the Gospel was an invitation to readers to imitate her faith and response. Though she is not named among the 12 disciples, she fulfills all the criteria for discipleship and could even be understood as the first evangelist to those outside Judaism, as she faithfully preached to her entire town. In the church today, her story should be told with this same theological purpose: to invite both women and men to imitate her faithful response to Christ.

Conclusion

"Feminist and Reformed theologians share a conviction that tradition is not a fixed and unchangeable body of truths received from our predecessors to be handed on intact but rather a human cultural product that is always being reshaped through its transmission in new circumstances."[48] We can acknowledge that many Reformation and modern interpretations of this story are deeply influenced by a

---

[46] Fehribach, 45–46.
[47] Beirne, *Women and Men in the Fourth Gospel*, 67.
[48] DeVries, "Ever to Be Reformed According to the Word of God," 57.

patriarchal worldview, which focuses on the woman's sexuality and presumes that she lacks understanding. Yet this does not mean we must dismiss the Scripture completely nor even disregard all historical interpretations of it. Rather, we can reengage this text with an eye to its purpose as Scripture, pointing to the transforming reality of Jesus and calling women and men to respond like the Samaritan woman.

Both feminist and pre-modern interpreters contribute to a faithful understanding of this text that opens an opportunity to hear this woman's story as an invitation to discipleship. The Samaritan woman's story need not be relegated to a place of shame, discounted because of her sexual history. Without denying the way her story has been misshaped throughout its history of interpretation, the theological readings offered here demonstrate how this narrative can be reclaimed for the church's transformation. As the Samaritan woman's story of discipleship and evangelism is heard anew today, it has the potential to help the church appropriate a vision of both women and men as models. Her story is about being a disciple—perhaps even an apostle—a foreshadowing of the church in which Jew and Gentile, male and female are united in Christ. Her story can become a means of grace for us today, through which we hear God's transformational call to the church: to become a discipleship of equals.

Bibliography:

Augustine of Hippo, *Tractates on the Gospel of John: 11–22.* Fathers of the Church, vol. 79. Washington, DC: The Catholic University of America Press, 1988.

Beirne, Margaret M. *Women and Men in the Fourth Gospel: A Genuine Discipleship of Equals.* New York: Sheffield Academic Press, 2003.

Calvin, John. *The Gospel According to St. John, 1–10.* Edited by David W. Torrance and Thomas F. Torrance. Grand Rapids: Eerdmans, 1961.

Chrysostom, John. *Commentary on Saint John The Apostle and Evangelist: Homilies 1-47.* Fathers of the Church, vol. 33. New York: Fathers of the Church, Inc., 1957.

Conn, Joann Wolski. "A Discipleship of Equals: Past, Present Future," *Horizons,* 14 no. 2, (Fall 1987).

DeVries, Dawn. "'Ever to Be Reformed According to the Word of God': Can the Scripture Principle Be Redeemed for Feminist Theology?"

In *Feminist and Womanist Essays in Reformed Dogmatics*, edited by Amy Plantinga Pauw and Serene Jones. Louisville: Westminster John Knox Press, 2006.

Fehribach, Adeline. *The Women in the Life of the Bridegroom: A Feminist Historical-Literary Analysis of the Female Characters in the Fourth Gospel*. Collegeville: The Liturgical Press, 1998.

Moore, Stephen D. "Are There Impurities in the Living Water that the Johannine Jesus Dispenses?" In *Feminist Companion to John*, vol. 1, edited by Amy-Jill Levine. London: Sheffield Academic Press, 2003.

Neyrey, Jerome. "What's Wrong with This Picture?" In *Feminist Companion to John*, vol. 1, edited by Amy-Jill Levine. London: Sheffield Academic Press, 2003.

O'Day, Gail. "John." In *Women's Bible Commentary*, edited by Carol A. Newsom and Sharon H. Ringe. Louisville: Westminster John Knox Press, 1998.

Origen, *Commentary on the Gospel According to John: Books 13-32*. Fathers of the Church, vol. 89. Washington, DC: The Catholic University of America Press, 1993.

Reinhartz, Adele. "The Gospel of John." In *Searching the Scriptures: A Feminist Commentary*, edited by Elizabeth Schussler-Fiorenza. New York: Crossroad, 1994.

Schneiders, Sandra M. *Written that You May Believe: Encountering Jesus in the Fourth Gospel*. New York: The Crossroad Publishing Company, 1999.

Schottroff, Luise. "The Samaritan Woman and the Notion of Sexuality in the Fourth Gospel." In *What is John?: Literary and Social Readings of the Fourth Gospel*, vol. 2, edited by Fernando F. Segovia. Atlanta, GA: Scholars Press, 1998.

Spencer, F. Scott. "You Just Don't Understand (Or Do You?): Jesus, Women, and Conversation in the Fourth Gospel." In *Feminist Companion to John*, vol. 1, edited by Amy-Jill Levine. London: Sheffield Academic Press, 2003.

Thompson, Marianne Meye. *John: A Commentary*. Louisville: Westminster John Knox Press, 2015.

CHAPTER 13

The God Who Elects Leaving

Alberto La Rosa Rojas

As a student in Dr. Boogaart's classes, I learned that good theology is always attuned to the cracks and wounds in creation through which the God of Israel often speaks to us in whispers. In his classes, we took pilgrimages into the strange and unfamiliar world of the Hebrew Scriptures, often accompanied by our tour guide Abraham Joshua Heschel. Each tour began with this important warning from Dr. Heschel that we would all do well to remember: "The principle to be kept in mind is to know what we see rather than to see what we know."[1] Each lecture took us to the valleys of darkness in the life of the people Israel, where the poor and the marginalized suffer the yoke of injustice, to the peaks of Mounts Hebron, Zion, and Carmel from where God's healing Word comes down. The hallmark of these journeys is always an encounter with the ineffable and infinitely knowable God of Israel, and an encounter with this God always destabilizes the structures that hold up our world. This essay attempts to honor the teaching, mentoring, and friendship which Dr. Boogaart so freely lavished on his students

---

[1] Abraham Joshua Heschel, *The Prophets*, 1st Perennial classics edition (New York: HarperPerennial, 2001), xxiv.

191

by going on a journey once again down to the valleys of suffering, into the strange world of Scripture, in the hope that the God of Israel would encounter us and change the way we see and act in the world. Thank you, Dr. Boogaart, for all the journeys and all the stories and for always committing to take us up the mountain to be transformed and transfigured before the face of God.

Narratives of Leaving

This essay aims to enter into the biblical narrative with the questions of the immigrant in mind. To enter the biblical narrative with the question of the immigrant is not equivalent to asking the Bible to provide the answers concerning the ongoing global migration crisis. As an immigrant, there is a set of moral questions about my life that the majority of social spaces I inhabit do not allow me to ask. Questions like: Is it a sin to leave one's family, community, and land behind in the act of migration? Is it possible to carry out the commandment to honor thy parents and love thy neighbor when thy neighbors and parental ancestors belong not only to two distinct communities but to two communities whose welfare and values are at times in direct conflict with each other? If leaving my home in Peru was a transgression in any way against my family and my community, would leaving my new home in the United States to return to Peru constitute a second transgression? To ask these questions is often to run the risk, on the one hand, of being labeled a privileged immigrant and a bigot, and on the other hand, of being labeled an opportunistic lawbreaker. This essay tries to carve out a space to reflect about these "unaskable" questions, resisting the urge to foreclose on an answer before the question even gets asked. In particular, this essay will focus on one question, which serves as a starting point for my reflection on my life as an immigrant: *Why did we leave?*

Before proceeding, I must make one important caveat. Each migration story bears a distinct set of questions, challenges, and consequences that refract each migrant or migrant group's cultural background as well as the particular material circumstances of their migration.[2] However, any reflection on migration that seeks not only

---

2   I use the word "immigrant" throughout this paper mostly in reference to myself or my family given that this is the most commonly used term to denote those who, like my family, are not refugees and therefore are categorized as economic migrants. The term "migrant" I use as an umbrella term to include anyone who has undergone a change in where they live resulting from crossing some significant

to be intellectually generative but also to address the concrete realities of migration ought to begin not with broad ideas and theories about migration (helpful though these can be) but rather with the concrete experiences of a particular migrant. As such, this essay explores a question prompted by my own immigrant journey. My hope is that the questions I bring to the Bible will serve to open up fresh frameworks for thinking about migration and new questions with which to critically reflect about the complex reality of migration, not only for Christians but also for anyone wishing to engage the conversation.

Introduction

This essay brings the question of "leaving"—a question that has marked my own immigrant journey—to the Joseph narrative found in Genesis 37-50. The primary question I will engage is: Why does Joseph leave his family and the land of Canaan? After providing an overview of the narrative leading up to Joseph's departure and the ways in which Joseph's brothers have often been given sole responsibility over Joseph's departure, the essay will engage the work of contemporary Jewish biblical scholar Avivah Gottlieb Zornberg and her reflections on the Joseph narrative as found in her acclaimed book *The Beginning of Desire: Reflections on Genesis.*[3] Through her deep engagement with various Jewish voices across time, Zornberg's work challenges any reductive interpretations of Joseph's narrative. More specifically, in the silent spaces between the words of the narrative, Zornberg unearths the angst of God's chosen people Israel and the struggle between a desire for rest and peace and the turbulent realities of life, which include leaving one's family and land. From this tension in the Joseph narrative between the righteous desire for rest and the constant reality of leaving and being unsettled emerges a scandalous question: Could it be that the shape of God's election of Israel inherently entails a life of always leaving but never settling, always seeking rest but never finding it? Drawing from Zornberg's reflections on the Joseph narrative, I conclude that God elects to assume no other story or people except the people Israel and their story, which is one shaped by the trauma of leaving. In order to

---

border. Migrant can include immigrants of any legal status, refugees and asylum seekers, in addition to those who, by virtue of their nation of origin, race, ethnicity, and language capacities, can pass off as "citizens" despite also having changed their place of residence across an international border.

[3]   Avivah Gottlieb Zornberg, *The Beginning of Desire: Reflections on Genesis* (New York: Schocken Books, 2011).

show that my claims do not exist in a vacuum but are held alongside those of other Jewish scholars, I conclude the essay by briefly engaging the work of Judith Butler in *Parting Ways: Jewishness and the Critique of Zionism*.[4] As a secular Jew, Butler does not employ the language of divine election; instead, she resorts to history to suggest that "the exilic—or more emphatically, the diasporic—is built into the idea of the Jewish"[5]

Bringing in the Accused: Joseph's Brothers

If asked why Joseph leaves his family in Canaan, many familiar with the story will answer that Joseph did not have a choice in leaving. The story of Joseph opens up in Genesis 12:8 with Jacob and his children as sojourners in the land of Canaan, waiting to inherit the land of Canaan according to God's promise to Abraham. However, this opening verse, which anticipates the fulfillment of the Abrahamic covenant, is quickly interrupted by the story of a 17-year-old shepherd boy named Joseph, the eleventh son of his father Jacob, and his troublesome dreams, which fuel the contempt of his older brothers. The story that follows is so enticing, scandalous, and inspiring that the opening line, "Jacob settled in the land where his father had lived as an alien, the land of Canaan"[6] soon fades into the background. The story quickly devolves into tragedy as the contempt of Joseph's brothers grows into a murderous plot: "They [Joseph's brothers] said to one another, 'Here comes this dreamer. Come now, let us kill him and throw him into one of the pits; then we shall say that a wild animal has devoured him, and we shall see what will become of his dreams.'"[7] Alas, Joseph is able to avoid death due to the intervention of Reuben, the eldest brother. However, for Joseph this glimmer of hope turns out to be a conduit for a crueler fate as the brothers spot a caravan of Ishmaelite traders. Upon Judah's suggestion, the brothers sell Joseph off to slavery for "twenty pieces of silver."[8] Why does Joseph leave for Canaan? A cursory reading of the text would suggest that his brothers are the sole and fully responsible agents in Joseph's departure. The reader is left then to sympathize with Joseph and to look with contempt toward Joseph's brothers. This reading of Joseph's departure that indicts Joseph's brothers can be summed up

---

4   Judith Butler, *Parting Ways: Jewishness and the Critique of Zionism* (New York: Columbia University Press, 2012).
5   Butler, 15.
6   Genesis 37:1.
7   Genesis 37:19-20.
8   Genesis 37:25-28.

well in the lines of Andrew Lloyd Webber's classic musical production of this text, *Joseph and the Amazing Technicolor Dreamcoat*: "Oh now brothers, how low can you stoop? You make a sordid group, hey, how low can you stoop? Poor, poor Joseph, sold to be a slave."[9]

This common way to frame the story of Joseph—perhaps the most well-known among Christians—is as a crime novella in which Joseph is an innocent victim and Joseph's brothers are presented as cowardly and morally bankrupt individuals. The narrative thus understood has its own integrity and structure, distinct from the other patriarchal narratives of the book of Genesis.[10] This renders the story capable of adaptation by way of extraction from its literary location, a matter that Tim Rice put to good use in writing the script for *Joseph and the Amazing Technicolor Dreamcoat*. Walter Brueggemann supports a version of this hypothesis, arguing, "The Joseph narrative offers a kind of literature which is distinctive in Genesis. It is distinguished in every way from the narratives of dealing with Abraham and Jacob."[11] Brueggemann contends that the Joseph narrative appears to be much more like a Davidic or Solomonic narrative wherein God's absence is a way of establishing "the hidden rule of God in the affairs of persons and nations."[12] However, this hypothesis about the composition of the Joseph narrative runs into three obstacles.

First, the Joseph narrative as self-enclosed narrative eschews the significance of the opening line "Jacob settled in the land of his father's sojourn."[13] The content of election and the Abrahamic covenant is, of course, present in the story but no longer as the controlling narrative. Instead, it is treated as a historical artifact or theological motif. Eschewing the first line of the narrative allows us to make Genesis 37; 39–50 a story primarily about Joseph and Joseph's virtues (which is to say, the virtues of the Israelite ruler) over against his treacherous brothers rather than a story about the unfolding election of the Abrahamic family, which the text's opening line points us to.

[9]   Tim Rice, "Poor, Poor, Joseph" in *Joseph and the Amazing Technicolor Dreamcoat*, (Van Nuys: Bellwin Mills, 1971).
[10]   Walter Brueggemann, *Genesis,* Interpretation: A Bible Commentary for Teaching and Preaching (Atlanta: John Knox Press, 1982).
[11]   Brueggemann, 288.
[12]   Brueggemann, 291.
[13]   Genesis 37:1; Brueggemann argues, "The movement of this narrative is from the initial dream of Joseph (37:5-9) to the secure settlement of Israel in the land under the governance of Joseph (47:27). To make the Joseph narrative a "continuous unit," Brueggemann brackets out Genesis 37:1. Brueggemann, 290.

Second, reading the story of Joseph as a self-contained drama apart from Israel's story of election renders the literary absence of God from the text as an occasion for the reader to arbitrarily determine which aspects of the narrative are God's will and which are not. God's hiddenness in the text, without the context of the election of the Abrahamic family, allows the divine will to become the substance of the reader's "dreams." In Webber's reinterpretation of the Joseph story, the moral of the story is spelled out in the lyrics to the prologue where the omniscient narrator sets out "to tell the tale of a dreamer like you / We all dream a lot / Some are lucky, some are not / But if you think it, want it, dream it, then it's real / You are what you feel."[14] In Webber's musical production, the content of Joseph's dreams (which I will later argue are unintelligible outside of an account of God's election of Israel) are filled in with whatever the reader "thinks," "wants," and "feels."

The same danger exists in theologically interpreting the Joseph narrative as a text about divine providence without properly anchoring God's providence in the election of the Abrahamic family. In his commentary on Genesis, Walter Brueggemann writes, "[The] narrative has an identifiable and singular intention. It urges that in the contingencies of history, the purposes of God are at work in hidden and unnoticed ways."[15] What Brueggemann argues may very well have been the intention of a pro-Solomonic redactor of the text precisely in order to assert and justify the power and divine authority of an Israelite monarch. However, Christians ought to be very wary about taking up a providential reading of the text without rooting it in the concrete election of Israel.

The story itself gives us precedence for questioning authoritative figures in the text when they declare to have knowledge of God's providential will. Joseph proclaims to his brothers, "Even though you intended to do harm to me, God intended it for good, in order to preserve a numerous people, as he is doing today."[16] But to what extent is Joseph a trustworthy source in the narrative? Having made the story primarily about Joseph and his virtues as an Israelite ruler, we begin to hold a blind trust toward Joseph. However, Joseph is a convoluted and ambiguous character throughout the text. The fact that, at Joseph's

---

[14]   Tim Rice, "Prologue," in *Joseph and the Amazing Technicolor Dreamcoat* (Van Nuys: Bellwin Mills, 1971.

[15]   Brueggemann, 289.

[16]   Genesis 50:19-20; Joseph makes the same claim to his brothers in an earlier passage, Genesis 45:5-8.

command, the Israelites and most other Canaanite peoples in the region are resigned to sell their land and livelihood to Pharaoh calls into question whether Joseph's actions in the story are always trustworthy and God ordained. It is possible that though Joseph can see the events surrounding God's family before they unfold, nevertheless, Joseph is not always a wise interpreter of the way the events correspond with the shape of the election of the Abrahamic family.

An alternative route of interpretation, which I will develop later in this essay, is that God's providence, while remaining a mystery and as such inscrutable, is revealed concretely, visibly, and intelligibly in the election of Israel. God's definitive action in history doesn't happen "*to* people;" it constitutes "*a* people." God's election reveals that God is not a *deus ex machina*, intervening in history secretly as an all-powerful outsider. Rather, God's action in history is precisely to bind Godself to the concrete people and history of Israel. Though Joseph summons God's name to give an explanation of the events as they have occurred, the only time in the story when God speaks for Godself is in comforting Jacob as he prepares to leave Canaan for Egypt, "I myself will go down with you to Egypt, and I will also bring you up again; and Joseph's own hand shall close your eyes."[17]

Finally, reading the story of Joseph as a self-contained drama apart from Israel's story of election renders unintelligible the actions of Joseph's brothers and, more significantly, of God in electing them as the patriarchs of Israel. It is one thing to note that God elects to work with flawed people; it is another to suggest that God elects as the source of the tribes of Israel a band of brothers for whom fratricide and betrayal are innocuous actions. This is what is implied in framing Genesis 37–50 as a story about "poor, poor Joseph" and his "sordid" brothers. We might wonder then why God had to wait for Adam and Eve to bear Seth instead of simply continuing the line of election with Cain. There is no need to exculpate the brothers who clearly erred gravely in what they did to Joseph. However, the narrative also opens up the possibility that the brother's actions are indeed intelligible when read in the context of the covenant history, and moreover, the narrative raises the possibility that Joseph is somehow implicated in his own departure from the land of Canaan.

---

[17] Genesis 46:4.

Cross-Examining the Witness: Joseph

According to the Jewish sages, Joseph's dreams were more than a just nuisance to his brothers; Joseph's dreams threatened the stability and integrity of the covenant family. To recognize this, it is important to note the clear echoes of the Joseph narrative to that of the preceding and proceeding narratives as tales of conflict within the covenant family. The immediately preceding narrative (Genesis 25–37) witnessed the scandal of Jacob, Esau's younger brother, receiving the firstborn's blessing from Isaac. This disordering of the natural family relations results in 20 years of family infighting and exile for Jacob. Before Jacob shockingly inherits the family blessing, Ishmael, the firstborn son and rightful heir of Abraham, is similarly exiled to the desert because of the threat he represented to Sarah and Isaac.[18] Near the end of the Joseph story, Joseph presents his two children Ephraim and Manasseh to receive the family's blessing from Jacob, a reiteration of the fact that Joseph, the eleventh born son, is to receive the firstborn's blessing. Joseph, in order to help his aging father, puts his children on Jacob's lap and places Jacob's hands on the heads of the two boys such that Jacob's hand rested on Manasseh, the eldest and rightful heir of Joseph. However, Jacob "stretched out his right hand and laid it on the head of Ephraim, who was the younger," and in so doing, Jacob incurs Joseph's rebuke. In the very moment of performing the unnatural shape of his own election by receiving the firstborn's blessing, Joseph shows that he has not yet understood the narrative of his own life and, as such, that of the people Israel. On the other hand, for Jacob, it took losing his favored son to Egypt and then having to leave the land of Canaan and settle in the strange land of Egypt to finally grasp the unfolding election of his family. The ability to interpret dream visions is one thing, but the capacity to understand the shape of God's election of Israel is another thing altogether, and Joseph lacks the latter ability.

In *Bereishis Rabbah*, it is written that "Joseph was worthy that twelve tribes should emerge from him just as they emerged from our father Jacob."[19] In similar manner to his ancestors Abraham, Isaac,

---

18   Genesis 21:8-9; It is no coincidence that it is a band of Ishmaelites who pick up Joseph and lead him to exile.

19   Many things of the events that occur in the story can be attributed to the sense that Joseph somehow emanated or bore the disposition of someone especially elected by God for great things. The Rabbis explain that it is this recognition of Joseph's divine election that drove Potiphar's wife to desire Joseph. Meir Zlotowitz and Nosson Scherman, eds., *Bereishis: Genesis, a New Translation with a Commentary*

and Jacob, Joseph was destined to be a patriarch of the people Israel in a way that his brothers were not.[20] As such, Joseph's dreams are not mere predictions of the future; they reveal a portion of the plot within which Abraham's offspring find themselves, a plot that unfortunately neither Jacob nor Joseph nor his brothers are at first able to fully discover. Joseph's second dream (Genesis 9–11) not only invites his brothers' contempt; it also precipitates a rebuke from Jacob his father. If Joseph had understood that his dreams were a part of a larger plot, then perhaps he would not have so glibly exposed his dreams to his brothers. Had Joseph understood his dreams, he would have noted that Abraham's election implicated leaving his family and the land of Ur to be a wanderer, that Isaac's election almost rendered him a sacrifice on Mount Moriah and later implicated the exile of his brother Ishmael, and finally, his own father's election evoked the wrath of his brother Esau and resulted in Jacob having to leave the safety of the family and live in exile for 20 years. Joseph might have then seen that his unnatural election would similarly indicate a foreboding future. But Joseph, it seems, wrongly reads the plot of his life.

The actions of Joseph's brothers, though grievously mistaken, nevertheless were not expressions of irrational evil and self-interest but rather reflected a legal pronouncement. The brothers see in Joseph the possibility of Cain, Esau, and Ishmael—a usurper of the natural roles and God mandated roles. [21] But it was not only the brothers who made a gross miscalculation when attempting to get rid of Joseph; Joseph himself misreads the plot and tactlessly incurs the contempt and judgment of his brothers. This itself does not exculpate Joseph's brothers and their tragic actions. It does, however, render Joseph as an actor with weight in the narrative, as another member of the family whose inability to understand the narrative plays a part in the entire family ultimately settling in Egypt. Does this mean Joseph and his brothers are co-responsible for Joseph's departure the land of Canaan?

Bringing in the Final Witness: The God Who Elects Leaving

In her acclaimed book *The Beginning of Desire*, Avivah Zornberg brings a third option to the table in examining the causes behind

---

Anthologized from Talmudic, Midrashic and Rabbinic Sources, 2nd ed., 2 vols., ArtScroll Tanach (Brooklyn: Mesorah Publ, 1986), 2: 1563.

[20] Joseph's two sons each become the founders of a tribe of Israel, a matter that marks out Joseph and his descendants from the rest of the covenant family.

[21] *Bereishis*, 2:1574–78.

Joseph's exile to Egypt, an option that entails reading the text not primarily as unfolding with respect to Joseph nor his brothers but as a narrative responding to Jacob. Zornberg opens her reflection on Joseph's narrative by noting a peculiar feature of many early rabbinical commentaries on the text: they pay close attention and give profound significance to the opening lines of the text, "Jacob settled in the land where his father had lived as an alien, the land of Canaan."[22] Though Genesis 37; 39–50 follows the events surrounding Joseph's life, the narrative remains in many ways as a sequel to Jacob's wrestling match with God at Peniel.[23] In this chapter of his life, Jacob wrestles between the desire to "settle in peace" and the reality of leaving, which does "leap upon him" through Joseph.[24] For Zornberg, Israel's patriarchs are careful readers of history, attentive to the ways in which God's promises to Abraham are being fulfilled and in what manner. "Jacob's settling" represents an attempt by Jacob to "appropriate his life ... he would like to 'settle down' in the Holy Land, after his years in exile and danger."[25]

You might say that Jacob reads the signs of the times. It had been told to father Abraham that there would be a period of exile as part and parcel of receiving the promised land. After 20 years of living in exile and with the occurrence of Esau leaving the land of Canaan to settle in Seir,[26] Jacob interprets this as the time of the fulfillment of God's promise to give the land of Canaan to Abraham and his descendants. Joseph's exile to Egypt means more than the loss of the most beloved son of Jacob; it is a signal that Jacob has misunderstood the plot of the story. Zornberg writes, "Jacob wants to compose a whole world of his own: 'He sought to settle in peace' indicates a cognitive aesthetic ambition to see history resolved, sojourning's over, in this world. What 'leaps upon him' is the wild animal that tears Joseph apart."[27] Joseph's exile from Canaan forces Jacob into a narrative plot not of Jacob's choosing but one that Jacob is familiar with. It seems now that, like his ancestors Jacob, Isaac, and Abraham, Joseph's life is shaped by trauma and experience of leaving home.

If Jacob does not choose the narrative in which he finds himself at the moment of Joseph's exile, then who is finally writing Israel's story?

---

[22]   Genesis 37:1; Zornberg, 243.
[23]   Genesis 32.
[24]   Zornberg, 244.
[25]   Zornberg, 244.
[26]   Genesis 36:8.
[27]   Zornberg, 247.

On this question, which gets to the heart of the tensions between divine and human agency, the rabbinical tradition offers no consensus. On the one hand, Zornberg notes that, for Rashi, this chain of events can be traced to a very human cause: the "narcissism of youth" implicitly found in the opening lines which describe that "Joseph was seventeen years old."[28] In the end, Joseph's immaturity, his father's favoritism, and his brothers' hatred all combine to set up the perfect conditions for Joseph's unavoidable exit from Canaan. On the other hand, another rabbinical interpretation opens up the possibility that Jacob's life resembles that of another famous biblical figure, Job, in that the tragic events that fill both lives; even children dying (Job 1:13-18) is brought about by non-human agencies in the world.[29] This interpretation of Joseph's departure from Canaan suggests that "human beings [are] as participants in a drama of God's devising. Though ultimately not malicious, God's intents are inexorable, and human beings are for the most part unconscious actors in His plot."[30] What remains the common denominator in either circumstance is that God does not stay at a distance to the events surrounding the Abrahamic family. God is involved and implicated in Joseph's departure. Without seeking to resolve this tension, I would like to draw attention to the one verse in the narrative where God does speak, not surreptitiously but in a direct address to Jacob, precisely in the moment when Jacob is preparing to migrate with the entire family to Egypt in order to be closer to Joseph.

Nearing the end of his life, Jacob finally begins to understand the kind of narrative in which he finds himself, a narrative in which God has unconditionally determined to be bound to his family both in times of crisis and in times of blessing. Losing Joseph is not only a profound wound to Jacob's fatherly heart; it also throws into question Jacob's entire sense of the shape and nature of God's election of his family. If it is the case that it is the children of the promise—and not the natural firstborn children—who bear the covenant, then why is Joseph gone? Finding out that Joseph is alive not only reaffirmed Jacob's understanding of his family's election; it also must have made him reconsider his initial decision to settle in the Land of Canaan. After all, droughts do not last forever, and with Joseph alive and Esau still departed, nothing stood in the way of Jacob settling the land of Canaan. And yet with fearful heart and meditative mind following the unex-

---

[28] Genesis 37:2; Zornberg, 253.
[29] Zornberg, 257.
[30] Zornberg, 255.

pected course of events, Jacob makes his way to see Joseph after first asking the LORD if going down to Egypt truly was a part of the narrative through which the promises would be fulfilled. The possibility remained that Joseph, having grown up a large part of his life in Egypt, was no longer a righteous and true son of Israel, and, as such, his petition to have his family move down to Egypt might be one that went against not only Jacob's desire to settle in Canaan but also God's plan for Israel to settle in Canaan.

Preparing for yet another sojourn,[31] Jacob stops to offer sacrifices to God in Beersheba, and just as it happened at Peniel, God speaks—for the first and the only time in the entire Joseph narrative. "Then he [God] said, 'I am God, the God of your father; do not be afraid to go down to Egypt, for I will make of you a great nation there. I myself will go down with you to Egypt, and I will also bring you up again; and Joseph's own hand shall close your eyes.'"[32] If any doubts remained with Jacob that settling in the land of his father's sojourn was not the way in which history would be resolved, then God's words of comfort and hope vanish them. If any doubts remained as to whether Joseph was indeed the chosen son of the covenant despite not being the firstborn, then God's word vanish these as well. Evoking the language of the covenant, God utilizes this one and only time in the narrative to address not Joseph or the brothers but Jacob. Using words that echo the promises of the past, God tenderly and compassionately reminds Jacob once again that it is this family, this people, and this particular history—a history in which leaving is an unassailable reality—that God has elected to be bound to, to love, and to act through to fulfill the redemption of all things. The question we have been asking all along, why did Joseph leave?—a question which is complex and involves many intersecting and conflicting realities—is a question that is finally absorbed and assumed by the God of Israel. The God of Israel goes with Israel down to Egypt. God takes on the evil miscalculations of the brothers, the immaturity and narcissism of Joseph, the premature attempts to see history resolved by settling, and the trauma of leaving and makes all of these God's own story—God's own trauma—and God does all of this because God elects to make this family God's own.

---

[31]   Think here of Jacob's tired words before Pharaoh, "The years of my earthly sojourn are one hundred thirty; few and hard have been the years of my life. They do not compare with the years of the life of my ancestors during their long sojourn" (Genesis 47:9).

[32]   Genesis 46:4.

Leaving

God elects to assume no other story or people except the people Israel and their story, which is one marked by the trauma of leaving. God elects this story and no other story as the one through which the divine plan of redemption is to be carried forth. Jewish theologian Michael Wyschogrod puts it in these terms: "These are some of the puzzles that an external observer notices when he looks at the Jewish people. They add up, from the biblical perspective, to the conclusion that God is with this people in some special way, that they are peculiarly his property and that the fate of God in the human universe seem to be tied to this people."[33] In electing to be the God of Israel, God chooses to be implicated with the history of Israel, to be the God who is with and for a people who endure the trauma of leaving home and whose experience of leaving leaves a mark upon them, the mark of ceaselessly seeking rest, the mark of the foreigner living in a foreign land, indeed, the mark of bodies separated from their families and lands. Moreover, the questions evoked by the experience of leaving one's people and land, the tensions of life as a stranger in another's land, and the ongoing question of returning or settling down, are all questions that God assumes in and through and for the people Israel. In so far as Israel has to reckon with and make decisions in regard to these questions, God has to reckon with the question and decisions, not at a distance but with Israel, because God freely determines to "go down to Egypt" with Israel. As such, neither God nor Jacob and his family are passive witnesses in this drama, because God chooses to make Joseph and Jacob's departure from Canaan God's own sojourn. God is actively involved in bringing Israel's story to its redemptive fulfillment such that Israel's decisions and actions in the world have real theological and political weight, and they do so always with regard to God's covenant.[34]

While the idea that leaving and exile is part of the shape of Israel's election may seem scandalous to some who are rightly cautious about replicating the supersessionist, anti-Semitic ideology whose influence led to the Holocaust, it is nonetheless a familiar reading for many mem-

---

[33] Michael Wyschogrod, *The Body of Faith: God and the People of Israel* (Northvale: Jason Aronson, 1996), 11.

[34] This is why the question posed by the formation and establishment of the State of Israel and Zionism is always a theological question and one that all Christians who profess faith in the God of Israel as well as Jews must reckon with.

bers of the Jewish community. Both the rabbinical tradition and more modern, secular Jewish authors like Judith Butler affirm that God has elected Israel as a people on the move, because God is determined to be the God who is known by the decision to go with God's people into exile.[35] In *Parting Ways: Jewishness and the Critique of Zionism*, Butler argues against what she calls "a narrative lock down," which inseparably binds Jewishness with Zionism. She instead argues for an alternative account of Jewishness drawing from a long history of Jews living in diaspora and the corresponding politics of "making room for the other" that grow from this history. The shape of Jewish existence throughout history, Butler argues, has been that of diasporic existence, such that to be Jewish is "to be departing from oneself, cast out into the world of the non-Jew, bound to make one's way ethically and politically precisely there within a world of irreversible heterogeneity."[36] According to Butler, departing or leaving not only constitutes Jewish existence; the practices that result from leaving home and living in diaspora are at the foundation of a genuine Jewish politics, which Butler argues are antithetical to the settler-colonial practices often adopted by the State of Israel. In sum, Butler argues that Zionism gets the plot of the Jewish story wrong and therefore performs a vicious form of Jewishness. Instead, Butler argues that the correct plot of the Jewish people, not only descriptively but also normatively, is that of diaspora. It is one in which the traumatic reality of leaving is not only unavoidable but can be a determined force in constituting a just and peaceful order. If Butler's claims are right, and my reading of the Joseph narrative argues that they are, then Christians need to reckon with the implications of believing in the God of Israel, a God who goes into exile with God's people. Put in other terms, if, as Christian theologian Kendall Soulen suggests, "apart from a relationship to the people Israel, no relationship to the God of Israel is possible," then the very question of salvation and the question of how, as Christians, we relate to the stranger in our midst are more intimately entangled than we often appreciate.[37]

Why did we leave? On any given day, you might hear a distinct answer from me as to why my family and I left Peru. There are many reasons for why immigrants leave their families and their lands, none

---

[35]   I owe this insight to a colleague and dear friend, Gregory Williams.

[36]   Butler, *Parting Ways*, 15.

[37]   R. Kendall Soulen, *The God of Israel and Christian Theology* (Minneapolis: Fortress Press, 1996), 8.

of which we ought to unquestionably approve or condemn. Yet there is one story often only told in whispers by many migrants, one that needs to be heard and reckoned with.

Immigrants have to think carefully about what to bring with them and what to leave behind when they prepare to emigrate. My mother, a devout Roman Catholic, brought her 20-by-28-inch portrait of *el Sagrado Corazón de Jesús* with us when we immigrated to the United States. She has subsequently brought it to every home that we have lived in. She believes we would never have made it to the United States if God was not with us, indeed, if God was not for us. The portrait reminds her—during the worst days of struggling with sciatica while working at the factory, when facing prison for driving without a license, and when beloved church members express anti-immigrant slander—that at the end of the day, we left and God went with us. I'm certain some days she wonders if she made the right decision; most immigrants do. Yet the decision to return is not any easier than the decision to leave, both on practical and moral grounds. Leaving home is not easy for many migrants, particularly those who are considered as undesirable by their host communities. In the midst of this trauma, many pray—sometimes for the first time—asking God to protect them and their children. Upon making it to their destinations, many believe that God was with them bringing them to their new home. What are we to make of this narrative, which defies and resists the common sentiment we often hear in the public square?

As an immigrant, and especially as one who emigrated as a child, I have wrestled my whole life with the question of why my parents left Peru. Rarely was there space for me to ponder these questions either without feeling the judgmental weight of those who think that my parents left in the pursuit of their own self-interest without care for the rule of law or the common good or without the well-meaning folks who foreclose an answer on the question with before I can ask it, saying it does not matter why they left, because we are welcome. Although more complex, a similar logic is at play in people's minds who like to draw a facile line between forced migrants, or asylum seekers, and economic migrants, those who voluntarily migrate in pursuit of wealth and social advancement. One group's migration is always morally acceptable; the other's is always morally questionable. In the face of these answers, the Joseph narrative allows us to question why Joseph left and to reckon with the reality that the answer is not clear. But if I have learned anything from my mother's witness, it is that God goes with migrants in their sojourn. God goes with them to prison, God is with them in deportation buses, and God is certainly with them in their holding cells at the border. The God we find in the Joseph narrative is a God who elects to go into exile with God's people. When migrants like my mother pray, their faith and hope rests precisely in this God, the God of Jacob and Joseph, the God revealed in Jesus Christ.

CHAPTER 14

Francis of Assisi's Ministry of Example in *The Assisi Compilation*

John W. Coakley

"Preach the Gospel, sometimes with words." This saying, and variations of it, is commonly attributed to Francis of Assisi (1181/2–1226). Like some other admirable quotations ascribed to Francis, including the prayer that begins "Lord, make me an instrument of your peace,"[1] he did not actually say it. It is not to be found in his writings or in the early sources about him. Indeed, the saying appears to be of very recent origin, probably within the last 30 years,[2] and as a representation of Francis's thoughts, it is also a bit misleading, since he himself preached "with words" more often than just "sometimes." Nonetheless, the saying does preserve an echo of Francis's deepest concerns, as represented by the early traditions about him. For in those traditions,

[1] The prayer first appeared in a French devotional magazine, *La Clochette,* in 1912. Christian Renoux, *La prière pour la paix attribuée à saint François: une énigme à résoudre* (Paris: Editions franciscaines, 2001); "The Origin of the Peace Prayer of St. Francis," in *The Franciscan Archive,* accessed November 10, 2018, http://www.franciscan-archive.org/franciscana/peace.html.
[2] The website "Wikiquote" cites Charles Swindoll, *The Strong Family* (Portland: Multnomah Press, 1991), 9, as the earliest documented appearance of the quotation, accessed November 10, 2018, https://en.wikiquote.org/wiki/Francis_of_Assisi.

the concept of *example*—a rich concept that unites the inner and outer life of the person of faith and gives expression to paradoxical depths of the gospel—appears to have been crucial to Francis's understanding of himself and his mission, and, by implication, the Christian life.

This essay—which I offer in honor of Tom Boogaart and in fond memory of conversations about the grace of encountering the pre-modern worlds of our traditions—examines Francis's ministry of example as it appears in the early-fourteenth-century collection of stories known as *The Assisi Compilation*.[3] The stories are in the form of self-contained anecdotes about Francis, which are not connected to each other by a narrative line, as would be the case in a "vita" or biography. Instead, we are given in each case an isolated snapshot, or rather, a brief video, of an event in Francis's life, ostensibly as observed by friars who accompanied him in his lifetime, with attention to his words and actions and sometimes to their own feelings and reactions as well. From that viewpoint, the stories show us a very human Francis, who has to deal with personal illness, sometimes receives rude treatment from the others in his brotherhood, and is determined, sometimes at personal cost, to do what seems to him right. It is in some ways an un-idealized Francis that the stories show us—significantly, they relate few events that even to the medieval mind could be interpreted as miraculous[4]—yet the narrators' deep admiration for him, their conviction of his holiness, shines through. And the importance he attached to the setting of an example appears, to them, an important component of that holiness.

The Texts

A word is first in order about the texts themselves and how I shall read them.

---

3   I will cite these writings the Latin text of *The Assisi Compilation* (see below at note 6) as contained in the edition titled by Marino Bigaroni: *"Compilatio Assisiensis" dagli Scritti di fra Leone e Compagni su S. Francesco d'Assisi* [hereafter cited as "AC," followed by paragraph number and page number](Assisi: Edizioni Porziunola, 1975). The translations I give are my own. A translation of the whole of AC is to be found in *Francis of Assisi: Eary Documents* [hereafter cited as "ED"], 3 vols., eds. Regis J. Armstrong, A. Wayne Hellmann, and William J. Short (New York, London, and Manila: New City Press, 1999–2001), 2:113–230.

4   Those few events are the following: an apparently supernatural power forces the Bishop of Assisi out of Francis's cell, AC 54:122–24; food fortuitously appears when it is needed, AC 68:186–88 and AC 71:198; Francis hears heavenly music, AC 66:180–84; a disease among cattle is eradicated by application of water in which Francis has washed his hands, AC 94:280–82.

The question of the relation of the stories found in *The Assisi Compilation* to the actual historical Francis has been a major focus of scholarship about the saint for more than a century, and the answer is still inconclusive. [5] The collection itself is found in a manuscript located now in Perugia but almost certainly originally copied at Assisi around 1311.[6] Its contents, however, preserve earlier traditions. Almost surely, somewhere at the core of the collection are memories of the saint that were recorded by Francis's closest companions, including his confessor Brother Leo, in response to a call issued in 1244 by the General Chapter of the Franciscan Order and the Minister General at that time, Crescentius of Iesi, to be used in the writing of a new vita of the saint.[7] Indeed, several scholars have attempted to argue that a substantial portion of the collection in the Perugia manuscript—if one excludes some paragraphs that are demonstrably taken from the second vita of Francis by Thomas of Celano[8]—constitutes the actual "Leonine writings," that is, material sent by the companions to the Chapter, in more or less their original form.[9] The prevailing scholarly view, however, is skeptical that the stories in their preserved form can be trusted to be what the companions originally wrote. This is largely

---

[5]   Reviews of the history of scholarship on the question include: Rosalind Brooke, *Scripta Leonis, Rufini et Angeli Sociorum s. Francisci* (Oxford: Clarendon Press, 1970), 4–7; Jacques Dalarun, *The Misadventure of Francis of Assisi* (St. Bonaventure: Franciscan Institute Publications, 2002) 204–5; and Augustine Thompson, *Francis of Assisi: A New Biography* (Ithaca and London: Cornell University Press, 2012), 153–70, especially 164–66.

[6]   Brooke, 26–50, presents a detailed description of the manuscript at Perugia and considers its relation to other manuscript witnesses to the texts.

[7]   The call asked for stories about Francis from those who had known him to be used in the writing of a new vita to replace *The Life of the Blessed Francis* (hereafter cited as "1C"), written by Thomas of Celano in the wake of Francis's canonization in 1228 (in *Analecta Franciscana* [hereafter cited as "AF"], vol. 10 [Quaracchi: Collegium s. Bonaventurae, 1926–1941], 1–117; translation in ED 1:180–297) in view of the subsequent controversies that had emerged about the nature of the Order and thus about Francis's original intentions for it. Thomas wrote his second vita of the saint, *The Remembrance of the Desire of a Soul* (AF 10:127–268; translation in ED 2:239–393; hereafter cited as "2C"), at Crescentius's behest to incorporate material that the call had elicited. André Vauchez, in his narrative of the development of the early hagiographical sources, in *Francis of Assisi: The Life and Afterlife of a Medieval Saint,* trans. Michael Cusato (New Haven and London: Yale University Press, 2012), 188–96, helpfully places the call in context of those sources.

[8]   On the paragraphs taken from 2C, see Brooke, *Scripta Leonis,* 39. The paragraphs in question, which Brooke excludes from her edition, correspond to AC 1–3 and 23–49.

[9]   Brooke, *Scripta Leonis;* Jacques Cambell, *I fiori dei tre compagni* (Milan: Vita e Pensiero, 1967).

because in tone overall, as Augustine Thompson has written, they "present early Franciscan life as in overt or implicit contrast with a corrupt institutional Church and compromised Franciscan order"—a perspective that suggests ideological influence, direct or indirect, of the so-called "Spiritual" Franciscan party that was emerging in the late decades of the thirteenth century.[10] There can be little doubt that the stories convey a tradition of reflection on Francis—intimate in its perspective, eschewing any larger narrative framework to bring them together and attentive to his inner pain and conflicts—that was distinctively that of the companions. But by the time the stories were copied in the Perugia manuscript, that tradition had developed beyond its origins.

The stories of *The Assisi Compilation*, therefore, show us a version of Francis rooted in intimate memories of the man, which, however, were surely then conditioned and shaped over time by the experiences and reflections of a certain community of his followers. They cannot be viewed uncritically as representations of Francis as he truly was; and for that matter, even the genuine writings of the companions, if we could be sure we had them, would present us with memories that themselves would have been influenced by almost two decades of experience beyond the moment of the saint's death. Acknowledging all of this, I nonetheless will not attempt here to sift out the historical Francis from these stories. For the stories, in the form in which we have them, still provide us a genuine encounter—a literary encounter—with Francis, as, reading them, we observe and share their ostensible authors' engagement with him.[11] Here there is a parallel with how many of us read the Gospels. That is, without attempting to sift out the elusive historical Jesus from the things said about him, we value and listen attentively to the witness of each of the narratives that the tradition has given us, as firmly rooted in the memories of the man they present to us and yet also inseparable from the subsequent experience and reflection upon those memories by the communities that have preserved them and set them down in writing. And in Francis's case, that is how I read here the stories of *The Assisi Compilation*.

---

[10]   Thompson, *A New Biography*, 165–66; see also Vauchez, *Life and Afterlife,* 192–94, and Dalarun, *Misadventure*, 204–16.

[11]   I have not included consideration of the paragraphs that are manifestly from, in which, at any rate, I do not find the theme of exemparity to be conspicuous.

Francis as Self-Conscious Example

In most of the stories in *The Assisi Compilation* that picture Francis as an example to others, the focus is not directly on Francis's effect on those around him (although an effect is always implied) but rather on exemplarity as a concern of Francis himself. For him, exemplarity is a mode of relationship with others in which he can influence them not through any persuasion, instruction, coercion, or command on his part but rather solely through his behavior and comportment. Accordingly, to set an example becomes, for him, a matter of extraordinary self-scrutiny and self-discipline, and these constitute a major theme in the stories. For the narrators of the stories, then, Francis's exemplarity is not merely a personal quality or character trait or a by-product of natural virtue. Rather, it is a central object of his own desire and will, which required intentional effort, was directed to various ends, and came with a personal cost.

The stories make it clear overall that Francis regarded exemplarity to be his chief responsibility toward others and toward the brothers in particular. One of the stories pictures him in a moment of discouragement about the behavior of some of them, receiving a revelation from the Lord that

> "I did not choose you to be a literate and eloquent man to be over my family, I chose as someone simple, so that you would know, and others as well, that I am watching over my flock; but I placed you as a sign to them, so that they will see the works which I work in you, and will do them as well. ... Therefore, I say to you, do not be sad, but act as you act, and do the works you do...."[12]

Later, in the same narrative, the narrators report that after Francis resigned his prelacy over the Order (this was in 1220), in part because of illness, he would often say that now "I have no hold over the brothers but to exhibit a good example (*nisi exhibere bonum exemplum*)" and would add, in apparent reference to that earlier revelation, that

> it was revealed to me by the Lord and I know in truth that even if my infirmities had not excused me, the greater help I can weigh out to the brothers of [our] religion is if I give myself to daily prayer for it to the Lord, so that he will govern, conserve, protect

---

[12] AC 112:368.

and defend it. For in this I have bound myself to the Lord, namely that, if any brother of mine perishes from [my] bad example, I wish to be held by the Lord to give an accounting.[13]

Given that Francis considered the setting of an example to be at the core of his calling, the stories show him intent on it and thus on maintaining his own integrity. Thus, one story pictures him walking through the streets of Assisi accompanied by "many men" when a poor old woman approached him and asked alms. He "immediately gave her the coat which he had on his back"—a dramatic act of charity. But Francis had no sooner done this, than he turned to those around him and confessed that in the midst of his action he had "felt vainglory," that is, his motive had not been pure. And the narrators ("we who were with him") then remark that they "saw and heard many other similar examples ... [in which] the blessed Francis had a great and excellent zeal, namely *not to be a hypocrite before God* [emphasis added]."[14] The focus of the story is thus not on Francis's act itself but on his care not to conceal the impurity of his motives in performing it and thus to be completely honest to anyone observing him.

For the Francis of these stories, this determined effort "not to be a hypocrite before God"—to maintain his own integrity—was thus fundamental. It also involved a projection of how he would appear to others. Thus, another of the stories tells of one winter day when he was staying at a hermitage in the region around Rieti, and "because of the great cold" he patched both his own tunic and the tunic of his companion. And then on a day shortly afterward, he said "with great joy" to the companion, apparently alluding to his patching of both of their tunics,

> it is right that I be (*me oportet esse*) the form and example of all the brothers, since although it is necessary for my body to have a patched tunic, still it is right that I consider my brothers for whom the same thing is necessary but who do not or cannot have one. And so it is right that I come down (*condescendere*) to them

---

[13]   AC 112:370.

[14]   AC 82:234. The phrase "we who were with him (nos qui cum eo fuimus)" or some variation of it occurs in 21 of the 117 paragraphs of AC. Raoul Manselli, "We Who Were With Him: A Contribution to the Franciscan Question," trans. Edward Hagman, *Greyfriars Review* 14 (2000): suppl., 195. Manselli takes the phrase as strong evidence that the stories that contain it are "the most reliable and immediate testimonies we have about Francis of Assisi." Manselli, 37.

and the necessities that they suffer, and to suffer them myself, so that they, seeing this, are able to sustain greater things patiently.[15]

To this story, "we who were with him" add that they often saw him deny himself "necessities ... of food and clothing, so that they might tolerate neediness with greater patience" and thus, especially after he resigned from the prelacy of the Order, he taught them "more by works than words." Apparently, the comment is occasioned by the fact of the holes in the tunics rather than to the act of patching them; but in any event, the point is not just that he set an example of doing without "necessities" but that by doing so he intended to communicate a sense of solidarity and encouragement.[16]

Other stories illustrate this concern about the appearance of his actions, in concrete terms in particular situations. In one story set in winter, when he was suffering from the cold "because of the weakness of his spleen and a chill in his stomach," Francis's companion begged him to allow a piece of fox skin to be sewn on the inside of his tunic next to the affected parts of his body. Francis agreed but only on condition that a corresponding piece of the fur be sewn, visibly, to the *outside* of that part of the tunic as well, presumably so that he would be acknowledging his weak acquiescence to this bit of luxury.[17] Another story recounts that once in Assisi when recovering from a serious illness, he left his sick bed and, after returning from preaching to the people of the town, removed his clothes, and, naked, directed his companion to lead him back before them, by a rope around his neck, to confess as a penitent that "in my illness I ate meat and broth made from meat"—that is, that he had broken his ascetic discipline.[18] In yet another story, after being attacked

---

[15] AC 111:364–66.

[16] AC 111:366. In another story, in explanation to Cardinal Hugolino (the future Pope Gregory IX) why he has, to the cardinal's embarrassment, gone begging for alms before attending a dinner at the cardinal's house and shared the scraps of food he had obtained with the other's guests, Francis explains that he has been setting an example to the brothers so that they are not "held back by shame and a bad example" from asking alms themselves (AC 97:294). Or again, as the narrators explain at the end of a story about Francis's compassionate response in the early days of the brotherhood to a brother who was fasting excessively and awakened the others at night by crying out that he was "dying" of hunger, Francis himself claimed to be weak of body and to have a genuine need for substantial food, but "because it is fitting for me to be a form and example for all the friars, I wish to have, and be content with, scanty food and things, and not fine ones" (AC 50:114).

[17] AC 81:232–34.

[18] AC 80:226–30, (cf. AC 81:230–32, which alludes to other similar incidents). There are parallels to the episode in 1C 1.52 and in Bonaventure, *Legenda Maior* 6.2 (AF

by demons during a night spent in comfortable surroundings provided by a Roman cardinal, Francis interpreted the event as punishment for his having enjoyed luxury while some of his brothers "go through the world undergoing hunger and much tribulation and others who live in poor little huts and hermitages." He "must always offer them a good example, for this is why I have been given to them," he explained to the cardinal, who allowed him to leave his lodging and return to the brothers.[19] Or again, "we who were with him" tell how, on another occasion, after he had been staying in a cell that had been prepared for him by "a certain brother, a spiritual man, to whom Francis was very close," he abruptly abandoned it when one of the brothers spoke of it to him as "your little cell." He did this because "by his example he wished to have no house or cell in this world, nor to have one made for him"[20]— that is, because he worried that he would appear to be practicing a less than absolute poverty.

Another particularly touching instance of Francis's use of example pastorally is the story of his attentions to one of the brothers, "a spiritual man" who was "weak and ill." Francis knew full well, says the narrator, that (like himself) the brothers were committed to bear their illnesses with "cheerfulness and patience" rather than treat them with medicine or special diets. Still, he was "moved with tenderness" toward this particular brother and thought he would be helped by eating some ripe grapes. And so,

> on a certain day, he got up very early in secret and called that brother; and leading him to the vineyard which is next to the church, he chose a certain vine in which there were good sound grapes, ready to eat. He sat down with that brother next to the vine, and, so that the brother would not be ashamed to eat alone,

---

10:582-3; translation in ED:570-71). Hester Goodenough Gelber takes all three accounts as a starting point for an insightful analysis of Francis's exemplarity (as a biographical exercise, not a literary one) from the point of view of existential psychoanalysis in "A Theater of Virtue: The Exemplary World of St. Francis of Assisi," in *Saints and Virtues*, ed. John Stratton Hawley (Berkeley: University of California Press, 1987), 15–35.

19   And "we who were with him" (see note 13) then insert a comment about the effectiveness of Francis's example—i.e., they bring the actual effect of his actions on the brothers into the story—saying that when they or any other of the brothers who knew about his commitment to share their sufferings, think about this, they cannot hold back their tears, and find their own capacity for patience increased (AC 117:390–92).

20   AC 57:146–48.

he began to eat the grapes. And as they ate together, that brother praised God; and, for as long as he lived, he often recalled to the other brothers with great devotion and many tears the mercy that the holy father had showed him.[21]

The crux of Francis's pastoral action here is the initiative he takes to begin eating the grapes himself, this being the setting of the example, which here is not so much a matter of offering encouragement or of making sure that his own behavior did not become a stumbling-block, as in the other instances we have seen; rather it is a matter of direct compassion and empathy.

If the Francis of these stories can present himself as example in order to express his care of individuals, he can also do so for ends of a more strategic nature to further his own work and the brotherhood. Thus, in another of the stories, when the brothers asked him for a privilege from the pope to bypass the authority of bishops (who were often delaying or withholding altogether their permission to brothers to preach in their dioceses), Francis, rebuking them, told them, "You are keeping me from converting the whole world in the way that God wants." For, he said, he intended that the bishops themselves would be converted "through humility and reverence," and afterward they would not just permit but would "implore" the brothers to preach to their people. And then he said, "The privilege I want is from the Lord himself—namely, the privilege not to have any privilege from humans, unless it be to show reverence toward all and, through obedience to the holy Rule, to convert everyone through example rather than word."[22]

If the stories make clear that Francis's exemplarity was no mere by-product or incidental effect of his virtue but something highly intentional on his part to which he devoted strenuous effort, they also suggest that he paid a personal price for it, or rather, for the renunciation of any other power than that of example. Again, his resignation from the office of prelate of the Order was, for the authors of these stories, a crucial event. For after describing it—and noting that Francis afterward asked for one of the brothers who were his companions to be appointed as a kind of vicar for the minister general to whom Francis could be immediately subject to all the time, thus highlighting his obedience to authority—"we who were with him" add the comment that

---

[21] AC 53:120–22.
[22] AC 20:61–62.

many times, when the other brothers did not give satisfaction to him in his needs or said something to him which could give offense (*per quod solet homo moveri ad scandalum*), immediately he went into prayer and afterward did not say in recollection, "such-and-such a brother did not treat me well (*talis frater michi non satisfecit*)" but rather [only] that he "said such and such to me (*dixit me tale verbum*)." The closer he came to his death, the more solicitous he was in all perfection to consider how in all humility and poverty he might live and die.[23]

The narrators appear to be saying that even, or maybe even especially, within the brotherhood itself, he could be on the receiving end of unkind behavior, to which, in exemplary fashion, he would not retaliate or complain.

The Reception of Francis's Example

Though on the matter of Francis's exemplarity, the stories of *The Assisi Compilation* mainly focus on the person of the saint himself, telling us about Francis's efforts and putative intentions, they also at a few points witness to how those efforts were received—that is, what effect Francis's example actually had on others. In the process, they address the question of what it meant for those observing him to call him "saint," and, not incidentally, they sometimes picture Francis also reacting to peoples' actual responses—that is, not just formulating his intentions but also reflecting on the results.

One story in particular vividly illustrates the way others could understand and react to Francis's exemplarity. The events of the story took place shortly before his death, which occurred in April of 1226. Francis, we know, had been ill for several years with both a virulent form of conjunctivitis that had begun to threaten his eyesight and an advanced case of malaria that would indeed soon lead to his death.[24] Now, as he was staying with some other brothers in the town of Begnara some 40 kilometers' journey eastward from his home town of Assisi, his feet and legs began to swell: likely, a sign of kidney failure brought on by the malaria. Word got back to Assisi that Francis was dying. In response, the city sent knights to conduct him home immediately. Why? Because,

---

[23]   AC 111:364–66.
[24]   On Francis's final illnesses, see Raoul Manselli, *St. Francis of Assisi* (Chicago: Franciscan Herald Press, 1985), 248.

we are told matter-of-factly, if he died elsewhere, "others would have his most holy body." That would not do, for Assisi considered it a foregone conclusion, even then before his death, that their Francis was a saint—a great saint, even—whose place of burial would be a place of renown and miracle.

The heart of the story, then, is something that happened on the trip home. The knights, with Francis and his companions in tow, stopped in a "certain town belonging to the commune of Assisi"—apparently the town of Satriano, roughly halfway on the journey—to find food. Francis himself "rested in the house of a certain man who received him with joy and great charity." In other words, he receives hospitality from someone who was honored to provide it, apparently (so the context of the story would suggest) on the basis of Francis having begged, that is, asked for alms in his usual way, "for the love of God." Meanwhile, the knights had been going "through the town" trying to *buy* themselves something to eat, and when they were unsuccessful, they came back to Francis and said to him "jokingly (*quasi ludendo*)" that he would have to give them some of his alms. Francis, however, replied seriously to them that they should beg alms themselves: "You didn't find anything, because you trusted in your 'flies,' that is, your coins, and not in God. Go back to the houses where you went looking for something to buy, and without being ashamed ask them for alms for the love of God, and the Holy Spirit will inspire them and you will receive abundantly." So they went and asked for alms, "for the love of God," and they received food "in abundance." They returned again to Francis and reported this. Then the story concludes with the words: "They took this for a great miracle, considering that what he had predicted to them came true to the letter." [25]

I take this story as another case of Francis providing an example to others, even though it is true that, uncharacteristically here, he did not just rely on his own actions—in this case, his begging of alms—to convey that example but actually proposed to the knights that they follow it. Nonetheless, when he spoke to them, he was pointing to his own example, not simply telling them what to do. And they followed that example, with success.

But the story takes another turn at the end, when Francis's effort at engaging the knights through his own example apparently backfired, for the conclusion that the knights drew from Francis's successful

---

[25] AC 96:286–90.

experiment with them—the experiment born of Francis's determination to have them share in his experience, to share his subjectivity rather than make him a saintly object—was precisely to reinforce their notion of him as a saintly object. The lesson they drew was not that they should cease relying on their money but that Francis correctly predicted their success, and, accordingly, that this was a "miracle," proving again that Francis was a man of extraordinary powers. They missed the point, in (we might add) a long tradition of witnesses of holy people, going back to the Jesus of the Gospels and his clueless disciples. In this sense, the story ends in irony.

But if the story suggests a failure in that sense, it also does not question the knights' recognition of Francis's sanctity, his status as a "saint"; and about that status here, there is more to say. For Francis himself did not deny it. There is nothing here about Francis balking at being considered a saint or at the purpose of the journey itself—namely, to make his corpse available to the people of Assisi as a holy object. What are we to make of that?

Another story in *The Assisi Compilation* addresses this matter of Francis's own attitude toward being called a saint and suggests a gloss on the story of what happened at Satriano. In this other story, Francis did express distress at the appellation "saint," but he also, in a certain sense, accepted it. The place is a town called Terni. Francis had just preached to the people of the town, and the local bishop, who had heard the sermon, stood up and said to the people, "The Lord from the beginning when he planted and edified his Church, has always illuminated it with holy men, who have cultivated it by word and example. Now moreover in this latest hour he has illuminated it by this little man who is poor and despised and illiterate...." Later on, Francis prostrated himself before the bishop, thanking him for not calling him a saint. "For," Francis told him, "other men say [of me], here is a saint (*sanctus*)!—attributing glory and holiness to the creature and not the creator. But you, as a man of discretion, have separated the precious from the vile." The narrators then adduce some other quotations from Francis to explain what they believe he meant in commending the bishop's words. Thus, he sometimes would tell people that it was still possible that he might have "sons and daughters"—that is, that he might give up the chastity that was part of his saintly reputation; and more fundamentally to the point, he would make a distinction between himself and what God was doing in him. Thus, he would say that if and when "the Lord wishes to take his treasure from me, which he has given me, what would remain to me, except only the body and soul," which would make him no different from a "thief" or an "infidel." Or again he likened himself to a picture painted on wood, a picture of which may be "honored according to God's gifts" that have been bestowed upon it.[26]

This story of what happened at Terni is above all a humility story, in which Francis is pointing out that whatever God has done in him is God's doing and not his own. But even in this story Francis is not denying what God has done in him; and one can imagine him not denying it at Satriano either. For the overarching importance, for him, of being an example, means that whether he is a "saint" or not is beside the point. And so, I imagine him at Satriano saying, or thinking, something like this:

> I am a "saint": this is a given, if what you mean by it is that others call me one. I do not try to deny it; indeed, I accept that others see me that way. I have been known to point out that I may yet engender children, as though to remind everyone of my own fallibility, the possibility that I would lack staying power. That's all true enough. But even to say that, anymore—to make that mild rebuttal—feels to me as though it is just to call attention to the claim of sanctity, to say I have some stake in it. But I have no stake in it. Better, then, to live with it; better not to rebut. The point is that I have my own consistency to worry about, not for the sake of keeping up a "saint's" reputation but for the sake of my brothers and my neighbors: to encourage them, to respect their suffering and their consciences, and so above all things to set an example. So when the knights show up to bring me to Assisi so that I would not die anywhere else: I see it as a non-issue. Let the knights come, let them do what they have been charged to do. Ah, and let me do what I have been charged to do too—which, all unawares, they have let me do, as it turns out, and have now been implicated in it, and thus in the very undermining of the claim that some are saints, some are not. Their jest to me—asking for some of our alms—was based on that assumption, which they had not even thought about (knights not being about charity, so they assumed). But I challenged this: Why should they not ask alms for the love of God? The root of their failure to find food wasn't their status as knights, as though knight were a synonym for "not

---

[26] AC 10:26–28.

a holy man"; their failure was their faith in their money, a faith not peculiar to knights. I had them share the world with me for a moment, see it as I do, give up the distinction between saint and non-saint, and they did, for a moment—until, that is, they reflected on the whole matter and decided their success at alms was proof of my sanctity, and then we were back at the beginning again.

Conclusion: Example and Reflection

So the story of what happened at Satriano ends in irony. In another sense, though, this is not an ironic story. It is a witness to the social fact of Francis's sanctity—to the fact that people experienced him as a saint—and it has the charm of being written in the voice of some persons who believed they saw things, in effect, from the saint's point of view, who shared with him some measure of his motivation and sensibility—persons with whom, one might say, Francis had been more successful in sharing himself than he was with the knights. And those authors simultaneously witness to the fact of his saintly reputation and to the real means by which Francis attained it. For the authors are attempting to show us the *genesis* of the event that caused or, rather, reinforced the knights' conviction that he was a saint, and it does not have to do at heart with miraculous powers in the way they thought. Rather, as Francis himself said at Terni, it is a matter of the evident image painted by God on the mere flat wood of Francis and accordingly of Francis's determination to stand, with empathy and without hypocrisy, as an example for others, intent on exhibiting that image and relying on its own power to affect those around him. The narrators of the Satriano story are showing us that in this sense the knights did not miss the point, for Francis *was* indeed in that sense a person of holiness, and this meant the event *was* indeed a kind of miracle, emerging as it did from his quite extraordinary person; it is just that the writers of all these stories understand in some measure—as the knights did not, or did not care to—the way such a miracle came about.

The writings of *The Assisi Compilation* have much to say about Francis as example; indeed, the theme is everywhere in those writings and fundamental to the authors' ostensible experience of Francis. We should also note, however, as a coda to this essay, a rather striking *absence* in these stories—namely, an absence of much reference to Francis's own relation to Jesus Christ. Other of the early sources—the vitae by Thomas of Celano (1228 and ca. 1247), and especially the official vita by Bonaventure (1263)—began to develop the idea of Francis as someone whose life displayed a "conformity" to that of Christ, a conformity that was powerfully symbolized in the appearance of the stigmata, that is, of wounds on his hands and side, and (as Bonaventure charted out painstakingly) also visible in the progressive course of his inner experience—an immensely important vein of interpretation in the centuries to follow, in which the role of Francis as one who *set* an example is overshadowed by his role as the greatest *follower* of an example, that of Christ.[27] The authors of the stories no doubt knew of these interpretations in their early forms; furthermore, they report sayings of Francis in other contexts in which he adduces Christ as an example for himself, and they also do make one reference, though only one, to the stigmata.[28] But such large interpretation of Francis in Christological terms was foreign to their intent, which was to tell what they saw from day to day without reflecting much on it, or anyway without trying to tie it all together. For what the General Chapter of the Order had called for in 1244 was raw material for the writing of the life of Francis, not a finished product; and rich raw material is what these writings, even in the later form in which we have them, provide. But for us, this is no bad thing, for they are rich raw material for our reflection too.

---

[27] On Christ as model for Francis, see Vauchez, *Life and Afterife*, 205–28, and Jaroslav Pelikan, *Jesus through the Centuries: His Place in the History of Culture* (New York: Perennial Library, 1987), 133–44. I have discussed Bonaventure's development of the theme in "The Conversion of St. Francis and the Writing of Christian Biography, 1228–1263," *Franciscan Studies* 72 (2014): 67–68.

[28] AC 51:16, 57:148 (sayings); 94:280 (stigmata).

CHAPTER 15

Ben Zoma Shakes the World: Two Sources or Two Powers

Christopher Barina Kaiser

Introduction

Although Christians tend to focus on the six "days" of Genesis 1 and debate their nature, Jewish exegetes[1] have attended equally to the ten "God said" phrases (*wayyo'mer 'Elohim*) found there (e.g., Mishnah Avot 5:1; Babylonian Talmud Baba Batra 47a). All of the "God said" texts in Genesis 1 are followed by "God made/created," "God saw," or both. The pattern is repetitious enough to become almost hypnotic but varied enough to hold interest.[2]

---

[1] For readers who wish to explore early midrash on their own, the best place to start would be the Classics of Western Spirituality volume, *The Classic Midrash: Tannaitic Commentaries on the Bible*, trans. Reuven Hammer (New York: Paulist Press, 1995). That covers third- and fourth-century *midrashim* on Exodus, Leviticus, Numbers, and Deuteronomy. For the midrash on Genesis dated to the early fifth century that is the focus of this study, see *Genesis Rabbah*, translated in three volumes by Jacob Neusner (Atlanta: Scholars Press, 1985).

[2] On this general subject, I have benefitted greatly from discussions with my friend and colleague, Tom Boogaart. Tom patiently reminds me of the contingency of

More than a decade ago, Aron Pinker pointed out a problem with this apparently seamless pattern.[3] The "God said" texts in Genesis 1 are readily seen as stressing creation by the *fiat* (Vulgate Latin for "let there be"). In contrast to Babylonian and other creation stories, the LORD can create by a mere word—"without hands," as it were. The Creator God, who needed only to speak and it was so, is transcendent and non-anthropomorphic.[4] This image of the Deity is reinforced in parts of the Palestinian Targums (Aramaic paraphrases of the Hebrew Bible).[5]

However, the sequel to "God said" in each case is quite anthropomorphic (except, for obvious reasons, for the command to be fruitful and multiply). In half the instances, "God said" is followed by "God made/created" (the firmament, celestial lights, sea creatures and birds, land animals, and humanity). In cases where the emergence and behavior of creatures were spontaneous responses to God's command (light, seas and dry land, vegetation, and the consumption of vegetation), "God said" is followed by "God saw that it was good," which is equally anthropomorphic.[6] In three cases, the sequel to "God said" is both "God made/created" and "God saw" (celestial lights, sea creatures and birds,

---

God's creation and the risks of relying on source critical approaches to the Hebrew Bible, and I believe he will find a kindred spirit in Ben Zoma. I also wish to express my appreciation for Prof. Alan Segal's thoughtful suggestions and encouragement based on an earlier draft of this essay (email dated March 8, 2010). May his memory be a blessing.

3   Aron Pinker, "Ben Zoma's Query on Genesis 1:7: Was It What Drove Him Insane?" *Judaism* 55 (Fall-Winter 2006): 51–58.

4   Pinker here follows the standard interpretation of the "God said" phrases in Genesis 1; cf. Gerhard von Rad, *Genesis, A Commentary*, trans. John H. Marks, revised ed. (London: SCM Press, 1972), 51: "The idea of creation by the word preserves ... the most radical distinction between Creator and creature." For an alternative view, in which the divine speech becomes the animating principle of creation like the "spirit" in Genesis 1:2, see Mark S. Smith, *The Priestly Vision of Genesis 1* (Minneapolis: Fortress Press, 2010), 55–57, 66–67.

5   The Fragment Targum has the *"memra* (the word) of the LORD" make the creatures in Genesis 1. Instead of God seeing that the creatures were good, the Targums make it "manifest before the LORD" that they were good; ET in Michael L. Klein, *The Fragment-Targums of the Pentateuch* (Rome: Biblical Institute Press, 1980), 3–6. Targum Neofiti is less consistent; ET in Martin McNamara, *Targum Neofiti 1*: Genesis and Exodus, 2 vols. (Collegeville: Liturgical Press, 1992/1994), 1:52–55. Michael Klein argues that the Palestinian Targums are not as consistently anti-anthropomorphic as some scholars have assumed; Klein, "The Translation of Anthropomorphisms and Anthropopathisms in the Targumim," in *Congress Volume, Vienna, 1980: International Organization for the Study of the Old Testament Congress*, ed. John Adney Emerton, VT Supplement 32 (Leiden: Brill, 1981), 162–77 (177).

6   Cf. Job 28:27.

and land animals). The God of Genesis 1 who made and inspected what he had made is straightforwardly immanent and anthropomorphic.[7]

Pinker's article was not primarily about the text of Genesis but about a fascinating aggadic midrash on one of the verses (Genesis 1:7) that is associated with the name of the second-century Tannaitic sage, Shim'on ben Zoma[8] (Genesis Rabbah 4:6[7]). The early Rabbis (the sages) differed from most modern biblical exegetes in that they encouraged a range of interpretations of the text so long as they were based on actual features of the text. They often focused on slight shifts in spelling or characterization that would seem to us to be mere accident or artistic license (or editorial slippage). In its attention to detail, midrashic methods were something like the quest for indicators of different sources in modern source criticism. Pinker duly noted this similarity in Genesis Rabbah's characterization of Ben Zoma and concluded that the sage had himself discerned a duality of sources lying behind the text.[9] According to the midrash, this unprecedented discovery was radical enough for its time to "shake the world" and perhaps even cause the author to lose his mind.[10]

---

[7] Von Rad calls attention to the "terminological unevenness which persists clearly throughout the chapter" and attributes this discrepancy to two distinct "voices," one stressing the distance between Creator and creature, and the other bringing God's hands in direct contact with his subjects; Von Rad, *Genesis*, 53–54. Note that the creation of celestial lights and that of sea creatures involve both "God made/created" and "God saw."

[8] "Ben" is the Hebrew word for "son (of)," not to be confused with a nickname for "Benjamin." So the surname Ben Zoma means the son of Zoma.

[9] Pinker, "Ben Zoma's Query," 51. Pinker joins a long line of interpreters who go beyond the world of midrash to identify Ben Zoma's ideas. Ephraim Urbach interpreted Ben Zoma's exegesis of Genesis 1:2 (the way R. Joshua is reported to have heard it) in terms of various Alexandrian philosophies; Urbach, *The Sages: Their Concepts and Beliefs*, trans. Israel Abrahams (Cambridge: Harvard University Press, 1987), 191. Saul Lieberman interpreted it in terms of Sethian Gnostic texts; Lieberman, "How Much Greek in Jewish Palestine?" in *Biblical and Other Studies*, ed. Alexander Altmann (Cambridge: Harvard University Press, 1963), 123–41 (136, 139). Israel Efros interpreted it in terms of teachings attributed to Simon Magus; Efros, *Ancient Jewish Philosophy: A Study in Metaphysics and Ethics* (Detroit: Wayne State University Press, 1964), 58. Samson H. Levey interpreted it in terms of the Epistles of Paul and the Gospels; Levey, "The Best Kept Secret of the Rabbinic Tradition," *Judaism* 21 (1972): 454–69 (465–7). Henry Fischel interpreted it (tentatively) in terms of Thales and Epicurus; Fischel, *Rabbinic Literature and Greco-Roman Philosophy: A Study of Epicurea and Rhetorica in Early Midrashic Writings* (Leiden: Brill, 1973), 78–89. Christopher Rowland interpreted it in terms of the Apocryphon of John; Rowland, *The Open Heaven: A Study of Apocalyptic in Judaism and Early Christianity* (New York: Crossroad, 1982), 330. Methodologically speaking, such extraneous sources should be consulted only as a last resort.

There are several problems with this interpretation—historical anachronism being just one—but I believe Pinker has pointed the way to an even better solution, one that is more readily contextualized in the documentable concerns of Tannaitic midrash. To state my conclusion at the outset: what Ben Zoma discovered in the account of creation was not a duality of literary sources but a polarity in the divine the Creator—what in current academic parlance is called "two powers in heaven."[11] To support this reading, I shall first review two exegetical traditions associated with Ben Zoma elsewhere in rabbinic literature, then focus on the possibility of two powers in Genesis Rabbah 4:6, and conclude with some thoughts on how Ben Zoma's midrashic exegesis could possibly have "shaken the world."

Ben Zoma's Reputation for Exegetical Detail (Mishnah Berakhot 1:5)

The hermeneutical premise of this paper is that *midrashim* should be read in the context of associations made in early rabbinic discussions, available to us now in the form of Tannaitic and Amoraic literature. We cannot hope to reconstruct a "historical Ben Zoma" with any certainty, but we can explore the methods and interpretations habitually associated with his name.[12]

---

[10]   Pinker, "Ben Zoma's Query," 56. Early traditions concerning Ben Zoma's being "smitten" (*eino ba'olam*) in the Garden (*Pardes*) occur in Tosefta Hagigah 2:3–5, where it is implied that he feasted his eyes on something more than was appropriate for a mere servant. The earliest attestation to Ben Zoma's exegesis of Genesis 1:2 immediately follows (Tosefta Hagigah 2:6). Note, however, that the Yerushalmi parallel states that Ben Zoma died as a saint and his associate, Ben Azzai, was the stricken one (Jerusalem Talmud Hagigah 2:1, 77b).

[11]   Alan F. Segal, *Two Powers in Heaven: Early Rabbinic Reports about Christianity and Gnosticism* (Leiden: Brill, 1977). The role of "two powers" thinking in Ben Zoma traditions has been pointed out by Efros, *Ancient Jewish Philosophy*, 58–9 (regarding Genesis Rabbah 4:6 [7] and 5:4) and by Daniel Boyarin, *Border Lines: The Partition of Judaeo-Christianity* (Philadelphia: University of Pennsylvania Press, 2004), 143 (regarding Genesis Rabbah 5:4). I avoid the term "binitarian," used by Segal (*Two Powers*, 150) and Boyarin (*Border Lines*, 131) because of the theological resonances it has for many people. I would also differentiate the apocalyptic and *heikhalot* visions of a second divine power in heaven, which belong to exegetical traditions of ascent (*ma'aseh merkavah*), from exegetical traditions concerning a second divine power upon earth or over the waters (*ma'aseh bere'shit*).

[12]   As I have argued in *Seeing the Lord's Glory* (Minneapolis: Fortress, 2014), most early Jews learned their biblical traditions not by reading but through participation in performances. where the part of the biblical prophet or rabbinic sage was presented (present-ed in the literal sense) by an inspired leader. Even in a synagogue service with an open Torah scroll (*qeri'at ha-Torah*), the cantor would normally recite the text by heart.

One important feature of Ben Zoma's reputation was that he was credited with attention to minor details of the biblical text. Such attention is exhibited in the very first mention of his name in the Tannaitic literature, his interpretation of the "exodus from Egypt" in Mishnah Berakhot 1:5 (where it is treated as the third part of the Shema). In what would become a standard rabbinic exegetical move, Ben Zoma pointed to the single word "all" (*kol*) in Deuteronomy 16:3. In the biblical text, the LORD commanded the people to remember the exodus for all the days of their lives (*kol yemei hayyeikhah*). Why for "all the days" and not just for "the days of your lives"? Each word of Scripture must add significant meaning. Perhaps the word "all" was added to include the nights as well as the 12-hour days. Ben Zoma inferred that the exodus was to be recited (as the third part of the Shema) during nights as well as days.

As we shall see, the traditions associated with his name in Genesis Rabbah also involve attention to small details of the text. The rabbinic traditions concerning Ben Zoma exhibit consistency in terms of exegetical method and may be expected to exhibit consistency in other regards as well. There are three passages in Genesis Rabbah that depict Ben Zoma's methods of midrashic exegesis. Before turning to the text that Pinker focused on, let me briefly review the other two in order to discern the general picture of his distinctive approach.

Two Powers in Genesis Rabbah 2:4 (on Genesis 1:2)

The most widely discussed of these traditions is Ben Zoma's exposition of the account of creation (*ma'aseh bere'shit*) in the presence of Rabbi Yehoshu'a (Joshua) ben Hananiah.[13] The relevant part according to David J. Halperin's unembellished translation reads as follows:

---

[13]   As stated above, I regard the "Ben Zoma" of these traditions as a persona representing one side of the rabbinic conversation (not necessarily a sect or school of thought). I refer to his statements as midrash, not as actions of an historical figure. William Scott Green follows Jacob Neusner in allowing for rabbinic circles that identified themselves with particular masters and with others who adhered to his teachings; Green, "What's in a Name? The Problematic of Rabbinic 'Biography,'" in *Approaches to Ancient Judaism: Theory and Practice*, ed. William Scott Green, 6 vols., Brown Judaic Studies (Missoula: Scholars Press, 1978–85), 1, (1978), 77–96 (84). Hayim Lapin argues that blocks of source material in the Mishnah that were attributed to individual second-century Rabbis "may reflect the work of 'schools' or circles with special regard for those individuals." He also states, however, that "these corpora [may] not preserve the traces of distinct schools espousing their founders' theories and techniques ....."; Lapin, *Rabbis as Romans: The Rabbinic Movement in Palestine, 100–400 CE* (Oxford: Oxford University Press, 2012), 59.

Simeon ben Zoma was standing, rapt [in thought]. Rabbi Yehoshu'a passed by .... He [Ben Zoma] said to him, "I was gazing at *ma'aseh bere'shit* [the account of creation] and there is between the upper and the lower waters only the equivalent of two or three fingers. *And the spirit of God [ruach 'elohim] blowing* is not written here [in Genesis 1:2], but *[And the spirit of God] hovering*: like a bird which flies and flutters with its wings, its wings touching and not touching." Rabbi Joshua turned away and said to his students, "Ben Zoma has gone."[14]

The placement of this little drama in Genesis Rabbah (*parashah* 2) indicates an ongoing discussion concerning the exegesis of Genesis 1:2 in rabbinic circles. Clearly, there was something daring about Ben Zoma's exegesis: Rabbi Yehoshu'a's verdict that he had "gone" and a concluding line about his leaving this world within a few days[15] evidently meant (in rabbinic hyperbole) that Ben Zoma had contravened his colleagues' understanding of Genesis 1.[16] In fact, the parallel versions in Tosefta Hagigah 2:6 and Yerushalmi Hagigah 2:1 (77a-b) place the exposition in the context of explicit warnings concerning restricted topics like the exegesis of Genesis 1, the very topic that Ben Zoma expounds (see below on the double meaning of *ma'aseh bere'shit*). Accordingly, I shall focus on Ben Zoma's midrashic exegesis and leave various other intriguing aspects of this midrash to others.

Ben Zoma's opening contention was simple enough: the space between the upper and lower waters was originally only a few finger

[14]   David J. Halperin, *The Merkabah in Rabbinic Literature* (New Haven: American Oriental Society, 1980), 79–80. The Hebrew text is given in J. Theodor and Ch. Albeck, *Midrash Bereshit Rabba: Critical Edition with Notes and Commentary*, 3 vols. (Jerusalem: Wahrmann Books, 1965), 1:17, lines 4–18. I work with the midrashic version of this tradition (Genesis Rabbah 2:4) because it is most readily compared with the primary text of interest. Parallel translations of all four rabbinic versions are conveniently provided by Rowland (*Open Heaven*, 325-27) and more schematically by Halperin (*Merkabah in Rabbinic Literature*, 96–97).

[15]   Urbach, *Sages*, 189 ("Before many days Ben Zoma departed this world"); Levey, "The Best Kept Secret," 456 ("Only a few days remained for Ben Zoma in this world"); Rowland, *Open Heaven*, 326 ("The days were few for Ben Zoma to be in the world"). It is not necessary for our purposes to adjudicate the issue of strict exegesis (Halperin et al.) versus mystic transport (Rowland et al.). Suffice it to say that for serious rabbinic students the exegetical world was the real world. All exegesis was "mystical" and, at the same time, "rational." The divine between the two modes of knowing is our problem, not theirs.

[16]   Rowland (*Open Heaven*, 330) and Middleton ("Whence the Feet?" 66-67) both refer R. Joshua's comment to Ben Zoma's exceeding the boundaries of accepted rabbinic exegesis regarding creation.

widths, just enough for a small bird to fly through. But why should there have been even a few finger widths? All would agree that the space between the upper and lower waters was not opened until the creation of the great expanse (or firmament) on Day Two.[17] In view of Ben Zoma's reputation for attention to textual details, however, we can readily assume that he saw a preliminary separation already on Day One. There are two reasons for this. For one thing, the ruach (wind, breath, spirit) of God was hovering in between the upper and lower waters in Genesis 1:2 (evidently, searching for a place to perch; cf. Genesis 7:8-12). For another, we notice that heaven and earth are verbally balanced in a symmetrical pair.[18] If so, the expanse between above and below ("heaven") must have been present in a preliminary way even before its widening and naming on Day Two. In the same way, its companion ("earth") was present on Day One before its full formation and naming on Day Three.[19] As various commentators have pointed out, this cosmological view was not unique to Ben Zoma in rabbinic discussions: it is also attributed to a number of other Sages in Bavli Hagigah 15a. So there was nothing very risky here.[20]

For these reasons, Rabbi Yehoshu'a's concern about this exegesis must lie in Ben Zoma's (reputed) way of reading Genesis 1:2, not in his cosmology. The clue is found in his "not this, but that" reasoning; "not "blowing, but hovering." The ruach 'elohim was sometimes understood as a wind or breath that God blew over the lower waters (e.g., Genesis Rabbah 2:3). To the contrary, Ben Zoma points out that the verb in Genesis 1:2 is not "blew" but "hovered" (merachepet). It implies that the ruach described was not an impersonal wind but the Spirit of God in the form of a small bird.[21] The one other time that "hovering" is used

---

[17] Genesis 1:6-8.

[18] Genesis 1:1; cf. Genesis 2:1, 4.

[19] Middleton unaccountably states that Ben Zoma's conclusion lacks any scriptural authority; "Whence the Feet?' 67. Given the creativity of rabbinic exegesis, it is dangerous to say that any recorded midrash has no authority.

[20] Certainly, the Bavli has a more developed (and contextualized) perspective than Palestinian *midrashim*, but I infer that the exegesis was already widely accepted in earlier generations: it is not likely that these parallel interpretations were adduced merely to support (or imitate) the view attributed to Ben Zoma.

[21] Hyam Macoby argues that Ben Zoma read *ruach* in Genesis 1:2 as "wind" rather than "spirit"; Macoby, "Ben Zoma's Trance," *Journal of Progressive Judaism* 1 (1993), 103–108 (105n.2). His reasoning is that (a) Targum Onkelos regarded *ruach* as "wind"; and (b) Ben Zoma saw that the space between the waters was just large enough for a "hovering" wind (not an average-sized bird). On the other hand, Macoby understands the Bavli parallel to read *ruach* as the "Spirit of God" and even draws a parallel to Marduk in the Babylonian Genesis (*Enuma elish*); Macoby, "Ben Zoma's Trance," 108. Middleton rejects this latter possibility, noting that

in the Torah, it depicts the gentle action of a mother bird. According to the Song of Moses, the LORD cares for Israel "as an eagle ... hovers over [*yirachep*] its young."[22] Our midrash does not quote this text word for word, but it does appear in the Tosefta and Yerushalmi versions, and the intertextual allusion is pretty clear in view of the fact that these are the only two uses of the Hebrew verb *rachap* in the Hebrew Bible.[23] Such use (or assumption) of intersecting verses from other parts of Scripture (*petihta'ot*, "remote ones") was normal practice among the Rabbis.[24]

I conclude that the exegetical tradition associated with Ben Zoma interweaves the account of creation with the well-known theriomorphic)[25] depiction of the LORD in Israel's journey through the wilderness.[26] This depiction is hardly controversial in itself, but recall that the fiat verses in Genesis 1 portray *'Elohim* as transcendent and non-anthropomorphic (to say nothing of non-theriomorphic). Apparently, the midrash has associated Ben Zoma's name with the same dual representation of the deity that Pinker had discerned in the midrash on Genesis 1:7. Put this together with the sequel in the Song of Moses, "The LORD alone did guide him—no foreign god was with him,"[27] and you have the daring notion that the LORD was a demiurge or "second power" within the godhead: guiding Israel in the wilderness like a mother bird, guiding the early stages of creation as *ruach 'elohim*, and generally playing a role distinct from that of the *'Elohim* of "God said."[28]

Strack and Billerbeck find no strong parallels to the notion of the *ruach* as a dove in rabbinic literature; Middleton, "Whence the Feet?" 66n.17.

[22]   Deuteronomy 32:11.

[23]   The reason that Genesis Rabbah does not verbally quote Deuteronomy 32:11 may have to do with the image of the eagle. Middleton ("Whence the Feet?" 65–66) thinks the problem was that the eagle was associated with Roman dominion. A simpler interpretation can be developed within the terms of the midrash itself, if we assume with Genesis 11:20 and Genesis Rabbah 7:3 that the bird is was hovering in the expanse beneath the upper waters (so understood by R. Joshua ben R. Nehemiah in Genesis Rabbah 4:5). An eagle cannot fit in the allowed space of a few finger-widths! In fact, the hovering bird must be a very small one in the midrash.

[24]   Martin Jaffee, "The 'Midrashic' Proem: Towards the Description of Rabbinic Exegesis," in *Approaches to Ancient Judaism: Theory and Practice*, ed. William Scott Green, 6 vols., Brown Judaic Studies (Chico and Atlanta: Scholars Press, 1978–85), 4:95–112 (106-7).

[25]   Theriomorphic imagery describes the Deity using the attributes of various animals (eagles, lions, etc.).

[26]   Deuteronomy 32:11.

[27]   Deuteronomy 32:12.

[28]   One might ask whether rabbinic interpretations of the Song of Moses in terms of two powers might have had parallels in other early Jewish and Christian literature.

The idea of "two powers" within the godhead was sometimes regarded to be a dangerous exegetical move by the Rabbis, as Alan Segal has amply demonstrated.[29] While Ben Zoma is portrayed as an advocate of such risky ideas, it remains the case that he had an excellent reputation in rabbinic circles for his thorough knowledge of Torah. There is no reason to believe that he was regarded as unorthodox (a *min*). According to Mishnah Sotah (9:15), in fact, Ben Zoma was one of the last great expounders of Torah.[30]

Discussions of an apparent dipolarity in the deity of the Genesis narrative were evidently common enough, however, to warrant various cautions about their misuse. In the context of debates with Gnostics, Christians, and other "two-powers" advocates, this particular aspect of the Ben Zoma traditions was portrayed as going out on a limb, if nothing more.

Before turning to Genesis 1:7, there is one more exegetical tradition to consider that is associated with the name of Ben Zoma.

Two Powers in Genesis Rabbah 5:4 (on Genesis 1:9)

There is the brief statement in Genesis Rabbah 5:4 about an exegetical tradition concerning Psalm 29:3a, "The voice of the LORD is over the waters; [the God of glory thunders, the LORD, over mighty waters]." In its midrashic context (*parashah* 5), this psalm verse is cited to explicate the gathering of the waters into the seas on Day Three.[31] Jacob Neusner's translation reads as follows:

The "flinty rock" in Deuteronomy 32:13 was taken by Philo as designating Sophia, Wisdom; *Det.* 115–17; cf. *Leg.* II.86 on Deuteronomy 8:14. Philo's interpretations often reflected standard Alexandrian exegetical traditions. Furthermore, a variety of other verses from Deuteronomy 32 had been referred to "the Lord Christ" in the New Testament (e.g., Romans 10:19; 1 Corinthians 10:4, 22; 2 Corinthians 4:5; Hebrews 1:6; 10:30; 1 Peter 3:15; Revelation 1:18). But I have not found any "two powers" readings of Deuteronomy 32:12 itself.

[29] Segal, *Two Powers in Heaven*, summarizes the evidence on pages 146–48.

[30] According to Mishnah Sotah 9:15, after Ben Zoma died there were no more expounders of Torah. Here his name is set alongside such luminaries as R. Meir, R. Aqiva, and Yohanan ben Zakkai. Mishnah Avot 4:1 cites Ben Zoma's willingness to learn from all his teachers to gain understanding. Christopher Morray-Jones notes various traditions that viewed Ben Zoma (and ben Azzai) as a model of *talmid hakham* ("disciple of the wise"); Christopher Rowland and Christopher R.A. Morray-Jones, *The Mystery of God: Early Jewish Mysticism and the New Testament*, Compendia Rerum Iudaicarum ad Novum Testamentum (Leiden: Brill, 2009), 356–58. However, he then turns around and states that Ben Zoma was "suspected of unorthodox beliefs" (356).

[31] Genesis 1:9-10.

There are interpreters of Scripture such as Ben Azzai and Ben Zoma who explain that the voice of the Holy One, blessed be he, turned into a guide [*metatron*, variant, *metator*] for the water. That is in line with this verse: "The voice of the Lord is over the waters" (Ps. 29:3).[32]

In this case, the Genesis text is pure fiat—God says, "Let the waters under the sky be gathered together into one place .... And it was so."[33] Nothing is stated here about the LORD forcibly restraining the waters in the anthropomorphic sense.[34] However, the sequel in Genesis 1 does speak of 'Elohim inspecting the result and declaring it "good" (as is true for the other six days of creation, except for Day Two).

Again, given Ben Zoma's reputation for attention to minor details, the way was open for a demiurgic reading of the creative act itself, and the proof text from Psalm 29 made it clear that that work was delegated to the divine voice. Psalm 29:3ab describes the thunderous "voice of the LORD" over the tumultuous waters, in a way similar to the "spirit of God" hovering over the chaotic waters of creation in Genesis 1:2.[35] According to the Ben Zoma midrash, the voice of the Lord served as a guide for the waters. Such views are attributed to a variety of Sages, of which Ben Zoma was just a typical one. Unlike the conversation with Rabbi Yehoshu'a, no concern about riskiness is indicated here.[36]

---

[32] Jacob Neusner, trans., *Genesis Rabbah*, 3 vols. (Atlanta: Scholars Press, 1985), 1:48. The Hebrew text is given in Theodor and Albeck, *Midrash Bereshit Rabba* 1:34, lines 5–7.

[33] Genesis 1:9.

[34] Contrast Job 38:8-11; Psalm 33:7.

[35] According to the same psalm, the "voice of the LORD" was Hashem himself in his immanent, anthropomorphic mode, enthroned on the floodwaters (Psalm 29:3c, 10a).

[36] Peter Schäfer sees the issue debated here is to be whether anthropic features like a finger can be attributed to Hashem; Schäfer, *The Jewish Jesus: How Judaism and Christianity Shaped Each Other* (Princeton: Princeton University Press, 2012), 112; Schäfer, "Metatron in Babylonia," in *Hekhalot Literature in Context: Between Byzantium and Babylonia*, eds. Ra'anan Boustan, Martha Himmelfarb, and Peter Schäfer, TSAJ 153 (Tübingen: Mohr Siebeck, 2013), 29–39 (32). It is also possible that the issue is more along the lines of the "two powers" controversy. Medieval commentators like Nahmanides associated *metator* (the Latin word meaning one who marks something out) with the figure of Metatron; Elliot R. Wolfson, "The Secret of the Garment in Nahmanides," *Da'at* 24 (Winter 1990): 25–49 (English section, 38n.55). As Daniel Boyarin states (*Border Lines*, 143), "This extraordinary passage [Genesis Rabbah 5:4] 'remembers,' as it were, that such central rabbinic figures [as Ben Zoma], whose Halakhic opinions are authoritatively cited in the classic rabbinic literature, were ... champions of a distinct Logos [second power] theology ...."

However, there is a similar (slightly earlier) midrash on Deuteronomy 32:49, which is attributed to one Rabbi Eliezer. *Sifrei Devarim* 338 describes the "finger of the Holy One, blessed be he" as the guide (*metatron*) that showed Moses all the future borders of the tribes of Israel from Mount Nebo.[37] Surely, such a comprehensive vision required supernatural aid of some sort for Moses. Rabbi Yehoshu'a shows up here as well and offers an opposing interpretation of the text: "Moses saw it all by himself. How so? God gave power to Moses' eyes, which enabled him to see from one end of the world to the other."[38] Ben Zoma's midrash was at least as risky as Rabbi Eliezer's.

A fairly consistent picture of the exegetical traditions associated with the name of Ben Zoma emerges from these two midrashim. Various verses in Genesis 1 could be understood in terms of two powers—a di-polarity—within the Godhead, particularly when read in conjunction with other parts of the Torah and Psalms. There was no attempt to systematize terminology. On Day One, the work was delegated to the *ruach* (spirit or breath) of God, which hovered over the waters of creation. On Day Three, the divine agent was the voice of the LORD that guided the waters to their proper place. As we shall see in third Ben Zoma midrash, the work of Day Two, making the firmament and separating the waters, is attributed to the word of the LORD as well as the *ruach*. All this was within the bounds of good rabbinic methodology yet pushing the envelope on the nature of the Godhead.

We turn back now to the text with which Aron Pinker was concerned, Ben Zoma's midrashic exegesis of the work of Genesis 1:7.

Two Powers in Genesis Rabbah 4:6 (on Genesis 1:7)?

Our principal midrash, Genesis Rabbah 4:6, states that Ben Zoma "shook the world" with his interpretations of Scripture verses. One such verse is singled out here, Genesis 1:7, "So God made the dome [or firmament]," which was the work of Day Two.[39] According

---

[37] Reuven Hammer, trans., *Sifre: A Tannaitic Commentary on the Book of Deuteronomy*, Yale Judaica 24 (New Haven: Yale University Press, 1986), 347; cf. Schäfer, "Metatron in Babylonia," 32.

[38] Hammer, 338.

[39] There are actually three occurrences of "and God made" (*vayya'as*, Genesis 1:7, 16, 25). We know that Ben Zoma was credited with citing the first of these (the making of the firmament) because Parashah 4 is dedicated to the work of Day Two (Genesis 1:6-8). Moreover, the intersecting verse, Psalm 33:6a, describes the creation of the heavens. If the second part of Psalm 33:6 was also in view, Ben Zoma's "and God made" might have encompassed the making of the sun, moon, and stars (Genesis 1:16) as well.

to Christopher Rowland's translation, the midrash reads: "This is one of the verses with which Ben Zoma shook the world—"and God made" [Genesis 1:7a]. [This is a strange thing.] Is it not by a command [*ma'amar*]?"[40] The midrash closes with a supporting psalm verse, Psalm 33:6, "By the word of the LORD [*davar YHWH*] the heavens were made, and all their host by the breath [*ruach*] of his mouth."

Unlike the two other midrashim we have studied, Ben Zoma's interpretation is not stated explicitly, but it had something to do with the difference between "God said" and "God made" in Genesis 1:6-7. The follow-up statement simply cites Psalm 33:6 to point out that the heavens were made by the command (*ma'amar*) of the LORD.[41] The same verse was cited in the previous chapter (Genesis Rabbah 3:2) as evidence that God did no hard work in creating but relied on a mere word. So we are forced to infer that Ben Zoma was puzzled by the wording of Genesis 1:7 (Pinker uses the word, "dumbfounded"[42]).

As various commentators have noted, it is not clear whether the supporting verse Psalm 33:6 was attributed to Ben Zoma himself or was simply added as a supplement to a question that was associated with his name.[43] Neither is it clear whether the psalm verse ("by the word of the LORD ... were made") is thought to avoid the anthropomorphic "God made" or to spell it out in terms of an anthropomorphic *logos*.[44] It does not really matter. On either reading, discussion centered around the problem that Ben Zoma saw in Genesis 1:7: a hands-on act of creation is attributed to the divine, not mere fiat. So the "two-powers" solution could be associated with Ben Zoma's line of questioning even if the solution was understood as a later development. Classic midrash was not greatly concerned about issues of authenticity and attribution that have absorbed so much attention since the Italian Renaissance.

To sum up our findings thus far, the traditions associated with the name of Ben Zoma include:

---

[40]   Christopher Rowland, *Open Heaven*, 331. The Hebrew text is given in Theodor and Albeck, *Midrash Bereshit Rabba* 1:30, lines 1-2. I have bracketed the English words that are only implied in the Hebrew text.

[41]   "Word" (*davar*) is equivalent to "command" (*ma'amar*) in texts like Psalm 147:15. It is also paralleled by "spirit/wind" (*ruach*) in Psalm 147:18.

[42]   Pinker, "Ben Zoma's Query," 51.

[43]   As Rowland points out (*Open Heaven*, 495n.46), it is not clear whether this sequel to the original question is meant to be taken as part of a Ben Zoma midrash or as a later comment. Pinker ("Ben Zoma's Query," 51-52) suggests that the citation of Psalm 33:6 was support for the original sequence of questions.

[44]   Wisdom of Solomon 18:15 and traditions assumed in Philo, *Conf.* 146; *Somn.* I.239; cf. Segal, *Two Powers in Heaven*, 169, 185.

(a) The recognition of some sort of polarity in the operation of the Godhead in Genesis 1.

(b) Elucidation of this polarity by reference to verses elsewhere in the Torah (Deuteronomy 32:12) and in the Psalms (Psalms 29:3; 33:6).

(c) The attribution of the demiurgic role to the spirit/breath, voice, or word/command of the Lord.

This consistency among Ben Zoma traditions confirms Pinker's point about the duality of God-portraits in the midrash but provides an interpretation, I believe, that is more contextually appropriate than appeals to source criticism are.

In What Sense Did Ben Zoma's Exegesis Shake the World?

So much for the exegesis associated with the name of Ben Zoma. In what way could he be said to have "shaken the world," as stated in our very principal midrash, Genesis Rabbah 4:6 (Genesis 1:7 was "one of the verses with which Ben Zoma shook the world")?

There are two fundamentally different ways to read this arresting line. It is frequently taken to mean that Ben Zoma caused a commotion or upheaval in the world of rabbinic scholarship (as in the Soncino edition, Fischel, and Pinker).[45] But it can also be taken to mean that Ben Zoma literally caused the earth to tremor or even to quake (as in Neusner).[46] There is no clear way to decide between these two readings; both may have been intended in a genre that thrived on double (and triple) meanings. As we have seen, however, there is no evidence of any unorthodoxy in traditions associated with Ben Zoma as usually assumed by those who support the former reading (commotion and upheaval).[47] According to the Talmud, in fact, anyone who saw Ben Zoma in a dream was promised the gift of wisdom (also associated with dreams of Solomon, Ezekiel, and Rabbi Yehudah in Babylonian Talmud Hagigah 57b).[48] The prevalence of the first reading appears to

---

[45] The standard Soncino edition, *Midrash Rabbah* 1:31 ("the son of Zoma raised a commotion"); Fischel, *Rabbinic Literature and Greco-Roman Philosophy*, 87 ("seems to refer to his rhetorical eloquence and forcefulness"); Pinker, "Ben Zoma's Query," 56 ("Ben Zoma's grand upheaval," based on Nahmanides' reading).

[46] Jacob Neusner, trans., *Genesis Rabbah* 1:41 ("Ben Zoma caused an earthquake").

[47] The absence of any reputation for "unorthodoxy" is duly noted by Fischel, *Rabbinic Literature and Greco-Roman Philosophy*, 88; Macoby, "Ben Zoma's Trance," 105, 107.

[48] The parallel versions of this dictum are conveniently displayed by in Rowland and Morray-Jones, *The Mystery of God*, 359.

rest on an assumption, at least among modern biblical scholars, that novel exegesis is a matter of academic debate. It causes commotion, but "earthquakes" could only be a metaphor.

For a student of the New Testament, the latter reading should not sound so strange: an earthquake also occurred when Jesus cried out on the cross.[49] Similar disturbances occur in rabbinic texts where such calamities occur at the suffering and death of the pious Jews who are beloved of God. According to the Babylonian Talmud, earthquakes regularly occur in sympathy with the grief of the LORD over the suffering of his children.[50] One third of the world's wheat, olives, and barley was destroyed when a humiliating ban was pronounced on Rabbi Eliezer.[51] Heaven and earth trembled when Rabbi Ishmael's skin was being peeled off and he cried out.[52] In the rabbinic mind, at least, there was nothing unusual about God's servants causing earthquakes when they die or are about to die. And Ben Zoma was classified among the most prominent servants of his era: Me'ir, 'Aqiva', Yohanan ben Zakkai, Gamali'el the Elder, Yehudah ha-Nasi', and even Hanina' ben Dosa' (all of whose deaths were mourned in m. Sotah 9:15).

However, Ben Zoma was not noted as a martyr or even as one who suffered for his faith. It is true that Rabbi Yehoshu'a said he was beyond this world and that he soon died.[53] So one could imagine a causal chain extending from Ben Zoma's exegesis to his death, from his death to God's grief, and from divine grief to an earthquake.[54] However, the "shaking the world" in Genesis Rabbah 4:6 seems to be a more direct result of his daring reading of Genesis. If so, what was it about Ben Zoma's exegesis that called for such a response from the orders of creation?

I believe the answer lies in the double meaning of *ma'aseh bere'shit*. On one hand, it is the story of creation and the work of interpreting it. But it is also the unfolding of creation itself, and rabbinic exegesis has a performative aspect that conjures and reconnects with the events envisioned in the text. For the basic idea, we need look no further than

---

[49]   Matthew 27:51.

[50]   Babylonian Talmud Berakhot 59a.

[51]   Babylonian Talmud Bava Metsi'a 59a-b.

[52]   *Midrash Elleh Ezkerah.* For a convenient translation of the "Story of the Ten Martyrs," see David Stern and Mark J. Mirsky, eds, *Rabbinic Fantasies: Imaginative Narratives from Classical Hebrew Literature* (New Haven: Yale University Press, 1990), 147–61 (my citation on 152).

[53]   Genesis Rabbah 2:4 and parallels.

[54]   According to Jerusalem Talmud Hagigah 2:1 (77b), Ben Zoma's death was "precious in the sight of Hashem" (Psalm 116:15).

the Jerusalem Talmud version of restricted topics like *ma'aseh bere'shit*.[55] Just before the story about Ben Zoma's exposition before Rabbi Yehoshu'a, there is a parallel incident in which Rabbi El'azar ben 'Arakh expounded the chariot chapter (Ezekiel 1) before Rabbi Yohannan ban Zakkai. As Rabbi El'azar discoursed on the "work of the chariot" (*ma'aseh merkavah*), fire fell from heaven, angels danced (in the fire), and the trees sang a psalm verse about the return of the LORD, as foreseen by Ezekiel.[56]

If the traditions attributed to Ben Zoma can be placed on the same level of profundity as that of Rabbi El'azar, his exegesis of Genesis 1 must have reproduced at least some of the primordial conditions of the first three days of creation. In the same way that Rabbi El'azar's exegesis reactivated the fiery angels of Ezekiel 1:4-5 (*ma'aseh merkavah*), Ben Zoma's threatened the return the world to the watery world of Genesis 1:2. By going back to the first two Days, when the Spirit and word of the Lord were active in separating and gathering the waters,[57] Ben Zoma returned to a time when the firmament and the earth were not yet fully stabilized. By re-invoking the thunderous "voice of the LORD over the waters" of Day Three,[58] Ben Zoma was effectively "shaking the wilderness."[59] For the time being, most biblical scholars may write off such rabbinic ideas as exaggerations. For the early Rabbis, however, they foreshadowed divine redemption, and New Testament writers seem to be closer to the Rabbis on this score. All of us would benefit from taking their writings seriously.

---

[55] Slightly further afield, note Babylonian Talmud Bava Metsi'a 85b, where R. Hiyya and his sons shook the world on a special fast day simply by beginning the *'Amidah* blessing of the One "who raises the dead." Ben Zoma is the mirror image of R. Hiyya: his exegetical pronouncements conjured the chaos of creation, whereas the latter's liturgical prayer conjured that of the eschaton.

[56] Jerusalem Talmud Hagigah 77a, citing Psalm 96:12; cf. Ezekiel 1:4-5; 43:2.

[57] Genesis 1:2, 6-7; Psalm 33:6-7.

[58] Cf. Psalm 29:3.

[59] Psalm 29:8.

CHAPTER 16

Divine Immanence, Newton's Metaphysics, and Just-So Stories *As Models*: The Boogaartian Challenge at the Science/Theology Boundary[1]

Stephen J. Wykstra

Both Catholics and Protestants in the late middle ages shared a cosmology, one forged by Thomas Aquinas. As their drawings and catechisms reveal, they believed that the hand of God was on the crystalline spheres and that God distributed life-giving power to the earth through these spheres. The discoveries of Galileo shattered these crystalline spheres, and Christians have struggled ever since to pick up the pieces and explain how the hand of God touches the world. Acknowledging the scientific discoveries of Galileo and others, theologians forged a new cosmology, a universe with two non-overlapping spheres: a spiritual sphere in which God resides and to which God draws humankind and a material sphere which is a self-contained system of matter and motion.

Thomas Boogaart, "The Hand of God and the Evolution of Life"[2]

[1] For helpful suggestions in developing this paper, I'm grateful to Nick Wolterstorff, Jen Zamzow, Ariel Dempsey, Kelly James Clark, Charles Huttar, and Dustyn Keepers. For proofreading and some great advice on writing, a big thanks to Mark Lewison at Hope College's writing center. And for our enlivening discussions over the past three years, I thank Tom Boogaart together with *all* the members of our Wednesday Science/Religion discussion group.
[2] Thomas Boogaart, "The Hand of God and the Evolution of Life," unpublished April 29, 2016, lecture for Calvin College *Christian Perspectives on Science* series 1.

With Aristotle's laws of motion overthrown, no role remained for a Prime Mover, or for Moving Spirits. The hand of God, which once kept the heavenly bodies in their orbits, had been replaced by universal gravitation. ... Governed by precise mathematical and mechanical laws, Newton's universe seemed capable of running itself.

T.H. Greer, *A Brief History of the Western World*[3]

For nearly three years, I've had the privilege of meeting weekly with a small interdisciplinary group to discuss questions at the boundary of science and theology. Tom Boogaart is a long-standing member of that group, which began some decades ago by his seminary colleague physicist-theologian Christopher Kaiser and Hope College astrophysicist Peter Gonthier. Tom now joins Christopher and me in our "radical sabbatical" from classroom teaching. To both honor him and further our ongoing research, I propose to explore here one of the persistent concerns Tom has brought to our Wednesday discussions, connecting it to my own background in history and philosophy of science. And as befits its conversational origins, my essay is exploratory and will freely mix informality with footnotes for further follow-up.

In the above quotation, Tom expresses his sense that we moderns and post-moderns have lost something important. In the ancient cosmology of Hebraic Scripture, Tom finds an affirmation of what he sometimes calls a "middle world"—a realm through which there is a porosity between the material and the spiritual. Tom sees a version, or perhaps remnant, of this in the "crystalline spheres" of the Thomistic synthesis of Judeo-Christian theology and Aristotelian natural philosophy: moved by "the hand of God," those immutable celestial spheres carrying the planets mediated God's "life-giving power" to the terrestrial realm.

But the crystalline spheres, Tom finds, were shattered by the astronomical revolution begun by Copernicus in 1543, and over the next two centuries, the realm of matter and of spirit became disjoined. For many today, the world of *matter* has thus acquired a certain autonomy. In the passage I've quoted by T.H. Greer, we thus find a common characterization of "Newton's universe": by Newtonian "gravitational

---

Handout and audio available at http://www.calvin.edu/admin/provost/seminars/ CPiS%20Contents/2016/2016.html.

[3] T.H. Greer, *A Brief History of the Western World*, 4th ed. (New York: Harcourt Brace Javonovich, 1982), 364.

attraction," the world of matter became viewed as "capable of running itself" by "mechanical laws." This disjoining of matter and spirit, Tom worries, has turned God's transcendence into remoteness if not utter absence while also reinforcing "current economic practices" running counter to God's vision for a just and flourishing creation.

A key challenge, Tom thus ventures, is to recover a sense of the *immanence* of God *within* creation. In our Wednesday group, we thus regularly return, in our cork-screwy way, to this challenge and to the opportunity Tom senses in the evolutionary sciences:

> The secure findings of the evolutionary sciences offer Christian theologians ... an opportunity to recover a more integrated and biblical cosmology. The story of the emergence of life and consciousness on our planet suggests that God's relationship to the material sphere is much more intimate and glorious than the two-sphere cosmology allows, and this emergence of life comports well with various biblical images of God creating and sustaining the orders of creation.[4]

This challenge—of re-conceptualizing the Hebraic sense of divine immanence in light of the "secure theoretical findings" of today's evolutionary sciences—is a daunting one. Getting a good grasp of these findings—and discerning how secure (or insecure) they *are*—is well beyond the ability of any single person or discipline. So, too, is learning to discern what, in this connection, the ancient Hebrew Scriptures have here to teach us. But Tom has helped me and others to see the challenge also as an opportunity and to take it to heart. Here, then, I'll call it "the Boogaartian Challenge."

As we try to address this Boogaartian Challenge relative to the sciences of today, Tom's erstwhile colleague Chris Kaiser, we shall see, challenges us to learn from how past thinkers have addressed it relative to the sciences of their own day. Taking a cue from Chris, I shall here reconsider an important strand in the thought of Isaac Newton (1642–1726).[5] In "Newton's universe," according to T. H. Greer, "the hand of God" was "replaced by gravitational attraction." But while some

---

[4]   Boogaart, "Hand of God," 2.

[5]   For a treatment of relevant Newton passages precluded by present space constraints, see Stephen Wykstra, "Should Worldviews Shape Science? Toward an Integrationist Account of Scientific Theorizing," in *Facets of Faith and Science, Vol. II: The Role of Beliefs in Mathematics and the Natural Sciences*, ed. Jitse van der Meer (Lanham: University Press of America, 1996), 123–71.

such replacement characterizes later Enlightenment thinkers claiming Newton's mantle, it does not hold of Newton himself. As Edward Davis argues in his "Newton's Rejection of the "Newtonian Universe,"[6] serious Newton scholarship has—ever since the groundbreaking work of J.E. McGuire[7]—increasingly revealed a Newton who, throughout his life, sought to guide his physics by a theistic vision affirming God's intimate concourse with the material world. Indeed, McGuire and John Henry in a recent paper recommend Newton's quest to the attention by contemporary thinkers seeking to "combine rigorous and up-to-the-minute science with belief in God" so as "to uphold the values of both science and religion."[8]

Encouraged by this recommendation, I here make a preliminary effort to connect several passages by Newton to the Boogaartian Challenge. The passages highlight a distinctive theistic metaphysics of

[6]   Edward B. Davis, "Newton's Rejection of the 'Newtonian World View': The Role of Divine Will in Newton's Natural Philosophy." In *Facets of Faith and Science, Volume 3: The Role of Beliefs in the Natural Sciences*, ed. Jitse M. van der Meer (Lanham: University Press of America, 1996), 75–96, taken (with minor changes) from *Fides et Historia*, 22 (1990): 6–20. Davis's essay (from which I've gleaned the apt Greer quotation above) is a valuable counterpoint to the view expressed by his graduate professor and premier Newton scholar Richard S. Westfall in "Newton and Christianity," in *Facets*, vol. 3: 363–74. Davis's perspective on Newton aligns with much recent Newton scholarship: Cf. James E. Force, "The Nature of Newton's Holy Alliance Between Science and Religion: From the Scientific Revolution to Newton (and Back Again)," in *Rethinking the Scientific Revolution*, ed. Margaret J. Osler (Cambridge: Cambridge University Press, 2000), 247–70.

[7]   See especially J.E. McGuire, "Force, Active Principles, and Newton's Invisible Realm," *Ambix* 15 (1968); 154–208. The paper remains a *locus classicus* of Newton scholarship: it is, for example, cited as providing "excellent guidance in contextualizing the theological dimensions of the Queries" by Steffan Ducheyne in his "Newton on Action at a Distance," *Journal of the History of Philosophy*, 52, Number 4 (2014): 278. Along with other key papers in the McGuire corpus, McGuire's "Newton's Invisible Realm" is now available in J.E. McGuire, *Tradition and Innovation: Newton's Metaphysics of Nature* (Springer, 1995). (Full disclosure: Ted McGuire was one of my esteemed professors in the Department of History and Philosophy of Science at the University of Pittsburgh.

[8]   John Henry and J. E. McGuire, "Voluntarism and Panentheism: The Sensorium of God and Isaac Newton's Theology," *The Seventeenth Century*, 33:5 (2018): 587–612. Henry and McGuire see Newton's thought as especially to the recent flourishing of what is now called *panentheism*—the "belief that the Being of God includes and penetrates the whole universe" while also being "more than, and not exhausted by, the universe." This label, they urge (page 600), "fits Newton's theology to a tee": Newton "can be seen as effectively a panentheist, and the development of modern panentheism can help us see why he chose to develop this kind of theology." For an able critical survey of positions within the diverse panentheistic family, cited by Henry and McGuire, we now have Calvin Seminary professor John W. Cooper's *Panentheism: The Other God of the Philosophers* (Downers Grove: InterVarsity Press, 2007).

"active principles" by which Newton sought to construe gravitational attraction and other action-at-a-distance forces as modes of divine immanence in the material world. In reflecting on Newton's metaphysical hypotheses, I want also to reconsider the significance for us today of the characteristic diffidence or humility with which he proposed them. Newton clearly recognized that his metaphysical hypotheses conspicuously lacked the virtues requisite for warrantable assertion within an "experimental philosophy" like physics. They were, in this sense, little more than "just-so stories." In nevertheless advancing them for consideration, Newton's implicit *epistemic* insight was that such hypotheses can nevertheless have legitimate and important functions within genuine inquiry. To illuminate this implicit insight and make it more available to us, I shall here try to connect the notion of "models" within twentieth-century mathematics to positive functions of hypotheses that are "just-so stories" in the above sense.[9]

Backdrop for Bridge-Building

Kaiser on Divine Immanence: A Patristic Starting Point

Before turning to Newton, let's take a brief glance at what earlier Christian theology said about divine immanence. Realizing how little

---

[9]   I shall here use "just-so story" to refer to hypotheses that, while illustrating how a larger conceptual scheme may explanatorily apply to some phenomena, falls short—to date—in those qualities requisite for warranted scientific *assertability* within some disciplinary context. That sense, I must stress, deviates from the dominant current pejorative usage by being relatively neutral, leaving as an open question whether the proffering of some such just-so story, on some particular occasion by some particular person, is serving a legitimate and valuable role in serious scientific (or other) inquiry. The neutral use contrasts with the far more common pejorative usage that has, ever since Stephen Jay Gould's "Sociobiology: the Art of Story Telling" (*New Scientist*, November 16, 1978: 530–33) and other essays, steadily gained polemical cachet. In its pejorative use, the term is applied to particular ways of offering some proposal that the term-user takes to involve some serious intellectual vice. *What* vice, however, is often a matter of some unclarity. In using the term in the more neutral sense stipulated here, my aim is to promote clarification as to what differentiates creditable and discreditable uses of hypotheses that, in various disciplinary contexts, admittedly lack the full virtues requisite for warranted assertability. In this I find precedent in James Lennox, "Darwinian Thought Experiments: A Function for Just-So Stories," in T. Horowitz and G. Massey, eds., *Thought Experiments in Science and Philosophy* (Savage: Rowman and Littlefield, 1991), 223–46. Without dismissing its pejorative application to "fraudulent uses of plausible stories posing as confirmed explanations," Lennox himself clearly uses the term in a neutral sense when arguing (pages 238 ff.) that "Just-So Stories may have a number of legitimate roles to play in evolutionary biology."

I know about this, I suddenly mourn our Wednesday group's loss of Christopher Kaiser, who in late 2016 absconded from Holland to Kalamazoo. What, I wonder, would Chris tell us?

But perhaps Chris can—like a Newtonian particle—act on me at a distance through his writings! So I now pull off my shelf his 1982 book *The Doctrine of God: A Historical Survey*. This little book, like his 1991 *Creation and the History of Science*, is a marvel of pithy comprehensiveness. So now looking at his Index of Names and Topics, under "Attributes of God," I find … oh dear, I find a dozen page numbers for "transcendence"— but nothing for "immanence"!

But wait, perhaps all is not lost. Checking the Table of Contents, I see that his third chapter—on the patristic doctrine of God—has a section on "The Existence and Attributes of God." And flipping to that section, I discover—page 48—a subsection, "Transcendence and Immanence." And here Chris says:

> The absolute transcendence of God does not contradict his immanence in the world. Following the ideas of the Old Testament, the fathers described God as "filling" or "containing" (*chōreō*) all things while he himself is uncontained (*achōretōs*) by any or even all things together.[10]

And this "paradoxical relation" of transcendence and immanence, Chris now says, was "given its most exquisite articulation" by Hilary of Poitiers, who in about 359 A.D. wrote these words:

> It was written that in all born and created things God might be known within them and without, overshadowing and indwelling, surrounding all and interfused through all, since palm and hand, which hold, reveal the might of His external control, while throne and footstool, by their support of a sitter, display the subservience of outward things to One within Who, Himself outside them, encloses all in His grasp, yet dwells within the external world which is His own. In this wise does God, from within and from without, control and correspond to the universe; being infinite He is present in all things, in Him Who is infinite all are included. In devout thoughts such as these my soul, engrossed in the pursuit of truth, took its delight.[11]

---

10   Christopher Kaiser, *The Doctrine of God: A Historical Survey* (Westchester: Crossway Books, 1982), 49.

11   Kaiser, *Doctrine of God*, 50. The passage is from Hilary of Poitiers, *De Trinitate*, in *Nicene and Post-Nicene Fathers: Second Series, Volume IX, Hilary of Poitiers and John of Damascus*, ed. Philip Schaff (Peabody: Hendrickson Publishers, 1995), 42.

Thank you, Chris Kaiser! In at least some patristics, there is a strong sense of God as "indwelling" and "interfused" through all of creation.

Kaiser on Reformation theology: "Unresolved Tensions"

But what about Reformed theology? I eagerly turn to Chris Kaiser's chapter on the Reformation. But here, alas, I find no explicit mention of divine immanence. I learn that Calvin himself balanced some things (e.g., "the divine attributes of transcendence and personality, or sovereignty and love"), but divine immanence is mentioned only in connection with later Pietists (Philipp Jakob Spener) and Neoplatonists (Henry More, Jakob Boehme, Samuel Coleridge). In these thinkers, Chris finds a stress on "the immediacy of God's presence in the world"—but he also sees them "tending in some cases to pantheism."[12]

The compactness of Chris Kaiser's book, however, warns me not to make any inference from silence. For more clues, I open his 1991 *Creation and the History of Science*. There I find that Calvin articulated God's relation to nature by doctrines of both particular and universal providence. Particular providence sought to acknowledge the role of secondary causes while also securing "the immediate, regular operation of God in nature and history." Within a largely Aristotelian conception of nature, Calvin saw the regularities of nature, especially various "strategic forces affecting human life" (e.g., the stability of the earth), as "indications of God's immediate and continuous providence."[13] At the same time, Calvin's doctrine of God's *universal* providence "provided some justification for the theoretical investigations of natural philosophers."[14]

Chris finds several strands of Reformation creationist thought—"creationist" in its broad sense of affirming the goodness of the universe of which God is creator and sustainer[15]—as bearing a complex relation

---

12   Kaiser, *Doctrine of God*, 100, 103.

13   These themes in Calvin get worked out in scholastic detail within later seventeenth-century Reformed Orthodoxy and Puritan theology, especially in orthodox Calvinists who followed the "premotionist" theory of concurrence of Aquinas and the Dominicans, on which it is only by the continuous concurrent activity of God that a secondary natural cause—say, fire, with its power to burn flesh—has causal efficacy.

14   Christopher Kaiser, *Creation and the History of Science* (Grand Rapids: Eerdmans, 1991), 134. For a more detailed treatment, see Susan Schreiner, *Theater of His Glory: Nature & the Natural Order in the Thought of John Calvin* (Grand Rapids: Baker Books, 2001).

15   And distinct from the parochial sense, dominant today, that opposes evolutionary and Big Bang theories.

to the nascent revolution to modern science. Kaiser identifies several unresolved tensions within the tradition, highlighting their potentially pivotal role:

> While there was little that was new theologically in the seventeenth century, there was ample concern for the viability of the inherited themes of the creationist tradition. Insofar as pious Christian natural philosophers were unable to resolve these issues, many eighteenth-century thinkers abandoned the creationist tradition as an interpretive scheme for their life and work.

And what Chris says next gives my essay here its main rationale:

> Consequently, the examination of the controversies of the seventeenth century is more than an academic exercise. One cannot help but be impressed with the degree to which theology was a vital factor in the scientific development throughout this phase of the scientific revolution. One must also ask why the theological tradition that inspired such accomplishments had become so shaky that it rapidly lost its credibility in the following century. [16]

Within those "unresolved tensions" of the past, I hear Chris suggesting, may lie keys to our theological future!

Back to the Future

Even as Newton the mathematical physicist profoundly shifted our conception of the material world by his theory of universal gravitation, Newton the creative "*meta*-physicist" found in this new theory scope for far-reaching rumination on the relation between the physical world and God. I'll here briefly probe two of his ruminations: one from his most mature work, the other from among (arguably) his most youthful. From the mature Newton, I focus on several passages from Query 31 of Newton's *Opticks* in its third (1721) edition.[17] The Queries,

---

[16]   Kaiser, *Creation and the History of Science*, 152–53.

[17]   Isaac Newton, *Opticks, or Treatise of the Reflections, Refractions, Inflections, and Colours of Light* (New York: Dover Publications, 1952). The fourth posthumous edition is identical with the third edition apart from minor handwritten corrections inserted by Newton before his death. The *Opticks* comprises three "Books." In Book I, Newton explains and theoretically interprets those groundbreaking prism experiments on light by which he established that white light is a composition of rays of—so to speak—"different colours." In Book II, he similarly uses experiments with thin

which Newton revised throughout the last decades of his life,[18] are deemed by Ernan McMullin as "perhaps our significant source" for "the most general categories of matter and action that informed Newton's research."[19]

The Query 31 passages can be usefully juxtaposed with passages by a more youthful Newton, from the very posthumously published manuscript *De Gravitatione et æquipondio fluidorum* (*On Gravity and the Equilibrium of Fluids*).[20] While scholars have fluctuated as to when Newton wrote *Gravitatione*, the evidence now tilts many scholars back to judging it composed by Newton while still in his twenties—some two decades before publishing his gravitational theory.[21] J.E. McGuire, in his groundbreaking 1968 essay "Forces, Active Principles, and Newton's Invisible Realm," deemed *Gravitatione* "the first sustained expression of Newton's philosophy of nature" and as "containing in embryonic form"

---

plates to support and develop a particulate theory of light that would, for the next century, maintain ascendency over the rival wave theory of his contemporary Christiaan Huygens. On Newton's theory, light consists of particles, streaming from a luminous body, that interact with ordinary matter by short-range forces. Book III consists of the "Queries," in which Newton uses the interrogative form to put forward his own best conjectures regarding the ultimate constitution of matter.

[18] In its 1704 first edition, the *Opticks* had only 16 Queries taking up six pages of text; by the 1721 third edition, these had grown to 31 Queries taking up some 70 pages: see Steffen Ducheyne, "Newton on Action at a Distance," *Journal of the History of Philosophy*, 52, Number 4 (2014): 676.

[19] Ernan McMullin, *Newton on Matter and Activity* (South Bend: University of Notre Dame Press, 1978), 3.

[20] Isaac Newton, "On Gravity and the Equilibrium of Fluids," in *Unpublished Scientific Papers of Isaac Newton*, eds. A. R. Hall and Marie Boas Hall (Cambridge: Cambridge University Press, 1962), 90–156. *Gravitatione* was first transcribed and translated by Rupert and Marie Boas Hall for publication in this volume. It is now also available in A. Janiak, ed., *Newton: Philosophical Writings* (Cambridge: Cambridge University Press, 2004).

[21] In their introduction to *Gravitatione* (pages 90–91), the Halls argued for a dating "between ... 1664 and 1668." (It's worth noting that in the Latin title of the essay, "gravitatione," is still used in its medieval sense of *weight*, not in Newton's later sense of "gravitational attraction" of all matter toward other matter as defended in his 1687 *Mathematical Principles of Natural Philosophy*. Scholars have fluctuated on the dating, but the evidence now tilts many back to the early dating given it by the Halls. While my story here assumes the earlier dating, a later dating would not change the moral of the story. For more detail on the issues, see J.E. McGuire, "The Fate of the Date: The Theology of Newton's Principia Revisited," in *Rethinking the Scientific Revolution*, ed. M. J. Osler (Cambridge: Cambridge University Press, 2000), 271–96; and John Henry, "Gravity and De Gravitatione: the development of Newton's ideas on action at a distance," in *Studies in the History and Philosophy of Science* 42 (2011), especially pages 23–26.

all the "main approaches to the ontological problem of causation" that Newton would explore over the next 50 years.[22]

Query 31 of the *Opticks*: Newton on Super-Hardness

Within Book III of the *Opticks*, Newton offers, in the guise of tentative "Queries," his considered thoughts on the ultimate constitution of matter and its relation to God. Of the Queries, Query 31 is the last, the longest, and the most revealing of Newton's metaphysical orientation.

The Context

Newton opens Query 31 with what I shall call his central question:

> Have not the small particles of bodies certain powers, virtues, or forces, by which they *act at a distance*, not only upon the rays of light for reflecting, refracting, and inflecting them, but also upon one another for producing a great part of the phenomena of nature?[23]

Newton's overall question, then, is whether particles of matter have "powers, virtues, or forces" by which they "act at a distance." To pursue this, Newton makes two moves. First, instancing "gravity, magnetism, and (static) electricity" as examples of *attractive* powers, he argues that since nature "is very consonant and conformable to herself," there "may be in nature many more attractive powers besides these." And he then—secondly—immediately qualifies his use of the term "attraction":

> How these attractions may be performed, I do not here consider. What I call attraction may be performed by impulse, or by some other means unknown to me. I use that word here to signify only in general any force by which bodies tend towards one another, whatsoever be the cause.

As I understand him, Newton is stipulating that he is using the word "attraction" in a *neutral* sense so as to leave open how to answer his central question: Are such ostensibly "attractive" tendencies due to some unseen, aetherial mechanism working by pure *contact-action* (or

---

[22]   J.E. McGuire, "Newton's Invisible Realm," 156.
[23]   This and the next two quotations are from Newton, *Opticks*, 375–76.

"impulse"), or are they due to something involving genuine "action at a distance" across empty space?[24] But he immediately makes clear that this neutrality is not meant to be permanent:

> For we must learn from the phenomena of nature what bodies attract each other, and what are the laws and properties of the attraction, before we enquire the cause by which the attraction is performed.

Accordingly, in the next 25 pages of Query 31, Newton surveys dozens of relevant chemical and other phenomena, thus preparing the way for his preliminary judgment on the central question.[25]

Newton's Metaphysical Proposal: the First Half

We now come to what I'll call the two "key paragraphs" of Query 31. The first begins as follows:

> All these things being considered, it seems probable to me, that God in the beginning formed matter in solid, massy, hard, impenetrable,[26] moveable particles, of such sizes and figures, and with such other properties, and in such proportion to space, as most conduced to the end for which he formed them; and that these primitive particles being solids, are incomparably harder than any porous bodies compounded of them; even so very hard, as never to wear or break in pieces—no ordinary power being able to divide what God himself made one in the first Creation.[27]

---

[24] There is currently renewed vigorous debate about what exactly Newton meant by "action at a distance" and what his stance toward it was. I discuss the issues in Wykstra, "Should Worldviews Shape Science?" For an entrance to the current debate see the previously cited papers by Steffan Ducheyne ("Newton on Action at a Distance") and John Henry ("Gravity and De Gravitatione") and by John Henry, "Newton and Action at a Distance," in *The Oxford Handbook on Isaac Newton*, eds. Eric Schliesser and Chris Smeenk (Oxford: Oxford University Press, forthcoming). In our Wednesday group, remarks by Peter Gonthier have caused me to wonder whether Newton took it that on his law of universal gravitation, gravity—if due to genuine action-as-distance powers— would need be propagated "instantaneously." I'm inclined to think not, for in Query 21 (*Opticks*, 351) Newton ventures a hypothesis that gravity is due to a density gradient in a rarified aether of particles acting on each other by a short-range repulsive force. This, it seems to me, would entail a certain gravitational "lag time."

[25] I take Newton to mean these 25 pages not as delivering the goods as to "the laws and properties" just mentioned but as a mere qualitative survey allowing a preliminary considered judgment on the central question.

[26] I take "impenetrable" to mean impenetrable to *each other*: no two of them can occupy the same space at the same time.

[27] The two key paragraphs are sequential. Newton, *Opticks*, 400–401.

Newton here begins his statement of what to him "seems probable" in the light of the preceding 25 pages. The first half of the sentence is at once about God, about God's act of creating "in the beginning," and about *what* God then created. Among this *what*: *what* God in the beginning created were *particles*—"primitive particles," he calls them—which are "solid, massy, hard, impenetrable, moveable," each with some size and shape, and also with "such *other* properties" and—in total—in "such proportion to space,"[28] as "most conduced to the end" for which God formed them.

For the *most* part, Newton is here echoing what was already accepted by thinkers like Robert Boyle and Christiaan Huygens, who endorsed a view of nature that Robert Boyle called "the Mechanical Philosophy" or "Corpuscular Philosophy." On that view, the material world is made of tiny particles that have some size, shape, and motion and behave in conformity with certain basic "laws of motion" of the sort first adumbrated by Descartes. But among these *orthodox mechanists* (as I'll call them), there was serious debate on one issue, and in the second half of the sentence, Newton zooms in on it. The issue was whether the corpuscles of matter are infinitely divisible.[29] Some mechanists—notably Descartes and his followers—argued they must be: any particle, after all, must take up *some* volume of space that is mentally divisible; hence, any such particle can, in principle, always be split into two smaller corpuscles, each occupying *less* space. But other mechanists, among them Gassendi and followers, asserted the contrary: cut finely enough, they argued, and you'd reach particles that are in principle "uncuttable." Call these the "atomists" ("atom" being Greek for "uncuttable.")

So on this issue, Newton here is staking out a position that tilts strongly toward the atomists. It is probable, he thinks, that there is indeed a bottom level at which the most basic particles are "so very hard" as to "never wear or break in pieces." They are particles with, let's call it, *super*-hardness. But notice how Newton stakes out his position: it is, I

[28]   Reflecting his sense of the importance of action-at-a-distance forces, Newton hesitantly ventured that all the matter in the solar system might "fit into a nut-shell." On the significance of his proposal and its later fortunes, see Arnold Thackray, "Matter in a Nut-Shell: Newton's *Opticks* and Eighteenth-Century Chemistry," *Ambix* 15:1 (1968): 29–53.

[29]   A closely related issue was whether all space is filled with matter, with atomists affirming a "void" of empty space between atoms, and plenists like Descartes seeing infinitely divisible matter as filling (or even as identical with) space. See Daniel Garber on "Descartes Against Indivisibility" in his *Descartes' Metaphysical Physics* (Chicago: University of Chicago Press, 1992), 266 ff.

would suggest, in a *diffident—a theistically* diffident—manner that is quite characteristic of Newton. For rather than saying that the basic particles are *in principle* indivisible, he posits that they are so "incomparably hard" that "no ordinary power" is able to divide them. And here the opposite of "*ordinary* power" seems to be that *divine* power that is "from first Creation" the source of this super-hardness.

Frosting on the cake?

Is Newton's God-talk here just—to use John Hedley Brook's metaphor—a veneer prettying up what had already been decided on other grounds?[30]

I think not. There is an argument worthy of respect going on here, and it is doing real work. The conclusion of the argument is not, I think, that there *is* a bottom level of particles that *are* in the ordinary course of nature uncuttable. So read, the argument is circular, as it requires as a premise the claim that in first creation, each basic particle *was* "made one" by God—which would assume the very thing in question. It is, rather, an argument aiming to defeat *another* argument—the atomists' *a priori* argument, already mentioned, that since any material particle takes up some volume that is *mentally* divisible, it must also in principle be physically divisible in two. Against this, we may see Newton as arguing that it is surely within God's *power* to give any *mentally* divisible particle a super-hardness such that nothing earthly can *physically* split it. Newton thus needn't assert that God *has* chosen to do this. It's enough to argue that it is within God's *power* to do it, leaving the question of whether God *has* so done it—i.e., whether matter *has* such super-hardness—to be settled on empirical or other grounds.

A Detour to De Gravitatione: the Youthful Newton on God and Matter

Newton's Query 31 so far may seem to bear out Greer's picture of "Newton's universe": in saying that God, in the very beginning, endowed material particles with super-hardness and other properties, is not Newton at least implying a universe that is thereafter—as Greer puts it—"capable of running itself"?

---

[30] The "veneer thesis" is explored in John Hedley Brooke, "Religious Belief and the Natural Sciences: Mapping the Historical Landscape," *Facets of Faith and Science, Vol. I: Historiography and Modes of Interaction*, ed. Jitse van der Meer (Lanham: University of Press of America, 1996), 1–26; and Stephen Wykstra, "Have Worldviews Shaped Science? A Response to Brooke," in *Facets of Faith and Science, Vol. I*, 91–111.

That Newton is not saying this will become clearer as Query 31 unfolds. But to glimpse why—and how *deeply*—Newton opposes this so-called "Newtonian" picture, it will be useful to detour to a passage from Newton's youthful *Gravitatione*.

The Context: A Just-So Story

In *Gravitatione*, Newton offers an extended critique of Descartes's metaphysics, in the course of which he develops his own views of space, time, and matter. Space, he famously argues, is God's "sensorium"; as such, it has a certain kind of necessary existence and character, flowing from God's very nature. In contrast, he argues, matter "does not exist necessarily but by divine will," and for this reason "the explanation of it must be more uncertain," for

> it is hardly given to us to know the limits of the divine power, that is to say whether matter could be created in one way only, or whether there are several ways by which different beings similar to bodies might be produced.[31]

We see, even in this youthful Newton, that "theistic diffidence" noted earlier, as he now continues:

> I am reluctant to say positively what the nature of bodies is, but I rather describe a certain kind of being similar in every way to bodies, and whose creation we cannot deny to be within the power of God, so that we can hardly say it is not body.

Newton will thus offer, to himself at least, a story about one way—a way we cannot rule out—by which God *might* be constituting material particles. It will not be offered as an assertion of how things are or even as a speculative possibility that one might someday put to empirical test. It is in this way no more than—indeed, considerably less than—what today's academics routinely belittle as a mere "just-so story."

Newton's Proposal: Matter as Freeze-Thawed Space

Newton begins with *human* agency—with our capacity to bring about things. That capacity depends upon *will* and *thought*: each of us "is conscious that he can move his body at will"; we also take it that

---

31   My quotations here and in what immediately follows are, more or less sequentially, from Newton, *De Gravitatione*, 138–40.

other humans "enjoy the same power of similarly moving their bodies by thought alone." Here "will" and "thought" work together: *willing* my arm to reach above my head typically involves forming a *thought* of doing so. So, too, for God. But *God's* faculty of will and thought are "infinitely more powerful and swift"—so to God we must attribute "the power of moving any bodies whatever by will." And Newton now brings this to bear on the nature of matter: "It must be agreed that God, by the sole action of thinking and willing, can prevent a body from penetrating any space defined by certain limits."

The idea here is that God has the power to, as it were, "freeze" a certain region of space so that it is impervious to approaching material bodies. Were God to do this, Newton continues, that region of space would, to our senses, have many features of a material body,

> for it will be tangible on account of its impenetrability, and visible, opaque and colored on account of its reflection of light, and when struck it will resound because the neighboring air will be moved by the blow.

It will indeed, Newton thinks, "assume all the properties of a corporeal particle, except that it will be motionless." But now, Newton continues, imagine that God wills

> that this impenetrability not always maintained in the same part of space, but can be transferred hither and thither according to certain laws, yet so that the amount and shape of that impenetrable space are not changed.

The idea, then, is that God might, as it were, momentarily "freeze" a certain region of space and then an instant later thaw it while freezing an immediately adjacent region of the same shape, and then simply continue this process in certain regular way—say, other things being equal, along a straight path at a constant speed. (The freeze-thaw metaphor is mine, not Newton's—and must not be pressed too hard.) In that event, Newton says,

> There will be no property of body which this does not possess. It will have shape, be tangible and mobile, and be capable of reflecting and being reflected, and no less constitute a part of the structure of things than any other corpuscle.

Lastly, he asks us to imagine that if all those things comprising the material corpuscles of the world were so constituted, the world would appear to us just as it does appear:

In the same way if several spaces of this kind should be impervious to bodies and to each other, they would all sustain the vicissitudes of corpuscles and exhibit the same phenomena. And so if all this world were constituted of this kind of beings, it would hardly seem to be any different.

On the conception Newton is proposing, what we imagine as various bits of moving matter are nothing but a divine activity by which God is continuously "freeze-thawing" successive bit-shaped regions of space.

Newton on the Usefulness of his Proposal

"What a wild-eyed idea!" a physicist might think.[32] And theologically, it seems as far from a deistic picture as one can imagine; it seems more—as Nicholas Wolterstorff exclaimed on reading it—like "occasionalism gone berserk."[33] But not so for Newton, who instead commends it for its usefulness:

> The usefulness of the idea of body that I have described is brought out by the fact that it clearly involves the chief truths of metaphysics and thoroughly confirms and explains them.[34]

And what "chief truths of metaphysics" does he have in mind? One is the truth that matter depends radically upon God for its continuing existence:

> If we say that extension is body, do we not manifestly offer a path to atheism, because we can have an idea of it [body] without any relationship to God. Indeed, however much we cast about we find almost no other reason for atheism than this notion of bodies having, as it were, a complete, absolute, and independent reality in themselves, such as almost all of us, through negligence, are accustomed to have in our minds from childhood (unless I am mistaken), so that it is only verbally that we call bodies created and dependent.

---

[32] Or perhaps not. At the physical level, it bears a resemblance to the "geometrodynamic" ontology proposed by renowned physicist J.A. Wheeler, on which "there is nothing in the world except empty curved space"—with what we call matter being nothing but the property of a "knotted-up region of high curvature" being "passed on from one portion of space to another." J.A. Wheeler, "Curved Empty Space-Time as the Building Material of the Physical World," in *Logic, Methodology and Philosophy of Science*, eds. Ernest Nagel, Patrick Suppes, and Alfred Tarski (Stanford: Stanford University Press, 1962), 361.

[33] Conversation with author, January 2019.

[34] My quotations here in following are from Newton, *Gravitatione*, 142–43.

So most of us "from negligence" have from childhood imagined that matter, once created by God, has a "complete, absolute, and independent reality" of its own—a conception Newton deems faulty and also finds, in more sophisticated form, in Descartes's identification of matter with "extension."[35] Either way, Newton thinks, we have "only verbally" called matter dependent on God and so opened the door to atheism. Newton thinks his account, by making matter continuously depend on God, keeps that door closed.

Worries and Models

But here we might puzzle. Newton *began*, we saw, by admitting he had little idea of what matter actually is—making his proposal, we noted, seem little more than a just-so story. Can his proposal be *useful* even while leaving so up in the air whether it is *true*?

Just-So Stories as Models

Perhaps, for a just-so story might—for Newton or us—play a role akin to that played by *models* in twentieth-century abstract mathematics. Here we must distinguish the mathematician's sense of "model" from the physicist's sense. In physics, the target is some actual reality, and a model is some deliberately oversimplified representation of it—for example, the Bohr solar-system model of the atom. In mathematics, by contrast, the target is some abstract proposition or formal axiomatic system, and the model of it is something more concrete—or even some actual reality. The model of some uninterpreted formalism might be the actual (or some hypothetical) system of rivers, creeks, and ditches in Ottawa County, which gives us, as put by Gerard Venema (with axiomatic formal systems in view),

> a particular way of giving meaning to the undefined terms in the system. An interpretation is called a model for the axiomatic system if the axioms are correct (true) in that interpretation.[36]

---

[35] Newton should not here be taken as a reliable exegete of Descartes's metaphysics, on which in fact—as one Descartes scholar puts it—"God sustains the world through his continual recreation, and continually sustains the motion he placed in it in the beginning." See Daniel Garber, *Descartes' Metaphysical Physics*, 266; and Daniel Garber, "How God Causes Motion: Descartes, Divine Sustenance, and Occasionalism," *Journal of Philosophy*, 84 (1987): 567–80.

[36] Gerard Venema, *The Foundations of Geometry*, 2nd ed. (Upper Saddle River: Pearson Prentice Hall, 2002), 19. For more on models see Wilfrid Hodges, "Model Theory," in *The Stanford Encyclopedia of Philosophy*, ed. Edward N. Zalta (Fall 2018 ed.), <https://plato.stanford.edu/archives/fall2018/entries/model-theory/>.

Models in this mathematician's sense, as well as giving meaning to "undefined terms" in a purely formal system, can also fill in meaning for a partially defined abstract term—a term such as "depends radically on" (as it occurs in our target proposition "matter depends radically on God"). That target proposition is, as mathematicians like to say, "true *in the story*" that Newton gives—so were that story true, the more abstract proposition would be true too. Now the great thing about such story-models is that they can be *useful* in various ways even if we don't know whether the story is true—or even if we know it is false. For example, if we can clearly see that some concrete story is merely *possible*, this is enough to demonstrate that the target proposition, modeled by the story, is logically *coherent*.

In a similar way, the account of matter in *Gravitatione*—even if Newton leaves its truth up for grabs—might be useful in various ways, including perhaps the way Newton specifies: it might help lessen the hold of a default conception of matter that "through negligence" we have held since childhood.

A Worry About Newton's Freeze-Thaw Model

So says one part of me. But here, I confess, I'm conflicted. Another part of me is the boy chemist. (From about fifth grade through junior high school, chemistry was my chief passion.) And boy-chemist Steve here says, "Not so fast."

Consider, first, just the sheer number of gas molecules in, say, an empty five-gallon gasoline can. By Avogadro's Number, there are about 10^{23}—that is, 100,000,000,000,000,000,000,000—of them. Each one is zooming around at about a thousand miles per hour, banging into around 50 of its neighbors every *ten billionths* of a second.[37] Now on Newton's just-so story, each one of these is not so much a single little enduring particle as a continuous, infinite series of events of God's freeze-thawings of successive regions of space. Keeping track of falling sparrows is one thing; this is quite something else. Does it not, worries

---

[37] I here draw on John Polkinghorne—but Sir John says every ten-billionth (or "one ten-thousand millionth") of a second. (John Polkinghorne, *Serious Talk: Science and Religion in Dialogue* [London: SCM Press, 1996], 80.) By my calculations, using an online calculator and plugging in relevant parameters, this is too small by two orders of magnitude. I've thus turned his one ten-billionth into ten one-billionths. In our Wednesday group, I'm grateful to mathematics professor Tim Pennings for repeating Polkinghorne's apparent mistake in print and later agreeing that Polkinghorne seems to have shifted a decimal point two places over. It, of course, doesn't affect Polkinghorne's larger thesis.

boy-chemist Steve, make God too *busy*—too *tediously* busy? Far better, he is inclined to think, for God to bring bits of matter into full *existence* as real enduring things with real properties and let them *really* zoom around and bang into each other.

Not everyone will share this worry of boy-chemist Steve; he might even be argued out of it. "Is God really the sort of being," he might be asked, "who could find it 'tedious' to simulate little particles—however many zillions of them—by freeze-thawing successive regions of space?" Perhaps we could convince young Steve that he has been unduly influenced by sermons on texts about God getting "weary" of this or that and help him outgrow a certain naive anthropomorphism about God's nature. Even so, however, the just-so story qua *model* will have been useful in bringing our underlying assumptions to the surface for scrutiny and for possible revision. But suppose he instead convinces us: saddling God with massive universe-wide micro-routine tasks does fit ill with the divine attributes. In that event, might not this shortcoming of the model begin to cast doubt on the more abstract proposition it seeks to model? More precisely: if we were to agree that Newton's freeze-thaw model has the liability that young Steve finds in it, *and* we were also then to find no model that does better, might this give us some serious reason to think that the target notion (of matter's radical dependence on God) is more conceptually precarious than we thought? I'm not sure. But if so, just-so stories *qua* models are yet more useful, being—despite their epistemic modesty—a double-edged sword.

Newton did not publish—or, so far as I know, ever refer to—his *Gravitatione* essay or its account of matter. What reservations might *he* have had about it? Here—as a mere just-so possibility—I recall another lesson from Chris Kaiser. The Genesis narrative depicts God as creating our universe by a temporally staged differentiation of chaotic flux into ordered stuff— real stuff, in real kinds, with real causal powers. And at each stage, God pronounces it *good* stuff and tells it to do its causal thing. Genesis 1:11 thus depicts God not as creating grass *ex nihilo* but as, at the proper time, unleashing as it were an implanted power of earth: "Let the *earth* bring forth grass." Chris Kaiser explains how, in such Scriptures, thinkers in the patristic period found an affirmation of the "relative autonomy of nature." Chris here quotes Basil of Caesarea:

> For the voice that was then heard and this command were as a natural and permanent law (*nomos phuseos*) for it; it gave fertility and the power to produce fruit for all ages to come. [38]

[38]   Kaiser, *Creation and the History of Science* (Grand Rapids: Eerdmans, 1991), 19.

By this term "the relative autonomy" of nature, says Kaiser,

> We mean the self-sufficiency nature possesses by virtue of the fact
> that God has granted it laws of nature. Like all laws, the laws of
> nature may come to be viewed as enslaving and inflexible, but, in
> their original sense, they were viewed as liberating (from chaos)
> and life-giving. The autonomy of nature is thus "relative" in the
> sense of being relational (to God), as well in the sense of not being
> self-originated or entirely self-determined.[39]

And for these patristic thinkers, as for earlier Jewish thinkers like
Aristobulus, created things possessed real causal powers by virtue of
"laws of nature"—and "the very regularity of natural law was a sign of
God's presence and activity."[40]

Query 31 Continued: Newton on "Active Principles"

I interrupted our consideration of Query 31 with a detour; let
me now explain why. Were Newton to have stopped with the Query
31 passage as quoted so far, his "Newtonianism" might seem to fit
Greer's picture; it would seem to attribute to matter, once created, a
continuing "on-its-own" existence making for a universe "capable of
running itself." That picture, we can now see, is deeply at odds with that
radical dependence on God envisioned by the model of his youthful
Gravitatione. But perhaps Newton's youthful articulation of that early
model led him—as it has just led us, *via* 14-year old Steve—to wonder
if it was not *too* radical.[41] Might not a better model affirm matter's

---

[39]   Kaiser, 15.

[40]   Kaiser, 18. Drawing on but extending Kaiser, Howard Van Till finds the patristic
       church fathers providing a rationale by which Christians can—in effect as
       "methodological naturalists"—endorse and pursue the search for natural causes
       characteristic of the evolutionary sciences. See Howard Van Till, "Basil, Augustine,
       and the Doctrine of Creation's Functional Integrity," *Science and Christian Faith* 8, no.
       1 (1996): 21–38. Van Till's use of the patristic Fathers finds a vigorous counterpoint
       in William A. Dembski, Wayne J. Downs, and Justin Frederick, eds., *The Patristic
       Understanding of Creation* (Riesel: Erasmus Press, 2008).

[41]   While this method always risks whiggishly projecting our present concerns into the
       past, I am in this case encouraged by Henry and McGuire's remarks on pages 201–
       202 on the "current flourishing of panentheism, especially among those religious
       believers who not only do not wish to reject the sciences, but also wish to keenly
       endorse them (or even tot contribute to them)." Seeing this current flourishing as
       motivated by a cultural situation not unlike Newton's, they urge that this resurgent
       panentheism by "those who want to uphold the values of both science and religion"
       can "surely provide the historian with new insights into the development of
       Newton's thought."

continuing dependence on God while still somehow seeing created things as having full-blooded causal powers?

Our detour, I thus hope, offers a dialectical context that may help us better appreciate how Newton—still honoring the core intuition of his youthful self—now continues to unfold his ideas within Query 31. Close on the heels of the above passage, he continues:

> It seems to me farther, that these Particles have not only a Vis inertia, accompanied with such passive Laws of Motion as naturally result from that Force, but also that they are moved by certain active Principles, such as is that of Gravity, and that which causes Fermentation, and the Cohesion of Bodies. These Principles I consider, not as occult Qualities, supposed to result from the specific Forms of Things, but as general Laws of Nature, by which the Things themselves are formed; their Truth appearing to us by Phenomena, though their Causes be not yet discovered.[42]

Newton thus draws a contrast. In addition to "passive laws of motion" countenanced by strict mechanists, he thinks that the primitive particles of matter are "moved by certain active principles," which manifest themselves in the various phenomena he has surveyed and by which "the Things themselves are formed."

And what *are* these so-called active principles? The pioneering research of J.E. McGuire, in extensive analysis of Newton's writings, finds in Newton's ontology of active principles a window into the theology behind his physics. In a draft passage for the Latin edition of *Opticks,* McGuire notes, Newton wrote:

> Life and will are active principles by which we move bodies, and thence arise other laws of motion not yet known to us. ... If there be an universal life, and all space be the sensorium of a immaterial, living, thinking being, who by immediate presence perceives all things in it ... the laws of motion arising from life or will may be of universal extent.[43]

Notice that here, as in *Gravitatione,* Newton begins with an analogy: just as we humans can "by life and will" can bring about certain effects within our bodies, so also the living God can bring about effects within that universe that is his "sensorium." But the mature Newton sees

---

[42]   Newton, *Opticks,* 401.
[43]   Quoted by McGuire, "Newton's Invisible Realm," 205.

God as doing this by intermediate "active principles": it is now these active principles, which we earlier saw he considered "as general Laws of Nature," that are the means by "by which" God has this agency.

McGuire recognizes that Newton's analogy here is vexing—showing, he thinks, Newton's "difficulty in clarifying how active principles affect natural phenomena." But it does seem to show, as McGuire says, "the extent to which Newton connected active principles with the volition of an active agent":

> Thus "mechanical causation" in the senses of Hobbes or Locke did not constitute, for Newton, causation at all: it did not involve agency, but was merely a description of events, like the "passive laws of motion." God's immanence and power are reflected by the analogies, and since Newton held that God actively governed the world, "universal life" was omnipresent. [44]

The theologically construed notion of active principles, McGuire thus argues, underlies Newton's sense—as Newton put it in some Query drafts—that "we cannot say that all nature is not alive."[45] For Newton, God is an omnipresent living being: his law-like active principles, underlying gravitational and other phenomena, are of "universal extent," and at the same time "are intimately connected with the causation of Divine agency." As I understand him, McGuire sees Newton as favoring genuinely action-at-a-distance forces grounded in law-like active principles by which the living God is everywhere active in the world. In this sense "laws of nature sustain the physical order" only "by virtue of God's concurrence with secondary causes."[46]

It is worth seeing, finally, how Newton's affirmation of active principles feeds back into his earlier proposal regarding God's endowing basic particles with "super-hardness." For note that Newton takes these God-sustained active principles to lie behind not just gravity and fermentation but also the "cohesion of bodies." Within the long survey of phenomena within Query 31 that we have not here covered, Newton

[44] Quoted by McGuire, "Newton's Invisible Realm," 205.
[45] McGuire, "Newton's Invisible Realm," 171.
[46] Note that in the second key passage from Query 23, active principles are for Newton closely connected to—perhaps even identified with—the "General Laws of Nature." The metaphysical status of laws of nature may be crucial for our understanding of Newton's thought—and for any appropriation of it that we might make in addressing the Boogaartian Challenge today. In our Wednesday group, I have benefited here from persistent ruminations of astrophysicist Peter Gonthier on the nature and status of fundamental laws of nature.

argues that a body's degree of hardness is a function of the degree of *cohesion* of its spatially distinct parts. His view, then, is that what we've called "super-hardness" is essentially a matter of super-cohesion. Hence, if cohesion depends on an invisible realm of law-like active principles mediating God's ongoing concourse with creation, so also does such super-hardness, making it still—for the mature Newton of Query 31 as for the youthful Newton of *Gravitatione*—"a sign of God's presence and activity in the world."[47]

Newton's mature—if still provisional—metaphysics of active principles can thus be seen as avoiding one weakness of his youthful freeze-thaw model while preserving its strength. His active principles—and the "General Laws of Nature" they implicate—have a full reality of their own as secondary causes, yet they also reflect God's sustaining moment-by-moment "concurrent activity" within the law-like active powers of matter itself.[48] McGuire and Henry stress that Newton does not *identify* God with these active powers: they show Newton "eschewing pantheism as tantamount to atheism" due to his commitment to God's transcendent sovereign will and transcendence. Rather, they find in Newton a compelling version of what nowadays is called *panentheism*, on which God is "continually present and active in the world" at its deepest physical levels.[49] By the active principles of what McGuire calls "Newton's Invisible Realm," Newton thus regained—at least for a time in his own day—a scientifically plausible "middle world" of the sort that Tom Boogaart finds imperiled by Tycho Brahe's shattering of the crystal spheres of the Thomistic synthesis.

---

[47]   Though space limitations preclude treatment of them here, both empirical and conceptual considerations are interspersed within the 25 preceding pages in Query 31 along with questions that would be pursued throughout the eighteenth century by both physicists like Jean Bernoulli and theologians like Jonathan Edwards. The questions include: What would hardness need to be like, if the laws of collision are to avoid violating a principle of discontinuity (by, say, changing velocity one value to another without going through all the intermediate velocities)? And by what sort of action or activity might God instill in a truly fundamental particle such super-hard cohesiveness that no ordinary power could knock a chip off it? On Bernoulli, see Scott Wilson, *The Conflict between Atomism and Conservation Theory, 1644 to 1860* (New York: Elsevier, 1970). On Edwards, see Antonia LoLordo "Jonathan Edwards's Argument Concerning Persistence," *Philosophers Imprint* 74, no. 23 (July 2014): 1–16. I take up some of these themes in Stephen Wykstra, "Religious Beliefs, Metaphysical Beliefs, and Historiography of Science," in *Science in Theistic Contexts: Cognitive Dimensions*, eds. Margaret Osler and Jitse van der Meer, *Osiris*, 16 (2001): 29–46.

[48]   Henry and McGuire, "Voluntarism and Panentheism," 603.

[49]   Henry and McGuire, 603.

Transplanting Newton

While Newton's theistic metaphysics for a time gained followers, it would soon be submerged by the rising tides of eighteenth-century Enlightenment thought. At the scientific level, to be sure, Newton's quest to quantify action-at-a-distance forces and mechanisms would reset the agenda for research programs within both the physical and life sciences.[50] But at the meta-scientific level, Enlightenment Newtonians would increasingly see these forces as simply one more property inherent in matter rather than as signs of God's abundant presence and activity in the material world.[51]

Still, might there not be within Newton's metaphysics something worth recovering and transplanting into our own twenty-first-century scientific context, helping us bridge the current gap between the ancient Hebraic vision and the findings of the evolutionary sciences?

To be sure, Newton may have never imagined that his theistically construed "active principles" could underlie what the evolutionary sciences now unveil: a gradual unfolding, out of a material substrate, of myriad species of ever-increasing levels of ordered complexity and functionality.[52] Nor is such gradual unfolding envisioned by the Hebraic creation narratives. But in his book *The Ethos of the Cosmos*, William P. Brown finds within those narratives an underlying metaphysics that

---

[50] For two still-solid treatments of eighteenth-century Newtonian research programs, see Arnold Thackray, *Atoms and Powers: An Essay on Newtonian Matter Theory and the Development of Chemistry* (Cambridge: Harvard University Press, 1970); and Robert E. Schofield, *Mechanism and Materialism: British Natural Philosophy in an Age of Reason* (Princeton: Princeton University Press, 1970).

[51] For more on this shift, see chapter 4 ("The Heritage of Isaac Newton: From Natural Theology to Naturalism") in Kaiser, *Creation*, 188–271; Thomas H. Broman, "Matter, Force, and the Christian Worldview in the Enlightenment," in *When Science and Christianity Meet*, eds. David C. Lindberg and Ronald L. Numbers (Chicago: University of Chicago Press, 2003), 85–100; and William B. Ashworth, Jr., "Christianity and the Mechanistic Universe," in *When Science and Christianity Meet*, 61–84.

[52] In *Query 31*, indeed, Newton seems to adamantly resist any Descartes-style speculation that increasingly ordered complexity of our universe might—even by Newton's divinely sustained active powers of matter—have evolved from relatively simple beginnings. He writes (*Opticks*, 402):

> Now by the help of these Principles, all material Things seem to have been composed of the hard and solid particles above-mention'd, variously associated in the first Creation by the Counsel of an intelligent Agent. For it became him who created them to set them in order. And if he did so, it's unphilosophical to seek for any other Origin of the World, or to pretend that

may have deep concinnity with that evolutionary perspective. Speaking of that priestly vision of God's creative process, Brown writes:

> The process is the point. For every step of the creative process, formal approbation is rendered. The distribution and use of power cut to the heart of the Priestly ethos limned in this remarkably irenic cosmogony. First and foremost, God is a creator of an order par excellence. Yet an omnipotent creator does not make a powerless and slavishly dependent creation. The basic elements of creation, as well as their respective inhabitants, also share a level of power that is altogether constructive when prompted by divine command. God's royal word calls forth, prompts, and brings to fruition the various potencies borne by these elements to engage constructively in the ongoing process of creation.[53]

What Brown here finds in the Hebraic creation vision—a kind of constructive power-sharing into which God calls the "various potencies" of even the "basic elements of creation"—seems to me to fit well with Newton's notion of active principles. If Brown's reading of the narratives is right, then Newton's metaphysics may be relevant to that challenge and that opportunity to which Tom calls us.

And *is* Brown's reading right? I confess I'm not sure. If discerning what lies within Newton's words is a great challenge, even more is doing so for these ancient Hebrew Scriptures. A team approach is clearly in order. But Brown is clearly addressing the Boogaartian Challenge. But, persuaded by Tom that this is indeed a challenge vital for us to undertake, I am on the team—and listening.

---

it might arise out of a Chaos by the mere Laws of Nature; though being once form'd, it may continue by those laws for many Ages.

But Newton's journey on such questions is complex; see Pierre Kerszberg, "The Cosmological Question in Newton's Science," *Osiris*, 2 (1986): 69–106.

[53] William P. Brown, *The Ethos of the Cosmos: The Genesis of Moral Imagination in the Bible* (Grand Rapids: Eerdmans, 1999), 47. I'm grateful to Tom for introducing me to Brown's work.

CHAPTER 17

"History" and "State" in Karl Barth: Elements of an Ontology of Human Being

Christopher Dorn

If the preacher's role is to serve as a transmission tower to communicate the ancient world of the Bible to the people who live in the world today, then the seminary professor's role is to show how challenging it is for those signals to traverse the divide. Tom Boogaart, who enjoyed a long and productive career as professor of Old Testament at Western Theological Seminary, performed the latter convincingly for me, as well as for many of my fellow students, when I had the privilege of sitting in his classes. He guided us skillfully into the "strange new world" of the Old Testament, illustrating the ancient Hebrews' understanding of the cosmos and their place in it in the presence of their God. What we discovered on our tour, if we were attentive enough to our surroundings, led many of us to conclude that their world has few parallels with our own. Indeed, Tom confirmed this conclusion by arguing that the success of the natural sciences in providing answers to our questions about reality, reduced to matter in motion, has rendered it extremely difficult for the church to give a plausible account of how God is involved in our world today.

For this reason, Tom has insisted on the need for theologians to incorporate the findings of the natural sciences into their work. He has complained that most seem to have neglected this task, with potentially disastrous consequences for the church. Early signs include the increasing alienation from the faith of the younger generations, who do not seem to believe that the church has anything meaningful to say about our place and purpose in the universe and so dismiss the assumed cosmology of Christian theology as an outmoded relic of a bygone era. Boogaart has made a plea to the church to recruit specialists from a wide range of disciplines to join theologians in a dialogue about how to develop a cosmology that integrates both the findings of the natural sciences and the data of Scripture.

In this essay, I want to suggest Karl Barth (1886–1968) as a theologian worthy to participate in such a dialogue. Barth read widely in the sciences of his time in the course of completing his doctrine of creation, which fills four large volumes (III/1–4) in his magisterial *Church Dogmatics* (*CD*). Since, in both formal and informal settings, Tom and his colleagues have often discussed the problem of the origins and nature of the human being, I propose that it is worth exploring two concepts that Barth introduces in the context of his discussion of the ontology of the human being, which he develops in the second part-volume of his doctrine of creation in a section called "Real Man."[1] Barth designates these two concepts as "history" and "state" and applies them to clarify what the human being "really" is. I suggest that they open up a space in which theologians and scientists can pursue dialogue with one another. Before explicating their content, however, it is important to understand Barth's position on the relationship between science and theological anthropology generally.

Theological Anthropology and What Science Cannot Teach Us

Barth affirms the legitimacy of the scientific disciplines, provided that they adhere to their objects and the methods of investigation appropriate to them. In this sense, theology, too, can qualify as a science, since its object is the Triune God in his self-revelation. Theology systematically investigates the divine self-revelation as it is attested in the data of Scripture.[2] Those natural sciences that have the human

---

[1]   Karl Barth, *Church Dogmatics* (hereafter "*CD*"), III/2 (Edinburgh: T&T Clark, 1960), 132–202.

[2]   See Daniel J. Price, *Karl Barth's Anthropology in Light of Modern Thought* (Grand Rapids: Eerdmans, 2002), 107, 116.

being as their object attempt to determine the particularity of the human being among all the creatures in the cosmos. That is, they aim to establish what makes the human being unique. The question that guides their investigations concerns what properties or characteristics can be predicated of *homo sapiens* so that we can grasp the human being in distinction from all other creatures.

It is worth pointing out that this question can be posed even more sharply today than in middle twentieth century when Barth was writing. Definitions of the human being in terms of the capacity to reason, to engage in moral decision-making, or to enter into personal relationship have served as traditional boundaries for marking off the human from the non-human spheres. But these boundaries have become blurred in recent decades in light of developments in primatology, neuroscience, and evolutionary psychology. New hypotheses have been formulated about the cognitive capacities of animals, especially of non-human primates. For example, there is an expanding body of research that suggests that chimpanzees have a "theory of mind."[3] Frans de Waal has shown that "aiding others at the cost or risk to oneself is widespread in the animal kingdom."[4] And the evolutionary psychologists R.B. Byrne and N. Corp have argued that the roots of the capacity for personal relatedness lie in "neocortical expansion as it has been driven by social challenges among the primates."[5]

Advances in these fields of investigation, however, do not in principle constitute a threat to theological anthropology in Barth's perspective. They neither lead us farther from the goal of identifying the "real" human being nor do they bring us any closer to it. The issue for Barth does not consist in the results of any particular investigation, which could be "relevant, interesting, important, legitimate ... and even instructive for us."[6] It lies, rather, in the starting point from which such an investigation proceeds. "For the point at issue is who is the man who wants to know himself and thinks he can? How does he reach

---

[3]   Richard W. Byrne and Andrew Whiten, *Machiavellian Intelligence: Social Expertise and the Evolution of Intellect in Monkeys, Apes and Humans* (Oxford: Clarendon Press, 1988).

[4]   *Good Natured: The Origin of Right and Wrong in Humans and Other* Animals (Cambridge and London: Harvard University Press, 1997), 216–17.

[5]   "Neocortex Size Predicts Deception Rates in Primates," Proceedings of the Royal Society in London (2004). See also Malcolm Jeeves, "Brains, Minds, Souls and People: A Scientific Perspective on Complex Human Personhood," in *The Depth of the Human Person: A Multidisciplinary Approach*, ed. Michael Welker (Grand Rapids: Eerdmans, 2014), 93–108.

[6]   Barth, *CD* III/2, 79.

the platform from which he thinks he can see himself?"[7] Even if the researcher thinks she has succeeded in isolating those properties whose distinctiveness convinces us that we have identified the "real" human being and "therefore the difference of his being from other beings," from what standpoint can we be sure that her conclusion is final? Since we cannot answer this question conclusively on the basis of the natural sciences, then all such phenomena in principle are "neutral, relative, and ambiguous. ... In themselves, they may equally well point to the essential unity of man with surrounding reality as to his difference from it."[8]

Barth denies that on our own we can break free from the vicious circle into which our attempts at such investigations entrap us. What is needed is a standard or criterion by which to determine the "real" human being that the data of our investigations in themselves cannot provide. In keeping with Barth's earlier image, we can say that we need a platform that we cannot build ourselves. Only from the view afforded by this platform can we interpret the phenomena we discover in our scientific investigations as "symptoms of the human," which point to our differences from other creatures. The standard or criterion comes from revealed truth and therefore from the domain of theological anthropology.

The Real Human

Barth's explanation of the "true being" or reality of the human being in terms of "history" and "state" occurs in the broader context of his central anthropological claim that the determination of our true being results from the fact that Jesus Christ is like us. According to Barth, "The likeness between him and us means that what he alone is, is valid for [us] too, that this is the light in which [we] not only stand outwardly, but are inwardly and essentially."[9] We have already seen that this "likeness" between Jesus and us cannot be established by independent investigation; there is no "third thing" to use as a basis of comparison for the humanity of Jesus and our humanity that allows the researcher to arrive at a common "humanity" in which we and Jesus share. Rather, it is God's self-revelation as attested in the message of the Bible that establishes Jesus's ontological significance for us (cf. Hebrews 4:15; Philippians 2:7).

---

7   Barth, 75.
8   Barth, 76.
9   Barth, 161.

What we can deduce first from the fact that Jesus has appeared with and among us according to the biblical message is that in him we have a counterpart. More precisely, in him we have a "human Neighbor, Companion and Brother."[10] This applies to all—both to those who were before and after him. Barth can predicate this universal significance of Jesus because in the biblical message about him, it is clear that his existence concerns everyone and constitutes the ground on which everyone is to be regarded and addressed. Everyone as such is the fellow-human being of Jesus. Put otherwise, the "real" human being is a being with Jesus.

But it is not enough to say that in Jesus we have a mere human neighbor, companion, and brother. For the human Jesus is at the same time the "bearer of the uniqueness and transcendence of God." "He is the one creaturely being in whom God is present as such in his saving action, in the vindication of his glory, in his lordship and in the fulfillment of his will."[11] In this respect, Jesus is both the one human being wholly turned to God and the one in whom God has wholly turned to us. Viewed from the latter angle, it appears that in all his likeness to us, there is an even greater unlikeness, stemming from the incarnation of the eternal Son. This very fact allows Barth to assert that in Jesus we have not only a human but also a divine counterpart. Human being as a being with Jesus, then, is essentially also a being with God. On this basis, Barth can conclude that it is a "transcendent and divine Other that constitutes man, from which he has his being, and in light of which he can be known as real man"[12]

Barth must anticipate an objection here: In what sense can we say that being with Jesus and therefore with God is distinctive to human being? How is it that this distinguishes human being from that of all other creatures? Cannot the same be said of all God's creatures?

Barth has to affirm this to be the case. All creatures have this same ontological basis (cf. John 1, Ephesians 1, Colossians 1). But we simply do not know what it means to them that they have this basis.[13] Here Eberhard Busch finds Barth's doctrine of creation noteworthy in view of the contemporary insistence on the need to shift from an anthropocentric to a biocentric approach to creation in order to preserve planetary life. Barth assumes a posture of modest agnosticism in the

[10]   Barth, 133.
[11]   Barth, *CD* III/2, 135.
[12]   Barth, 134.
[13]   Barth, 136–38.

face of non-human creatures, "in profound respect of their mystery and of the fact that the meaning of their existence is not exhausted in the human relation to them."[14] But the fact is that the God who is also their God did not become like them. Rather, he became like us in Jesus Christ. Therefore, only in our sphere do we find the bearer of the uniqueness and transcendence of God, as distinct from other creatures even as he is for them too.

That God enters the human sphere in Jesus Christ and thereby determines the "reality" of the human being is directed to a goal. It is in this regard that Barth unfolds what he calls the positive content of the ontological claims that he has been making about human being. He does this along four lines. To be human means (1) to be with the one who is the true elect of God; (2) to be addressed by the Word of God; (3) to be in gratitude to God; and (4) to be in responsibility before God. Of these, it is (2) that is most germane to the concepts of "history" and "state," and therefore we may confine our attention to it.

Barth draws a distinction between the Word of God *ad intra* and *ad extra*. The eternal Word of God is the divine Logos by which God "thinks himself" and "speaks with himself" in the inner Trinitarian being. But this Word is no less than that by which God created the heavens and the earth. When God utters the Word *ad extra*, God "thinks and speaks the cosmos."[15] At the heart of the cosmos is the person of Jesus Christ himself. In him, God not only reveals himself as its creator and Lord; he also acts as its savior and deliverer. To be with Jesus and therefore with God means being "in the sphere of the Word that has spoken and continues to speak in and through the existence of this man [Jesus]."[16] As "spoken," the Word incarnate *is* the divine address and summons. As "speaking," he is the "Bearer" and "Instrument" of this divine address. Finally, in his humanity, the Word makes the divine address to each of us real by hearing it and responding to it. It is especially this last aspect that is critical for grasping the distinction between "history" and "state."

History and State

It is important to clarify at the outset that "history" and "state" add nothing materially to what has gone before. Barth intends only to

---

[14]   *The Great Passion: An Introduction to Karl Barth's Theology* (Grand Rapids: Eerdmans, 2004), 192–93.

[15]   Barth, 147.

[16]   Barth, 148.

recapitulate in these abstract terms the theological insights that he has gained thus far. But a close analysis of their meaning will yield their potential for advancing the dialogue between science and theology, as we will now show.

In light of the fact that, in Jesus Christ, God has entered into our sphere, Barth can say that human being is a "history." In this context, this word is to be understood as a technical term, defined in opposition to that with which it is paired. If "state" refers to something "static," history, in contrast, refers to something in "movement."

In elaborating the former, Barth speaks of a something "completely insulated within itself" and therefore limited in its "possible changes and modes of behavior." Barth hastens to add that this does not imply a "conception of a motionless uniformity." There are, in fact, "states" that are very much in movement. Nevertheless, they do not develop beyond the closed circle of the "changes" and "modes of behavior ... intrinsic to themselves" to which they are therefore bound and must conform. Indeed, they are "never capable of more than these.... Even the concept of the most mobile state is not therefore equivalent to history."[17]

In a brief excursus, Barth draws on concrete examples to illustrate the point that he is making here. It will be helpful for the sake of clarity to reproduce it in its entirety:

> For example, we do not really know what we are talking about when we speak of the history of a plant or animal, because what we know of plants or animals can appear to us only as fixed circles of change and modes of behavior. Nor have we yet realized the history of man if we envisage only the plenitude—limited plenitude—of his characteristic movements in their juxtaposition and sequence, continuity and causal connection, so that what we have before us is only the nature of man—his nature regarded as the sum total of his possible and actual changes and modes of behavior.[18]

The above reveals the sense in which Barth affirms the continuity between non-human and human forms of life. Barth contends that history does not occur for a being—human or otherwise—when it is involved only in the changes or modes of behavior that are proper

---

[17]　Barth, *CD* III/2, 158.
[18]　Barth, 158.

to the sort of being that it is. Rather, it occurs only when something from without takes place upon it, that is, when something "new and other than its own nature befalls it."[19] Again, we allow Barth to explain himself in his own words here:

> The history of a being begins, continues and is completed when something other than itself and transcending its own nature encounters it, approaches it and determines its being in the nature proper to it, so that it is compelled and enabled to transcend itself in response and relation to this new factor. The history of a being occurs when it is caught up in this movement, change and relation, when its circular movement is broken from without by a movement towards it and a corresponding movement from it, when it is transcended from without so that it can and must transcend itself outwards.[20]

This concept of being as history is embodied in the existence of the human Jesus. To speak concretely, his history is actualized in his own encounter with the transcendent and divine Other, in which there takes place a movement from the Creator to the creature, and a corresponding movement from the creature to the Creator.[21] It is important to add that what happens in this double movement is decisive for those who came before Jesus and those who came after him. In this regard, we may say that he is the narrative pattern that has chronological priority for some human beings but (onto)logical priority for all. The history of this one "true man" Jesus lifts us all above "mere state," making our being also a "history" in virtue of our being with him.[22] The new and other that God is directly for the man Jesus, God is for us, too, insofar as we are with Jesus. Barth spells out the consequences of this dynamic in a rather difficult passage that we may nonetheless regard as a useful summary statement of what is entailed in designating human being as a "history" as opposed to a "state."

> Man is what he is as a creature, as the man Jesus, and in him God himself, moves towards him, and he moves towards the man Jesus and therefore towards God. Man is as he is engaged in this movement in this "to him" from without and "from him"

---

[19]   Barth, 158.
[20]   Barth, 158.
[21]   Price, *Karl Barth's Anthropology in Light of Modern Thought*, 121.
[22]   Barth, *CD* III/2, 161.

outwards. Because this fact is his Whence and Whither, it cannot be interpreted as a self-centered movement, and therefore a state.[23]

From this passage, we see what Barth means when he defines history as "movement": in the last analysis, it is self-transcendence. It is significant for Barth that this is no less the case for God than it is for human beings. God comes out of himself to encounter the human being, who in turn goes out of itself in response. It is in this double movement that history consists.

Concluding Observations

Barth does not develop the implications of this theological anthropology for a conception of human being that accords with that of the natural sciences even though the concepts of "history" and "state" are pregnant with these implications. It is worth asking how far these concepts have opened up a space in which to entertain hypotheses concerning the nature and origins of the human being that are compatible with contemporary science as well as theology. For example, can we envisage humanity as a "state" at a phase prior to the encounter that God initiates with them, after which they acquire a "history" and therefore a "being" that is "human" in the proper sense? Put otherwise, can we, on the one hand, view prehistoric human beings as we would plants and animals, but on the other, regard the former as no less *materia inhabilis et indisposita* for human being not yet encountered and addressed by God and therefore not yet human being in the strict sense?

There seem to be a number of intriguing possibilities here, even as we must acknowledge that Barth imposes strict limitations on both the natural sciences and theology as disciplines with their own respective objects and methods of study. If it is outside the domain of the natural sciences to determine our "true being" or "reality" and therefore our place and purpose in the universe, as we have seen, it is beyond the competence of theology to single out a specific scientific cosmology as the one most adequate to its own object. Barth is firm in his insistence that the "Word of God does not contain any cosmology of heaven and earth themselves."[24] For this reason, it does not allow the theologian to deduce from "doctrine of the creature" a "doctrine of the universe, a cosmology."[25]

---

[23] Barth, 162.
[24] Barth, 6.
[25] Barth, 19.

In a final evaluation, we may pose the critical question: Does Barth force one domain to cede too much ground to the other? Many will raise doubts that the proper object of theological anthropology as Barth has defined it—the relation of God and humanity in the divine Word—is separable from cosmology. And from the opposite end, many will protest that the proper object of those natural sciences that study the human being extends farther than its "phenomena." Indeed, to assert otherwise is to contradict the self-understanding of these sciences. The advantage, however, in demarcating firm boundaries between the two domains allows the scientific researcher and the theologian to pursue their respective investigations in relative freedom from undue intrusion by one another. At the same time, the methodological clarifications and the delimitations of the respective aims of these domains allow and even demand that the practitioners respect what each other is doing. Mutual respect seems to us to be a prior condition for genuine dialogue. However the critical question may be answered, it is certainly the case that Barth gives the scientific researcher and the theologian who wish to enter into dialogue with each other much to consider.

CHAPTER 18

The Saving Work of Christ: Three Offices or Three Pilgrim Feasts?

David L. Stubbs

The saving work of God through Christ and the Spirit has often been talked about in terms of "atonement theories." A perennial problem with atonement theories is that they, in spite of the best intentions of those who use them, can quickly narrow the work of Christ and the Spirit in a way that Scripture does not. Furthermore, as they do so, they can tend to drift away from their scriptural moorings.

For example, a person might try to sum up the problem that needs to be overcome between God and humanity by starting with Paul's statement that "all have sinned and fall short of the glory of God."[1] This is how the famous "four spiritual laws," written by Bill Bright of Campus Crusade for Christ in 1952, explain the gospel.[2] However, when the "spiritual law" that Christ's saving work fulfills is explained, Bright's words, not Paul's, summarize the underlying logic: "This diagram illustrates that God has bridged the gulf that separates us from Him by sending His Son, Jesus Christ, to die on the cross in our place

---

[1] Romans 3:23.
[2] Bill Bright, "Four Spiritual Laws," (Orlando: Bright Media Foundation, 2013–2016).

to pay the penalty for our sins." After 2.5 billion pamphlets distributed and many, many lives converted to God, there is obviously truth to be found here and celebrated—a truth that will be revisited and affirmed in a different way below. Given a modern mechanistic worldview in which it "makes sense" that there could be a "spiritual law"—like a Newtonian law of physics—that even God must obey in order to save us, and given the retributive understandings of justice that surround us in our penal systems and law codes, such a summary explanation of the gospel has been seen as plausible to many modern people. But is it the best way? Does it narrow the work of God in Christ too far? Does this explanation of the gospel drift too far away from the worldview of the scriptural writers? Is it the most scriptural way of summing up God's saving work through Christ and the Spirit?

These comments and questions lead me to the work of Dr. Tom Boogaart. One of the central concerns of Dr. Boogaart in his teaching, writing, and living has been to help others rediscover the strange and glorious world of the Old Testament. For us modern people, such a rediscovery is not an easy thing. Take the words of Paul above: "all have sinned and fall short of the glory of God." Tom's eyes would immediately go to and ask questions about the meaning of "the glory of God." Could Paul be imagining that in some way, we as human creatures, even our bodies, and even the entire creation, are called to participate in God's glory and yet fall short?[3] How does Christ overcome our falling short and allow us to participate once again in such glory? Can we see glimmerings of that participation even now? Tom might ask precisely such questions.

How quickly our modern eyes tend to pass over such an important word like "glory" in that passage and narrow Christ's work into strictly a legal matter. Much of Tom's work has been to help give students new eyes for reading Scripture by immersing them in the social imaginary of the scriptural writers. In that way, his students and those who read his writings are able to experience more deeply the depths of Scripture and thus be more truly guided in their practice and belief. I hope this chapter continues in the spirit of Tom's work and brings honor to his substantial legacy.

So in thinking about the saving work of God, how might we go deeper into the richness of the scriptural witness while still organizing our understanding in a way that is simple and teachable? A familiar

---

[3]   See Romans 8:18-23.

way in the Reformed tradition is to use the fact that Christ fulfilled the Old Testament anointed offices of prophet, priest, and king as a kind of rubric or scheme for organizing our thinking about Christ's identity and saving work.

I have been greatly influenced by this way of thinking and have used it with benefit in my teaching. Given the fact that it understands the work of Christ in light of a positive vision of the Old Testament, I would think that Dr. Boogaart would be pleased with such an understanding. And yet as I have researched more deeply into the ways those offices functioned in the Old Testament and in the lives of the Hebrew people, my sense of unease has increased about the way that schema is often used in Christian theology. It, too, has the potential to narrow and distort.

Another option is suggested by the work of Dr. Boogaart. One aspect of Dr. Boogaart's work has been to attend not simply to Old Testament texts and themes but more importantly to the larger narratives of Scripture as well as to the embodied religious life of the people of Israel. A prime example of such a narratival and embodied aspect of Israel's life is the three pilgrim feasts. As commanded by God in the Law, the narrative and the central meanings of God's saving work were put into practice through the embodied performance of the three pilgrim feasts at the temple in Jerusalem. These pilgrim feasts were also important for the authors of the New Testament. They came to understand God's saving work through Christ and the Spirit as fulfillments of or in typological relationship to their main meanings and central symbols.

The following is an appreciative yet cautious evaluation of the three offices as a way to approach the saving work of God through Christ and the Spirit and also a proposal that the three pilgrim feasts of the people of Israel might offer a better way to organize our thinking about God's saving work.

The Saving Work of Christ and the Three Offices

The idea of Christ as the fulfillment of the three offices of prophet, priest, and king is a biblical idea. Even though no New Testament writer speaks directly of "the three offices," Christ is portrayed as fulfilling the anointed callings of Old Testament prophets, priests, and kings throughout the New Testament. As an explicit conceptual approach to Christ's identity, it has a history of use in theology before the Reformation. In part because of Calvin's use of it in his *Institutes*, it became a regular feature within Reformed theologies and confessions as well as contemporary theology.[4] Geoffrey Wainwright, in the second half of his book *For Our Salvation: Two Approaches to the Work of Christ*, made good use of this "approach" to speak of both the identity and work of Christ as well as the vocation of the church.[5] It plays a role in Herman Bavinck's *Reformed Dogmatics* as well as in providing the structure of Karl Barth's *Church Dogmatics*, volume four.[6] Recent Reformed work that features the threefold office as a way to approach and organize one's understanding of the work of Christ includes Robert Sherman's *King, Priest, and Prophet* as well as Michael Horton's *Lord and Servant: A Covenant Christology*.[7]

One of the many positive results of this approach is that it broadens the saving work of Christ beyond one primary mode or way of thinking about "atonement." Gustaf Aulén's important work, *Christus Victor*, was influential in moving work on atonement theology past the supposedly dichotomous poles of the "moral influence" theory of Abelard, favored by some Protestant liberals, and the "satisfaction" theory of Anselm, or "penal substitution," favored by conservative Protestants.[8] He helped to bring back into the discussion the common early church motif of Christ as a victor over the evil powers that hold humanity captive. In its wake, many have related Aulén's trichotomy, or improved variations of it, to the threefold office of Christ. It becomes a way of not arguing for simply one way of understanding atonement but instead holding together the many facets of God's saving work. It also is a way to highlight positive links between the Old Testament and the New Testament—something Dr. Boogaart would applaud.

And yet, questions arise. The first has to do with the basis of the threefold structure itself. Why should there be three basic aspects of God's saving work that neatly correspond to each of those three offices, especially when those three offices in the Old Testament are not very neatly delineated or structured? Wainwright and John Henry Newman

---

4   For example, John Calvin, *Institutes of the Christian Religion*, II/XV (Philadelphia: The Westminster Press, 1960).

5   Geoffrey Wainwright, *For Our Salvation: Two Approaches to the Work of Christ* (Grand Rapids: Eerdmans, 1997).

6   Karl Barth, *Church Dogmatics*, IV/1–3; Herman Bavinck, *Reformed Dogmatics*, vol. 3 (Grand Rapids: Baker Academic, 2006), 364–68.

7   Robert Sherman, *King, Priest, and Prophet: A Trinitarian Theology of Atonement* (New York: T&T Clark, 2004). Michael Horton, *Lord and Servant: A Covenant Christology* (Louisville: Westminster John Knox, 2005).

8   Gustaf Aulén, *Christus Victor: An Historical Study of the Three Main Types of the Idea of the Atonement* (New York: Macmillan, 1960 [1931]).

suggest that those three offices "seem to contain in them the three principal conditions of mankind" that Christ redeems us from.[9] Karl Barth linked the three offices to the doctrine of Christ being "two natures in one person" with again links to particular sinful conditions. Robert Sherman instead links the three offices to the three persons of the Trinity.[10] I appreciate the humility of Michael Horton who says that he is simply following Calvin in his presentation and that "one advantage of this approach is that it integrates the person and work of Christ."[11] There certainly is wisdom and intriguing connections contained in these threefold structures. But especially given the messiness of the Old Testament offices of king, priest, and prophet—which do not seem to have been given to Israel to heal three different aspects of the sinful human condition—I wonder if the search for a neat structural scheme based on the three offices is sometimes taken too far.

Furthermore, as one drills down into, for example, the priestly office, one finds that there is not simply one thing that priests do, nor is "sacrifice" simply one thing—in either the Old or New Testaments. There are five different types of public sacrifices in Israel that affect the relationship between God and Israel in different ways, with at least two or three major categories of these, and New Testament writers link Christ's sacrificial life and death to more than one of them. The three-office structure often subtly pushes one toward "summing up" what, for example, sacrifice is and accomplishes in one particular way, usually around the sin or guilt offering. A good example of this is Barth's *Church Dogmatics* IV/1. In that part volume, the "priestly" aspect of Christ's work is considered in part under the rubric, "The Judge Judged in our Place."[12] The whole of priestly work and sacrifice is summed up not through an exploration of Old Testament sacrifice but, rather, through moving us into the world of the legal courtroom, where justice and judgment are explored in a re-working of a penal substitutionary model of atonement (albeit a brilliant one). My complaint is that there is more than one kind of sacrifice, and Barth's procedure obscures that.

Sherman's work is an interesting example of this as well. In the detailed middle part of his chapter on Christ's priestly work, we find a very expansive notion of what it means for Christ to be both "priest"

---

[9]   Wainwright, *For Our Salvation*, 120. Citing Newman, *Sermons*, 54. Quoted in Sherman, 30.
[10]   Sherman, 15–16.
[11]   Horton, *Lord and Servant*, 208.
[12]   Barth, *CD* IV/1, §59.2.

and "sacrifice." He rightly points out that "sacrifice" at the temple had a variety of meanings. In the middle of the chapter, he organizes his thinking around three major kinds of sacrifice:

> Three general categories are evident. Sacrifices could function as gifts or tributes to God, as an offering of daily "sustenance" intended as a means "of forging or reaffirming ties of kinship or alliance," or as expiation.[13]

The first type includes "firstfruit" offerings, the firstborn, as well as the most typical "whole burnt offering" sacrifice. The Passover lamb has important ties to this first type of sacrifice. The second type is a kind of communion with God in which covenant bonds are reaffirmed and the shalom of God's kingdom is celebrated. The third type involves "sin" and "guilt" offerings as well as the important sacrifices on the Day of Atonement. He goes on to show how Christ "as priest and sacrifice fulfills yet also redefines these three fundamental meanings of sacrifice."[14]

All this I wholeheartedly affirm. I also find links between these three different kinds of sacrifice and the main meanings of the three pilgrim feasts—Passover, Pentecost, and Booths—which I will point out below.

However, at the beginning and end of his chapter, in key summary statements, he seems to conflate all of these into the third type, or at least he greatly emphasizes it to the detriment of the first two. At the beginning of the chapter, he writes,

> In a world corrupted by human sin, the eternal Son himself became human and, representing humanity, took upon himself its guilt and bore the punishment that was its due, even as he provides the means for overcoming this corruption.

His final phrase in that summary paragraph describes the goal of priestly work as "to reconcile us to God and grant us access to him."[15] Toward the end of the chapter, he writes,

> Just as the affirmation of Christ as king means that God the Father reclaims our context from bondage to alien and evil powers, so,

---

[13]   Sherman, 183. Here he draws upon his own work and that of T. H. Gaster and Roland de Vaux—all have various threefold divisions.

[14]   Sherman, *King, Priest, and Prophet,* 186.

[15]   Sherman, 170.

too, the affirmation of Christ as priest means that God the Son also reclaims us from our own sinfulness and guilt.[16]

And finally,

> The priestly/sacrificial understanding of the atonement assumes primarily that humans are separated from God not because of bondage to "powers and principalities" opposed to God, but because of their own failings and transgressions.[17]

What happened to his threefold understanding of sacrifice? Priestly work tends to get reduced to simply making sin/guilt offerings.

The same phenomena can be spotted in discussions about the roles of the prophetic and royal offices in his work as well as in others'.

Michael Horton resists the temptation of narrowing each office to only one particular facet of Christ's work; they instead become categories within which more complicated discussions take place. Part of the impetus of his writing is, in fact, to overcome the way that past debates for and against satisfaction and penal substitutionary models have obscured important parts of Christ's work:

> Conceding the usual Reformed objection that Anselm's theory is weakened by insufficient attention to the resurrection, the active obedience of Christ, recapitulation, covenant, and the cosmic dimensions of salvation, my goal ... is to do greater justice to these essential elements.[18]

But these more complicated discussions about the overlaps between and multiple meanings of each office seem to undermine one of the most attractive features of the three-office approach: its elegant simplicity. This raises the question: Is this the best way of summing up God's saving work through Christ and the Spirit?

God's Saving Work in Light of the Three Pilgrim Feasts

Surely, there is much potential in reflecting on the way God saves humanity through Christ and the Spirit based on the three offices. The richness of the work of Bavinck, Barth, Wainwright, Sherman, and Horton, among others, have all shown us that. But I would also suggest

[16]   Sherman, 210.
[17]   Sherman, 213.
[18]   Horton, *Lord and Servant*, 208.

that reflecting on God's saving work in light of the three pilgrim feasts of *Pesach* (Passover), *Shavout* (Pentecost), and *Sukkot* (the Feast of Booths) has just as much, or even more, potential.

Why? Here are two preliminary reasons.

First, the three pilgrim feasts are a God-commanded, central way of summing up God's saving work in the Old Testament. Arguably, they also partly organize the witness to God's saving work in the New. Those are bold statements, but it is noteworthy that the commandment to celebrate the pilgrim feasts—and in that way to remember, recommit to, and anticipate God's saving work—is an important part of the Law given on Mount Sinai to God's people.[19] In Exodus 23:17, God commanded Moses, "Three times in the year all your males shall appear before the Lord God." It is as if God wanted to teach Israel something about how best to understand God's saving work among them and to shape their proper response to it.

That commandment did indeed shape the people of Israel. Those three festivals became central events that structured the national life of Israel at the time of Christ. As Oskar Skarsaune writes, "The Torah commandment to visit Jerusalem on the three festivals ... is the key to understanding life in Jerusalem in the Second Temple period."[20] They were the central means by which the theology, identity, and worldview of the people of Israel were shaped and by which they understood God's salvation. As Rabbi Samuel R. Hirsch claimed, "The Jew's calendar is his catechism."[21]

In the New Testament, seen as a canonical whole, God's saving history likewise moves from the Passover—the festival during which Christ was crucified according to the four Gospels—through Pentecost— which in Acts 2 is the festival during which the Spirit is poured out— and moves toward the trumpets, judgment, atonement, and final feast (the main symbols of the eschatologically-oriented Feast of Booths) of the book of Revelation. This movement through the three feasts is biblical through and through.

Second, the narrative structure of these feasts is a natural way to organize one's thinking about God's saving work. The feasts point to,

---

[19] Those celebrations are commanded and outlined in Exodus 23:10-19; Leviticus 23:4-44; Numbers 28:16-29:40; and Deuteronomy 16:1-17.

[20] Oskar Skarsaune, *In the Shadow of the Temple: Jewish Influences on Early Christianity* (Downers Grove: Intervarsity Press, 2002), 89.

[21] Quoted in Harold Kushner's foreword to Hayyim Schauss, *The Jewish Festivals: A Guide to Their History and Observance*, trans. S. Jaffe (New York: Schocken, 1962), ix.

summarize, and give meaning to God's saving work in the Exodus, the giving of the Law on Mount Sinai, and movement to God's promised future. New Testament writers understood God's saving work through Christ and the Spirit as the typological fulfillment of that narrative marked out by the three feasts. The narrative structure holds richer possibilities than a single reductive "theory of atonement."

Think of "narrative" as opposed to "covering law." In the modern world especially, progress in knowledge, especially in the physical sciences, is often marked by discovery of "laws" or "theories" that describe or cover the phenomena being examined. Social sciences, such as economics, also speak of "laws" of human economic behavior, and the mathematization of economic theory has been seen as progress in that field. So, too, in theology, where covering laws having to do with the requirements of justice have structured many people's thinking about God's saving action—such as in the four spiritual laws.[22] But here at the end of the modern world, these ways of thinking have been called into question—especially in the biological and human sciences—and the category of "narrative" has been recovered as a perhaps more fitting approach to knowledge about the identity, character, and motivations of human beings and the ways of God.[23] So perhaps our knowledge about God's saving action is best increased through an analysis of the recurring narrative patterns, "types," and "images" through which the character and "ways" of God are seen.[24]

As an aside, frustration with modern biblical and theological methods has been a characteristic of Dr. Boogaart's career. In his teaching of Hebrew and the Old Testament, he instead found that helping students "indwell," "soak in," and even perform the narratives of Scripture are more deeply transformative approaches than many modern methods. They give students a different kind of knowledge of the Scriptures and of the God they witness to.

---

[22]   This is my understanding of the impulses behind the rise of modern "systematic" theology. For example, Friedrich Schleiermacher's *Christian Faith* is partially structured around an analysis of supposedly universal structures of human religious experience—these "laws" then provide a kind of foundational structure to his "system" of theological knowledge. On the other hand, knowledge about biblical texts was understood to be increased by applying the "laws" or "method" of historical science.

[23]   This is one of the central insights of, for example, Hans Frei, in his groundbreaking *The Eclipse of Biblical Narrative* and especially in his *The Identity of Jesus Christ*.

[24]   See for example, *Scripture, Metaphysics and Poetry: Austin Farrer's* The Glass of Vision *with Critical Commentary*, ed. Robert McSwain (New York: Routledge, 2016).

While the three-offices approach links the Old and New Testaments together in typological fashion, the three-feasts approach draws us even more directly and closer to the image-logic and type-logic of the biblical narrative and thus resonates even more strongly with the concerns and insights of Dr. Boogaart.

So in the following, I will briefly point to the central meanings of the three feasts and a few of their implications for atonement theology. While some of those central meanings are still contested, given the constraints of this paper, I cannot argue for them here (but have done so elsewhere).[25] Consider this a first foray into this way of organizing a larger theology of atonement.

Passover

The three pilgrim feasts were understood by the people of Israel to be, in large part, celebrations of events within the larger saving work of God. They were not simply nomadic or agricultural festivals. At the very least, they were understood in this way at the time of Christ.[26]

God's saving work was remembered as beginning with the exodus of Israel from Egypt, as celebrated at the Passover festival. The central meanings of *Pesach*, or Passover, are tied to three central symbols: bitter herbs, the Passover lamb, and unleavened bread.

During the Passover celebration meal, bitter herbs are eaten. The symbolism here is straightforward. The herbs symbolize the bitterness, oppression, and affliction Israel experienced in Egypt. Eating them caused Israel to ponder this bitterness. Such a ritual may seem unnecessary—slavery is obviously a horrible thing, right?—but during their sojourn toward the promised land, rebellious Israel often looks back with a wistful eye to that time of slavery.[27] They longed for a way of life that was easier than the way of salvation that God offered them.

Relating this to the saving work of Christ, perhaps one of the first aspects of our salvation is the revelation that we are caught in sin—that we are indeed in a bitter situation. The rejection of Christ by

---

[25]   I am drawing from both my work on the three pilgrim feasts, laws concerning sacrifice, and implications for understanding Christ's saving work in both Stubbs, *Numbers*, Brazos Theological Commentary on the Bible (Grand Rapids: Brazos Press, 2009), especially 80–104, 214–26; and Stubbs, *Table and Temple: The Jewish Roots of the Lord's Supper* (Grand Rapids: Eerdmans, forthcoming).

[26]   Arguments for this are made in Stubbs, *Numbers*, 215–16. There was an older scholarly consensus that they began as nomadic and agricultural festivals, but there is no evidence for that.

[27]   Numbers 11:5, 18, 20; 14:3; 21:5.

his people and ultimately the crucifixion of Christ reveals the extent of our predicament.[28] And just as Moses lifted up the serpent in the wilderness[29]—which may be interpreted as a revelation of whom Israel was truly following (the serpent)[30]—part of the "lifting up" of Christ is precisely this prophetic critical work which influences us morally by helping us see, admit, and reject the bitter fruits of this old way of life.

God's saving work through Christ can also be related to the second central Passover symbol: the unleavened bread. The unleavened bread has two central, related meanings. The first meaning is tied to the haste with which Israel had to leave Egypt. A different, but related, meaning comes from the emphasis on it having no leaven. "For seven days no leaven shall be found in your houses," the Lord tells Moses in Exodus 12:19.[31] Leaven for Israel was a powerful symbol of something unseen that has great effects, like a habit, disposition, or vice. The Passover ritual of cleaning out the leaven from a house and then burning it right before the start of the festival thus represents a cleaning out of old habits and ways of living and a creating an opportunity for a new start in a household's habits, practices, and inner principles. Leaving behind the old and starting fresh because of God's deliverance—these are the central meanings wrapped up in the symbol of unleavened bread.

The sacrifice of the Passover lamb is a complex symbol, both in the original Passover sacrifice before Israel left Egypt and also in the Passover celebrations at the temple. While I cannot make a full argument for its meaning here, let me simply say that I understand the key to its meaning is found in its connection to the replacement of the "firstborn" and to the *Aqedah*, the binding of Isaac by Abraham.[32] The "firstborn" is a symbol of what Israel, and indeed all of humanity, is to offer to God. They are to offer themselves, as living sacrifices, wholeheartedly to God. They do not. God graciously and mercifully provides a substitute for this, and it is in a mysterious way through their identification with the life-pattern (not death) symbolized by this substitute, be given to God, that they are delivered from their slavery.[33]

"The blood of the Lamb"—the Passover lamb—thus becomes a symbol of God's gracious deliverance, which happens in a certain way:

---

[28]   John 1:11; 12:37-43; 19:13-19.
[29]   John 3:14-17.
[30]   Stubbs, *Numbers*, 165–172.
[31]   Cf. Exodus 12:15, 20; 13:7; Deuteronomy 16:4.
[32]   I offer a full argument in *Table and Temple*.
[33]   Or alternatively, their identification with the pattern of self-offering seen in the act of offering the firstborn.

God provides a symbolic substitute, a representative life, for something they have not (yet) given—namely, their obedient lives. This symbol is also a symbol of their vocation as God's "firstborn" people. They are to be a "priestly people"[34] who offer themselves to God and thus model a different, "saved" way of life. It is through the sheer mercy of God that they are delivered and put on this vocational path.

In this way, the Passover sacrifice is not about atonement for sin, at least if "atonement" is narrowly understood as a substitutionary punishment of some kind. Richard Hays in his *1 Corinthians* commentary says this quite clearly: "To repeat what has been said above, the Passover festival has nothing to do with atonement for sin and everything to do with deliverance from the powers of oppression. This fact has wide-ranging implications for the way we think about Christology and about our own communal identity."[35]

Relating this to God's saving work in and through Christ, this pushes us to see that the foundation of God's saving work in Christ is not vicarious punishment but rather vicarious active obedience and self-offering. While there is a "sin offering" aspect of Christ's work that is "typed" in the three pilgrim feasts—namely, in the Day of Atonement rites during the Feast of Booths—that is not a central meaning of Passover.

The three main Passover symbols can be thus be seen as fitting types of the beginnings of God's saving work in and through Christ. While we were caught in sin, God, out of sheer mercy, has provided a new start for humanity. This new start begins with a rejection of the old, a throwing out of the old "leaven" in humanity as a whole—and in each individual's life. The new start is provided by God. This is how God saves us. Christ, our Passover lamb, is a new Adam. He is the new "firstborn." In his life, we see the obedience and the way of life that all humanity and God's people in particular are called to live.

Pentecost

But there is more. After Israel is saved from their life of slavery, God does not simply free them from the old and promise the new; he enters into a covenant relationship with them. That covenant with its "law" specifies the way of life they should live with God as their king. Fifty days after their deliverance from Egypt, Israel arrives at Mount

---

[34]   Exodus 19:6.
[35]   Richard Hays, *1 Corinthians* (Louisville: Westminster John Knox, 2011), 90-91.

Sinai, where the covenant is given to them. In it, specifics of their vocation as a "priestly people and holy nation"[36] are outlined.

The yearly pilgrim Feast of Pentecost celebrates this covenant.[37] The two central symbolic acts of the feast are the presentation of firstfruits offerings by individual Israelites and the corporate wave offering of two loaves of bread at the feast. The distinguishing aspect of these loaves is that they are leavened. These are the only leavened bread ever used in corporate sacrifices at the temple. Just as care is taken at Passover to make sure that there is no leaven in the bread, here the fact that the loaves must be leavened is stressed.

These loaves arguably have two central meanings. First, the fact that they are *leavened* carries connotations over from Passover. Just as Israel is to have left behind the "leaven" of Egypt, here they celebrate a new "leaven," new principles of action and life that should spread throughout their lives as a people. What is this leaven? On Mount Sinai Israel is given the Torah—patterns of life that detail their relationship with God, with each other, and with the rest of creation. The law contains the patterns of the kingdom of God. Such a word, or law, will shape and form them into the people suited for their covenant relationship with God, a way of living in sharp contrast to the ways of Egypt. This "way" is given to Israel so that they might bear fruit and prosper.

The second meaning of the two loaves corresponds to the fact that they are leavened *bread*. Such bread—similar to the bread of the presence in the Holy Place, and similar also to the firstfruits offerings—is a representative of the realized blessings of God that flow from that covenant life with God.

Thus, through these symbols and other parts of the Pentecost celebration, Israel remembered, gave thanks for, rededicated themselves to, and celebrated the fruits of their covenant relationship of God. This covenant relationship was a further aspect of the way that God brought salvation to God's people.

Relating this to the salvation of God through Christ and the Spirit, in the Gospels, Christ is not only empowered by the Spirit to live his exemplary life which fulfills the Law, but he also shares the Spirit with his disciples.[38] Through receiving the Spirit, Christ's disciples are

---

[36]   Exodus 19:6.
[37]   Yet again, there has been debate about if and when this feast was associated with the covenant. For arguments for the connection at the very least at the time of Christ, see Stubbs, *Numbers*, 221–222.
[38]   John 20:22; Acts 1:5.

united to Christ, and they participate in this renewed human way of life that Jesus pioneered. Through the Spirit, the "law," or "way" of life, that God intended for humanity is written not only on stone tablets, as in the Old Covenant, but first on the humanity of Christ and then also on the hearts of Christ's disciples. As a result of the Spirit's work, the blessings, fruits, and spiritual gifts of this new, abundant, eternal Kingdom life begin to be experienced (e.g., Acts 4:32-35).

Booths

In the seventh month of the year, Israel celebrated the greatest of the three pilgrim feasts at the temple: *Sukkot*, the Feast of Booths. Its central themes and images are all connected with God's actions at the close of the year and the close of the age. It leans into the future. It is an eschatological feast.

During the first convocation at the temple, called the Feast of Trumpets, or *Rosh Hashannah*, trumpets were blown and sacrifices made, anticipating the coming of God to judge. Nine days after this announcement of judgment was the Day of Atonement, or *Yom Kippur*. On that day, Israel experienced the mercy of God. The sins of the people that were uncovered in judgment are covered over during the elaborate ceremonies and sacrifices at that important event.

After *Yom Kippur*, the final part of the festival sequence, call the Feast of Booths, the Feast of Ingathering, or simply, the Feast, lasted a week. More sacrifices were made during this feast than during all the other festivals put together. The details and meanings of the symbols and rites associated with this weeklong feast and the final "eighth day" feast that followed it are many. But most centrally, and more than in any other feast, the celebrants longed for the end of the age and celebrated a foretaste of the great feast to come when God's reign will be fully realized on earth.

We can again relate this festival sequence to the salvation of God through Christ and the Spirit shadowed forth in this pilgrim feast. The Feast of Trumpets that begins the festival finds its fulfillment first in the advent of Christ incarnate—as John the Baptist announced (e.g., Matthew 3:1-12)—but ultimately in the second coming of Christ, the great day of judgment "when all ... must appear before the judgment seat of Christ."[39] Such judgment is anticipated in the life of the church in a "now and not yet" manner whenever the presence of Christ is encountered, most centrally in Word and sacrament. Paul writes about

---

[39]   2 Corinthians 5:10.

this, for example, in his critique of the Eucharistic practices of the Corinthian church: "For all who eat and drink without discerning the body, eat and drink judgment against themselves."[40]

But just as in the Festival of Booths, judgment is not the last word. God's work through Christ and the Spirit is not ultimately for the sake of judgment but, rather, salvation. The Day of Atonement is the next step in that feast. Similarly, the work of Christ—especially his death on the cross—can be seen as the fulfillment of the Day of Atonement rites at the temple. Such connections are seen in Scripture, for example, in Paul's statement in Romans 3:24-25, when he speaks of "the redemption that is in Christ Jesus, whom God put forward as a sacrifice of atonement by his blood, effective through faith." In the book of Hebrews, the significance of Christ's saving death is explicitly and at length seen in terms of Old Testament rites at the temple, above all the rites of the Day of Atonement (e.g., Hebrews 9:23-28).

It is here—as fulfillments of these Day of Atonement rites—that discussion of concepts such as "penal substitution" belongs. It should be noted that there are several ongoing theories about how the Israelites understood how the "sin offering" expiated sins, one of them being akin to penal substitution. Scripture is not entirely clear *how* the sin offering expiates sin, only *that* it does so.

But the Feast of Booths tells us that salvation is not completed by "forgiveness of sins" but, rather, by the great feast that follows. In many places in the Gospels, Jesus likens the goal of God's saving work to a "wedding feast" or "banquet" or meal around a table (e.g., Matthew 25:1-3; Luke 12:35-38; Matthew 8:11; Luke 13:29). And he symbolically enacted this goal of his work in the meals he shared and the miraculous feedings of thousands (e.g., Mark 2:15-17, 6:30-34, 8:1-10; John 6:3-15). Even though salvation will be finally complete only in the new creation, we gain a foretaste of this even now, most centrally at the Lord's Supper. Balai, a fifth-century Syrian leader of the church, wrote of this in a hymn he composed for a dedication of a church:

> His altar is ready, and he takes his meal with us;
> His glory is offered to men, and they take their place at table;
> We eat with him at our table; one day he will eat with us at his.[41]

---

40   1 Corinthians 11:29.

41   From the German translation by P. S. Langersdorfer in *Ausgewählte Schriften der syrischen Dichter*, vol. 6 of *Bibliotek der Kirchenväter* (1913), 13. Quoted in Wainwright, *For Our Salvation*, 57.

Conclusion

What does this brief tour through the three pilgrim feasts and their main rites and symbols show us? Primarily, that thinking about God's saving work in this way is a biblical, satisfying, compact, yet comprehensive structure for contemplating and speaking about salvation and God's work to make us "at one" with God and God's purposes for us as his sinful yet beloved creatures. Insights gained from reflecting on Christ's priestly, royal, and prophetic work are not lost but, rather, placed within a larger narrative that helpfully grounds them.

A few final observations about this approach.

First, I think it is important to note that in this larger narrative of salvation, the "vicarious new humanity" of Christ and our union with him through the Spirit is at the center of the narrative rather than vicarious punishment. This certainly would affect how one understands and shares what "the gospel" is. It also fits well with a certain tradition within Reformed theology, exemplified in the writings of John McLeod Campbell and the Torrances.[42] This pilgrim feast narrative certainly reserves a special place for the "sin offering" of Christ corresponding to the Day of Atonement. However, it also shows that there is more than one offering or sacrifice involved in God's salvific work. The providing of the vicarious Passover lamb by God is just as important as the Day of Atonement rites and even has a certain narrative priority. There is a narrative relationship between the two sacrifices—namely, that we are first freed to follow and participate in the life of the "firstborn" through the power of the Spirit, and then at the conclusion of our lives, our sins are atoned for. I am not suggesting a temporal *ordo salutis* but, rather, noting the narrative logic. This narrative logic reminds me of Bonhoeffer's words about grace as presupposition versus grace as conclusion in *Discipleship*:

> I am liberated from following Jesus—by cheap grace, which has to be the bitterest enemy of discipleship, which has to hate and despise true discipleship. Grace as presupposition is grace at its cheapest; grace as a conclusion is costly grace.[43]

---

[42]   E.g., John McLeod Campbell, *The Nature of the Atonement* (Grand Rapids: Eerdmans, 1996 [original 1856]); and James B. Torrance, *Worship, Community and the Triune God of Grace* (Downers Grove: IVP Academic, 1997).

[43]   Dietrich Bonhoeffer, *Discipleship*, DBW vol. 4 (Minneapolis: Fortress Press, 2001), 51.

The good news is first that we are freed from bondage to the ways of the sin, the world, and the devil and freed to follow Christ as the Holy Spirit unites us to him. And, especially as we come to the end of our life of discipleship, we are also assured that Christ's once-for-all sacrifice atones for our sins.

Second, this three-pilgrim-feast approach reveals that the most basic scriptural place for grounding current discussions and disagreements about penal substitution is the Day of Atonement and its rites. Not the courtroom.

Finally, if conversations about salvation and atonement would be approached in this way, it would require a renewed emphasis on the positive relationship between the Old and the New Covenants, and a renewed recognition that most Christians are wild olive shoots that have been graciously engrafted onto the tree and root of Israel.[44] This approach would "work" only as lingering anti-Judaism and certain forms of supersessionism are overcome. And it would involve the need for Christians to once again "soak" in the Scriptures, to soak in the images and symbols of the Exodus, the giving of the Law and Jewish festivals such as the Feast of Booths.

Perhaps such an approach would seem to not work very well given our culture. But such worries, which were precisely the worries of the main players within Protestant liberal theology, no longer seem worth worrying about to me. They sought to translate the kernel of the biblical message into the modern worldview, because they thought the "ugly ditch" that lay between our modern culture and the worldview of biblical times made those narratives and thought-forms implausible. That project was, in my opinion, ultimately destructive for the theology and the faith of many.

Rather, given our late-modern or post-modern times, concepts and realities such as slavery and oppression, creating a new way of life, discipleship, indwelling, glory, judgment, sacrifice, bread, and feasting do not seem all that foreign or implausible to me. Instead, what I find implausible is the way that the gospel was presented by many "liberals" on the one hand and, on the other hand, by more "conservative" approaches such as the "four spiritual laws."

The work of Tom Boogaart and the generations of students that have benefitted from his teaching has shown us such a transformation of our imaginations is possible. Dr. Boogaart's work has shown that

---

[44]   Romans 11:17.

deeply engaging with the narratives and thought patterns of the Israelite people is not only possible but deeply satisfying, illuminating, and spiritually transformative. For his example and his friendship in such a cause, I am deeply grateful.

Index

2017 Millennial Impact Report, 153

Abelard, 278
Ahab of Samaria, 162
Alternative Trade Organization, 74
Ambrose of Milan, 98
Ammerman, Nancy, 148
And God Said, 28
Anselm, 278
Aristobulus, 258
Aristotle, 240
Art of Biblical Performance: Biblical Performance Criticism and the Genre of the Biblical Narratives, The, 40
Assis, Elie, 146, 154
Assisi, Compilation, and exemplarity of Francis of Assisi, 211–16; and reception of examples, 216–20; relation of, to real Francis, 209–210
Assisi Compilation, The, 208
Ateek, Naim Stifan, 166
atonement theories, problems with, 275–76
Augustine, 86–87, 93, 98; and the Samaritan woman, 184–85
Aulén, Gustaf, 278
authority, Reformed view of biblical, 44–46

Bands of Syria, The, 28; development of from 2 Kings 6, 22–27
Barbezat, Daniel, 54
Barker, Jeff, 38, 40; essay by, 13–29
Barker, Karen, 16
Barth, Karl, 278, 279; and science with theology, 266–73; and the real human, 268–70; history and state, 270–72
Basil of Caesarea, 257
Bavinck, Herman, 278
Bechtel, Carol M., essay by, 1–11
Becker, Ernest, 127
Beginning of Desire: Reflections on Genesis, The, 193, 199
Ben Azzai, 232
ben Hananiah, Rabbi Yehoshu'a (Joshua), 227
Ben Zoma, Shim'on, and Genesis, 225–26; exegesis shakes the world, 235-37; reputation of, for exegetical detail, 226–27; traditions associated with, 234–35
Berding, Kenneth, 6
Bereishis Rabbah, 198
Bible, and culinary encounters with God, 43–44; and curricular competition, 7; and methodological barriers to reading, 7–8; and

transformation, 65–66; as a book,
33–35; centrality of, 4; decline in
knowledge about, 1–2; General
Synod statement on, 4–5; kind
of person to read the, 93–95;
metaphors about the, 32–33; ,
reading for entertainment, 4;
reading, virtues for, 96–103;
reasons for not reading, 6–8. *See
also* hospitality; performance;
Scripture.
biblical cosmology. *See* reality,
sacramental view of.
biblical performance, criticism, 38–
40; Jeff Barker's start with, 16–18;
Tom Boogaart's start with, 16
Biblical Theology Bulletin, 39
*Billy and Dave: From Brokenness to
Blessedness*, 96
Boehme, Jakob, 245
Boff, Clodovis, 159
Boff, Leonardo, 158, 159
Bonaventure, 221
Bonhoeffer, Dietrich, 155, 290
Boogaart, Judy, 17
Boogaart, Tom, 9, 47, 105, 113,
135, 157, 175, 191, 208, 239, 291;
and Bible study, 7–8; and biblical
authority, 45; and centrality of
coram Deo, 82; and cosmology,
240–41; and formational
teaching, 66; and Hebrew cur-
riculum at WTS, 34–35; and
incorporating the sciences into
theology, 265–66; as scholar, 64;
as steward of WTS, 63–75; central
theme of teaching, 276, 283–84;
implications of biblical approach,
38–46; nature and style of, 91–92;
on career, 77–78; style of teaching
Hebrew, 52–53; teaching style, 32–
33, 49–50, 58, 59–62; translation
of 2 Kings 6:8-23, 13–15, 26;
Boogaartian Challenge, 241–43
Booths, Feast of, and Christ, 288–89
Boyle, Robert, 250
Brahe, Tycho, 261
Brookfield, Stephen, 53

Brook, John Hedley, 251
Brother Leo, 209
Brown, Bill, 46; and Helen, 96
Brown, Timothy, 16; essay by, 91–104
Brown, William P., 262
Brownson, James V., essay by, 105–112
Brueggemann, Walter, 162, 195, 196
Bultmann, Rudolf, 177
Busch, Eberhard, 269
Bush, Mirabai, 54
Bush, Pam, essay by, 49–62
Butler, Judith, 194, 204
Byrne, R.B., 267

Calvin, John, 44, 46, 47, 245; and the
Samaritan woman, 185–86; and
the Spirit, 45; and three offices of
Christ, 277
Camino de Santiago de Compostela,
78
Campbell, John McLeod, 290
"Canaanites, Cowboys, and Indians",
170
Christ, and Feast of Booths, 288; and
Passover, 284–86; and Pentecost,
286–88; and the three pilgrim
feasts, 281–89; three offices of,
277–81; vicarious new humanity
of, 290
Christians in Theatre Arts con-
ference, 28
Christus Victor, 278
Church Dogmatics, 278, 279
Civil War, 109
Coakley, John W., essay by, 207–21
Cohick, Lynn, 181
Coleridge, Samuel, 245
Community Kitchen, 74, 83, 105
compassion, and reading the Bible,
96–97
Confessions, 98
Conner, Benjamin, essay by, 63–75
Conn, Joann Wolski, 173
Copernicus, 240
coram Deo, 50, 63, 66, 67–69; 92;
and Tom Boogart's teaching,
82–87
Corp, N., 267

corpuscular philosophy, 250
cosmology, and Tom Boogaart, 240–41. *See also* reality, sacramental view of.
Courage to Teach, The, 42
Crescentius of Iesi, 209
"Crisis of Biblical Illiteracy,The", 6
Cruz de Ferro, 87

Davis, Edward, 242
Day of Atonement, 288–89, 290–91
Dean, Diane, 138
death, and triumphalism, 125–27
Denial of Death, The, 127
Descartes, René, 250, 252
DeVries, Dawn, 176
de Waal, Frans, 267
"Dialogue Concerning the Two Chief World Systems", 108
Discipleship, 290
"Discipleship of Equals: Past, Present, and Future, A", 173
dispossessed, preferential option for, 161–62
divine immanence, 243–45
Dorn, Christopher, essay by, 265–73
Drescher, Elizabeth, 145, 149, 151
Dykstra, Craig R., 63, 70

Early One Morning, 28
earthquakes, and the sympathy of God, 236
El'azar, Rabbi, 237
Eliezer, Rabbi, 233, 236
Enlightenment, the, 41
epistomology, and the Bible, 40–44; Hebraic, 43. *See also* knowledge.
Ethos of the Cosmos, The, 262
exclusivism, in Jonah, 10
exegesis, embodied, 38–40
exemplarity, as responsibility of Francis of Assisi, 211–16; reception of, 216–20
experience, and biblical interpretation, 107–109, 112

Farley, Edward, 66, 70
feasts, as God-commanded, 282; as organizational structure, 282–83

Fehribach, Adeline, 182, 188
Fierce, Victoria, 151
"Forces, Active Principles, and Newton's Invisible Realm,", 247
formation. *See* hospitality.
For Our Salvation: Two Approaches to the Work of Christ, 278
Foster, Richard, 79
Francis of Assisi, 78, 81; and conformity to Christ, 221; as self-conscious example, 211–16; story of his death, 216–18
Friendship House, 83
funeral, purpose of, 123–24

Galileo, 108, 110, 239
Gelber, Hester Goodenough, 214
Genesis, Rabbah 2:4, two powers in, 227–31; Rabbah 4:6, two powers in, 233–35; Rabbah 5:4, two powers in, 231–33
God, immanence of, within creation, 241
God, who elects leaving, 199–202
Gonthier, Peter, 240
Gravitatione et æquipondio fluidorum, De, 247, 252, 257
Greer, T.H., 240, 241
Gutenberg captivity of the Bible, 34, 47
Gutierrez, Gustavo, 158, 160, 161

Hageman, Howard, 9
Hall, Bradford, 139
Halperin, David J., 227
Hamman, Jaco J., essay by, 135–56
Hays, Richard, 286
Hebrew, and performance, 175; curriculum at WTS, transformation of, 34–35; sense of time in, 19–20
Hebrew Bible, the Old Testament, and Historical Criticism, The, 8
Henry, John, 242, 261
Heschel, Abraham Joshua, 43, 65–66, 80, 91, 93, 95, 100, 101, 146–47, 191
Hesselink, I. John, 45, 62
Hilary of Poitiers, 244

Hirsch, Samuel R., 282
history and state, for Barth, 270–272
Holy Spirit, in the Reformed
    tradition, 45
hooks, bell, 51, 55–56, 57, 61
Horton, Michael, 278, 279, 281
hospitality, and Bible metaphor,
    33, 35–38; and pedagogy, 69; at
    center of formation, 72; of the
    heart, 59; participation in, 73;
    transformational power of, 44–46
House of Cards, 4
"How Clear Is Our Vocation Lord", 6
"How We Gather", 144
humility, and reading the Bible,
    99–101
Huygens, Christiaan, 250

imago Dei, 85
immigrant, and biblical narrative,
    192–93; questions of an, 192
internalization, and the Bible, 36–37
Introducing Liberation Theology, 159
Ishmael, Rabbi, 236

Jefferson, Thomas, 92
Jezebel, 162
Joel, accountability in, 150–52; and
    blessing, 153–55; and the Spirit,
    148–50; discovering God in,
    146–48; life-giving community in,
    144–46; locusts and loss, 142–44;
    narrative in, 140–42; pastoral
    reading of, 155
John Chrysostom, 93; and the
    Samaritan woman, 185
John Paul II, 81
Jonah, and Bible study, 9–11; and
    biblical performance, 39–40
Joseph, and understanding God's
    election, 198–99
*Joseph and the Amazing Technicolor
    Dreamcoat*, 195
Joseph's Brothers, 194–197
Joseph narrative, 193
Joshua, 163
Judson University, 29
Jung, Carl, 103

just-so stories, as models, 255–56;
    meaning of, 243

Kabuki, style of, 19
Kaiser, Christopher Barina, 92, 240,
    241, 257; essay by, 223–37; on
    divine immanence, 243–45; on
    Reformation theology, 245–46
Keepers, Dustyn Elizabeth, essay by,
    173–89
kindness, and reading the Bible,
    97–99
King, Priest, and Prophet, 278
knowledge, 43; focal, 41; nature of,
    64–65; reciprocal nature of, 43;
    tacit, 41

land, in the history of Israel, 157
leadership research at Western in
    2012, 53–54
leaving, and God's election of Israel,
    203–205
Lee, Rob, 136
Levenson, Jon, 8, 34
Levine, Arthur, 138
Lewis, C.S., 100, 101, 103
liberation, Palestinian theology of,
    166; theologies of, 159–60
liberationist reading of 1 Kings 21
    and Joshua 10–12, 162–69
Lincoln, Abraham, 92
Literal Translation (by Young), 20, 26
*Lord and Servant: A Covenant
    Christology*, 278
Lord of the Rings, The 86
love, as pedagogy, 50–51; for the
    subject, 58–60; in the classroom,
    60–62; of students for each other,
    57–58; of teachers for each other,
    51–54; of teachers for students,
    54–57

MacIntyre, Alasdair, 63
marriage, 178–81
Mary Magdalene, 28
McClintock, Barbara, 42
McGuire, J.E., 242, 247, 259, 261
McMullin, Ernan, 247
"Mea Culpa", 66

mechanical philosophy, 250
meekness, and reading the Bible, 101–102
Melrose, Ron, 28
memorization, and internalization, 36–37
Mere Christianity, 103
millennials, and the contemporary church, 136–38
Millennials Rising: The Next Great Generation, 138
Moore, Stephen, 182
More, Henry, 245

Naboth, 162
narratives, in popular culture, 139
Neusner, Jacob, 231
Newbigin, Lesslie, 42
Newman, Elizabeth, 73
Newman, John Henry, 278
Newton, Isaac, 241–43; and Query 31, 248–51, 258–61; on God and matter, 251–55
"Newton's Rejection of the "Newtonian Universe, 242
Neyrey, Jerome, 181
NIV Application Commentary, 177
Northwestern College, 16
Nouwen, Henri, 50, 52, 57

O'Connor, Flannery, 83
O'Day, Gail, 187
Origen, and the Samaritan woman, 184
Osterhaven, Eugene, 67, 68, 86

Palmer, Parker, 42, 51, 55, 59–60, 65, 69
Parting Ways: Jewishness and the Critique of Zionism, 194, 204
passover, and Christ, 284
patience, and reading the Bible, 102–103
Paul the apostle, and reading the Bible, 94–95
pedagogy, and interactive learning environment, 55; goal of, 69; practices at the center of, 70–71; socially embodied, 69–75

pentecost and Christ, 286–288
performance, and Bible, 38–39
"Performance Criticism: An Emerging Methodology in Second Testament Studies", 39
pilgrim feasts, 281–289
pilgrimage, and sacramental view of reality, 78; as practice for rootedness, 81–82
Pinker, Aron, 224–226, 233, 235
plagues, types of in Joel, 143
play, distinguished from story, 17–18
Polanyi, Michael, epistomology of, 41–42
Polkinghorne, John, 85
Pope John Paul II, 78
Poppen, Zac, essay by, 157–171
practices, Christian, at center of pedagogy, 70–72
prayer, peace, of Francis of Assisi, 207
Present Shock: When Everything Happens Now, 140
Prudentius, 93–94
Psychomachia, 93

Raheb, Mitri, 166, 168
rationalism, objective, 65
reality, sacramental view of, 82–85, 86
Reformation theology, 245–46
Reformed Dogmatics, 278
Reformed pietism, 67, 74, 86
Reformed slogan, 109
relativism, subjective, 65
resurrection, failure to educate about, 123–25; teaching the larger story about, 130–31
ressurection of the body, and current ministry, 127–29; in 1 Corinthians, 119–23; in 1 Thessalonians, 117–19; in contemporary teaching, 113–17; in Paul, 116–23
Return of the Prodigal Son, 75
Rhoads, David, 39
Rice, Tim, 195
Rojas, Alberto La Rosa, essay by, 191–206
Roosevelt, Theodore, 92

Rowland, Christopher, 234
Rushkoff, Douglas, 140

Sagrado Corazón de Jesús, el, 205
Satriano, and Francis of Assisi, 218–21
Schart, Aaron, 141, 151
Schneiders, Sandra, 178–79, 182, 187
Schottroff, Louise, 180–81
Schreiber, Mordecai, 151
Schumacher, E.F., 61
science, and theology, 266
Screwtape Letters, 100
Scripture, and experience, 107–109;
    divisions over interpreting, 105–106;
    why it says what it says, 109–112;
    women in, 174–75. *See also* Bible.
Sega, Alan, 231
Seitz, Christopher, 146
sexual ethics, 111, 111–12
Shakespeare, William, 4
Sherman, Robert, 278, 279
Skarsaune, Oskar, 282
slavery., 108–109
Small, Kyle J.A., essay by, 77–89
Smith, David, 72
Smith, James K. A., 72
"Some Thoughts on Playwriting", 18
Song of Moses, 230
soul, immortality of the, 116
speed-reading, not appropriate for
    Bible, 102–103
Spencer, F. Scott, 179, 182
Spener, Philipp Jakob, 245
spiritual formation, 88–89
spiritualities, changing, iin the
    church, 136
Stevens, Wallace, 89
Stubbs, David L., essay by, 275–292

Tehom, 50, 51, 58, 59
Temple Mount, Jerusalem, 103
Teresa of Avila, 78
ter Kuile, Casper, 144
Terni, and Francis of Assisi, 218–20
The Bridge, 74, 83, 105
theological education, and forma-
    tion, 66–67; and the academy, 70
theology, primary genre of, 66

Theresa of Avila, 81
Therese of Lisieux, 51
Thomas of Celano, 209, 221
Thompson, Augustine, 210
Thurston, Angie, 144
Tolkien, J.R.R, 86
Torrance, James B., 290
Touching the Altar, 16
Toulmin, Stephen, 84
Trible, Phyllis, 147
Troxel, Ronald, 150

Valdes of Lyon, 5
Vander Broek, Lyle, essay by, 113–33
VeggieTales, 3
Venema, Gerard, 255

Wainwright, Geoffrey, 278
Waldensians, 5
Warrior, Robert Allen, 170
Washington, George, 91
Watkins, Gloria Jean. *See* hooks, bell.
"We Are the Pirates Who Don't Do
    Anything.", 3
Webber, Andrew Lloyd, 195, 196
Weber, Hans-Ruedi, 34
West, Travis, essay by, 31–47
Whyte, David, 79
Wilder, Thornton, 18
Williamson, Marianne, 50–51
Wolterstorff, Nicholas, 254
woman, Samaritan, and marriage,
    178–81; as a disciple, 186–88; at
    the well, 175–78; conversation
    with Jesus, 181–83; past theo-
    logical readings, 183–86; ordi-
    nation of, 106–107, 173–74
Word. *See* Bible.
Wormwood, 100
Wuthnow, Robert, 136
Wykstra, Stephen J., essay by, 239–63
Wyschogrod, Michael, 203

Young, Arthur, 73
Young, Frances, 73
Young, Robert, 20

Zornberg, Avivah Gottlieb, 193,
    199–200

Publications in the Historical Series of the Reformed Church in America

The following Historical Series publications may be ordered easily through the Faith Alive web site at www.faithaliveresources.org

The home page has a search the site box. Either enter the specific title or author, or enter "Historical Series" to search for all volumes available. Titles will appear with the option of adding to cart. Books may also be ordered through your local bookstore.

You may also see the full list of titles on the RCA website at:

www.rca.org/series

1. *Ecumenism in the Reformed Church in America*, by Herman Harmelink III (1968)
2. *The Americanization of a Congregation*, by Elton J. Bruins (1970)
3. *Pioneers in the Arab World*, by Dorothy F. Van Ess (1974)
4. *Piety and Patriotism*, edited by James W. Van Hoeven (1976)
5. *The Dutch Reformed Church in the American Colonies*, by Gerald F. De Jong (1978)
6. *Historical Directory of the Reformed Church in America, 1628-1978*, by Peter N. VandenBerge (1978)
7. *Digest and Index of the Minutes of General Synod, 1958-1977*, by Mildred W. Schuppert (1979)
8. *Digest and Index of the Minutes of General Synod, 1906-1957*, by Mildred W. Schuppert (1982)
9. *From Strength to Strength*, by Gerald F. De Jong (1982)
10. *"B. D."*, by D. Ivan Dykstra (1982)
11. *Sharifa*, by Cornelia Dalenburg (1983)
12. *Vision From the Hill*, edited by John W. Beardslee III (1984)
13. *Two Centuries Plus*, by Howard G. Hageman (1984)
14. *Structures for Mission*, by Marvin D. Hoff (1985)

15. *The Church Speaks*, edited by James I. Cook (1985)
16. *Word and World*, edited by James W. Van Hoeven (1986)
17. *Sources of Secession: The Netherlands Hervormde Kerk on the Eve of the Dutch Immigration to the Midwest*, by Gerrit J. tenZythoff (1987)
18. *Vision for a Christian College*, by Gordon J. Van Wylen (1988)
19. *Servant Gladly*, edited by Jack D. Klunder and Russell L. Gasero (1989)
20. *Grace in the Gulf*, by Jeanette Boersma (1991)
21. *Ecumenical Testimony*, by Arie R. Brouwer (1991)
22. *The Reformed Church in China, 1842-1951*, by Gerald F. De Jong (1992)
23. *Historical Directory of the Reformed Church in America, 1628-1992*, by Russell L. Gasero (1992)
24. *Meeting Each Other in Doctrine, Liturgy, and Government*, by Daniel J. Meeter (1993)
25. *Gathered at Albany*, by Allan J. Janssen (1995)
26. *The Americanization of a Congregation*, 2nd ed., by Elton J. Bruins (1995)
27. *In Remembrance and Hope: The Ministry and Vision of Howard G. Hageman*, by Gregg A. Mast (1998)
28. *Deacons' Accounts, 1652-1674, First Dutch Reformed Church of Beverwyck/Albany*, trans. & edited by Janny Venema (1998)
29. *The Call of Africa*, by Morrill F. Swart (1998)
30. *The Arabian Mission's Story: In Search of Abraham's Other Son*, by Lewis R. Scudder III (1998)
31. *Patterns and Portraits: Women in the History of the Reformed Church in America*, edited by Renée S. House and John W. Coakley (1999)
32. *Family Quarrels in the Dutch Reformed Churches in the Nineteenth Century*, by Elton J. Bruins & Robert P. Swierenga (1999)
33. *Constitutional Theology: Notes on the* Book of Church Order *of the Reformed Church In America*, by Allan J. Janssen (2000)
34. *Raising the Dead: Sermons of Howard G. Hageman*, edited by Gregg A. Mast (2000)
35. *Equipping the Saints: The Synod of New York, 1800-2000*, edited by James Hart Brumm (2000)
36. *Forerunner of the Great Awakening*, edited by Joel R. Beeke (2000)
37. *Historical Directory of the Reformed Church in America, 1628-2000*, by Russell L. Gasero (2001)
38. *From Mission to Church: The Reformed Church in America in India*, by Eugene Heideman (2001)
39. *Our School: Calvin College and the Christian Reformed Church*, by Harry Boonstra (2001)

40. *The Church Speaks, 2*, edited by James I. Cook (2002)
41. *Concord Makes Strength*, edited by John W. Coakley (2002)
42. *Dutch Chicago: A History of the Hollanders in the Windy City*, by Robert P. Swierenga (2002)
43. *Doctors for the Kingdom*, Paul Armerding (2003)
44. *By Grace Alone*, Donald J. Bruggink (2004)
45. *Travels of an American Girl*, June Potter Durkee (2004)
46. *Letters to Hazel*, Mary Kansfield (2004)
47. *Iowa Letters*, Robert P. Swierenga (2004)
48. *Can Hope Endure, A Historical Case Study in Christian Higher Education*, James C. Kennedy and Caroline J. Simon (2005)
49. *Elim*, Robert P. Swierenga (2005)
50. *Taking the Jesus Road*, LeRoy Koopman (2005)
51. *The Netherlands Reformed Church, 1571-2005*, Karel Blei (2005)
52. *Son of Secession: Douwe J. Vander Werp*, Janet Sjaarda Sheeres (2006)
53. *Kingdom, Office, and Church: A Study of A. A. van Ruler's Doctrine of Ecclesiastical Office*, Allan J. Janssen (2006)
54. *Divided by a Common Heritage: The Christian Reformed Church and the Reformed Church in America at the Beginning of the New Millenium*, Corwin Smidt, Donald Luidens, James Penning, and Roger Nemeth (2006)
55. *Henry J. Kuiper: Shaping the Christian Reformed Church, 1907-1962*, James A. De Jong (2007)
56. *A Goodly Heritage, Essays in Honor of the Reverend Dr. Elton J. Bruins at Eighty*, Jacob E. Nyenhuis (2007)
57. *Liturgy among the Thorns: Essays on Worship in the Reformed Church in America*, James Hart Brumm (2007)
58. *Old Wing Mission*, Robert P. Swierenga (2008)
59. *Herman J. Ridder: Contextual Preacher and President*, edited by George Brown, Jr. (2009)

60. *Tools for Understanding*, edited by James Hart Brumm (2009) 404 pp. ISBN: 978-0-8028-6483-3

"Beginning with Donald Bruggink's own notion that 'history is a tool for understanding,' the dozen essays in this volume are tools for understanding four areas of his life and his fifty-five years of ministry. While all the contributors to this volume have benefited from Bruggink's friendship, teaching, and ministry, the first and last essays are by the contributors he has known longest, who had a formative role in his life"

— Eugene Heideman and I. John Hesselink.

61. *Chinese Theological Education*, edited by Marvin D. Hoff (2009) 470 pp. ISBN: 978-0-8028-6480-2

This book offers insight into the emergence of the Christian church after Mao's Cultural Revolution. While reports of Communist oppression have dominated American perceptions of church and state in China, this is an increasingly dangerous view as China changes. Dr. Marvin D. Hoff, as executive director for the Foundation for Theological Education in Southeast Asia, traveled at least annually to China for the period covered by this book. The original reports of his encounters with Chinese Christians, especially those involved in theological education, are a historic record of the church's growth—and growing freedom. Interspersed with Hoff's accounts are reports of essays by Chinese and other Asian Christians. Introductory essays are provided by Charles W. Forman of Yale Divinity School, Daniel B. Hays of Calvin College, and Donald J. Bruggink of Western Theological Seminary.

62. *Liber A*, edited by Frank Sypher (2009) 442 pp. ISBN: 978-0-8028-6509-0

Liber A of the Collegiate Church archives contains detailed seventeenth-century records of the Reformed Dutch Church of the City of New York, including correspondence, texts of legal documents, and lists of names of consistory members. Especially significant are records pertaining to the granting in 1696 of the royal charter of incorporation of the Church, and records relating to donations for, and construction of the church building on Garden Street. The full Dutch texts have never before been published.

63. *Aunt Tena, Called to Serve: Journals and Letters of Tena A. Huizenga, Missionary Nurse to Nigeria*, edited by Jacob A. Nyenhuis, Robert P. Swierenga, and Lauren M. Berka (2009) 980 pp. ISBN: 978-0-8028-6515-1

When Tena Huizenga felt the call to serve as a missionary nurse to Africa, she followed that call and served seventeen years at Lupwe, Nigeria, during a pivotal era in world missions. As she ministered to the natives, she recorded her thoughts and feelings in a diary and in countless letters to family and friends--over 350 in her first year alone. Through her eyes, we see the Lupwe mission, Tena's colleagues, and the many native helpers. Aunt Tena (Nigerians called all female missionaries

"Aunt") tells this profoundly human story. Interesting in its own right, the book will also prove invaluable to historians, sociologists, and genealogists as they mine this rich resource.

The extensive letters from Tena's brother Pete offer marvelous insights into the Dutch Reformed subculture of Chicago's West Side. Because his scavenger company later evolved into Waste Management Inc., those letters are especially valuable. Pete's winsome descriptions and witty dialogue with his sister add a Chicago flavor to this book.

64. *The Practice of Piety: The Theology of the Midwestern Reformed Church in America, 1866-1966*, by Eugene P. Heideman (2009) 286 pp. ISBN: 978-0-8028-6551-9

"With the instincts of a historian and the affection of a child of the RCA, Gene Heideman has accessed both Dutch and English sources in order to introduce us to the unique theology and piety of the Midwestern section of our denomination from 1866 to 1966. Through the words of pastors, professors, and parishioners, he has fleshed out the Dutch pilgrims of the 19th century who found their roots in the Netherlands but their fruit in America. Accessing the Dutch language newspaper *De Hope*, and the writings and lectures of a century of Western Seminary professors, the history of the RCA in the Midwest has come alive. This book is a gracious and winsome invitation to its readers and other scholars to dig deeper and understand more fully the theological and ethnic heritage of those who have helped ground our past and thus form our future."

— Gregg A. Mast, president, New Brunswick Theological Seminary

65. *Freedom on the Horizon: Dutch Immigration to America, 1840 to 1940*, by Hans Krabbendam (2009) 432 pp. ISBN: 978-0-8028-6545-8

"It's been eighty years since the last comprehensive study of the Dutch immigrant experience by a Netherlands scholar—Jacob Van Hinte's magisterial *Netherlanders in America* (1928, English translation 1985). It was worth the wait! Krabbendam has a firmer grasp of American history and culture than his predecessor, who spent only seven weeks on a whirlwind tour of a half-dozen Dutch 'colonies' in 1921. Krabbendam earned an M.A. degree in the USA, is widely traveled, versed in American religious culture, and has written the definitive biography of Edward W. Box (2001). *Freedom on the Horizon* focuses on the ultimate meaning of immigration—the process by which one's inherited culture is reshaped into a new Dutch-American identity. 'Only the steeple was retained,'

Krabbendam notes in his tale of a congregation that tore down its historic church edifice in favor of a modern new one. This is a metaphor of the Dutch immigrant experience writ large, as told here in a masterful way."

— Robert D. Swierenga, Kent State University

66. *A Collegial Bishop? Classis and Presbytery at Issue,* edited by Allan Janssen and Leon Vanden Broek (2010) 176 pp. ISBN: 978-0-8028-6585-4

In *A Collegial Bishop?* classis and presbytery are considered from a cross-cultural, indeed cross-national, perspective of the inheritors of Geneva and Edinburgh in their contemporary contexts in the Netherlands, South Africa, and the United States.

"Dutch theologian A. A. van Ruler compares church order to the rafters of a church building. Church order sustains the space within which the church is met by God, where it engages in its plan with God (liturgy), and where it is used by God in its mission in and to God's world. Presbyterian church order intends to be faithful to its root in God's Word, as it is shaped around the office of elder and governed through a series of councils of the church."

Alan Janssen

— Pastor, Community Church of Glen Rock, NJ

67. *The Church Under the Cross,* by Wendell Karssen (2010) 454 pp. ISBN: 978-0-8028-6614-1

The Church Under the Cross: Mission in Asia in Times of Turmoil is the illustrated two-volume account of Wendell Paul Karsen's more than three decades of cross-cultural missionary work in East Asia.

In one sense a missionary memoir of Karsen's life and ministry in Taiwan, Hong Kong, China, and Indonesia, the work also chronicles the inspiring story of the Christian communities Karsen served—churches which struggled to grow and witness under adverse circumstances throughout years of political turbulence and social upheaval.

68. *Supporting Asian Christianity's Transition from Mission to Church: A History of the Foundation for Theological Education in Southeast Asia,* edited by Samuel C. Pearson (2010) 464 pp. ISBN: 978-0-8028-6622-6

"This volume, telling the story of how one North American ecumenical foundation learned to move from a 'missions' stance to one of 'partnership,' is at once informative, intriguing, and instructive for anyone curious about or interested in the development of contextual theological education and scholarship in China and Southeast Asia. It traces the efforts of Protestant churches and educational institutions emerging from World War II, revolution, and colonization to train an indigenous leadership and to nurture theological scholars for the political, cultural, and religious realities in which these ecclesial bodies find themselves."

— Greer Anne Wenh-In Ng, Professor Emerita, Victoria University in the University of Toronto

69. *The American Diary of Jacob Van Hinte*, edited by Peter Ester, Nella Kennedy, Earl Wm. Kennedy (2010) 210 pp. ISBN: 978-0-8028-6661-5

"This is a charming translation, scrupulously annotated, of the long-lost travel diary of Jacob Van Hinte (1889–1948), author of the monumental Netherlanders in America. Van Hinte's energetic five-week sprint in the summer of 1921 from "Dutch" Hoboken up the river by dayliner to Albany and on to the Dutch-settled towns and cities in the Midwest convinced him that the "migration to America had been a blessing" to the Dutch. But in his brief sojourn among the descendants of the immigrant generation, he also became aware of the "tales of misery" and the "noble struggles" of the settlers that will put readers of all ethnic backgrounds to wondering about their own poignant histories."

— Firth Fabend, author of Zion on the Hudson: Dutch new York and the New Jersey in the Age of Revivals

70. *A New Way of Belonging: Covenant Theology, China and the Christian Reformed Church, 1921-1951*, by Kurt Selles (2011) 288 pp. ISBN: 978-0-8028-6662-2

"As someone who spent much of my childhood on the mission field described in this book, I anticipated having my early memories refreshed by reading it. I did indeed find the book to be an accurate and thorough account of the work of the CRC China Mission as I remember it, but—more surprising—I also learned a good deal of new information. Kurt Selles has performed an important service for the history of missions by uncovering so much new information and doing such impressive research under difficult circumstances. Although the events took place more than a half-century ago, Selles has been able to retrieve a vast amount of detail. His analysis of the cross-cultural dynamics of this work is insightful. Anyone interested in the successes and failures of Christian mission should find this study interesting and informative."

— J. William Smit, professor of sociology, Calvin College, child of CRC China missionary Albert Smit

71. *Envisioning Hope College: Letters Written by Albertus C. Van Raalte to Philip Phelps, Jr., 1857-1875*, edited by Elton J. Bruins and Karen G. Schakel (2011) 556 pp. ISBN: 978-0-8028-6688-2

These letters between the colony's leader and the first president of Hope College in Holland, Michigan, are sequentially placed in historical context and richly footnoted. They offer an intimate view of Van Raalte as he seeks funding for his college from the Dutch Reformed Church in the east, as well as insights into his pioneer community in the midst of conflagration and war.

72. *Ministry Among the Maya*, by Dorothy Dickens Meyerink (Dec. 2011) 434 pp. ISBN: 978-0-8028-6744-5

Dorothy Meyerink entered her ministry among the Maya of Chiapas, Mexico, in 1956, and spent her entire service there. *Ministry Among the Maya* is an exciting account of persecution and success, relating the story of how, through the faithful witness of the laity and the early ordination of Mayan ministers, a strong, large, indigenous church was established and continues to flourish. Meyerink interweaves her personal experiences and the history of the church with reflections on the effective application of church growth principles.

73. *The Church Under the Cross, Vol. 2*, by Wendell Karsen (Dec. 2011) 802 pp. ISBN: 978-0-8028-6760-5

See volume 67.

74. *Sing to the Lord a New Song: Choirs in the Worship and Culture of the Dutch Reformed Church in America, 1785-1860*, by David M. Tripold (2012) 304 pp. ISBN: 978-0-8028-6874-9

As their privileged status evaporated in America's melting pot, the Dutch Reformed Church was forced to compete with a host of rising Protestant denominations in the New World. Survival became linked to assimilating within a new American way of life, with its own distinct language, culture, and religious practices. Gradually, organs, hymns and institutional church choirs were added to the traditional singing of the Psalter—innovations that altered the very fabric of Dutch Reformed religious life in America.

Sing to the Lord a New Song examines how choirs in particular revolutionized the Dutch Reformed Church in the nineteenth century, transforming the church's very nature in terms of worship, ecclesiastical life, institutional structures, and even social, fiscal, and moral practices. Moreover, the book examines how choirs helped break social barriers, particularly those regarding the status and role of women in the church.

Includes audio CD.

75. *Pioneers to Partners, The Reformed Church in America and Christian Mission to the Japanese*, by Gordon Laman (2012) ISBN: 978-0-8028-6965-4

Beginning with Japan's early exposure to Christianity by the very successful Roman Catholic mission to Japan in the sixteenth and seventeenth centuries, and the resultant persecution and prohibition of Christianity, Laman lays the groundwork for understanding the experience of nineteenth-century Protestant missionaries, among whom those of the Reformed Church in America were in the forefront. The early efforts of the Browns, Verbecks, Ballaghs, and Stouts, their failures and successes, are recounted within the cultural and political context of the anti-Western, anti-Christian Japan of the time.

Verbeck's service to the government helped bring about gradual change. The first Protestant church was organized with a vision for ecumenical mission, and during several promising years, churches and mission schools were organized. Reformed Church missionaries encouraged and trained Japanese leaders from the beginning, the first Japanese ministers were ordained in 1877, and the Japanese church soon exhibited a spirit of independence, ushering in an era of growing missionary/Japanese partnership.

The rise of the Japanese empire, a reinvigorated nationalism, and its progression to militarist ultranationalism brought on a renewed anti-Western, anti-Christian reaction and new challenges to both mission and church. With the outbreak of World War II, the Japanese government consolidated all Protestant churches into the Kyodan to facilitate control.

Laman continues the account of Reformed Church partners in mission in Japan in the midst of post-war devastation and subsequent social and political tensions. The ecumenical involvement and continued clarification of mutual mission finds the Reformed Church a full participant with a mature Japanese church.

76.   *Transatlantic Pieties*, ed by Hans Krabbendam, Leon van den Broeke, and Dirk Mouw (2012) 359 pp. ISBN: 978-0-8028-6972-2

Transatlantic Pieties: Dutch Clergy in Colonial America explores the ways in which the lives and careers of fourteen Dutch Reformed ministers illuminate important aspects of European and American colonial society of their times. Based on primary sources, this collection reexamines some of the movers and shakers over the course of 250 years. The essays shed light on the high and low tides, the promises and disappointments, and the factors within and beyond the control of a new society in the making. The portraits humanize and contextualize the lives of these men who served not only as religious leaders and cultural mediators in colonial communities, but also as important connective tissue in the Dutch Atlantic world.

77.   *Loyalty and Loss, the Reformed Church in America, 1945-1994*, by Lynn Japinga (2013) ISBN: 978-0-8028-7068-1

Offering a meticulously researched yet also deeply personal history of the Reformed Church in America throughout much of the twentieth century, Lynn Japinga's *Loyalty and Loss* will be of intense interest to the members of the RCA, reminding them of where they have come from, of the bonds that have held them together, and of the many conflicts and challenges that they have together faced and ultimately surmounted.

For those outside the RCA the questions of identity raised by this book will often sound very familiar, especially, perhaps, in its account of the church's struggle throughout recent decades to reconcile the persistently ecumenical spirit of many of its members with the desire of others within the denomination to preserve a real or imagined conservative exclusivity. Others may find the conflicts within the RCA reflective of their own experiences, especially as they relate to such issues as denominational mergers, abortion, the Viet Nam war, and women's ordination.

78.   *Oepke Noordmans: Theologian of the Holy Spirit*, Karel Blei (tran. By Allan Janssen) (2013) ISBN: 978-0-8028-7085-8

Oepke Noordmans was one of the major Dutch theologians of

the twentieth century, whose recovery of a vital doctrine of the Holy Spirit placed him at the center of thought on the nature of the church and its ministry.

In this volume Karel Blei, himself a theological voice of note, has provided a lucid introduction to and summary of Noordmans's thought and contextual impact. The book also includes substantial excerpts of Noordmans's writing in translation, offering a compact representation of his work to an English-speaking audience.

79. *The Not-So-Promised Land, The Dutch in Amelia County, Virginia, 1868-1880*, by Janet Sjaarda Sheeres (2013) 248 pp. ISBN: 978-0-8028-7156-5

The sad story of a little-known, short-lived Dutch immigrant settlement.

After establishing a successful Dutch colony in Holland, Michigan, in 1847, Albertus Van Raalte turned his attention to the warmer climes of Amelia County, Virginia, where he attempted to establish a second colony. This volume by Janet Sheeres presents a carefully researched account of that colonization attempt with a thorough analysis of why it failed. Providing insights into the risks of new settlements that books on successful colonies overlook, this is the first major study of the Amelia settlement.

A well-told tale of high hopes but eventual failure, *The Not-So-Promised Land* concludes with a 73-page genealogy of everyone involved in the settlement, including their origins, marriages, births, deaths, denominations, occupations, and post-Amelia destinations.

80. *Holland Michigan, From Dutch Colony to Dynamic City* (3 volumes), by Robert P. Swierenga (2013) ISBN: 978-0-8028-7137-4

Holland Michigan: From Dutch Colony to Dynamic City is a fresh and comprehensive history of the city of Holland from its beginnings to the increasingly diverse community it is today.

The three volumes that comprise this monumental work discuss such topics as the coming of the Dutch, the Americans who chose to live among them, schools, grassroots politics, the effects of the world wars and the Great Depression, city institutions, downtown renewal, and social and cultural life in Holland. Robert Swierenga also draws attention to founder Albertus Van Raalte's particular role in forming the city—everything from planning streets to establishing churches and schools, nurturing industry, and encouraging entrepreneurs.

Lavishly illustrated with nine hundred photographs and based on meticulous research, this book offers the most detailed history of Holland, Michigan, in print.

The volume received the Historical Society of Michigan 2014 State History Award in the Books, University and Commercial Press category

81. *The Enduring Legacy of Albertus C. Van Raalte as Leader and Liaison*, edited by Jacob E. Nyenhuis and George Harinck (2013) 560 pp. ISBN: 978-0-8028-7215-9

The celebration of the bicentennial of the birth of Albertus C. Van Raalte in October 2011 provided a distinct opportunity to evaluate the enduring legacy of one of the best-known Dutch immigrants of the nineteenth century. This book of essays demonstrates his unique role not only in the narrative of the migration to America but also in the foundation of theological education for Seceders (Afgescheidenen) prior to his emigration. These essays were all presented at an international conference held in Holland, Michigan, and Ommen, Overijssel, the Netherlands, with the conference theme of "Albertus C. Van Raalte: Leader and Liaison." Three broad categories serve as the organizing principle for this book: biographical essays, thematic essays, and reception studies.

Van Raalte began to emerge as a leader within the Seceder Church (Christelijk Afgescheidene Gereformeerde Kerk) in the Netherlands, but his leadership abilities were both tested and strengthened through leading a group of Dutch citizens to the United States in 1846. In his role as leader, moreover, he served as liaison to the Reformed Protestant Dutch Church in America in the eastern United States (renamed the Reformed Church in America in 1867) to the Seceder Church in the Netherlands, and to the civil authorities in the United States, as well as between business and their employees.

These fifteen essays illuminate the many facets of this energetic, multi-talented founder of the Holland kolonie. This collection further enhances and strengthens our knowledge of both Van Raalte and his Separatist compatriots.

82. *Minutes of the Christian Reformed Church, Classical Assembly, 1857-1870, General Assembly, 1867-79, and Synodical Assembly, 1880*, edited and annotated by Janet Sjaarda Sheeres (2014) 668 pp. ISBN: 978-0-8028-7253-1

"Janet Sheeres, noted scholar of the Dutch in North America, here turns her skill to the early years of the Christian Reformed Church in North America. She has painstakingly researched all the individuals who attended denominational leadership gatherings and the issues discussed and debated at these meetings. Her extensive annotations to a new translation of the minutes provides unprecedented and cogent insight into the early years of the denomination and the larger Dutch trans-Appalachian immigration of the nineteenth century. The annotations reflect Sheeres's characteristically detailed research in both Dutch and English. Scholars of immigration, religion, Dutch-American immigrants, and the Christian Reformed Church will benefit from data in this book, and the appendix of biographical data will be invaluable to those interested in family research."

— Richard Harms, archivist of the Christian Reformed Church

83 *New Brunswick Theological Seminary: an Illustrated History, 1784-2014.* John W. Coakley (2014) ISBN: 978-0-8028-7296-8

This volume marks the 230th anniversary of New Brunswick Theological Seminary and the reconfiguring of its campus by retelling the school's history in text and pictures. John Coakley, teacher of church history at the seminary for thirty years, examines how the mission of the school has evolved over the course of the seminary's history, focusing on its changing relationship to the community of faith it has served in preparing men and women for ministry.

In four chapters representing four significant eras in the seminary's history, Coakley traces the relationship between the seminary in New Brunswick and the Reformed Church in America, showing that both the seminary and the RCA have changed dramatically over the years but have never lost each other along the way.

84. *Hendrik P. Scholte: His Legacy in the Netherlands and in America.* Eugene P. Heideman (2015) 314 pp. ISBN: 978-0-8028-7352-1

This book offers a careful contextual theological analysis of a nineteenth-century schismatic with twenty-first-century ecumenical intent.

Hendrik P. Scholte (1803-1868) was the intellectual leader and catalyst of a separation from the Nederlandse Hervormde Kerk. Leaving the state church meant being separated from its deacon's funds, conflict with the laws of the state, and social ostracism. Due to poverty, Scholte emigrated with a group that settled Pella, Iowa. Schismatic tendencies continued in this and other nineteenth-century Dutch settlements with the most notable division being between those who joined the

Reformed Church in America and those who became the Christian Reformed Church in North America.

As Heideman says: "Although this book concentrates on what happened in the past, it is written with the hope that knowledge of the past will contribute to the faithfulness and unity of the church in the future."

85. *Liber A:1628-1700 of the Collegiate Churches of New York, Part 2*, translated, annotated, and edited by Frank J. Sypher, Jr. (2015) 911 pp. ISBN: 978-0-8028-7341-5

See volume 62.

86. *KEMP: The Story of John R. and Mabel Kempers, Founders of the Reformed Church in America Mission in Chiapas, Mexico*, by Pablo A. Deiros. 558 pp. ISBN 978-0-8028-7354-5

"This faithful story reveals God's power to transform thousands of people's lives through a couple committed to spreading God's message of love and devotion. The Kempers' commitment to their slogan "Chiapas para Cristo" was evidenced in all that they did. They were our surrogate parents, mission colleagues, and mentors."

— Sam and Helen Hofman, career RCA missionaries in Chiapas, Mexico.

"Employing a creative narrative style, Pablo Deiros has fashioned a fully documented biography into a compelling story of the lives and witness of John and Mabel Kempers. *Kemp* is a must read for those who are interested in the intersection of the Christian Church and the social revolution in Mexico during the twentieth century, the struggles of Maya cultures in Chiapas, and the transformative impact of the gospel of Jesus Christ among the people of Chiapas. *Kemp* is an inspiring and engaging history."

— Dennis N. Voskuil, Director, Van Raalte Institute

87. *Yes! Well...Exploring the Past, Present, and Future of the Church: Essays in Honor of John W. Coakley*, edited by James Hart Brumm. 324pp. ISBN: 978-0-8028-7479-5

In this volume, authors from around the world present essays in honor of John W. Coakley, L. Russell Feakes Memorial Professor Emeritus of Church History at New Brunswick Theological Seminary in

New Jersey. Following the pattern of Coakley's teaching, the contributors push readers to think about aspects of the church in new ways.

Contributors include: Thomas A. Boogart, James Hart Brumm, Kathleen Hart Brumm, Jaeseung Cha, James F. Coakley, Sarah Coakley. Matthew Gasero, Russell Gasero, Allan Janssen, Lynn Japinga, Mary L. Kansfield, Norman J. Kansfield, James Jinhong Kim, Gregg A. Mast, Dirk Mouw, Ondrea Murphy, Mark V. C. Taylor, and David W. Waanders

88. *Elephant Baseball: A Missionary Kids Tale*, by Paul Heusinkveld. 282 pp. ISBN: 978-0-8028-7550-1

This fascinating book recounts the up-and-down experiences of a missionary kid growing up overseas away from home in the 1960s. A sensitive autobiographical exploration of the universal trials of adolescence, Paul Heusinkveld's *Elephant Baseball* luxuriates in narrative fluidity—truly a riveting read.

89. *Growing Pains: How Racial Struggles Changed a Church and a School,* by Christopher H. Meehan. 240 pp. ISBN: 978-0-80287-570-9

In the 1960s, black parents from Lawndale Christian Reformed Church in Chicago tried to enroll their children in an all-white Christian school in the suburb of Cicero. A power struggle ensued, taking the matter to synod and inspiring the creation of the Office of Race Relations.

90. *A Ministry of Reconciliation: Essays in Honor of Gregg Mast,* edited by Allan J. Janssen. 272 pp. ISBN: 978-0-80287-598-3

Respect and affection for Gregg Mast permeates this volume of essays written by his colleagues across the fruitful years of his ministry. He certainly has much to show for his years of labor; the list of his accomplishments is long. But it is his heart that impresses me the most. I consider it a privilege to number myself as one of his colleagues, and I can attest, along with many others, to his generosity of spirit, kindness of speech, and faithful persistence of character. This book is a fitting tribute to his impact, and I warmly commend it to a wide readership.

Leanne Van Dyk
President and Professor of Theology
Columbia Theological Seminary
Decatur, Georgia

91. *For Better, For Worse: Stories of the Wives of Early Pastors of the Christian Reformed Church*, by Janet Sjaarda Sheeres. 224 pp. ISBN: 978-0-80287-625-6

    In *For Better, for Worse*, Janet Sjaarda Sheeres highlights the lives of the wives of the first ten pastors of the Christian Reformed Church. Beginning in 1857, when the CRC was founded, Sheeres proceeds in the order in which the first ten pastors joined the church.

    Drawing on genealogical and census data, church records from congregations their husbands served, and historical information about the position of women at the time, Sheeres brings the untold stories of these women's lives to light.

92. *In Peril on the Sea: The Forgotten Story of the William & Mary Shipwreck*, by Kenneth A. Schaaf. 382 pp. ISBN: 978-0-98914-696-8

    "Historian Ken Schaaf has mined the rich holdings of the Library of Congress, the National Archives, and research facilities on both sides of the Atlantic to uncover the amazing story of the eighty-six Frisians who boarded the William & Mary en route to America. After weeks of sailing, they found themselves abandoned at sea by captain and crew aboard their sinking vessel. Readers interested in transatlantic passages under sail will not be able to put this book down. The story grabs the emotions and will not let go."

    —Robert P. Swierenga, Senior Research Fellow,
    Van Raalte Institute

93. *Jack: A Compassionate Compendium: A Tribute to Dr. Jacob E. Nyenhuis, Scholar, Servant, Leader*, edited by Donald A. Luidens and JoHannah M. Smith. 366 pp. ISBN: 978-0-98914-697-5

    A tribute to Dr Jacob E. Nyenhuis, scholar, servant, and leader. Nyenhuis served as a professor of Classics at Hope College (Holland, Michigan) and later served as its Provost, before becoming the director of the Van Raalte Institute.

94. *A Commentary on the Minutes of the Classis of Holland, 1848-1876: A Detailed Record of Persons and Issues, Civil and Religious, in the Dutch Colony of Holland, Michigan*, edited by Earl William Kennedy (three volumes). 2,080 pp. ISBN: 978-0-98914-695-1

    "This much-anticipated, annotated edition in English of the Dutch-language minutes of the Classis of Holland (Michigan)-- the seminal regional assembly of Dutch Reformed immigrants in the Midwest--is extraordinary for its scope and detail. Every substantive theological and ecclesiastical issue, whether Netherlandic or American in origin, is rooted in the foundational Synod of Dort (1618-19) and the Later (Nadere) Reformation. In addition, Kennedy provides biographical sketches of virtually every ministerial and elder delegate, likely hundreds of churchmen. Only a scholar grounded in Reformed theological and ecclesiastical history, fluent in languages, and skilled in genealogical search engines could have written such an extensive work. This multivolume sourcebook will be indispensable to anyone interested in Reformed church history."

—Robert P Swierenga, Research Professor, A. C. Van Raalte Institute, Hope College

95. *Hope College at 150: Anchored in Faith, Educating for Leadership and Service in a Global Society*, Jacob Nyenhuis et alii (two volumes).1,414pp. ISBN: 978-1-950572-00-7

A comprehensive survey and history of 150 years of Hope College, edited by Jack Nyenhuis with contributions by James C. Kennedy, Dennis N. Voskuil, Robert P. Swierenga, Alfredo M. Gonzales, John E. Jobson, Michael J. Douma, Thomas L. Renner, and Scott Travis. The two volume set includes many full-color images of the buildings on the campus and the history of Hope's architecture as well as lists of alumni, faculty, enrollment data, summaries of student life and housing, ending with a plan for the future.

96. Remembrance Communion and Hope: Essays in Honor of Allan J. Janssen, edited by Matthew van Maastricht. 286 pp. ISBN:978-1-950572-01-4

A volume in celebration of the life, teaching, and ministry of Allan Janssen. Essays included by Daniel M. Griswold, Micah L. McCreary, Gregg Mast, John W. Coakley, Daniel J. Meeter, Eugene P. Heideman, Karel Blei, Abraham van de Beek, Christo Lombard, Leon van den Broeke, Leo J. Koffeman, Carol M. Bechtel, and Paul Janssen.